Volunteer Administration:
Professional Practice

Editor
Keith Seel, Ph.D., CVA

Council for Certification in
Volunteer Administration

LexisNexis®

Volunteer Administration: Professional Practice
© LexisNexis Canada Inc. 2010
June 2010

Members of the LexisNexis Group worldwide

Canada	LexisNexis Canada Inc, 123 Commerce Valley Dr. E., MARKHAM, Ontario
Australia	Butterworths, a Division of Reed International Books Australia Pty Ltd, CHATSWOOD, New South Wales
Austria	ARD Betriebsdienst and Verlag Orac, VIENNA
Czech Republic	Orac sro, PRAGUE
France	Éditions du Juris-Classeur SA, PARIS
Hong Kong	Butterworths Asia (Hong Kong), HONG KONG
Hungary	Hvg Orac, BUDAPEST
India	Butterworths India, NEW DELHI
Ireland	Butterworths (Ireland) Ltd, DUBLIN
Italy	Giuffré, MILAN
Malaysia	Malayan Law Journal Sdn Bhd, KUALA LUMPUR
New Zealand	Butterworths of New Zealand, WELLINGTON
Poland	Wydawnictwa Prawnicze PWN, WARSAW
Singapore	Butterworths Asia, SINGAPORE
South Africa	Butterworth Publishers (Pty) Ltd, DURBAN
Switzerland	Stämpfli Verlag AG, BERNE
United Kingdom	Butterworths Tolley, a Division of Reed Elsevier (UK), LONDON, WC2A
USA	LexisNexis, DAYTON, Ohio

Library and Archives Canada Cataloguing in Publication

Volunteer administration : professional practice / Council for Certification in Volunteer Administration.

Includes bibliographical references and index.
ISBN 978-0-433-46222-4

1. Voluntarism—Management. 2. Volunteers—Management. 3. Nonprofit organizations—Personnel management. I. Council for Certification in Volunteer Administration

HN49.V64V636 2010   658.3   C2010-902969-0

Printed and bound in Canada.

PREFACE

WHAT IS CCVA AND WHY THIS BOOK?

The Council for Certification in Volunteer Administration (CCVA) was established in 2006 in order to sustain the CVA (Certified in Volunteer Administration) credential originally developed by the Association for Volunteer Administration (AVA). This credential recognizes practitioners in the field of volunteer resources management who meet specified standards as measured through an exam and performance-based portfolio. CCVA also promotes six core values in volunteer resources management as detailed in *Professional Ethics in Volunteer Administration*, and views these principles as an essential part of competent leadership and management. Candidates for the CVA credential are required to affirm their intent to uphold these ethical standards.

Most would agree that the impact of volunteer engagement is maximized when it is competently led and managed by individuals with the appropriate skills, knowledge, and values. The past 50 years have brought a steady evolution of professionalism to this function, as evidenced by the growth of professional associations, publications, training classes and conferences, academic-based courses and certificates, standards of practice, ethical principles, and an international credential. Nevertheless, the nonprofit, government, and philanthropic sectors have been agonizingly slow to embrace the principles of effective volunteer management on a large scale.

THE CONTENT AND AUTHORS

The practice of volunteer administration is inherently complex and diverse, involving knowledge and skills drawn from many other disciplines. Despite the extensive variety, breadth, and depth of activity, there is a set of common elements and core competencies which forms the foundation for effective practice. There are many books currently available which address the "how to" of leading and managing volunteer engagement. Some focus on particular sub-sectors of the field, while others provide very practical tips and tools about specific aspects of volunteer management. Most are written by practitioners, trainers, or consultants. So why publish yet another book?

Our intent is not to duplicate what already exists, but rather to enhance the body of literature about volunteer administration by adding a comprehensive reference book. More specifically, *Volunteer Administration: Professional Practice* is:

- based on the five Core Competencies detailed in the CCVA Body of Knowledge (based on a 2008 Practice Analysis study of the field);

- supported by related research and academic theory;

- focused on content appropriate for a professional practitioner with a minimum of three years' experience;

- the primary text to support the CVA credential;

- relevant for NGOs, public sector agencies, and all volunteer organizations — regardless of setting; and

- internationally applicable, not country-specific.

To this end, the Table of Contents is structured around the CCVA Core Competencies. Contributing authors were selected from the United States and Canada, and include individuals who have earned the CVA credential, emerging thought-leaders, and academics whose area of scholarly research is in the area of volunteer administration. The writing of these 21 "prac-ademic" authors provides a solid theoretical framework and professional context for the more tactical aspects of how we do our work with volunteers. Readers will find that some of the content will offer opportunities for further professional development. It was the intent to have contributions that would stretch the thinking on volunteer administration.

Note that for consistency of style, the publisher has used Canadian spelling throughout all of the chapters.

INTENDED USE

As stated earlier, this textbook now becomes the primary reference on which the CVA credential is based. It will be required reading for all CVA candidates, ensuring their thorough understanding of the concepts and principles which define them as managers, leaders, and professionals.

In addition, the book provides voluntary sector educators with a tool for ensuring curriculum development consistent with real-world practice as verified by a credible Practice Analysis process. In the absence of a current, comprehensive text, instructors have had to piece together their reading list with a number of more narrowly focused materials. *Volunteer Administration: Professional Practice* fills this gap.

Consultants and trainers may find this book helpful as a core reference on which to base their work, and to share with clients. It also serves as an appropriate companion reference for the larger disciplines of public administration and nonprofit management, which has seen tremendous growth in the last two decades.

Finally, this textbook sends a powerful message to employers, supervisors, and practitioners, reinforcing the need for skilled, competent leadership of volunteers in order to achieve desired results. When the elements of effective practice are in place, organizational credibility increases, community image improves, volunteer commitment is sustained, and important work gets done.

We are proud to offer *Volunteer Administration: Professional Practice* to a field whose time has come.

Katherine H. Campbell, CVA
CCVA Executive Director

ABOUT THE EDITOR

Keith Seel, Ph.D., CVA is the Director of the Institute for Nonprofit Studies at Mount Royal University. Through the Institute, Keith is engaged with other researchers in three broad research streams focused on Canada's nonprofit sector: governance of the sector, policy development and analysis, and sustainability issues.

Keith has been associated with the profession of volunteer administration since 1993 and has held board positions with the Association for Directors of Volunteer Resources and the Association for Volunteer Administration. He has been a volunteer board member for 30 years largely in the human services field. Currently, he holds appointments to two provincial boards in Alberta focused on education and children.

Keith is the Chair of the national Human Resources Council for the Nonprofit Sector, which examines labour force issues particular to the nonprofit sector in Canada.

As an author, Keith has been widely published in books and journals. He co-authored the AVA Statement of Ethics, and he was a major contributor to a management series by John Wiley & Sons, New York. For the same publisher, Keith has also written on ethics and its impact on management, and the risks and opportunities associated with commercial ventures by nonprofit organizations, governance issues for boards of directors, and sustainable development for the charitable sector.

TABLE OF CONTENTS

Chapter 1

TERMINOLOGY

Jeffrey L. Brudney, Ph.D.
Cleveland State University

Melissa A. Heinlein, MA, MS, CAVS
Philadelphia VA Medical Center

INTRODUCTION

Volunteers are valued and recognized for their great contribution to society. Between September 2008 and September 2009, 63.4 million people aged 16 and older volunteered throughout the United States, representing 26.8 per cent of the population (Bureau of Labor Statistics, 2010). According to the Independent Sector Organization (2008), in 2007 total charitable giving reached $306.39 billion. In 2005, nonprofit organizations employed 12.9 million individuals, or 9.7 per cent of the U.S. economy. Despite the size of the sector, those who "mobilize, lead, and manage volunteers" (Brudney, 2001) — administrators of volunteers — tend to be overlooked and not accounted for as they work to fulfill the missions of nonprofit organizations. Without them, these organizations and others that rely on volunteers would accomplish far less.

Administrators of volunteers are the unsung heroes who marshal, mobilize, and motivate an unpaid workforce to serve nonprofit organizations, government agencies, and the broader society. As Brudney (2001, p. 329) observes:

> Each day, countless volunteers stream into the offices of a huge number of organizations. They settle into their places and begin to perform jobs that contribute substantially not only to the internal operations of the agency but also the delivery of goods and services to clients and constituents.... Such a smooth integration of volunteers into the workplace does not happen by accident or without considerable planning and preparation on the part of the sponsoring organization. As societies have grown increasingly dependent on volunteer labor to meet popular demands for goods and services, especially those provided by government and nonprofit organizations, a profession has emerged concerned with introducing unpaid citizens and sustaining their constructive participation. The field of volunteer administration is dedicated to the effective, ethical involvement of volunteers for the benefit of host organizations, their clientele, and the volunteers themselves.

This chapter assesses the professional development of the field of volunteer administration. Given the estimated 1.6 million registered nonprofit organizations in the United States (and many more non-registered), as well as the myriad religious institutions and government agencies that utilize volunteers in the areas of arts, culture, and humanities; education and research; environmental and wildlife services; human services; international and foreign affairs; and public and societal benefit (Independent Sector, 2008); one would anticipate that a great many people would call their profession volunteer administration. According to survey research, three out of five charities in the United States (62%) report that they have a paid staff person whose responsibilities include management of volunteers (Urban Institute, 2004). In the public sector the percentage appears to be much lower (Brudney, 2005). Regardless of sector, administrators of volunteers are constantly defending their positions — to volunteers, paid staff, organization leadership, and the community — as a credible profession.

Organizations sometimes fail to appreciate the range of important activities performed by administrators of volunteers (Brudney, 1992, p. 272). A human resources department will likely have several employees to assist with the intake and processing of new (paid) hires, but an administrator of volunteers may have to act as her or his own department to carry out all of the associated tasks while at the same time managing large numbers of volunteers. Important human resources tasks from recruitment and marketing strategies to "sell" the nonprofit organization to volunteers, to screening new volunteers, to providing appropriate training, placement, management, and recognition may all emanate from a "department of one" — a single administrator of volunteers. In a recent survey of the Pennsylvania Society of Directors of Volunteer Services in Healthcare, Inc. (PSDVS), for instance, a sample of n=107 administrators of volunteers led 16,201 volunteers and provided supplemental care to almost 4.1 million patients. The economic contribution to hospitals in 2008 was an estimated $27 million saved in almost 30 counties across the Keystone State.

This chapter also assesses the status of the field of administration of volunteers in becoming a profession. In classifying administration of volunteers as a profession, administrators might be recognized for their valuable contributions to nonprofit organizations, religious institutions, and government agencies. Other disciplines such as social work and sociology have studied the field(s) related to volunteer involvement, but not from the perspective of this official. The chapter highlights the role and importance of the administrator of volunteers and evaluates the path toward professionalization of the field. The particular lens on this development is the terminology associated with what we acknowledge as the profession of volunteer administration.

THE TERMINOLOGICAL TANGLE IN THE FIELD OF THE ADMINISTRATION OF VOLUNTEERS

"Language is messy by nature, which is why we must be careful in how we use it" (Senge, 1998, p. 17). The field of administration of volunteers provides an apt illustration. Examining this field leads to a terminological tangle. No one accepted job title dominates the field; instead, a number of titles are used. In the absence of this basic classificatory device of an accepted (single) job title, it is challenging to obtain reliable data to describe and elaborate the parameters of the field, including such key factors as size, compensation, benefits, career paths, *etc*. As the author of a recent study lamented, "The study is not at all representative — we simply do not know how many volunteer managers there are, so drawing a sample to reflect the diversity of roles, organizations and so on would be nigh on impossible. In fact, I am using two surveys to compare findings which emphasize this point" (Howlett, 2009, p. 1).

The variety of terms used in the field is responsible in part for the tangle in which administrators of volunteers struggle to be seen and recognized as a profession.

We carried out an exhaustive Internet search of the main terms used to describe practitioners in this field. The terms included:

- Volunteer Administrator;

- Administrator of Volunteers;

- Volunteer Coordinator;

- Coordinator of Volunteers;

- Volunteer Manager;

- Manager of Volunteers;

- Director of Volunteers;

- Volunteer Director; and

- Community Organizer.

We searched for the terms on websites on which one would expect to encounter them, such as: Google, Points of Light Institute, Association for Research on Nonprofit Organizations and Voluntary Action (ARNOVA), Standard Occupational Code, EBSCO host, and Energize, Inc. The results, shown in Table 1, reveal only limited penetration of these terms into websites important to find and/or raise the profile of volunteer administration, or to acquaint new people to the field. Susan Ellis (2006, p. 1) writes, "What's the best title for the person who is designated as the leader of volunteers? Even more important, is there a name/term on which we can all agree as a label for our profession? ... Evidently there is no right answer, since we've been having this debate for decades and are no closer to agreement than before."

Table 1: Common Terms for the Administrator of Volunteers

Title Searched	Google	ARNOVA	SOC	Points of Light	Energize	EBSCO
Volunteer Administration	✓				✓	
Administrator of Volunteers	✓				✓	
Director of Volunteers	✓				✓	
Volunteer Director	✓				✓	
Coordinator of Volunteers	✓				✓	
Volunteer Coordinator	✓				✓	
Manager of Volunteers	✓				✓	
Volunteer Manager	✓				✓	
Community Organizer	✓				✓	

Controversy typically centres over whether the term "volunteer" is necessary to precede the job title, as in "volunteer administrator." In our view this construction has presented an obstacle to the field in establishing its legitimacy as paid work: the popular (mis)conception is that the position is not salaried. Such flawed reasoning may account for the unfortunate result that despite our persistent research efforts to uncover one, any paid position overseeing a volunteer department or program (regardless of title) is not found in *any* industrial classification code.

The American 2000 Standard Occupational Classification (SOC) System provides a wealth of employment data useful to many groups, including researchers, human resource/labour relations/personnel specialists, job seekers, and students and others considering career options. The Unites States Bureau of Labor Statistics website <www.bls.gov/soc> for Standard Occupational Codes contains the code 21-000 listings which include Community and Social Services Occupations. However, it does not include a title for Administrator of Volunteers or a similar listing (for example, Volunteer Services Administrator). Code 11-000 lists management occupations, but a Director of Volunteers again is not found. Canada's Occupational List (2001) enumerates Code A for Management Occupations and Code E for Occupations in Social Science, Education, Government Service, and Religion. In none of these sources is Administrator of Volunteers or similar title acknowledged. Similarly, on a Department of Veterans Affairs hospital employee survey the occupation code for "Chief, Voluntary Service" is *not* listed but lumped instead under "administrative, technical, or professional employee." By contrast, housekeeper, educator, physician, dentist, social worker, chaplain, *etc.*, each has its *own* occupational classification or code. For an individual interested in practice or a career in the field of administration of volunteers, this omission presents a definite obstacle.

In 2004, the Points of Light Foundation published "The Changing Nature of the Volunteering Field: Keeping Abreast of Current Trends." The goal of the research was to understand how "those who work in the field of volunteering feel about issues." Yet, "those who work in the field" were not granted a title; they remained nameless. According to the Federal Register (1995), the SOC does *not* provide a mechanism for identifying administrators of volunteers. "The SOC may be used to classify volunteers" for analysis of contributed economic value, "but occupations unique to volunteer settings were *not* included in the 1980 SOC" (Federal Register, 1995, p. 10999).

With such varying titles, what does this individual who delicately takes care of an unpaid workforce do? Managers of volunteers "analyze the mission of a nonprofit to find ways for volunteers to help" (Crosby, 2001, p.12). They weave volunteer skills, interests, and talents with the needs and mission of the organization. In addition, administrators of volunteers are knowledgeable and skilled in strategic planning, marketing, fundraising, supervision and human resources, management, operations, leadership, and program development (Crosby, 2001, p. 13). Burkham and Boleman (2005) describe four main roles essential to managing volunteers:

1.   Project coordinator;

2.   Advisor/mentor;

3.   Event coordinator; and

4.   On-going activity coordinator.

Yet, in job classification codes and job descriptions, it is only *volunteers* who are recognized as fulfilling these roles in organizations, *not* those who supervise or direct them, *i.e.*, administrators of volunteers.

According to the findings of a study on the "Dynamics of Occupational Prestige: 1975-2000" (Goyder, 2005), administration of volunteers has been overlooked. On a listing of professions in Goyder's (2005) study — which included firefighter, housekeeper, plumber, trailer truck driver, physicist, lawyer, and physician — no mention of administrator of volunteers or like title appears. For practising administrators of volunteers this result must be discouraging.

In 2000, volunteerism experts Susan Ellis and Steve McCurley engaged in a debate, "Should volunteer administrators be a profession?" According to Ellis, "volunteerism practitioners are broad enough in scope to deserve our own category." This view offers an endorsement of the profession. Ellis (2000) maintained that one of the most detrimental issues facing administrators of volunteers is the sense that "this is a dead-end job" (p. 2). Yet, the valuable skills learned as an administrator of volunteers (see above) could be transferred across settings to facilitate career advancement and mobility — if the field were understood and recognized as a profession. Ellis drives home the point that "our success comes from learning both the *science* and the *craft* of volunteer leadership" (p. 2). This success, which is a sign of a profession, is "the ability to transmit knowledge to new practitioners" (Ellis, p. 2).

McCurley (2000) takes a different stance. "If you want respect, you have to earn it in the trenches" (p. 1). He recommends that administrators of volunteers develop high-impact volunteer positions in order to be accepted and embraced within the organization. McCurley does not favour the term "profession" since he believes it gives the "impression of building walls, being overly serious, and unimaginative" (2000, p. 1). The Ellis-McCurley debate could lead practising administrators of volunteers to question the future of the field, and perhaps, even deter new career aspirants from entering.

Below we examine the merits and obstacles to volunteer administration in becoming a profession. Before we do so, based on the scant research that has been undertaken on them, we briefly present a profile of administrators of volunteers.

ADMINISTRATORS OF VOLUNTEERS: A PROFILE

According to Perlmutter (1982, p. 97), Braithwaite focused on the role of the administrator of volunteers as early as 1938. For over 70 years the paid (or sometimes nonpaid) individual who recruits, interviews, orients, trains, and matches skill sets with the needs of the organization, as well as administers the other facets of the volunteer program, has gone by various titles (and additional responsibilities). Ellis (2006) and Scheier (1988) agree that it is too easy for an executive or someone who knows little about volunteers to label the volunteer administrator as the one who is "only responsible for volunteers." Often this position also attracts in-kind resources and represents the organization to the community. In "The Case for Hiring a Manager of Volunteers," Hawthorne (2004) shows that the position carries out a variety of other important tasks, such as agency promotion and public relations and risk assessment and management. What Naylor stated in 1976 still holds true in 2010 — that most of the people employed in many fields to administer volunteers work quite alone or with very few associates who understand the profession and its pressures and constraints (1976, p. 47). The emergence of a profession could help to unite isolated practitioners and give them a shared occupational identity.

Perlmutter (1982) notes that administration of volunteer programs is both paid and nonpaid, and that neither classification should be overlooked. However, her study focuses on paid administrators of volunteers and finds that their background, both in terms of education and experience, is highly varied (Perlmutter, 1982, p. 99). There are no requirements defined for the administrator of volunteers. Although in the 1982 study administrators reported flexibility and creativity in developing their own department of volunteers, no uniform guidelines exist for the field. The administrator usually operated apart from others, often feeling unsupported in her or his organization (Perlmutter, 1982, p. 99).

According to a study conducted by Stubblefield and Miles (1986), administrators of volunteers attain relatively high levels of formal education. At the time of their study no national list of administrators existed. Therefore, Stubblefield and Miles relied on membership lists of Directors of Voluntary Action Centers, Association of Volunteer Administration, and the National School Volunteer Program to obtain their data. In their sample (n=1042) of full-time salaried administrators of volunteers, 32.6 per cent held less than a bachelor's degree, 38.8 per cent held a bachelor's degree, 28 per cent held a master's degree, and less than one per cent held a doctorate degree.

In a Survey of Volunteer Administrators, 1992 and 2000, conducted for the Association for Volunteer Administration (AVA), Brudney and Schmahl (2001) again documented high levels of formal education among the people who work in the field of volunteer administration. The 1992 Survey reported that 34.4 per cent of administrators of volunteers held a bachelor's degree, 14.2 per cent had completed some college courses, 21.4 per cent held a master's degree, 18.8 per cent had completed master's degree level courses, and 1.7 per cent held a doctoral degree. In the 2000 Survey, 64.5 per cent held a bachelor's degree, and 26.7 per cent had attended or completed graduate school.

Whether or not administrators of volunteers feel supported in their organization for the work they do with volunteers and the programs they establish, salary seems to be an issue. In the 2000 Survey of the Profession, 35.2 per cent of respondents stated that their salaries were lower or much lower than those received by their counterparts in the organization. On average, administrators of volunteers reported a comparatively low average salary of $30,000-$39,000. General wage discrimination against women may be a factor — the great majority of administrators of volunteers in the 2000 survey were white females (91.9%). Only 8 per cent of the administrators reported receiving a salary of $50,000-$59,000, and just 4.2 per cent reported a salary of $60,000 or more. The 2004 Nonprofit Salary Survey conducted by the *Nonprofit Times* (2004) confirms a low average salary of $37,857/$35,868 for 2003/2004, far lower than for any other nonprofit official polled in the survey with the exception of "webmaster" ($35,147/$39,659).

In 1989 the Educational Needs in Volunteer Administration Survey conducted by the Association for Volunteer Administration with support from VOLUNTEER — the National Center, concluded that administrators of volunteers have more training opportunities at the beginning of their career, rather than at the later stages. Still, only about one-quarter of a large sample of administrators of volunteers (24.5%) had received training in the field prior to employment (Brudney and Brown, 1990, p. 23). By contrast, a startling 80 per cent of respondents indicated that they would appreciate the opportunity to attend in-depth, advanced courses in volunteer management in topics relating to planning, evaluation, training employees to utilize volunteers, recordkeeping, and public relations. A majority of the respondents to the AVA Membership Survey (1992) and the Survey of the Profession (2000) stated that they had not received training in the administration or management of volunteers before entering the field. Only a few administrators of volunteers had completed a certificate or degree program in volunteer administration at a college or university (12.4%) or college or university course(s) in this field (12.8%). Whether for lack of training opportunities or organizational support, the need for continuing education for administrators of volunteers seems manifest.

The facts that most entrants to the field do not have prior training in administration of volunteers and have difficulty acquiring it on the job suggest the need for greater professionalization in the field. As a result of lack of training, Bradner (1999) points out, no matter how capable an administrator might be to lead a workforce of volunteers, she or he is not usually aware that proven techniques of volunteer management already exist. In the absence of such basic knowledge that training might impart that volunteers need to know what they are expected to do, and to be assigned appropriately, oriented and trained, supported, guided, and recognized for their talents and achievements (Bradner, p. 10), newcomers to the field are likely to waste their time and energy and, perhaps, risk burn-out. To alleviate this problem Table 2 provides a brief listing of useful Internet resources for administrators of volunteers. Other chapters in this text supplement these resources significantly.

Table 2: Selected Internet Resources for Administrators of Volunteers

General Resources	URL (Location)	Description
Bureau of Labor Statistics	www.bls.gov	Statistics on volunteers
CharityChannel®	www.charitychannel.org	Resource connecting to other nonprofit colleagues
Council for Certification in Volunteer Administration	www.cvacert.org/index.htm	Profession and practice of volunteer resource management
United States Department of Labor	www.dol.gov	Laws applicable to volunteers
Energize, Inc.	www.energizeinc.com	Resources, advice, discussion boards, articles
E-Volunteerism	www.e-volunteerism.com	Articles, discussions, resources on topics relating to volunteer administration
Idealist	www.idealist.org	Idealist is an interactive site where people and organizations can exchange resources and ideas, locate opportunities

General Resources	URL (Location)	Description
Institute for Volunteering Research	www.ivr.org.uk	Aspects of volunteering at a variety of levels, research maximize the policy and practice impact
National Service Resource	www.nationalserviceresources.org/	Tools and training for volunteer and service programs
Nonprofit Good Practice Guide	www.npgoodpractice.org	Research on philanthropy, volunteerism and nonprofit management
Nonprofit Risk Management Center	Nonprofitrisk.org	Risk management practices for volunteers
VolunteerMatch	www.volunteermatch.org	Database to post volunteer opportunities
VolunteerToday	www.volunteertoday.com	Information about volunteer administration, professional development opportunities
United States Resources		
Association for Healthcare Volunteer Resource Professionals	www.ahvrp.org	Healthcare administrators of volunteers
Corporation for National and Community Service	www.nationalservice.org	Resources to support the American culture of citizenship, service and responsibility
Council on Foundations	www.cof.org	A national nonprofit association of grant-making foundations and corporations
Independent Sector	www.independentsector.com	Research, dollar value of volunteer time, research on volunteering, giving
Points of Light Institute	www.pointsoflight.org	Engages individuals, corporations, nonprofit organizations, and government agencies in developing volunteer and community partnership opportunities
ServiceLeader.org	www.serviceleader.org/new/virtual/	Provides information on all aspects of volunteerism

General Resources	URL (Location)	Description
International Resources		
International Association for Volunteer Effort	www.iave.org	A global network of volunteers, volunteer organizations, national representatives and volunteer centres, with members in over 70 countries, and in all world regions
European Volunteer Centre	www.cev.be	European umbrella organization of 27 national and regional volunteer centres across Europe
Volunteer Canada	volunteer.ca/en/en-home	Volunteer Canada leads the advancement of volunteerism in strengthening society and improving quality of life in Canada
OzVPM	www.ozvpm.com/index.php	OzVPM focuses on volunteerism, primarily as it relates to the Australasian region, but we are also proud to work regularly with leaders of the international volunteering community
Volunteering Australia	www.volunteeringaustralia.org/html/s01_home/home.asp	Volunteering Australia is the national peak body working to advance volunteering in the Australian community
Volunteering England	www.volunteering.org.uk	Volunteering England works to support and increase the quality, quantity, impact and accessibility of volunteering throughout England
World Volunteer Web	www.worldvolunteerweb.org	A comprehensive website offering continuing news of worldwide volunteer efforts

General Resources	URL (Location)	Description
Volunteer Opportunities		
1-800-Volunteer.org	www.1-800-volunteer.org/ 1800vol/openindexaction.do	National database of volunteer opportunities
Online Volunteering	www.onlinevolunteering.org /en/index.html	Connects volunteers with organizations working for sustainable human development
United Way	www.unitedway.org	Worldwide network to advance community well-being
VolunteerMatch	www.volunteermatch.org	Online services to support civic engagement; preferred Internet recruiting tool for more than 65,000 nonprofit organizations

Criteria for Professionalization of a Field

Researchers and practitioners have long been concerned about the definition or criteria for an occupation, vocation, or field to become a profession. Although Brubacher (1962) traces the word profession to the sixteenth century, professions were not researched systematically until the middle of the twentieth century. Elliot (1972, p. 5) defines profession as "... a specialized skill and service, an intellectual and practical training, a high degree of professional autonomy, a fiduciary responsibility with the client, a sense of collective responsibility for the profession as a whole." Pieczka (2000) and Houston (2008) maintain that the way practitioners can demonstrate their value to clients is through professionalization.

Despite the value that its practitioners contribute to clients, organizations, and communities every day, the field of administration of volunteers has not yet achieved the status of a profession. Silver and Melsh (1999, p. 1) maintain, "Despite widespread agreement that involvement of the public as volunteers is essential for the health and well being of society and community life, volunteers and the people who engage them are still largely taken for granted."

Houle (1980) describes a process of professionalization to guide occupations and vocations, such as the administration of volunteers, to develop the characteristics of a profession (see Fisher and Cole, 1993, pp. 160-163). Houle (1980) presents 14 criteria that describe an occupation emerging as a profession. The first five criteria focus on the role of practitioners in advancing the occupation as a profession; the remaining nine criteria are directed to what the vocation as a whole must do to attain this status:

1. Clarify the defining function of the profession.

2. Master information and theory for the knowledge base of the profession.

3. Use theoretical bodies of knowledge to solve problems.

4. Have available and use a substantial body of knowledge and techniques developing out of hands-on applications.

5. Enhance application through study of topics not directly related to the profession's occupation.

6. Establish formal procedures to transmit bodies of knowledge and techniques to practitioners before they enter service and throughout their careers.

7. Use formal means to test the capability of individual practitioners.

8. Create a subculture with distinctive attributes.

9. Use legal support and formal administrative rules to protect rights and privileges of the profession.

10. Encourage public awareness of the work done by practitioners.

11. Establish a code of ethical practice.

12. Establish and enforce standards of practice.

13. Establish and maintain clear relationships with allied occupations.

14. Define relationships between practitioners and those who use their services.

Vollmer and Mills (1966) present similar criteria to Houle (1980) for a field to become a profession, such as: knowledge based on scientific theory, service orientation, defining function, and standards of education and training. We focus on Houle's criteria because they offer guidance to practitioners having ownership of their career as well as to the vocation or occupation as a whole having a parallel responsibility to advance the field.

Although administrators of volunteers may feel alone in their struggle to become accepted as a profession, other fields such as rehabilitation counselling, teaching, and public relations are also working to become recognized and respected. Stebnicki (2009) is concerned about the field of rehabilitation counselling, where due to retirement, part of the history, knowledge, and energy for moving the field forward has been lost. As a result, "we are in a state of transition concerning our personal and professional identity" (Stebnicki, 2009, p. 133).

Some believe that teaching is a profession like law or medicine, although others consider the field a craft like journalism, which is learned principally on the job (Levine, 2006, p. 33). Observers differ regarding whether teaching should be regarded as a profession (Myers, 2008; Houston, 2008). In public relations, professionalization is linked to a body of knowledge, ethics, and certification, which are understood as defining criteria of a profession (Pieczka, 2000, p. 212). Public relations professionals are challenged, as are administrators of volunteers, to offer value to paid staff, the community, and society. The *knowledge* that public relations practitioners possess is a "powerful source of the profession's status and power" (p. 211). Nevertheless, the field struggles to convince others of its role and status.

As in these other fields, administrators of volunteers are also seeking recognition for their contribution to clients, organizations, and the larger society. Houston (2008, p. 25) raises questions about the field of teaching which may be applicable to the administration of volunteers as well:

> 1) Should teaching be a profession? 2) Does it matter? 3) Does being called a professional change status, income, effectiveness, mode of conduct, or procedures? 4) Will having an agreed-on definition of teaching as a profession make a difference in the quality of preparation, practice, or compensation?

In the following section we compare the field of administration of volunteers against Houle's (1980) criteria to establish its status and movement toward becoming recognized as a profession. In making this comparison we need to adjust our expectations to the observation noted by Fischer and Cole (1993, p. 160) that of the thousands of occupations in contemporary society perhaps only 30 to 40 have been fully professionalized.

ADMINISTRATION OF VOLUNTEERS: PROGRESS TOWARD PROFESSIONALIZATION

Houle (1980) proposes that professionalization of a field is the responsibility of both individual practitioners and the vocation as a whole. Using Houle's criteria (listed above) we assess the progress of the field of administration of volunteers toward professionalization.

1. "Clarify the defining function of the profession": In general, administrators of volunteers and researchers in the field have succeeded in elaborating the functions, responsibilities, and organizational role of those who involve and integrate volunteer and other community resources. Even though practitioners and researchers understand this set of job responsibilities as a distinct profession, the public is not well aware of its existence — an issue which calls for further professionalization of the field.

A poignant example emanates from the immediate aftermath of the 9/11 Tragedy in New York City — a time when volunteer administrators should have been at the forefront of relief and recovery efforts. The New York Mayor's Voluntary Action Center was involved for coordination, "But, the extensive and diverse number of volunteer program managers in New York have not been tapped for their expertise" (Ellis, 2001, p. 2). Instead, an investment banker was appointed to head the relief effort, who "was amazed to learn that there was a profession of volunteer management" (Ellis, 2001, p. 2). Ellis laments: "How could this happen? Is it really necessary to re-invent the basics of volunteer management in the middle of this sort of crisis? Why did no one in charge call upon one (or many) of the civilian volunteerism experts in the city? The answer, I'm afraid, is that they didn't even think of it."

Because they are related, we combine our evaluation of Houle's (1980) criteria: 2. "Master the essential information and theory that constitute the knowledge base of the profession"; and 3. be able to "use theoretical bodies of knowledge to solve problems" that arise in practice. In addition to the general body of literature that addresses volunteerism and volunteer administration, administrators of volunteers also need to be aware of the particular context(s) in which they work, for example, healthcare, social work, arts and culture, recreation, *etc.* Recognizing and absorbing the considerable breadth and depth of pertinent knowledge that exists not only in volunteer administration but also in their particular substantive area pose challenges for practitioners. Fisher and Cole (1993, pp. 166) also point out the difficulties professionalization can create through the tendency to standardize or unify "best" or "correct" practices across organizational or policy realms that are quite different.

4. "Have available and use a substantial body of knowledge and techniques that has grown out of practical application": Administration of volunteers is a hybrid field that draws useful contributions from social work, psychology, education, management, and other disciplines. As

such, its practitioners tend to be masters of improvisation who apply techniques and methods with which they feel comfortable and have served them well in the past. They are accustomed to drawing on diverse applications. Given the breadth and fragmentation of the field across diverse organizational settings, however, the danger exists that administrators of volunteers may not always be aware of the range of applicable techniques and/or their respective strengths and limitations.

5. "Enhance application through the study of topics not directly related to their occupation": Because volunteer administration is a highly applied field, and administrators of volunteers must demonstrate to their various stakeholders (and skeptics) that the methods and procedures they employ are effective, they need to become proficient in the policy contexts of the organizations in which they work. The motivation, thus, exists for them to become knowledgeable about their particular policy domain, from "a" (for example, arts administration) to "z" (for example, zoo management). We expect that many administrators of volunteers have become experts in their respective substantive areas. Nevertheless, it is not possible to draw a precise inference of how widely spread their knowledge extends beyond volunteer administration.

6. "Establish formal procedures to transmit the essential body of knowledge and technique in the field": The publication of the *International Journal of Volunteer Administration* (IJOVA, successor to the *Journal of Volunteer Administration* or JOVA) is a highly positive development in transmitting and disseminating knowledge to the field. Other journals also publish research relevant to the field (for example, *Nonprofit and Voluntary Sector Quarterly*, *Nonprofit Management and Leadership*, *Voluntas*, etc.). The prominent websites in volunteer administration (see Table 2) and the availability of training at professional meetings contribute to the dissemination of a knowledge and practice base for the field. Given our admittedly rudimentary estimates of the size of the profession, however, these media likely reach only a small fraction of practitioners, in particular, those who know of their existence and are most strongly socialized to seek out useful resources. Ironically, the practitioners who might benefit most from the resources may be least aware of them.

7. "Use formal means to test the capacity of individual practitioners" to perform their duties and to license them: Brudney and Stringer (1998) found that very few formal university curricula and courses exist that would qualify individuals in the administration of volunteers. No clear baccalaureate or two-year programs of study exist. Although

certifications are available such as the Certified Volunteer Administrator (CVA) and the Certified Administrator of Volunteer Services (CAVS) through the Association of Healthcare Volunteer Resource Professionals (formerly known as the American Society of Directors of Volunteer Services), they attract relatively few adherents. Practitioners often question what is to be gained from earning certification (for example, higher salary). Formerly offered through the Association for Volunteer Administration (AVA), the CVA certification is continued through its sponsorship by the Council for Certification in Volunteer Administration. Beginning in 1967, AVA awarded this performance-based credential to members who demonstrated proficiency in a set of competencies essential to successful administration of volunteers (Brudney and Stringer, 1998, p. 96).

In our experience, many people "fall" into the field of volunteer administration (for example, as an extension or "promotion" in their other job duties), rather than begin (and remain) in the field as a result of a self-conscious career intention to serve as an administrator of volunteers. "Because it is not yet widely possible to prepare for this profession through formal academic schooling, you will find that administrators of volunteers come from a wide variety of backgrounds" (Ellis, 1996, p. 64). Stubblefield and Miles (1986) confirm that substantial numbers of administrators of volunteers come to the job without a strong background in the field and do not profess strong commitment to it as a career (compare Brudney, 1990).

8. "Create for its members a distinctive subculture": Some support networks are available to administrators of volunteers, such as DOVIAs (Directors of Volunteers in Agencies) and other associations and chapters of practitioners in various locations. At the local level, practitioners may find general associations of volunteer administrators, such as the Delaware Valley Association of Volunteer Administration, spanning many types of organizations, as well as associations distinctive to particular substantive domains, such as administrators of volunteers in the arts, healthcare, or museums. At one time volunteer programs in state government maintained a national association, and the federal government had a federal interagency task force on volunteers linking multiple agencies.

9. "Use legal support and formal administrative rulings to promote and protect the profession": This type of activity is rare even among professions; the foremost examples include doctors and lawyers. It is not evident for administrators of volunteers.

10. "Encourage the general public to be aware of the work done by practitioners": The fact that administrators of volunteers have to struggle to gain legitimacy in many organizational contexts suggests that the field has not succeeded in promoting the acceptance and recognition of the profession and the work of its practitioners. The popular media routinely extols the contributions of volunteers in both human (*i.e.*, help and value to individual clients) and financial (*i.e.*, aggregate dollar value of contributed time) terms, yet overlooks the proficient and valuable efforts of administrators of volunteers in bringing about these results. Volunteers have captured the public eye — but not the professionals who enable and facilitate their impressive achievements. The creation and promotion of a professional association such as AL!VE — the Association of Leaders in Volunteer Engagement (2009) — could be most helpful in publicizing and promoting the field to the media, the public, and practitioners. The mission of AL!VE is to "enhance and sustain the spirit of volunteer engagement in America by fostering collaboration and networking, promoting professional development, and providing advocacy for leaders in community engagement."

11. "Establish a tradition or code of ethical practice": With its code of Ethics and Standards, the Association for Volunteer Administration was forthright in promoting ethics in volunteer administration (Fisher and Cole, 1993, pp. 177-178). That Code is still in force and has been updated by the Council for Certification in Volunteer Administration. As well, other literature and training in volunteer administration typically remind and reinforce the concept and value of ethical practice. In addition, those who enter the field from other client-oriented professions, such as social work, nonprofit administration, public administration, leisure studies, *etc.*, are normally exposed to ethical precepts and practice in their studies.

12. "Establish and enforce standards of practice" that result in penalties for those who are incompetent or fail to uphold ethical standards: Short of legal action that might ensue in the most egregious of cases, administrators of volunteers lack an association, accrediting body, or governmental entity to perform this policing function. Such a criterion signals a very mature profession.

13. "Establish and maintain clear relationships with allied occupations": In the absence of strong identification, acceptance, and recognition of the field of administration of volunteers, its relationship with allied occupations is unclear. In fact, because administrators of volunteers may have been educated in allied occupations and trained in

a variety of disciplines, and hold a variety of job titles across organizations, their relationships with other professions are more often mixed than distinct. These officials are more likely to borrow and share across disciplines than to be concerned about the "permeability" versus "purity" of their field versus other occupations.

14. "Define the relationship between practitioners and those who use their services": Although administrators of volunteers must satisfy a variety of important stakeholders (host organizations, partnering organizations, community groups, people served, *etc.*), they are well aware of their principal clientele: people interested in donating their time and talents to worthwhile causes of every description. Without them, a field of volunteer administration would cease to exist. Administrators of volunteers are the experts in recruiting, motivating, and sustaining this group in volunteering. These administrators understand that to fulfill this defining function of their profession (the first requirement for becoming a profession, according to Houle (1980)) they must be highly sensitive to the needs, preferences, and capabilities of their main clientele, current and prospective volunteers.

CONCLUSION

Our review of the criteria for professionalization with regard to the administration of volunteers suggests prospects as well as problems for the field. The field embraces a strong, innovative group of practitioners who seem adaptable and energetic to the demands of becoming a profession. The field boasts a journal (IJOVA), and other journals address volunteerism and administration of volunteers to inform research and practice. The emergence of a new professional association should also assist in the dissemination of knowledge to the field and promote engagement with the media and the public. Yet, the field must confront long-standing issues, such as a unifying name or title for its practitioners, creation of identifiable educational programs and career tracks, and inclusion in major occupational classification codes.

According to the Standard Occupation Code (SOC), "the principles adopted in the new SOC should be relevant to the existing world of work. It should realistically reflect the current occupational structure of the United States" (1995, p. 10999). If the administration of volunteers is to become recognized as a profession, it must make its way onto the Standard Occupational Code listing. No mean feat, this accomplishment would correct an inaccurate characterization of the valuable work carried out by these professionals. Moreover, it would offer a clear signal and guidepost for new entrants to the field as well as seasoned practitioners of the value and contribution of the administrator of volunteers. If the SOC were to list administration of volunteers as a credible profession, more individuals may be drawn to the career as a meaningful way to contribute to society through working with volunteers.

In Spring 2009, President Barack Obama signed the *Serve America Act*, which is intended to triple the number of AmeriCorps participants, allocate $5.7 billion to the Corporation for National and Community Service through 2014, and stimulate much greater volunteer activity. The Act will increase opportunities for Americans of all ages to serve. If millions more Americans are encouraged to volunteer and assist communities, the need for capable administrators of volunteers to provide the experiences and results they seek should rise in importance.

This official is responsible for administering volunteer programs to achieve the best outcomes for clients, organizations, and volunteers. The stakes are high, for negative experiences for any of these constituencies can demean volunteerism as a response to community needs and interests and restrict the flow and number of volunteers into service. Progress toward professionalization will help the field prepare for and adapt to the new service initiatives.

In our view, the path toward professionalization is difficult, but worth the effort. We need a profession to match the serious social problems that volunteers confront and the inspiring motivation and commitment they bring to these endeavors.

REFERENCES

ALIVE – the Association of Leaders in Volunteer Engagement. (2009). Available at http://www.associationofleadersinvolunteer engagement.org/index.php. Retrieved June 15, 2009.

Association for Healthcare Volunteer Resource Professionals. (2009). Available at http://www.ahvrp.org/ahvrp/about/association.html. Retrieved June, 15, 2009.

Bradner, Jeanne. (1999). *Leading volunteers for results: Building communities today*. Winnetka, Illinois: Conversation Press, Inc.

Brubacher, J.S. (1962). The evolution of professional education. In N.B. Henry, *Education for the profession: The sixty-first yearbook of the National Society for the Student of Education* (pp. 47-67). Chicago: University of Chicago Press.

Brudney, Jeffrey L. (1990). *Fostering volunteer programs in the public sector: planning, initiating, and managing voluntary activities*. San Francisco: Jossey-Bass.

Brudney, Jeffrey L. (2001). Volunteer administration. In J. Steven Ott (Ed.), *Understanding nonprofit organizations* (pp. 329-338). Boulder, CO: Westview Press.

Brudney, Jeffrey L. (2005). Utilizing volunteers in the workplace. In Stephen E. Condrey (Ed.), *Handbook of human resource management in government* (2nd ed.) (pp. 215-238). San Francisco: Jossey-Bass.

Brudney, Jeffrey L., & Brown, Mary. (1990). Results of a major survey and challenges for the field: Educational needs in volunteer administration. *Voluntary Action Leadership*, Summer.

Brudney, Jeffrey L., & Schmahl, Sandra. (2001). Surveys of volunteer administrators, 1992 and 2000: Trends for the profession. *The Journal of Volunteer Administration*, *20*(1), 6-14.

Brudney, Jeffrey L., & Stringer, Gretchen E. (1998). Higher education in volunteer administration: Exploring – and critiquing – the state of the art. In Michael O'Neill & Kathleen Fletcher (Eds.), *Nonprofit management education: U.S. and world perspectives* (pp. 95-109). Westport, CT: Greenwood/Praeger.

Bureau of Labor Statistics. (2010). Volunteering in the United States, 2009. Bureau of Labor Statistics. Available at http://www.bls.gov/ews.release/olun.nr0.htm. Retrieved April 26, 2010.

Burkham, A., & Boleman, C. (2005). *Volunteer administration in the 21st century: Understanding and managing direct and episodic volunteers.* Agricultural Communications: The Texas A&M University System.

Crosby, Olivia. (2001). Helping charity work: Paid jobs in charitable nonprofits. *Occupational Outlook Quarterly*, Summer, 11-23.

Elliot, P. (1972). *The sociology of the professions*. New York: Herder and Herder.

Ellis, Susan. (1996). *From the top down: The executive role in volunteer program success* (2nd ed.). Philadelphia, PA: Energize, Inc.

Ellis, Susan. (2000). Should volunteer administration be a profession? Yes … *e-Volunteerism*, *1*(1), (Fall), 1-2. Available at http://www.e-volunteerism.com/subscriber/quarterly/00fall/roffull1yes.html. Retrieved February 18, 2009.

Ellis, Susan. (2001). A volunteerism perspective on the days after the 11th of September. Available at http://www.energizeinc.com/hot/1oct.html. Retrieved June 1, 2009.

Ellis, Susan. (2006). What's in a name … or a title? Available at http://www.energizeinc.com/hot/2006/sept06.html. Retrieved February 8, 2009.

Fisher, James, & Cole, Kathleen. (1993). *Leadership and management of volunteer programs: A Guide for volunteer administrators.* San Francisco: Jossey-Bass.

Goyder, John. (2005). The dynamics of occupational prestige: 1975-2000. *Canada Review of Sociological Anthropology, 42*(1), 1-23.

Hawthorne, N. (2006). The case for hiring a manager of volunteers. In *Nonprofit agenda* (pp. 6-7, 10). Washington, DC: The Center for Nonprofit Advancement, April/May. Available at: http://www.nonprofit advancement.org/usr_doc/Apr-May_06_agenda_final.pdf. Retrieved June 11, 2009.

Houle, C. O. (1980). *Continuing learning in the professions.* San Francisco: Jossey-Bass.

Houston, W. Robert. (2008). Third response to "The Teacher as a Service Professional," by Donald A. Myers: Defining professionalism does not make it so. *Action in Teacher Education, 30*(1), 21-25.

Howlett, Steven. (2009). Global volunteer management survey, summary report: People first – total solutions (2008): A look at the findings. *e-Volunteerism, IX*(3) (April 15-July 14), 1-5. Available at http://www.e-volunteerism.com/subscriber/quarterly/09apr/09apr-researchfull.html. Retrieved May 22, 2009.

Independent Sector. (2009). U.S. charitable giving reaches $295.02 billion in 2006. Available at http://www.aafrc.org/press_releases/gusa/20070625.pdf. Retrieved February 15, 2009.

Levine, Arthur. (2006). Educating school teachers (Report No. 2). Washington, DC: Education Schools Project.

McCurley, Steve. (2000). Should volunteer administration be a profession? No … *e-Volunteerism, I*(1), (Fall), 1-2, Available at http://www.e-volunteerism.com/subscriber/quarterly/00fall/proffull1no.html. Retrieved February 18, 2009.

Myers, Donald. (2008). The teacher as a service professional. *Action in Teacher Education, 30*(1), 4-11.

Naylor, Harriet. (1976). *Leadership for volunteering.* New York: Dryden Associates.

Nonprofit Times. (2004). Special report: NPT salary survey 2004: Raises beat inflation, newly filled positions pay less. Available at http://www.nptimes.com/Feb04/specialreport.pdf. Retrieved June 1, 2009.

Perlmutter, Felice D. (1982). The professionalization of volunteer administration. *Nonprofit and Voluntary Sector Quarterly, 11*(1), 97-107.

Pieczka, Magda. (2000). Objectives and evaluation in public relations work: what do they tell us about expertise and professionalism? *Journal of Public Relations Research, 12*(3), 211-233.

Points of Light Foundation. (2004). The changing nature of the volunteering field: Keeping abreast of current trends. *Observations from the Volunteering Frontline 1*(1), 1.

Scheier, Ivan. (1988). Empowering a profession II: Seeing ourselves as more than a Subsidiary. *Journal of Volunteer Administration, 7*(1), 29-34.

Senge, Peter. (1998). The practice of innovation. *Leader to Leader, 9,* 16-22.

Silver, N., & Melsh, M. (1999). *Positioning the profession: communicating the power of results for volunteer leadership professionals.* Richmond, Va.: Association for Volunteer Administration.

Standard Occupational Classification, Revision Policy Committee, Notice. (1995). *Federal Register, 60*(39), 10999-110002. Available at http://www.bls.gov/soc/soc_feb28.pdf. Retrieved April 30, 2009.

Standard Occupational Classification User Guide. (2009). Available at http://www.bls.gov/soc/socguide.htm. Retrieved on May 4, 2009.

Stebnicki, Mark. (2009). A call for integral approaches in the professional identity of rehabilitation counseling. *Rehabilitation Counseling Bulletin, 52*(2), 133-137.

Stubblefield, Harold, & Miles, Leroy. (1986). Administration of volunteer programs as a career: What role for higher education? *Nonprofit and Voluntary Sector Quarterly, 15*(1), 4-12.

Urban Institute. (2004). *Volunteer management capacity in America's charities and congregations: A briefing report.* Washington, DC: Urban Institute. Available at http://www.urban.org/UploadedPDF/410963_VolunteerManagment.pdf. Retrieved May 11, 2009.

Vollmer, H., & Mills, D.L. (1966). *Professionalization.* Englewood Cliffs, NJ: Prentice Hall.

Chapter 2

ETHICS — CONCEPTS AND DEFINITIONS

Kathleen McCleskey
University of North Texas
KM Consulting and Training Connection

HISTORY

In the mid-1990s the Association for Volunteer Administration (AVA) developed the first code of ethics for the profession of individuals who manage volunteers. Members of AVA shared a commitment to the effective leadership of voluntary efforts and to that end produced a professional code of ethics. AVA used the six pillars of core ethical values from the Josephson Institute. These pillars are (The Josephson Institute of Ethics, 1993):

1.   Citizenship and Philanthropy

2.   Respect

3.   Responsibility

4.   Caring

5.   Justice and Fairness

6.   Trustworthiness

In 2006, the Council for Certification in Volunteer Administration (CCVA) updated the ethics for the profession. The core principles from the original AVA document were incorporated. The Code of Ethics for Volunteer Administrators defines those who mobilize citizens as individuals who (Council for Certification in Volunteer Administration, *Professional Ethics in Volunteer Administration*, 2006, p. 2):

- Create a social climate which makes the meeting of human needs possible;

- Provide for the involvement of people in the decision making process;

- Contribute to creative and responsible social development and change; and,

- Enhance and extend the work of employed persons in many fields and settings.

The current code of ethics carries this tradition of helping members of the profession to become strong and principled leaders who make decisions that are founded on core ethical principles.

Jim Collins, the author of *Built to Last* and *Good to Great*, stated:

Our research points to one essential element in any successful company. Those that are the best have built a set of core values and lived by them.

(John C. Maxwell, *Ethics 101: What Every Reader Needs to Know* (New York: Center Street, 2003), pp. 68, 69.)

INTRODUCTION

CCVA supports an ethical approach to managing volunteer resources. To that end, the Council wants to ensure members of the profession understand the meaning of ethics, how ethics relate to the overall values or guiding principles of the nonprofit, and the importance of making ethical decisions.

While many for-profit and public sector organizations have codes of ethics, few nonprofit organizations have a code of ethics. Few people or organizations know the profession of volunteer administrators has a Code of Ethics. This chapter will explore professional, individual, and organizational ethics as well as offering definitions important to understanding a variety of terms. It will also explore the core values and principles for volunteer administrators.

The terms "values", "ethics", and "code of ethics" can be confusing. In 2005, the Association for Volunteer Administration defined the following terms.

- Values are: A set of core beliefs and attitudes that guide actions.

- Ethics are: A particular code of values about how someone behaves.

- Code of Ethics: Formal rules that govern behavior of a group.

(Kathy Perun, CVA, and Katie Campbell, CVA, *The Relevance of Professional Ethics* (Charlottesville, VA: Custom Publishing, 2005), p. 10.)

Another part of determining what ethics means comes from an individual's frame of reference. Individual values are most often shaped by family, society, religion, culture, and the community in which the volunteer administrator developed their value systems. During this development, a frame of reference for ethical behaviour began and became the core of how they view workplace situations, decision-making, and how to manage a volunteer program. This is why it is important to consider one's individual frame of reference for ethics as well as professional ethics. One does influence the other.

There are some questions that individuals might consider when examining what ethics means to the role of a volunteer administrator:

- What is an example of an ethical person? What makes them ethical?

- What do I think constitutes ethical behaviour in my professional role?

- How might unethical behaviours affect my profession and my organization and what are the consequences?

The above questions go to the core of some of the issues associated with discussing ethics. Problems with an ethical dimension that volunteer administrators may encounter include how to treat clients or interact with members of the staff — paid or volunteer. This relationship can cover dimensions such as trust, responsibility, caring, and fairness. Other areas might include determining how to mesh volunteer wants versus nonprofit needs or adhering to policies and procedures strictly or using them as guidelines or ensuring ethical practices and organizational policies are mutually supportive and not in conflict. When these problems are considered, they can lead to other questions:

- Whose perspective on ethics are being discussed — the organization's; the individual's; the client's; or the profession's?

- Are professional ethics applied only when there is a problem or as part of how things are generally done?

- How are my professional ethics viewed by others I work with, *e.g.*, other professions, or different religious or cultural groups?

- How do my professional ethics mesh with the nonprofit organization's statement of values or statement of ethics, if the nonprofit has one? If the nonprofit does not have one, what do I compare my professional ethics to?

- How will my obligations to the professional code of ethics guide my response to unethical behaviour in the workplace?

As a professional, a volunteer administrator takes the responsibility of adhering to the CCVA code of ethics as they make decisions for their volunteer program. The volunteer administrator is responsible for establishing a clear pattern of behaviour and actions for them self and their program. This will lend credibility to the volunteer program. It is incumbent on the volunteer administrator to not only be aware of and understand their individual ethics but understand those with whom they are working and with whom they will come into contact. This examination includes determining when to apply ethical concepts.

When faced with ethical dilemmas, such as clearly identified unethical behaviour, the code of ethics can act as a guide. For example, if a court-ordered volunteer is "padding" their hours and this comes to the attention of the volunteer administrator, do they consider their professional ethics (*e.g.*, responsibility), the nonprofit's code of ethics (*e.g.*, upholding policies and procedures regarding recording time), or do they simply ignore the breach? Depending on workplace ethics or cultural differences, the volunteer administrator must examine their role as a volunteer administrator in light of their professional ethics, any organizational ethics statements, and their individual perspective on ethics. Through the examination of professional ethics the volunteer administrator is better able to determine their course of action. In this case they might refer to the CCVA Professional Code of Ethics and determine that it does matter because it is their responsibility to uphold organizational policies and procedures that dictate accurate accounting of court-ordered volunteer hours. Reflective activity such as this provides improved clarity about the profession of volunteer administration's expectations of professional conduct and the obligations a practitioner has to act in a particular manner.

Understanding individual perceptions about ethics in relationship to the profession of managing volunteer resources contributes to the effective management of a volunteer program. One outcome of this understanding is recognition that professional ethics takes precedence over personal ethical preferences — something that can pose very real challenges for some practitioners. Knowledge about individual ethical perceptions will assist the volunteer administrator to bridge with the professional codes of ethics when working with stakeholders such as the executive director, paid and volunteer staff, the board, and the community as a whole. Professional ethics will enable the volunteer administrator to examine their actions toward the overall management of volunteers, the nonprofit organization's stakeholders, and in the decision-making process. For example, consider the case of confidentiality of volunteer information. Generally, this may be known to be good practice because of the legal consequences that may result if confidential information becomes public. While responding to the legal consequences (*e.g.*, penalties) may motivate a manager to protect confidential information by securing it in a locked filing cabinet, this is a minimal standard. A volunteer administrator who views the protection of confidential information as an ethical responsibility (*e.g.*, part of being responsible and trustworthy) may consider a much higher standard. For example, instead of just locking confidential information away, a professional volunteer administrator may also consider information collection systems and processes of which information security is a small part.

Definitions of Ethics

Ethics are a set of standards by which individuals judge one another, organizations, and everyday occurrences. Over the centuries, the definition of ethics or what constitutes good ethics has been debated. Some people sum ethics up simply as the "Golden Rule" framed by some as "do unto others as you would have them do unto you." Organizations, individuals, families, and society as a whole have behaviours that govern how they will complete their job, interact with one another, and determine right from wrong.

Professions develop formal ethical standards to assist the members of that profession in upholding collective standards of behaviour to be followed by those who have proven themselves (by meeting some standard) to be a professional. These standards do not circumvent individual perspectives on ethics or organizational ethical standards but do take precedence for the practising professional. They help to guide a course of action that a professional can take; in some cases for some professions are even directive regarding expected behaviour in a specific set of circumstances.

Table 1 shows some of the words used to describe ethical behaviour for individuals, organizations, and professionals. In moving from left to right, the ethical perspective broadens from the individual, to a single organization and finally to the profession as it stands around the world.

Table 1: Examples of Individual, Organizational, and Professional Ethical Standards

Individual Perspective on Ethical Standards	Organizational Ethical Standards	Professional Ethical Standards for Volunteer Administrators
Privacy	Commitment	Trustworthiness
Dignity	Responsibility	Responsibility
Respect	Client focused	Respect
Fairness	Treated staff equability	Justice and Fairness
Caring	Caring	Caring
Being a citizen and giving back	Belong and Relationships	Citizenship and Philanthropy

The broadening of the ethical perspectives as we move to the professional level of ethical standards means that a wider range of considerations is expected of volunteer administrators. For example, as an individual, you may not have to do much in the way of explaining your rationale for your beliefs. An organization may not have to explain its standards very widely either. However, as a profession, volunteer administration has to apply across a wide variety of organizations, in multiple community contexts and set a standard of practice consistent across uncountable individual differences of its certified professionals. A profession does have to explain to its members, to organizations, and the wider community why professional standards are important and what they mean in terms of volunteer engagement or client service.

As you can see by Table 1 some ethical standards cross the continuum and are often understood no matter the context — individual, organizational or professional. Caring is one example. The commonality of each lies in the human focus no matter which area is being examined. The explanation of what professional ethics mean can be put in terms that are understood by addressing individual and organizational ethics and how they relate to professional ethics. For example, many organizations set the standard of treating all employees equally. As individuals people relate to that because they like being treated in a reasonable and fair manner. That easily transcends over to the professional ethical standard of justice and fairness. When discussing the professional code of ethics it is important the volunteer administrator is able to make the connection in terms of the three areas to ensure those with whom they work can understand the importance in relationship to volunteerism.

The professional ethical standards set by CCVA provide guidance for the most appropriate course of action. When a situation arises in the context of professional practice and the volunteer administrator feels pressure to make the right decision, the Professional Ethics in Volunteer Administration are there to help guide them. When individual, organizational, and professional ethics collide, this can lead to ethical dilemmas.

Professional and Organizational/Workplace Ethics

Professional ethical standards are guidelines for best practice. It is a common experience that professional ethics for volunteer administrators align with an individual's own personal sense of ethics. The core values in particular have been shown through workshops and feedback from CCVA certified professionals to resonate with individuals. The effect is that for most people professional practice is not at odds with individual values — most volunteer administrators report believing in caring, responsibility, trustworthiness, justice and fairness, respect, and citizenship and philanthropy. What is sometimes harder for individuals is truly appreciating that professional ethics — whether or not you personally agree with them — supersede both individual and organizational ethical perspectives. For a new professional this may result in many challenging questions about implementation or behaviour. For example,

- As an individual I do not believe that the choices of some of the volunteers that I work with are right. How am I supposed to respect and show caring to those volunteers when I think that what they are doing is fundamentally wrong?

- I believe that justice and fairness are more about the individual than the group. How am I supposed to act in the interest of the volunteer team when some individual volunteers may feel that I am treating them unfairly?

Volunteer administrators exhibit leadership when, using the Professional Ethics for Volunteer Administration to establish the standards of behaviour for the volunteer program. Leadership means ensuring volunteers are aware of what is expected of them and how they will perform whatever task they are assigned in an ethical manner. How the volunteers perform their assignments are viewed by those in the organization and the community. Thus, the volunteer administrator must exhibit and articulate what ethical behaviour is expected.

Risk of Unethical Behaviour

Behaving ethically is a basic and effective form of risk management. If a volunteer administrator or a member of the volunteer program does not behave in an ethical manner, the nonprofit organization is put at risk. The consequences may be severe and include:

- difficulty in recruiting and/or retaining volunteers;

- loss of program funding, sponsorships, or endorsements;

- legal action;

- termination of staff or volunteers role;

- unfavorable media coverage; and

- loss in reputation.

A breach of ethics can have long lasting effects on the nonprofit organization. The honesty of program staff or volunteers may come into question or the integrity of the nonprofit organization is undermined if there is a breach. A professional volunteer administrator should make the management of the nonprofit organization aware of the ethical standards for volunteer administration. Ideally this would take place on a regular basis as a topic at staff or management meetings. Discussing ethical considerations for the volunteer program is a form of organizational risk management. As a leader, the volunteer administrator is in a position to strengthen their organization by contributing program design elements that reflect the high ethical standard associated with volunteer administration.

CCVA CORE VALUES AND PRINCIPLES FOR VOLUNTEER ADMINISTRATION

CCVA in 2006 updated the ethics for volunteer administrators (CCVA, 2006). The following is a brief overview of the Core Values and Principles for Volunteer Administration. Under each Core Ethical Value there will be several supporting statements from the Core Values and Principles document and a brief discussion about some of the components. The following is reprinted with permission from CCVA.

Citizenship and Philanthropy

There are two ethical principles associated with the core ethical value of citizenship and philanthropy:

1. **Ethical Principle: Philosophy of Volunteerism**

   The Volunteer Administrator accepts the responsibility for the ongoing development of a personal, coherent philosophy of volunteerism as a foundation for working with others in developing volunteer programs.

2. **Ethical Principle: Social Responsibility**

   The Volunteer Administrator accepts responsibility to help create a social climate through which human needs can be met and human values enhanced.

(Association for Volunteer Administration, *Professional Ethics in Volunteer Administration* (2005), p. 5.)

Ideally, the volunteer administrator has a personal, coherent philosophy of volunteerism, as a foundation for working with others in developing the nonprofit organization's volunteer program. As part of the credentialing process associated with the Certified in Volunteer Administration (CVA) designation, aspiring professionals develop a personal philosophy statement. This philosophy continues to be developed and refined over a period of time and through many personal and educational experiences. Volunteer Administrators often recount working with their family in their community during holidays or at times of disaster or as part of their faith. Their philosophy of helping those in need is often formed at an early age. For others it may have been formed because of an event that affected their lives when someone else helped them. Still others choose to take a class to see what volunteer administrators do and from that point began to develop their philosophy.

Volunteer administrators should share their ideas about citizenship and philanthropy with the nonprofit organization, staff and the volunteers. A philosophy is a systematic way to view one's work. It is a continuous process of study and learning. It involves looking beyond the day-to-day and considering problems from the point of view of what repercussions or consequences actions may have on stakeholders inside and outside of the organization. A philosophy is a thought process that includes utilizing the skills of volunteers, to meet human needs. It means having an ethical basis through which they will develop their volunteer program and make decisions. The sharing of a philosophy means standing up, advocating, and mobilizing others toward the philosophy of utilizing the skills of volunteers to help others. This can be internal to members of the nonprofit or external to the community at large, the nation, or worldwide. By articulating their philosophy about volunteerism, the volunteer administrator will help others see the importance of utilizing the skills of volunteers.

In some nonprofit organizations, it may take a concerted effort to promote the mutual benefits of volunteers serving in the organization. An individual philosophical statement can help to promote the understanding that meeting human needs can be accomplished through the utilization of the skills of citizens in the community who can become volunteers. The articulation of the mutual benefit of utilizing volunteers can be an ongoing process. It means the volunteer administrator is diligent in behaving in a professional manner and keeping up-to-date on all the latest developments in the profession of volunteer administration.

For some the word philanthropy produces images of people giving money to a cause. Philanthropy also means giving service and time. From the ancient Greek the term philanthropy means to "love people." Individuals who work in a paid or nonpaid capacity in a nonprofit organization generally do so because they care about people. They want to assist those individuals the nonprofit organization serves. Volunteer administrators often cite the importance of giving of service and time to help others as a major motivation for volunteering. Being a citizen means having rights and responsibilities as a member of a community. For some this translates into giving back to the community through service and time, in other words, through volunteering. It means helping a community of people with whom you share a common concern or passion. The ethical pillars of citizenship and philanthropy mean the volunteer administrator must share their philosophy of citizen engagement. They must create a climate where clients can be served by volunteers.

Respect

There are four ethical principles associated with the core ethical value of respect:

1. **Ethical Principle: Self-Determination**

   The Volunteer Administrator accepts the responsibility to involve people in decisions that directly affect them.

2. **Ethical Principle: Mutuality**

   The Volunteer Administrator accepts the responsibility to promote understanding and the actualization of mutual benefits inherent in any act of volunteer service.

3. **Ethical Principle 2: Human Dignity**

   The Volunteer Administrator accepts responsibility for the development of volunteer programs and initiatives that respect and enhance the human dignity of all persons involved.

4. **Ethical Principle: Privacy**

   The Volunteer Administrator accepts the responsibility to respect the privacy of individuals and safeguard information including written, electronic, audio-visual and verbal formats identified as confidential.

(Association for Volunteer Administration, *Professional Ethics in Volunteer Administration* (2005), p. 6.)

Respect is the acceptance of or attitude toward ideas and people based on actions or behaviours. The volunteer administration brings respect to the volunteer program based on the program itself, how people are included, and how people are treated. Respect for people and programs is earned; not given. In the case of a volunteer program the volunteer administrator can earn respect by involving people, showing the benefits of the volunteer program to the nonprofit, communicating with stakeholders, and taking the responsibility to safeguard information about the volunteers in the volunteer program. The program gains respect by being well-run and successful.

A well-run volunteer program within an organization should involve paid staff, volunteer staff, and other stakeholders. Each nonprofit organization will have a different mix depending on its size, mission and programs. This working relationship with various stakeholders will lead the volunteer administrator to develop a well-run volunteer program by incorporating:

- volunteer tasks and position descriptions;

- performance expectations;

- policies and procedures;

- compliance with laws;

- ethical decision-making; and

- other facets of the volunteer program.

The input from stakeholders builds "buy-in" for the volunteer program; it assists those who will be working directly with volunteers to understand the expectations of the volunteers; it helps volunteers to understand decisions that affect what they are accomplishing for the nonprofit. In addition, it brings a variety of skills, knowledge, expertise, and perspective about any decisions that are being made. By involving stakeholders, the respect for the program will grow because there is an understanding of what is taking place and what the goals are of the volunteer program.

The volunteer administrator must understand how their program align with the overall mission of the nonprofit. Showing how volunteers can help to complete the mission of the nonprofit through a well-run and successful volunteer program brings respect for the volunteer program. To this end the volunteer administrator must be aware of the priorities within the nonprofit and how the volunteer program can align its activities to help complete the nonprofit's priorities. Without the strategic alignment of the volunteer program with the nonprofit's mission, it sometimes becomes a matter of "selling" the value of having a volunteer program. Communication helps stakeholders, both internal and external to the nonprofit organization, understand that volunteers help to complete the nonprofit's mission and accomplish priorities that are working toward helping the clients being served. Communication can be accomplished in a variety of ways, for example:

- website with information about the volunteer program;

- regular reports to the board about the outcomes the volunteers are producing; and

- evaluation data about the volunteer program.

By communicating accomplishments, the volunteer administrator is not only promoting the program but also indicating how the volunteer program is helping serve clients to the mutual benefit of the nonprofit. Communicating what is taking place and being accomplished by the volunteer program builds respect for the program, the volunteer administrators, and the corps of volunteers. Communication and respect tie directly into building trust and trust is built when information is shared, there is follow through, and everyone understands what is happening within the volunteer program.

While respect does not mean that a volunteer administrator has to like every volunteer they encounter, it does mean that they will need to acknowledge each person as a worthwhile contributor to the volunteer program and to the mission of the organization. Volunteer administrators will work with a variety of people from different backgrounds, age groups, and life experience. It is the responsibility of the volunteer administrator to work with each potential volunteer with respect in relationship to interviewing, placing, recognizing, and managing. Understanding that each potential volunteer is unique in their needs as a volunteer will assist the volunteer administrator in developing a plan and a philosophy of how to work with that individual to ensure they know they are a valued part of the nonprofit staff. Through the development and execution of a well-run volunteer program the staff will begin to respect the work of the volunteers and volunteer administrator and how the program helps the nonprofit accomplish its priorities and serve its clients. To accomplish this, the volunteer administrator consistently works toward developing programs that enhance individual skills and needs as well as serving the clients. This helps ensure the recognition of volunteer accomplishments and helps to distinguish the volunteer program as one that puts the needs of clients and other stakeholders it serves in a valued arena.

As a manager of human resources, volunteer administrators are responsible for the application of various state or provincial laws, such as those addressing privacy or the protection of vulnerable populations. They are also responsible, at an organizational level for policies, and procedures governing all aspects of handling volunteers as part of the overall human resource compliment of the nonprofit organization, such as protecting the confidentiality of personal information. This is no different than it would be for any paid staff member. This ensures the privacy of the individuals who volunteer for the nonprofit. All information pertaining to the volunteers should be reviewed by the volunteer administrator to see if it is confidential and requires special protection or treatment. From the minute an application or phone call is taken from a potential volunteer, the volunteer administrator must act in such a manner as to ensure the privacy of the volunteer. Respecting privacy and adhering to laws, policies, and procedures will build respect for the volunteer program.

Because volunteers in a nonprofit organization may be working with staff other than the volunteer administrator, efforts need to be made to ensure that paid staff are clear regarding confidentiality requirements. Client confidentiality is often a concern of paid staff when utilizing volunteers. To help mitigate this lack of risk tolerance, the volunteer administrator develops guidelines and training curriculum to help ensure volunteers understand the importance of client confidentiality. The volunteer administrator also works with paid staff to ensure the privacy of a volunteer's records; application, evaluations, *etc.* are confidential; any information about a volunteer is in a locked area that is secure and not accessible. All of this leads to ensuring that confidentiality is held in the highest regard. In order to reach this component of a well-run volunteer program a volunteer administrator must keep themselves up to date on legal changes and updates in the nonprofit and any change in terms of human resource management. The maintaining of confidentiality will gain the respect of the volunteer program by those who work with and in it.

The respect of a volunteer program and its volunteer administrator is earned. To earn that respect the volunteer administrator must communicate with and involve stakeholders at all levels. They must safeguard the privacy of the volunteers and indicate to the stakeholders how the volunteer program is beneficial to the nonprofit.

Responsibility

1.   Ethical Principle Staff Relationships

The Volunteer Administrator accepts the responsibility to develop a volunteer program that will enhance and extend the work of the organization's paid staff.

2.   Ethical Principle Professional Responsibility

The Volunteer Administrator accepts responsibility to contribute to the credibility of the profession in the eyes of those it serves.

3.   Ethical Principle Diligence

The Volunteer Administrator accepts responsibility to be reliable, careful, prepared, and well informed.

4. Ethical Principle Doing One's Best

The Volunteer Administrator accepts responsibility to pursue excellence even when resources are limited.

5. Ethical Principle Perseverance

The Volunteer Administrator will seek to overcome obstacles to excellence.

6. Ethical Principle Continuous Improvement

The Volunteer Administrator commits to improving his/her knowledge, skills, and ability to make judgments.

7. Ethical Principle Self-Disclosure and Self-restraint

The Volunteer Administrator commits to reflective decision making with the intent of advancing the long-term greater good.

(Association for Volunteer Administration, *Professional Ethics in Volunteer Administration* (2005), p. 8.)

Volunteer administrators are responsible for establishing a climate where the needs of the clients being served by the nonprofit are met through volunteer skills. At the same time, the volunteers in the program want to have a rewarding and fruitful volunteer experience. The volunteer administrator must create a climate that includes ensuring the tasks volunteers complete are on target to help the nonprofit complete its mission and service its clients as well as balance the needs of the volunteers who give of their time and talents.

Ultimately, the responsibility of the volunteer program rests with the volunteer administrator. This responsibility includes keeping stakeholders informed about the achievements of volunteers. The volunteer administrator is responsible for ensuring the volunteer program meets or exceeds the expectations of the program's stakeholders. To that end the volunteer administrator must be mindful of what is taking place in and around the volunteer program at all times. This enables the volunteer administrator to utilize volunteer skills to pursue a benchmark of excellence. To accomplish this, the volunteer administrator must ensure paid staff is informed and ready to accept volunteers. The preparation can include supervisory training, sharing of task/position descriptions, policies and procedures concerning volunteers, and inviting paid staff to participate in volunteer orientations. This preparation takes the mystery out of what volunteers are doing and establishes the groundwork for a good working relationship between paid staff and volunteer staff.

One of the best ways to pursue excellence is to ensure the components of a well-run volunteer program are in place. These components include:

- organizational management;

- human resource management;

- accountability; and

- leadership and advocacy.

These components make up a methodical process that take time to develop and are addressed in other chapters.

Upholding the principles of a well-run volunteer program is paramount to achieving excellence. It is the responsibility of a volunteer administrator:

- To ensure funding and resources are available to run the volunteer program.

- To develop well-defined operating procedures that are updated, reviewed, and known by all those who work with the volunteer program.

- To solicit feedback about the operations of the volunteer program on a regular basis.

- To be up-to-date on all priorities and strategic plans of the nonprofit.

- To be well-informed and understand all the aspects of managing a volunteer program in a confident and reliable manner.

- To become a life-long learner and teacher of new members of the profession.

- To make decisions that are thorough and thoughtful.

Many of these will be discussed in detail in other chapters.

The skills of managing a volunteer program are not static. The profession is ever evolving to keep abreast of the latest trends, the expectations of various generations of volunteers, and the changing environment of nonprofits. To that end the volunteer administrator must continuously be reading, conducting research online, attending professional development sessions, and networking the colleagues. These actions will help the volunteer administrator to continuously improve the volunteer program which will in turn better serve the clients. This continuous learning is the responsibility of the volunteer administrator to ensure their volunteer program is viable.

The position of volunteer administrator is one that has considerable responsibility. The responsibility falls to the volunteer administrator to do their best, be a life-long learner, and ensure relationships between the volunteer program and other members of the staff are such that the nonprofit's mission is reached. Finally, this responsibility means the volunteer administrator will keep the short-term and long-term priorities of the nonprofit in mind in all the work they do.

Caring

1. Ethical Principle Compassion and Generosity

The Volunteer Administrator assumes the responsibility to be kind, compassionate, and generous in all actions so as to minimize the harm done to others in the performance of one's duties.

(Association for Volunteer Administration, *Professional Ethics in Volunteer Administration* (2005), p. 9.)

The volunteer administrator works in an environment where helping others is the norm. At the same time, a volunteer administrator has the responsibility to be kind, compassionate, and generous in all they do inside the nonprofit and in the community. The ability to be compassionate and generous will reflect on people's impression not only of the volunteer administrator as an individual, the volunteer program, and ultimately the nonprofit as a whole. To achieve this, the volunteer administrator is conscious of all the work they perform within the nonprofit especially in the kinds and quality of relationships that they have with the people that they work with. They are also aware of how they treat potential and current volunteers. This interaction will affect that volunteer's experience and the overall quality of the volunteer program by ensuring that so-called "soft skills" are attended to. Soft skills include reflecting a concern for the well-being of others, acting to attend to how volunteers are feeling at any given time, or creating a welcoming, low stress environment. To that end, a volunteer administrator is compassionate and helps to prevent any harm or misunderstanding when volunteers are performing their tasks.

Justice and Fairness

1. Ethical Principle Procedural Fairness

The Volunteer Administrator assumes the responsibility to have an open and impartial process for collecting and evaluating information critical for making decisions.

2. Ethical Principle Impartiality

The Volunteer Administrator assumes the responsibility for having impartial and objective standards that avoid discriminatory or prejudicial behaviors.

3. Ethical Principle Equity

The Volunteer Administrator assumes the responsibility to treat all individuals with whom he/she works equitably.

(Association for Volunteer Administration, *Professional Ethics in Volunteer Administration* (2005), p. 10.)

Even though developing a well-run volunteer program is a methodical process, the outcome of that process is neither pre-determined nor permanent. Changes within the organization, the community or in the volunteers themselves will require the volunteer program be constantly reviewed and revised. The volunteer administrator is responsible for the continuous updating of information and evaluating the volunteer program. This includes checking with all stakeholders to examine any issues that have arisen and making decisions about those issues. This review will enable the volunteer administrator to collect information and evaluate it to ensure all facets of the volunteer program are being run in a fair and equitable manner. Consistency and standards in a volunteer program help to ensure a clear understanding of expectations and helps to avoid any discriminatory or prejudicial behaviours. The volunteer administrator must be prepared to make decisions that are tough and may not be popular. Decisions that are based on a clear understanding of written plans will help mitigate concerns of paid and volunteer staff. This creates an atmosphere of cooperation and teamwork to accomplish not only the goals of the volunteer program but the nonprofit as a whole. Having clear guidelines enables the volunteer administrator to make clear and equitable decisions.

Although volunteer performance standards, task descriptions, and evaluations are developed to ensure a well-run cohesive volunteer program, these should be reviewed regularly to ensure they are free from any barriers and uphold the highest ethical standards of the volunteer program. The continuous updating of information and feedback from stakeholders will enable the volunteer administrator to develop a program that not only states expectations and responsibilities for the volunteers and those who supervise them but also encourages a climate of open communication. The continuous feedback loop between the paid staff, board, volunteer staff, clients, and the volunteer administrator will assist in developing a program of excellence. Some organizations have review panels that consist of various stakeholders. Their mission is to annually review all documents and make suggestions about changes and help to close the gap in any discrepancies.

As with any organization, it is imperative the standards and policies that are developed are not discriminatory or prejudicial in any way. Many volunteer administrators base standards and policies for the volunteer program on those for the paid staff. This is one way to exhibit impartiality. Impartiality extends to other facets of the volunteer program as well. Recognition plans, for example, should be standardized for the entire volunteer program. This ensures those who have performed in such a manner as to deserve recognition are recognized in a consistent manner and thus avoiding the appearance of prejudice. The volunteer administrator must be perceived at all times as being impartial in all aspects of the volunteer program. Otherwise, the volunteer administrator and the program can lose credibility in the sight of the volunteer program's stakeholders. The idea of equity goes beyond areas such as recognition and extends to all aspects of the volunteer program. As the individual who is associated with the volunteers, the volunteer administrator is being observed to see how they interact with various stakeholders and make decisions. Their actions will be noted if they are not behaving in a judicious and fair manner.

The volunteer administrator is responsible for developing an atmosphere of teamwork and cooperation. The volunteer program's support of reaching common goals provides the opportunity for constructive feedback. It is the responsibility of the volunteer administrator to consider the feedback and ensure all aspects of the program allow volunteers to become more competent. The volunteer administrator must act in a judicious and fair manner when dealing with all stakeholders. These actions will help the volunteer administrator and the volunteer program to earn the trust of the nonprofit and the clients it serves.

Trustworthiness

1. **Ethical Principle Truthfulness**

   The Volunteer Administrator is committed to the truth and assuring that all verbal and written agreements and contracts for volunteers and staff are founded on the premise of open and honest interaction.

2. **Ethical Principle Candor**

   The Volunteer Administrator is committed to fairness and forthrightness.

3.   Ethical Principle Sincerity/Non-Deception

The Volunteer administrator will interact with all volunteers in a forthright manner with the upmost sincerity and good intent, never conducting business in a deceptive manner and continually promoting that principle throughout the organization.

4.   Ethical Principle Principled

The Volunteer Administrator understands and works to promote the core ethical values.

5.   Ethical Principle Moral Courage

The Volunteer Administrator will base his/her actions on core ethical values and will not compromise those values for convenience.

6.   Ethical Principle Reasonability of Commitments

The volunteer Administrator accepts the responsibility to be reasonable, realistic, and professional in determining the appropriateness of expectations or requests.

7.   Ethical Principle Clarity of Commitments on Behalf of the Organization, Staff and/or Volunteers

The volunteer Administrator accepts the responsibility to assure clear communication regarding commitments made on behalf of the organization, staff, or volunteers. In order to maximize success of everyone involved, the Volunteer Administrator accepts the responsibility to establish contracts and agreements that are understood and practice.

8.   Ethical Principle Limitations to Loyalty

The Volunteer Administrator understands personal and professional limits of his/her loyalty to his/her volunteers, clients and organization and prioritizes them clearly and appropriately to minimize liability and risk to everyone involved.

9.   Ethical Principle Addressing Conflicts of Interest

The Volunteer Administrator is responsible for identifying policies, procedures and circumstances that might result in a conflict of interest by appropriately and professionally addressing the issue at hand and eliminating it as a conflict.

(Association for Volunteer Administration, *Professional Ethics in Volunteer Administration* (2005), p. 11.)

Trustworthiness is about telling the truth, being honest and above board, and keeping commitments. To be trustworthy the volunteer administrator must also be sincere. This will enable the volunteer program to be seen as the program that completes what it says it will complete. The volunteer administrator's professional practice is founded on core values. The volunteer administrator will closely examine their actions beforehand and use ethical principles to guide them. They will understand "taking the easy or fastest way" to do something may not be ethical. Taking the ethical approach will help to ensure trust in the volunteer administrator and the volunteer program.

The Volunteer Administrator accepts the responsibility to assure clear communication regarding commitments made on behalf of the organization, staff, or volunteers. In order to maximize success of everyone involved, the Volunteer Administrator accepts the responsibility to establish contracts and agreements that are understood and practised. When an individual is contemplating volunteering for a nonprofit organization, they will consider if the organization will best serve or align with their interest and needs. When paid staff agrees to work with volunteer staff, they are considering if the individual they are supervising will be able to complete specific tasks and thus ultimately help the clients the nonprofit serves. The communication of responsibility, accountability, and standards rests with the volunteer administrator. Clear agreements will aid in this open and honest interaction. This process involves trust.

The volunteer administrator's role often places them between the volunteer staff and paid staff. They not only represent the volunteers but the volunteer program to the nonprofit organization. Thus, they must keep the interest of the volunteers and the nonprofit organization in balance. To aid in this understanding, the volunteer administrator must develop and adhere to any agreements, written or verbal, between the volunteer program, individual volunteers, and the paid staff. This develops trust between the staff and the volunteers. This trust is developed through open communication. Without information exchange it is hard to identify concerns. Open communication consists of who to keep informed about what, how to identify and check concerns, ideas, or grievances about volunteers or the volunteer program, and how information will be exchanged — face-to-face or electronically. Open communication means that feedback about the volunteer program is a 360-degree endeavour. All stakeholders in the volunteer program have an opportunity to present feedback, positive and negative, to all other stakeholders. Remember stakeholders in a nonprofit include the board, paid staff, volunteer staff, funders, clients, and the community as a whole. It is not a one way conversation. It is all around feedback. This openness of communication enables the volunteer administrator to review situations, examine behaviours, determine the impact, and make decisions. Devoting a concerted effort to open communication will exhibit fairness and candour in working with all stakeholders in the nonprofit. For example, consider a situation where a volunteer and a paid staff member are not working well together. The volunteer administrator needs to hear both sides of the situation to determine what to do. They may need to obtain information from both parties as well as share information they may have. In the end, the volunteer staff member and the paid staff member must be treated with impartiality and a decision must be made. The volunteer administrator cannot make assumptions about who is right or wrong but must instead, take the time to gather information and balance what was heard before taking action.

To achieve trusting interaction, the volunteer administrator works with the assistance of other staff and volunteers to develop the specifics of a well-run volunteer program including expectations, performance standards, and evaluation procedures. Developing these will help to ensure agreements that are made about tasks are clearly understood by paid and volunteer staff as to what work will be accomplished, in what time-frame, and who will be supervising and completing the tasks. The volunteer administrator must approach all situations with forthrightness. This means they communicate with candour and in an honest manner to avoid confusion. This assists paid and volunteer staff in understanding any written or verbal agreements that have been made with reference to the volunteer and the volunteer program.

Developing trust for the volunteer administrator means ensuring volunteers have what they need to accomplish the tasks they are given. The need can be anything from simple supplies, phone usage, computer accessibility, to explicit directions for completing a task. For volunteer staff to be successful the volunteer administrator must meet the needs of volunteers and the volunteer must trust all the resources they need to be successful are in place.

The volunteer administrator understands there are times when requests are made with reference to the volunteer program that may not be possible to fulfill. At these times, the volunteer administrator must act in a professional manner to decline the request and provide a reason for those affected. It is the volunteer administrator's responsibility to determine if the request can be fulfilled based on factors such as the timing of the request, number of volunteers available, and other pertinent factors. If a climate of trust has been developed, then the decision made by the volunteer administrator will be considered and agreed upon.

Trust also encompasses commitment. The volunteer administrator must ensure any commitments undertaken by the volunteer program are clear. The volunteer administrator must understand and be perfectly clear about any policies concerning conflict of interest, limits of personal and professional relationships, and other situations that might cause harm to the nonprofit. In order to accomplish clear commitments, the volunteer administrator must clearly communicate expectations, who is responsible, and who will be held accountable for any agreements that are made on behalf of the volunteer program. This will entail a continuous commitment to verbalizing the components of a well-run volunteer program and to the ethics of the profession. Even with a strong commitment to the ethics for the profession, the volunteer administrator may encounter situations that will call on them to be specific about any conflicts of interest that may arise. For example, a conflict of interest may arise that involves a board member, who is a volunteer. Perhaps they are seeking to use their position to secure a contract for printing brochures for a fundraiser from a company owned by their spouse. Clear boundaries of loyalties toward the volunteer staff, paid staff, board, clients, and other stakeholders must be beyond question. Without this clarity what may seen to be "no big deal" can quickly turn into front-page news. If it "smells", even a little, it may be time to examine the situation further and in more depth. If problems arise from any situation, it reflects on the nonprofit and can ultimately cause the nonprofit great harm in the form of lack of donations, lack of volunteers, and lack of community support. The volunteer administrator must address conflicts of interest, personal and professional relationships, and other situations by ensuring policies and procedures are in place for the volunteer program. If these are not adhered to, trust in the volunteer program in the eyes of the nonprofit, as well as the community, may decline.

CONCLUSION

Volunteer administrators are fortunate to have a well-developed, written set of professional ethics authored by CCVA to guide them in their role. The value of a professional statement of ethics is that it presents the guidelines by which a volunteer administrator can manage a well-run volunteer program and problems can be addressed in an ethical manner. Volunteer administrators ideally understand the ethics for the profession of managing volunteer resources and are aware of their individual code of ethics.

The benefit of employing professional ethics is that it will enable the volunteer administrator to base their professional practice and decisions on a solid foundation. Decisions and practice based on such a foundation:

- reduce the risk to the organization, the volunteers, clients, and the volunteer administrator;

- unify the profession of volunteer administration, giving a common language and practice base from which the profession can continue to grow;

- improve the contributions of volunteers to the mission of the organization and the the community generally;

- improve the accessibility of their volunteer program to diverse groups; and

- builds the public trust.

This foundation enables the volunteer administrator to have a driving force behind what they are doing and how they set priorities. Volunteer administrators wear many hats when it comes to developing a climate within their program so volunteers can productively work and help to achieve the mission of the nonprofit organization. Acknowledging and adhering to a code of ethics will enable the volunteer administrator to run a volunteer program that will be perceived as one that can be trusted.

REFERENCES

Association for Volunteer Administration. (1996). *Statement of professional ethics in volunteer administration* (2nd ed.). Boulder, CO.

Council for Certification in Volunteer Administration. (2009). *Professional ethics in volunteer administration*. Midlothian, VA.

Ethics Resource Center. (2010). Arlington, VA. Available at http://www.ethics.org.

Hammond, John S., Keeney, Ralph L., & Raiffa, Howard. (2002). *Smart choices: A practical guide to making better life decisions*. New York: First Broadway Books.

Josephson, Michael. (1993). *Making Ethical Decisions*. W. Hason (Ed.). Available at http://josephsoninstitute.org

Kidder, Rushworth M. (1996). *How good people make tough choices: Resolving the dilemmas of ethical living*. New York: Fireside.

Maxwell, John C. (2003). *Ethics 101: What every leader needs to know*. New York: Center Street.

Chapter 3

ETHICAL DECISION-MAKING

Cheryle N. Yallen
CNY Enterprises

INTRODUCTION

Ethics is the attempt to judge right from wrong, or good from bad. Ethical leadership pertains to how a volunteer administrator acts in a morally responsible way. Ethical dilemmas are conflicts of interest between two or more ethical interests. Frequently, such ethical dilemmas will occur where we have duties towards several different people at the same time, *i.e.*, towards the project's partners, the project's volunteers and the nonprofit organization all at the same time. An ethical dilemma is solved by analyzing the interests at stake, judging the moral implications of these interests and making a decision of the proper course of action.

- Volunteer administrators subscribe to a nationally-recognized code of ethics and create volunteer programs that meet the professional standards of the field. Volunteer administrators mobilize, direct and motivate volunteers and must be committed to the following core ethical values: (1) Citizenship and Philanthropy, (2) Respect, (3) Responsibility, (4) Compassion and Generosity, (5) Justice and Fairness, and (6) Trustworthiness.

These are discussed in detail in the previous chapter. Administrators of volunteer programs should base their decision-making on these core ethical values if they are to maintain a program that:

- is accessible to diverse groups;

- operates ethically with all stakeholders;

- strives for excellence;

- maintains the public trust;

- sustains a helping environment;

- is at low risk for legal actions against it. (Council for Certification in Volunteer Administration, 2006)

IDENTIFYING AN ETHICAL DILEMMA

Before we look at the types of ethical dilemmas an organization might face, it is helpful to identify what ethics is not. Manuel Velasquez, Claire Andre, Thomas Shanks, S.J., and Michael J. Meyer of the Markkula Center for Applied Ethics (1987) state:

- Ethics is not the same as feelings. Feelings provide important information for our ethical choices. Some people have highly developed habits that make them feel bad when they do something wrong, but many people feel good even though they are doing something wrong. And often our feelings will tell us it is uncomfortable to do the right thing if it is hard.

- Ethics is not religion. Many people are not religious, but ethics applies to everyone. Most religions do advocate high ethical standards but sometimes do not address all the types of problems we face.

- Ethics is not following the law. A good system of law does incorporate many ethical standards, but law can deviate from what is ethical.

- Ethics is not following culturally accepted norms. Some cultures are quite ethical, but others become corrupt or blind to certain ethical concerns. "When in Rome, do as the Romans do" is not a satisfactory ethical standard.

- Ethics is not science. Social and natural science can provide important data to help us make better ethical choices. But science alone does not tell us what we ought to do. Science may provide an explanation for what humans are like. But ethics provides reasons for how humans ought to act. And just because something is scientifically or technologically possible, it may not be ethical to do it.

Some ethical dilemmas are easy to recognize, while others are not. For example, Susan has a duty to get up in the morning and arrive on time for her volunteer job but she would rather sleep for a couple more hours. Compare this with Judy who is feeling very ill and possibly should not get out of bed and go to her volunteer assignment but insists on doing so anyway. Which is an ethical dilemma? Susan's desire to stay in bed itself is not an ethical interest — there is no real question of the proper course of action. The issue for the volunteer administrator is simply how to best resolve the conflict with the volunteer and demonstrating the importance of being on time. The situation with Judy, though, can be an ethical dilemma because the volunteer administrator will have to weigh several interests — Judy's health, her independence and the health risks to the clients served who would come in contact with Judy.

Volunteer administrators must first understand that certain rights and duties exist. A right is an ethical demand that you can make of other people, *e.g.*, the right to speak your opinion or the right not to be hurt or offended. A duty is an ethical demand that other people can make of you, *e.g.*, the duty not to hurt or offend others.

According to B.L. Toffler (1986) an ethical dilemma has six characteristics:

1. It is hard to name.
2. It is embedded in a specific context.
3. It may not be obvious.
4. It addresses the claims of multiple stakeholders.
5. It involves a situation where an individual wants to do the right thing but either does not know what that is or is not able to do it.
6. They frequently involve factors that make the right and wrong less than patently clear.

Ethical Decision-Making

To make an ethical decision we must understand five subjects — (1) the core ethical values and what they encompass; (2) the principle of tolerance and the role it plays in ethical decision-making; (3) the role of the volunteer administrator in ethical decision-making; (4) understanding ethical dilemmas; and (5) the process for making good decisions. Core ethical values and what they encompass is covered in the previous chapter. The second subject — the principle of tolerance — addresses each individual's comfort with conflict and/or disagreement.

When resolving an ethical dilemma the principle of tolerance comes into play. Simply put, this is the respect for differences. Disagreements are not resolved by becoming alike (*i.e.*, changing your preference, habit, norm, *etc.*), but rather by reaching a social agreement that accommodates everyone. The differences are not removed, but tolerated. Volunteer administrators interact with agency administration, other staff and the volunteers. Disagreements inevitably arise during the course of doing their job. There are times when some actions, preferences, norms, *etc.*, are so far outside the scope of being accepted by the profession of volunteer administration that they cannot be accommodated. The line between what you can accept and what you cannot is the boundary of tolerance.

Ethical behaviour can be risky because it aims to a have a higher standard in place regarding how people are treated. In organizations where there is resource scarcity or where there is an attitude of "just getting by," a strong advocate for higher service standards may challenge decisions by management or the board. Having the Council for Certification in Volunteer Administration (CCVA) professional ethical standards, however, provides a foundation for such advocacy.

By following these standards the dilemma becomes less confusing or fearful and decision-making clearer. As a volunteer administrator, the following must be considered when dealing with ethical dilemmas:

* What interests are at stake?

* Is it an ethical dilemma?

* What are my duties or obligations towards these interests?

* Which interest should have more attention/respect/right of way by comparing and judging them against each other?

There are numerous pressures in play when a volunteer administrator must make a decision. How do these pressures impact the volunteer administrator's ability to produce results? When pressure is applied to making decisions, individuals will act and react differently. Some will go with the status quo, some will examine various methods of decision-making, and others will just make a quick decision so they can get to the next task.

The pressure is decreased dramatically because the volunteer administrator must rely on their individual and professional code of ethics. A balanced decision regarding an ethical issue needs to take into consideration the perspectives of those people who will be affected by the decision made by the volunteer administrator, *e.g.*, the volunteer, clients, staff. Part of the decision-making process is a reflection on the real or perceived power that those who are participating in the process have. Volunteer administrators typically have formal power given to them by the organization related to the management of the volunteer program. Although they may have formal power, in order to have decisions that will obtain buy-in from others they want to act in such a manner that it instills trust in them and the decisions they must make. If they approach decisions from the "my way or the highway" perspective they will undoubtedly run into road blocks. Volunteer administrators want to have and use informal power which means they are trusted, they are seen as reliable, they use sound judgement and are ethical in their decisions. This informal power is not based on where they are on the organizational chart but instead on how they think and act.

When making a decision to resolve an ethical issue, a volunteer administrator must be:

- above board (transparent);

- avoid the perception of unethical behaviour (just and fair);

- avoid mistakes and own up to the ones that are made (responsible for their decision and its consequences);

- stand by what they say they will do (reliability);

- act in a responsible manner with sound judgement (integrity);

- help others understand what ethical decision-making is and its impact on the organization (responsible and caring); and

- promote the ethics of the profession (be a professional).

There are different approaches that can be considered when understanding ethical decision-making that complement the core ethical values within the professional code of ethics that is part of professional certification through CCVA. Velasquez *et al.* (2009) describe five such approaches:

The Virtue Approach

- Focuses on attitudes, dispositions, or character traits that enable us to be and to act in ways that develop our human potential.

- Examples: honesty, courage, faithfulness, trustworthiness, integrity, *etc.*

- The principle states: "What is ethical is what develops moral virtues in ourselves and our communities."

The Utilitarian Approach

- Focuses on the consequences that actions or policies have on the well-being ("utility") of all persons directly or indirectly affected by the action or policy.

- The principle states: "Of any two actions, the most ethical one will produce the greatest balance of benefits over harms."

The Rights Approach

- Identifies certain interests or activities that our behaviour must respect, especially those areas of our lives that are of such value to us that they merit protection from others.

- Each person has a fundamental right to be respected and treated as a free and equal rational person capable of making his or her own decisions.

- This implies other rights (*e.g.*, privacy, free consent, freedom of conscience, *etc.*) that must be protected if a person is to have the freedom to direct his or her own life.

- The principle states: "An action or policy is morally right only if those persons affected by the decision are not used merely as instruments for advancing some goal, but are fully informed and treated only as they have freely and knowingly consented to be treated."

The Fairness (or Justice) Approach

- Focuses on how fairly or unfairly our actions distribute benefits and burdens among the members of a group.

- Fairness requires consistency in the way people are treated.

- The principle states: "Treat people the same unless there are morally relevant differences between them."

The Common Good Approach

- Presents a vision of society as a community whose members are joined in a shared pursuit of values and goals they hold in common.

- The community is comprised of individuals whose own good is inextricably bound to the good of the whole.

- The principle states: "What is ethical is what advances the common good."

Each of the approaches above provides a good starting point to understanding what standards of behaviour can be considered ethical. There are still problems to be solved, however. The first problem is that we may not agree on the content of some of these specific approaches. We may not all agree to the same set of human and civil rights. We may not agree on what constitutes the common good. We may not even agree on what is a good and what is a harm.

The second problem is that the different approaches may not all answer the question, "What is ethical?" in the same way. Nonetheless, each approach gives us important information with which to determine what is ethical in a particular circumstance. And much more often than not, the different approaches do lead to similar answers.

CCVA's Professional Ethics in Volunteer Administration, as described in a previous chapter, expands on these standards by providing specific ethical principles to guide behaviour. The two problems described above are essentially eliminated because the professional standards are specific and leave little room for questions. Making good ethical decisions requires sensitivity to ethical issues and a practised method for exploring the ethical aspects of a decision and weighing the considerations that should impact our choice of a course of action. Having a method for ethical decision-making is absolutely essential. When practised regularly, the method becomes so familiar that we work through it automatically without consulting the specific steps.

The more novel and difficult the ethical choice we face, the more we need to rely on discussion and dialogue with others about the dilemma. Only by careful exploration of the problem, aided by the insights and different perspectives of others, can we make good ethical choices in such situations. Belonging to a local professional association is extremely helpful in these situations. The peer-to-peer networking and relationships that are developed provide the advantage of discussing ethical situations with like-minded professionals. Many of your colleagues have either already experienced the situation you find yourself in or, at a minimum, understands the dilemma. The volunteer administrator should encourage inquiry. Simple statements such as "let's talk about that idea" will encourage others to do just that — talk about their ideas. Being open to different ideas and possibilities is important whether leading a group decision-making process or making a decision alone.

The volunteer administrator should establish an environment:

- Where it is safe to disagree.
- Where all stakeholders ideas are equal.
- Where conflict around ideas is okay.
- Where the conflict is not about individuals but actions.
- Where the group is diverse and naysayers are allowed.

Starting Questions

The CCVA Code of Professional Ethics makes the point that not every issue is an ethical issue. For example, time, money, and the like are neutral. Ethical issues tend to derive from a conflict of values *or* behaviours inconsistent with ethical values. So how do we actually recognize when there is an ethical issue? There must be a framework for ethical decision-making. One such framework has been set forth by Velasquez *et al.* (2009). They start by asking the following questions:

- Could this decision or situation be damaging to someone or to some group?
- Does this decision involve a choice between a good and bad alternative, or perhaps between two "goods" or between two "bads"?
- Is this issue about more than what is legal or what is most efficient? If so, how?

Get the Facts:

- What are the relevant facts of the case? What facts are not known? Can I learn more about the situation? Do I know enough to make a decision?
- What individuals and groups have an important stake in the outcome? Are some concerns more important? Why?
- What are the options for acting? Have all the relevant persons and groups been consulted? Have we identified creative options?

Evaluate Alternative Actions

- Which option will produce the most good and do the least harm? (The Utilitarian Approach)
- Which option best respects the rights of all who have a stake? (The Rights Approach)

- Which option treats people equally or proportionately? (The Justice Approach)

- Which option best serves the community as a whole, not just some members? (The Common Good Approach)

- Which option leads me to act as the sort of person I want to be? (The Virtue Approach)

Make a Decision and Test It

Considering all these approaches, which option best addresses the situation? You can test your decision by considering the following: If I told someone I respect—or told a television audience—which option I have chosen, what would they say?

Act and Reflect on the Outcome

How can my decision be implemented with the greatest care and attention to the concerns of all stakeholders? Ensure that some thought is given to those who may experience a negative consequence resulting from making the decision. Also consider: How did my decision turn out and what have I learned from this specific situation?

At its best, ethical decision-making is a collaborative process. It is good to have support and input from those the decision will impact. They are ideally part of the process unless it is for a confidential matter. Often, though, volunteer administrators find themselves to be alone with the issue and needing to make a decision. The guidance of the CCVA Code of Professional Ethics will prove helpful in terms of both the core ethical principles of the profession and the process to make a good decision.

Decisions should be based on facts not opinions. That means information is gathered and analyzed. When decisions need to be made they should not be dwelled on nor shot from the hip. During the process participants need to consider how the decision will impact everyone involved, whether or not there is enough information to make a good decision, and will there be acceptance for the decision.

To increase the quality of decision-making several factors come into play:

- Understanding the styles of decision-making of others in the group.

- Understanding there are traps in decision-making.

- Understanding group dynamics.

- Understanding how to ask questions.

- Understanding how to facilitate the group.

Some decision-making traps to consider are:

1. Basing current decision on past decisions — relying too much on old data and not looking for new data.

2. Trying to maintain the status quo — it may be easier to resist change rather than stretching for new information or developing different solutions.

3. Not willing to admit a mistake has been made and a decision must be revisited — often because a lot of time and effort was put into the original decision people prefer to defend the decision rather than admit a mistake.

4. Only gathering information that supports one side and not gathering information and listening to dissenting points of view.

5. Framing the questions about the information gathered or the decisions as a win-lose.

6. Being overly confident knowing answers before gathering information.

7. Deciding not to decide which takes the control out of the hands of the group.

Inquiry is important in the decision-making process. The volunteer administrator should constantly ask questions, such as:

- Is there a quality requirement such that one solution is likely to be more rational than another?

- Do I have sufficient information to make a high-quality decision?

- Are there laws, policies, rules, *etc.* that can impact on the decision?

- Is acceptance of the decision by other stakeholders in the nonprofit critical to effective implementation?

- If you were to make the decision by yourself, is it reasonably certain that stakeholders in the nonprofit would accept it?

- Do the individuals that the decision will impact share the organization's goals? Have they been included in the process?

- Is conflict among subordinates likely if the decision is made alone? (Adapted from Vroom, V.H. and Yetton, P.W, 1973)

These questions will assist the volunteer administrator to frame and focus the discussion.

To create a climate that can question what is going on during the decision-making process the volunteer administrator helps the group to examine assumptions. The other skill the volunteer administrator must possess and use is the ability to help the participants "listen" to what others are saying. It is common to listen through an individual's filters. These filters are set by life experience and education. Questions can be asked that break through those filters, leading to a more open discussion and resulting decision.

Other skills the volunteer administrator needs to tap into include:

- ensuring the group is clear about the goal of the decision;

- developing decision-making criteria;

- ensuring all group members are participating;

- all points of view being heard; and

- a variety of alternatives being examined.

The types of ethical dilemmas a volunteer administrator might face are many. Here are a few examples:

1. A volunteer is very difficult to work with and makes life difficult for all those who work with her. She doesn't listen to instructions; she complains about the way the program is run; she gossips about staff. She is the wife of your board president. (CCVA Core Ethical Value 2 – Respect)

2. A volunteer complains to you that the staff member to whom you have assigned her is incompetent; screams at the clients; smokes on the job; and is generally obnoxious. (CCVA Core Ethical Value 3 – Responsibility)

3. You have two volunteers with highly professional skills. You believe they could be very helpful to a particular staff member. The staff member, however, says he doesn't want to work with volunteers. (CCVA Core Ethical Value 3 – Responsibility)

4. A court-referred volunteer who was given a sentence of 200 hours of community service for a DUI (driving under the influence) charge wants to volunteer for your organization. He has skills in marketing that you can use. Your boss doesn't want to involve court-referred volunteers. (CCVA Core Ethical Value 5 – Justice and Fairness)

5. A staff member complains that the group of volunteers you have assigned him are not responsible; waste time; and are "more

trouble than they are worth". You believe that you matched the volunteers pretty carefully and that they had talents that would help this staff member. (CCVA Core Ethical Value 6 – Trustworthiness)

6.   Your fundraiser asks you to provide some volunteers to help at a local for-profit business. The business has promised a big contribution to your agency if you will do this. (CCVA Core Ethical Value 5 – Justice and Fairness)

In these examples, a CCVA Core Ethical Value is suggested. As a reader with your own experiences, you may believe that another core ethical value is at the root of the dilemma. This is a common experience: different people see the same situation in different ways. What is important is that in working towards a solution the volunteer administrator identify a core ethical value from the CCVA Professional Ethics. Having the Professional Ethics as a basis for decisions will help ensure similar results even though starting points in the ethical decision-making process may vary.

A Framework for Ethical Decision-Making

When making an ethical decision the volunteer administrator must consider:

•   Who are the stakeholders?

•   What is the problem for each stakeholder in terms of core ethical values?

•   What actions can the volunteer administrator take on behalf of each stakeholder's concerns?

•   Make a decision choosing the option which on balance reduces harm and produces the greatest long-term good. (CCVA Professional Code of Ethics, 2006)

When evaluating the final decision the volunteer administrator, and participants, can test that decision against the following:

Golden Rule: is the decision treating others as you would wish to be treated?

Publicity: would you be comfortable with your reasoning and decision if it were to appear on the front page of tomorrow's newspaper?

Children in the room: would you be comfortable answering children's questions about the action? Are you practising what you preach?

(Michael Josephson, *Making Ethical Decisions*, 1993)

The following is a step-by-step process for making an ethical decision contained in the CCVA Professional Ethics (CCVA, 2006, p. 3):

Step 1 Identify the primary stakeholders in this situation, based on the mission of your organization and its primary clients. List all individuals that will be affected by your decision on the following worksheet.

Step 2 Identify the ethical issue/problem and define this in one or two sentences. Each stakeholder must agree that this is the issue/problem to be solved or you will find yourself solving the wrong problem with the ethical dilemma continuing to exist. Within the issue/problem identify the core ethical values or principles being violated in your ethical dilemma. Consider each stakeholder when identifying these values. You might find there are differing opinions about which core values are being violated and need attention. Record your thoughts on the worksheet.

Step 3 Determine the immediate facts that have the most bearing on the ethical decision you must render. What else do you need to know about the situation? All stakeholders must participate in this discussion because each might look at the problem differently and have a different set of facts. Once all facts and issues are on the table, draft an agreed-upon set of facts. Again, you want everyone solving the same problem.

Step 4 Generate a list of possible courses of action. Do this for each stakeholder because each has different needs. Always consider the option of doing nothing at all.

Step 5 Evaluate each possible course of action. For each course of action:

- Determine the pros and cons of each scenario.

- Test each course of action against the CVCA ethical principles.

Step 6 Make your decision including a statement of core ethical values, principles and stakeholders. Decide on the most ethical course of action by:

- Considering the interests of all stakeholders. Use the results on the worksheet to pick the course of action that produces the most positive consequences and the fewest negative consequences.

- Choosing a course of action based on core ethical values rather than those based on non-ethical values.

- Only violating a core ethical value if it is *clearly necessary* in order to advance another core ethical value that will produce a greater balance of good in the long run.

Step 7 Implement your decision. Draft a plan to implement the decision. Determine who is responsible for implementing each component of the decision and the timeline. The plan should also include the expected change that will occur as a result of the decision.

Step 8   Monitor and modify the decision as necessary. Questions to consider are:

- Are you seeing what you would expect? Has the problem been resolved?

- Are those responsible for certain components of the plan taking action?

- Will the plan be done according to schedule? If the plan is not being followed as expected, then consider: Was the plan realistic? Should more priority be placed on various aspects of the plan? Should the plan be changed?

(Adapted from Council for Certification in Volunteer Administration, 2006)

Ethical Decision-Making Worksheet

(*Use this worksheet to record your thoughts.*)

Step 1 Identify the primary stakeholders in this situation. List all individuals that will be affected by your decision.

Step 2 Identify the ethical issue/problem and define this in one or two sentences.

Identify the core ethical values or principles being violated in your ethical dilemma for each stakeholder. Record your thoughts on the first two columns of the following worksheet.

Step 3 List the agreed-upon facts that have the most bearing on the ethical decision you must make.

Step 4   Evaluate each possible course of action. Here you will consider each stakeholder and his/her needs.

STAKEHOLDER	CORE ETHICAL VALUE OR PRINCIPLE	POSSIBLE ACTIONS	POSITIVE CONSEQUENCES	NEGATIVE CONSEQUENCES

Step 5 Make your decision. Draft an action statement that incorporates the core ethical values, principles and stakeholders.

Step 6 Draft a plan to implement the decision. Determine who is responsible for implementing each component of the decision and the timeline. The plan should also include the expected change that will occur as a result of the decision.

Action	Person/Group Responsible	Deadline	Outcome (Expected Change)
Action 1			
Action 2			
Action 3			

CONCLUSION

Part of being a professional practitioner is applying the ethical principles of volunteer management. They are the foundation of professional behaviour and practice. Making decisions is never easy and is made more complicated when ethical dilemmas are involved. Key elements of the professional decision-making process include integrity, justice, fairness, truthfulness, responsibility, caring, and respect. In order the make the best decisions volunteer administrators have to use all the tools at their disposal. They have their professional code of ethics, the ability to consider a variety of approaches to the decision, and a framework to help them process information and data so they can make the best decision possible.

REFERENCES

Josephson, M. (1993). *Making ethical decisions*. Marina del Rey, CA: The Josephson Institute of Ethics.

Toffler, B.L. (1986). *Tough choices*. New York: Wiley.

Velasquez M., Andre, C., Shanks, T., S.J., & Meyer, M. (Fall 1987). What is ethics? *Issues in Ethics 1*(1).

Velasquez M., Andre, C., Shanks, T., S.J., & Meyer, M. (Winter 1987). Thinking ethically. *Issues in Ethics 1*(2).

Velasquez M., Andre, C., Shanks, T., S.J., & Meyer, M. (Winter 1996, Rev. May 2009). Thinking ethically: A framework for moral decision-making. *Issues in Ethics 7*(1).

Vroom, V.H., & Yetton, P.W. (1973). *Leadership and decision-making*. Pittsburgh: University of Pittsburgh Press.

Chapter 4

STRATEGIC MANAGEMENT OF VOLUNTEER PROGRAMS

F. Ellen Netting, Ph.D.
Virginia Commonwealth University

INTRODUCTION

In this chapter, we focus on ways in which volunteer administrators can understand the organizational and programmatic contexts in which they work in order to effectively manage volunteer programs. Differential approaches to management will be examined in terms of the focus, fit, and feasibility of volunteer programming within diverse organizational settings. Beginning with definitions of terms and a statement of guiding assumptions, the focus shifts to how important it is to understand the organizational and programmatic cultures in which one practices. Finally, we turn to different ways to plan and implement programs and how to use alternative strategies.

WHAT IS STRATEGIC MANAGEMENT?

A word of caution is in order and a brief historical perspective is needed in order to frame this chapter. Over the years, a hotly debated management issue has been who participates (and how much) in changing and managing programs and organizations. Organizational development (OD) and sociotechnical systems (STS) approaches have emphasized widespread involvement by all organizational members in planning and implementation processes. OD was most popular in the United States and STS in Europe, but both shared an ideology that participation was "an ethical imperative" and a "source of energy" in which collaboration needed to occur, and "the role of managers and other change agents was primarily to act as catalysts" (Dunphy, 2000, p. 123). Dunphy observes that in the 1980s, these participatory approaches were "successfully challenged by the proponents of strategic management" (p. 123) who shifted the locus of control to formal organizational leaders. "Consequently the strategic management school stressed managerial control of the … change process — or, in some cases, indulged in the rhetoric of empowerment while largely ignoring it in practice" (p. 124). This tension needs to be recognized by the professional volunteer manager because each paid staff person and each volunteer will have their own expectations and interpretations of where the locus of control is (and where it should be).

Over a decade ago, Mintzberg, Ahlstrand, & Lampel (1998) wrote: "The literature of strategic management is vast … and it grows larger every day." Thousands of articles and books focus on the subject in both the scholarly and popular literature. In the 1980s strategic management "became an academic discipline in its own right" (p. 18). Mintzberg and his colleagues take a broad view of the concept of strategic management that fits well with what volunteer administrators do. Being strategic can look very different, depending on who participates and what assumptions are held. It is important to keep in mind the word of caution that Dunphy puts forth about strategic management as dominance from the top-down. Thus, this chapter is titled "Different Strategies for Managing Volunteer Programs" to reflect Mintzberg's view that there are multiple ways to strategically manage.

Definition of Terms

Strategic management is a loaded term, in that some readers will continue to think of it as very "top-down" and others may see it more broadly defined. Even the terms "strategy" and "management" have different meanings. Strategy has its origins in military history and has been embraced by business. In both instances strategies involve finding approaches to keep people and organizations alive. Management is often used interchangeably with administration, but these are different terms. Administrators typically work at the executive level, making policy decisions and interfacing with the broader environment. Managers are the implementers of policies, "the person whose job it is to make the organization run in a productive and harmonious way" (Kettner, 2002, p. 3). Based on these terms and for the purposes of this chapter, strategic management is defined as those approaches, used by persons responsible for volunteer program implementation, to enhance capacity and move programs toward sustainability (survival).

Guiding Assumptions

This chapter is built on three assumptions. First, volunteer administrators often play multiple roles in the organizations in which they work, but they also do their work in diverse types of organizations. For example, they may be coordinating volunteers in a human service agency that targets a vulnerable population group such as frail elders receiving in-home care or children who are homeless. They may coordinate volunteers in a highly regulated healthcare institution or recruit volunteers for a social cause in an advocacy organization. Volunteer administrators may work for the local art museum or seek political volunteers for a campaign. The list is endless, but the point is that there are diverse roles in various settings, and one size does not fit all when it comes to managing in strategic ways.

Second, volunteer administrators are disempowered if they do not understand the programs and organizations in which they work and the arenas in which they are likely to spend much of their professional lives. If, for example, a manager of volunteers sees the need to change the manner in which volunteer orientation and training is done, this sounds simple enough. However, if a former manager (who is still at this organization) developed the current orientation and training program, one may encounter incredible resistance without knowing why. Or perhaps a board member feels particularly attached to a specific way of recognizing volunteers and you decide to be more contemporary, getting rid of plaques and certificates that are part of the long-expected norm. Then what seems like a small change becomes a huge stumbling block, symbolic of much more than volunteer recognition. Knowing the setting in which one operates, as well as its norms, is critically important to being able to strategically manage.

Third, volunteer administrators in these uncertain times must be astute at understanding their work setting in order to prioritize the things that need to change and the things that need to be sustained. Bolman and Deal (2003) say it well: "In a world of permanent white-water, nothing is solid and everything is in flux. It is tempting to follow a familiar path and rely on timeworn solutions, regardless of how much the problems have changed" (p. 431). They suggest that one has to get beyond what feels comfortable and orderly, that gives one a false sense of being in control. And they challenge the manager to "have the paradoxical capacity to stimulate change ... while simultaneously maintaining [one's] commitment to core ideology and values" (p. 431).

Based on these three assumptions, this chapter is built around four sets of skills that are needed for different purposes in strategic management practice:

- Understanding and Assessing Program Context;

- Planning Volunteer Programs;

- Focusing and Prioritizing; and

- Strategizing.

If a volunteer administrator develops these skill sets, then that person may be better positioned to manage in a strategic manner. Each of these four areas will be examined in detail.

UNDERSTANDING AND ASSESSING PROGRAM CONTEXT

Managing volunteers automatically means that you will work with groups, programs, and organizations, all of which are part of a constantly changing environment. As unexpected things happen, managers try to make sense and find meaning in what is occurring. Understanding the situation in its cultural context is critical to that sense-making process (Weick, 2000).

Organizational Culture

In order to understand change in context, it is helpful to know the culture in which you are working. Schein's definition of organizational culture is classic:

> A pattern of shared basic assumptions that was learned by a group as it solved its problems of external adaptation and internal integration, that has worked well enough to be considered valid and, therefore, to be taught to new members as the correct way to perceive, think, and feel in relation to those problems.

(Schein, 2004, p. 17.) Schein asserts that there must be a sense of shared experience in order for a culture to develop. Once a group identity forms, shared assumptions become so much a part of what the group is that these assumptions will influence how the members of that culture understand their environment and interpret why things happen. Cameron and Quinn (2006) say that an organization's culture is reflected by what is valued by its members, seen in the predominant leadership styles, reflected in the symbols and words used and in the routines and procedures, and is reified in how success is defined.

Typically, three levels of culture are identified — artifacts, values, and basic underlying assumptions (Schein, 2004). Artifacts are the tangible things and behaviours one observes including physical space, what is on the walls, written documents, interactions between staff and volunteers, what is said in hallway conversations, and a host of other possible actions in the course of people working together. Values are strongly held beliefs that are espoused or stated by members of the group, program, or organization including verbal and written forms. And basic underlying and taken-for-granted assumptions are the theories-in-use or worldviews that explain and make sense of what happens in the organization.

A metaphor often used to describe organizational culture is a tree. The artifacts are like leaves, visible, yet changeable in various seasons. Values are like the trunk, strong and visible, holding up the artifacts. The underlying assumptions are roots, not visible above the ground, but critically holding everything in place. Persons who hang on tenaciously to cultural assumptions and resist change guard the roots, but since the roots are underground, their resistance is not always evident. Thus an organization's culture can be viewed as a filter through which members look at the world and that provides stability. In times of overload or uncertainty, if this filter is challenged, it can be very unsettling because cherished assumptions are also challenged (Schein, 2004).

Basic Cultural Assumptions

Volunteer administrators, and other paid employees, bring assumptions to their programs and organizations. Volunteers bring assumptions too. Sometimes these assumptions are compatible with the program or organization's culture, and sometimes they are not. Everyone does not have to have the same assumptions (in fact, the world would be pretty boring if groupthink predominated), but it is important for managers to recognize that there will be differences and to consider how they may play out in practice.

The Competing Values Framework

Cameron and Quinn (2006) have studied organizational culture for many years. Their competing values framework has been very extensively used to help managers understand multiple settings. Formed by the intersection of two sets of values (stability/control versus flexibility/discretion, and internal focus/integration versus external focus/differentiation) the competing values framework reveals four types of organizational cultures: (1) the hierarchy culture, (2) the market culture, (3) the clan culture, and (4) the adhocracy culture. Remember that each is an ideal type for the purposes of understanding and that none of these cultures will present just as they do in theory.

The hierarchy culture is one in which the workplace is very formal and structured, with procedures that govern what people do on a daily basis. With efficiency-minded leaders, this is seen as a smoothly operating organization with programs that are clearly defined. Employee or volunteer success would be seen as focused on dependability, punctuality, and clear scheduling at the lowest possible cost. Predictability is a hallmark of this type of program or organization, so that people feel secure in their work environment (Cameron & Quinn, 2006). In this setting, the basic underlying assumptions are that stability/control and an internal focus/integration are important because the focus is on developing a close sense of shared, well-integrated operation. The manager of volunteers who works in this environment would be one who is rewarded for having a clearly defined and predictable program, one in which roles are clarified in tangible job descriptions and relationships conform to established protocols.

Cameron and Quinn's (2004) market culture is similar to the hierarchy culture in that they share a common assumption — stability/control is valued. Where the market culture differs from the hierarchy culture is in its basic assumption that external focus/differentiation is the way to go. Whereas the hierarchy culture maintains a focus on what happens internally, the market culture is focused beyond the walls of the organization itself and is highly competitive. In the market culture results are very important and what matters is getting the job done better than anyone else in the larger environment. People are very goal-oriented and highly competitive, with leaders being somewhat demanding and focused on change. In this hard-hitting competitive organization, volunteer administrators may need to think about how to recruit hard-charging volunteers who are very goal-oriented, visible, and motivated by competition and even conflict.

The clan culture is very different from the market culture because they share no common assumptions. The clan culture does share an assumption with the hierarchy culture in that both embrace internal focus/integration. Its second assumption, however, is that of flexibility/discretion (as opposed to stability/control). A family metaphor is often used to describe the clan culture which is a friendly place in which leaders serve more in mentor than manager roles. There is a strong sense of harmony and loyalty here with an emphasis on cohesion, development, and morale. Success has everything to do with how people are treated and respected, and a premium is set on teamwork, participation, and consensus (Cameron & Quinn, 2006). The manager of volunteers in a clan culture would be more of a coordinator than a manager because participation and input would be emphasized more than supervision and oversight. Creativity would be valued and different roles would likely emerge as volunteers with new skills are recruited.

Last, Cameron and Quinn identify what they call the adhocracy culture, a dynamic, entrepreneurial workplace in which people take risks and act in very innovative ways. At the intersection of flexibil-ity/discretion and external focus/differentiation, innovation is unlimited in this culture and success is defined as thinking outside the box. Individual freedom and initiative are encouraged. In this culture, the idea of a traditional form of management simply does not fit, and Farmer (1998) has gone so far as to call this "anti-administration" (p. 304). It is somewhat questionable as to whether one can manage in such a culture because the idea is for everyone to do what works for them.

Applying the Framework

The competing values framework has been used for years to di-agnose organizational culture particularly in the for-profit sector and it has been empirically tested (Cameron & Quinn, 2006). Building on this valuable framework, Macduff, Netting, and O'Connor (2006) applied these concepts to the management of volunteers, changing the focus from the organization to the program level. Trying to find terms that would be more user-friendly to persons working largely in programs based in nonprofit organizations, these four-type programs conform to the cultures described by Cameron and Quinn. They are: (1) traditional, (2) social change, (3) serendipitous, and (4) entrepre-neurial. O'Connor and Netting (2009) elaborate on these types for human service organizations.

The traditional volunteer program is congruent with a hierarchi-cal culture. For traditional programs, structure and control are the goals. Maintaining the status quo and only incrementally changing, this program is predictable and steady over time. Managing this program requires a planned, prescribed, gradual, and intentional approach. Program evaluation is consistent with outcome and perform-ance-based measurements.

The social change volunteer program is dedicated to conscious-ness-raising for change. The organization in which this program would most likely fit would be the market culture in which competitiveness is desired. For nonprofits, the competition is based on social change more than economic competitiveness, and volunteers would be needed to work on large scale advocacy efforts. Such efforts would involve conflict and collective mobilization of forces to change existing power differentials. Program success would occur when structural change is addressed.

The serendipitous volunteer program is focused on connection and collaboration, fitting nicely into the clan culture. There would be a flat, participatory structure in which volunteers would collaborate as colleagues with paid staff, respectful of their differences and working toward consensus. This type program would be a place in which volunteers would look for meaning and purpose as things emerged in process. Evaluation of success would heavily focus on how satisfied volunteers are in finding meaning in their connection to this program.

The entrepreneurial program is one in which individual empowerment reigns. Structure would be at a minimum. Macduff, Netting, and O'Connor (2006) indicate that persons who work from an entrepreneurial approach will not be corralled. Entrepreneurial volunteer programs are not very common, but individuals who act in an entrepreneurial fashion are more and more evident. An example of the results of entrepreneurial volunteerism is The PeopleFinder software system created by volunteers working independently and without what is usually understood to be formal supervision. The Internet and World Wide Web allow people to solve problems, create processes, and address issues without the involvement of nonprofit or volunteer programs. The fact that these entrepreneurs share these discoveries freely so that others use them as they wish is why they can be called volunteers. They, themselves may not label their work as volunteerism, but they are giving of their time freely to effect change. Table 1 provides an overview of the four types of programs.

Table 1: Types of Volunteer Programs and Their Assumptions

Culture	Underlying Assumptions
Traditional Volunteer Program	Structure and control is the goal Change is slow and gradual
Social Change Volunteer Program	Consciousness raising for change is the goal Transformative change is needed to change the system
Serendipitous Volunteer Program	Connection and collaboration is the goal Change is gradual and based on consensus
Entrepreneurial Volunteer Program	Individual empowerment is the goal Transformative change is needed to empower individuals

Source: Macduff, Netting, & O'Connor (2006).

For the professional management of volunteers, it is helpful to know what culture one prefers and how one's preferences fit with the organization in which one's program is lodged. In some cases, the organization may be the same as the program. It may be helpful to think about the following questions:

- Is your preferred culture traditional, social change, serendipitous or entrepreneurial?

- What type of culture does your group, program, or organization have?

- Are they congruent with your preferred culture? Why or why not?

Although these types have been presented as "ideal," the world does not conform to "ideal types." Studies using these or similar frameworks reveal that organizations tend to span types, perhaps leaning toward a preferred culture but not solely congruent with one (O'Connor, Netting, & Fabelo, 2009). This means that volunteer administrators (as well as others) work in paradox between competing values and underlying assumptions.

Examples of paradox are many. A program may develop in a friendly serendipitous culture in which there is a great deal of participation in decision-making. Volunteers are expected and encouraged to have input. But this same program may be a subculture in a traditional organizational culture that attempts to suppress the role of volunteers within a formal, bureaucratic structure. In another instance a mission statement for the organization may espouse great respect for individual choice and participation, but program outcomes are determined by experts. A social change volunteer program may focus on recruiting articulate volunteers who can work toward a social justice cause, yet there may be paid staff who think volunteers don't know their place and who are threatened by their assertiveness. In yet another example, hospice volunteers may be recruited to assist families in meaning-making at the end of life, only to be part of a hospital-based volunteer program in a culture that sees death as a failure of the system. In short, knowing the organizational culture you are in and recognizing when the program you are managing may have formed a different subculture is critical to strategic thinking. The major thing is to understand differences in assumptions, and when one's program is housed in an organizational culture that is different from one's program the manager of volunteers can find ways to creatively buffer paid staff and volunteers. Table 2 provides an overview of the material in this section and offers the manager of volunteers a list of questions to guide in understanding organizational and programmatic cultures.

Table 2: Understanding and Assessing Program Context

Questions to Guide Understanding and Assessing Program Context
1. Is this volunteer program embedded within a larger organization? If so, how would you describe the organization's culture? How would you describe the program's culture? How are the organizational and programmatic cultures similar or dissimilar?
2. What artifacts do you observe in the program's culture?
3. What values are espoused in the program's written documents and by its members?
4. What are the program's underlying assumptions?
5. Do you see any contradictions between program artifacts, values, and/or underlying assumptions? If so, what are they?
6. Do you think the program's culture is traditional, social change, serendipitous, or entrepreneurial? Or does it seem to have elements of all of the above?
7. Is your preferred culture traditional, social change, serendipitous or entrepreneurial?
8. How congruent is your preferred culture with the program's culture?
9. Are there paradoxes with which you work? If so, what are they?

PLANNING VOLUNTEER PROGRAMS

Beyond having skills in understanding and assessing the cultures in which they work, volunteer administrators must have program planning skills. They must make choices about how to plan and design programs from scratch, as in the case of being hired to develop a volunteer program for the first time or how to develop and change an existing program in which they have been newly hired. Most importantly, once you have been managing a volunteer program for some time, it is helpful to have skills in how to refresh the program within a constantly changing environment (even when one wants to batten down the hatches and ride out the wave of change).

Planning is an ongoing process as programs change, not just something that happens in the beginning. Planning also looks different in different organizational and programmatic cultures, so the manager of volunteers will want to know that there are different types of planning approaches available.

Different Ways to Plan

In 1979, Barclay Hudson compared several planning theories: synoptic (rational), incremental, advocacy, transactive, and radical. The synoptic tradition, often called rational planning, has dominated much of the planning literature for many years with popular program planning textbooks heavily relying upon this very linear approach (*e.g.*, Kettner, Moroney, & Martin, 2008; Pawlak & Vinter, 2004). In addition, the practitioner literature on how to design, plan, and manage volunteer programs has tended to be somewhat rational in using a business-related human resource management approach (*e.g.*, Ellis, 1996; Macduff, 1996; McCurley & Lynch, 2006; Wilson, 1976). This important literature has been needed in order to legitimize professional volunteer management in using well accepted approaches to planning.

But even though rational planning approaches have dominated, Hudson's recognition of other types is important in a multicultural organizational world. Incremental, advocacy, transactive, and radical planning theories were developed in reaction to the rational tradition. Incremental planning is associated with Charles Lindblom (1959) who criticized the rational planning tradition in his work on "the science of muddling through." His major criticism was that rational planning did not take into account just how political the planning process is, and without considering power and politics in one's efforts, the best laid plans could go awry. Incremental planning is particularly helpful when one is doing a pilot project or wanting to demonstrate a new way of doing business in that it involves compromises between competing groups and will change direction in process as needed.

Advocacy, transactive, and radical planning theories take into account the importance of including diverse constituencies and stakeholders in the decision-making processes. A basic value of these planning approaches is inclusiveness. Advocacy planning would mean including volunteers in determining program direction, but would not stop there. In all aspects of program management, including paid and volunteer staff would be paramount to the process. This would complicate and perhaps extend the process. The manager would have to be very skilled at managing power dynamics. Transactive planning is very relational, built on mutuality and face-to-face interaction, with the idea that consensus building is needed around solutions to problems. Radical planning, on the other hand, comes with a bias that systems are oppressive and that power inequities will rarely permit stakeholders full say in how things will be done. Therefore, the focus of radical planning is on liberating oppressed groups to transform the system, and conflict in this type of process is inevitable.

Netting, O'Connor and Fauri (2008) summarize the usefulness of these types, indicating that they are not mutually exclusive, but each has something to contribute. Whereas rational planning is used to develop services and sustain programs, there is no intent to fundamentally alter current ways of operating. "Incremental planning guides project development so that ideas can be demonstrated and powerful powers can be appeased, building programs one step at a time and even retracing one's steps if one runs into difficulty" (p. 19). On the other hand, advocacy planning casts a wider net, attempting to raise unheard voices so that they are part of the process. In this attempt to broaden the scope of who is included, advocacy planning may be a beginning step toward more structural change. In a similar way, transactive planning is highly process-oriented and sensitive to including all parties. Radical planning, then, is the most transformative in that it clearly seeks to change "what is" into what could be different at a system level and speaks to the oppressiveness of existing programs and organizations (pp. 19-20).

Fit with Culture

As you have read about these different planning approaches, you may have determined that some approaches will fit better in certain types of cultures. For example, the rational approach to planning is nicely aligned in traditional hierarchical organizational or programmatic cultures in which a clearly defined path is prescribed. Incremental planning, in which "muddling through" is expected and different paths will emerge in process, would work well in a clan or serendipitous volunteer program that seeks consensus and learns from process. Similarly, a transactive planning process in which face-to-face interaction is seen as critical to hearing everyone's views would work well in a clan culture. Advocacy planning, because it is focused on pulling in persons who have been left out, would likely work well in an entrepreneurial culture if the intent is to empower individuals. And radical planning could be aligned with a market or social change organization in which the goal is to alter the existing structure.

Note that the alternative theories to the rational planning process tend to be focused on participation and when one increases participation in the planning process it becomes more cumbersome, complex, and time-consuming. This is why the rational approach has been embraced so much — it is more efficient in getting things done. And this is why Dunphy (2000) was concerned that strategic management was often viewed as top-down, rather than encouraging participation. A traditional rational approach poses a dilemma for the volunteer administrator because the intent of a volunteer program by design is to bring in more people to the process (whatever tasks they are recruited to do), and in doing so, the work becomes more complex and power dynamics simply cannot be ignored.

Brody (2000) defined two basic planning processes: "forward-sequence planning" and "reverse-order planning" (pp. 77-78). Reverse-order planning starts at the end, by identifying a goal or outcome and working backward. This is what happens in rational planning. Forward-sequence planning begins by asking where you can start rather than where you want to go. This non-rational process occurs when an end state cannot be pre-determined. Sometimes if you determine the outcome first, it interferes with what emerges in the process. With forward-sequence planning, the process may go in unexpected directions. Netting, O'Connor, and Fauri (2009) suggest that there are basic approaches to program planning, both of which are equally appropriate: (1) rational planning and prescriptive approaches; and (2) interpretive planning and emergent approaches. Rational approaches have been dominant and they have tended to be directive, prescribing certain steps to take in a certain order. Interpretive planning is based on trusting things to unfold, even in unexpected directions. Table 3 provides questions to guide the planning process.

Table 3: Planning Volunteer Programs

Questions to Guide Planning Volunteer Programs
1.   What types of planning are used in your program? Give examples.
2.   With which planning type are you most comfortable?
3.   How congruent is the planning used in your program with the program's culture?
4.   How involved are volunteers in program planning? How involved do you want them to be?
5.   Can you give an example of when you used "reverse-order" (prescribed) planning?
6.   Can you give an example of when you used "forward-sequence" (emergent) planning?
7.   Can you give an example of when you started with one type of planning and moved to another type? Was that a conscious shift or one that just naturally occurred? What did you learn in the process?

FOCUSING AND PRIORITIZING

Understanding the setting in which one works and recognizing that there are different ways to plan can assist the manager of volunteers in knowing what may or may not work in a particular program or organization. But understanding is only a beginning step. The question is "where does one start?" Being able to focus and prioritize is a critical skill in strategic management.

Analyzing Situations

It is possible that you are in a program that works well. If that's the case, then you will want to focus on maintaining and sustaining what you have in place. If, however, you are managing a program that needs to change in some way or in which a problem arises, it is necessary to analyze the situation. In doing so, it is helpful to know the difference between a condition and a problem. A condition is simply "what is," whereas a problem is a condition that has been negatively labelled (Kettner, Moroney, & Martin, 2008). Case # 1 of Louis and the Museum Volunteers provides an example of how different people think of the same situation as simply a condition and others see it as very problematic.

Case # 1: Louis and the Museum Volunteers

A newly hired manager of volunteers (Louis) begins his job at a local art museum. The museum is known for being on the leading edge and for highlighting new, controversial artists. A recent show has been picketed by a local religious group who protested the work of a new artist whom they perceived as anti-religious, if not heretical. During a volunteer in-service, a heated controversy erupts among volunteers about this artist's work. Some volunteers are threatening to leave the museum, even though they have been there for years. Others see the nurturing of this young artist as a way to encourage self-expression and freedom of speech, and they feel very strongly that his work should be shown even if they personally don't find it appealing. Louis is faced with a contentious debate during what was supposed to be a regularly scheduled in-service on how to lead a guided tour of the gallery.

In this situation, there is disagreement. One group of volunteers is angry because they think the artist's work should not have been shown in their community. They see this show as an embarrassment. The other group does not see displaying the work as a problem — it is simply a condition — art museums display work from different artists all the time. The question for Louis is how to handle this disagreement. Whether he thinks it's a problem to display the work is not the problem with which he must deal. He must deal with contention and conflict among the volunteers that may lower morale, cause people to leave, make the program unattractive to new volunteers, leave permanent rifts in the group, and a host of other unintended consequences.

What one person or group perceives to be a condition can be a problem for another person or group, and vice versa. Because volunteer administrators are engaged in ongoing human resource management and the accompanying joys and challenges of working with people, many of the problems they will encounter will involve multiple perceptions of the same situation. Knowing how to analyze difficult situations is a necessary skill in being able to focus and prioritize. Table 4 provides a list of questions one might ask in analyzing a situation.

Table 4: Analyzing Situations

Questions to Consider in Analyzing Situations
1.   Who are the persons involved?
2.   What are the power dynamics in this situation?
3.   What is known about the history of the situation?
4.   Is there disagreement about whether this is a condition or a problem? What are the implications of your answer?
5.   Are there persons, theories, literature, records or other sources of information that might be useful in the analysis?

Determining the Focus

Once he has analyzed the situation, in the case of Louis and the Museum Volunteers, Louis has to determine how to focus. Possibilities include: (1) individual volunteers; (2) volunteers as a group; (3) the program; and (4) the larger organization. Louis may determine that his focus is on individual volunteers and how they go about their work. In this situation, Louis believes that working with the volunteers on how they function as a group is the focus. If this is the case, he may find ways to enhance volunteers' interpersonal relationships, use team building skills to promote rapport, and even set up a specific time to debate the issues so that everyone gets their feelings out. A program approach assumes a broader focus, in which Louis may have analyzed the problem only to discover that this is only the tip of the iceberg and that this unpleasantness is symptomatic of longstanding concerns that reflect deep-seated cultural norms that need to change. The focus, then is programmatic and may require a longer term intervention with the intent of embedding new cultural assumptions.

But Louis may have analyzed the situation and found that what is going on in his program is reflected in a much larger organizational (even community) dynamic in which there are contentious forces at play. The art museum may have a board of directors who were in disagreement over bringing this artist to town and displaying his work. And even if the board was in agreement and saw this as an opportunity to stretch convention, there may be groups within the community who hold strongly opposing views about what to do. In fact, the local paper may have carried a story about picketers at the museum, inflaming the controversy. If this is the case, then Louis as the manager of volunteers at the museum will not likely take on the whole debacle. But his focus on the volunteers will be contextualized in the broader issues so that he doesn't make the mistake of thinking this will go away if only he gets the volunteers to communicate with one another and agree to disagree. Table 5 summarizes focal options.

Table 5: Determining Focus

Questions to Consider in Determining Focus
1.   Is this an issue among individual volunteers?
2.   Is this an issue for a group of volunteers who are part of the program?
3.   Is this an issue for the volunteer program as a whole?
4.   Is this an issue that is broader than the program? Organization? Community?
5.   Is it all of the above?

Assessing Feasibility

Having considered the situation in context, volunteer administrators must now assess how feasible it is to attempt to change the situation — or to turn the problem around. One way to begin is to ask these questions:

- Within this culture, what can I control as the manager of volunteers?

- What adjustments can I make if I work with others?

- What do I have no control over (as least in the immediate future)?

Controllable valuables will likely be artifacts — changes in one's own behaviour and interactions, how one recruits volunteers, volunteer assignments, and a host of other things within one's immediate oversight. Contingencies may be artifacts and even values that can shift if others join with you in making changes. Constraints are those policies, procedures, regulations, standards, and other forces over which one has no control and to which one must conform at least for the time being.

In this situation, Louis does have control over this own behaviour within this program and he may want to model how to deal with conflict in a constructive manner. This is a controllable variable. Yet, there is no way he can influence volunteer behaviour without participation on the part of volunteers. Thus, a contingency is volunteer cooperation. Louis may actually form a task group to work on resolving the problem in-house, using the strengths of long-time volunteers to figure out how to intervene with the larger group. Similarly, Louis and his volunteers may change program artifacts enough that they open the way for better communication and demonstrate how the issues can be addressed in a professional manner. However, it is likely that neither Louis nor his volunteers will be able to leverage change in the larger community when it comes to strongly held feelings about the artist and his work. This is a constraint and focusing on a constraint of this magnitude would likely require Louis to step out of his role as volunteer coordinator and become involved in community politics that could cost him his job.

In Table 6, a series of questions tied to analyzing the situation, determining the focus, and assessing feasibility are provided. Examples of very different types of programs are provided below to further illustrate the skill set of focusing and prioritizing.

Table 6: Questions to Ask about Focusing and Prioritizing

Focusing and Prioritizing	Questions to Ask
Analyzing Situations	1. Who are the persons involved?
	2. What are the power dynamics in this situation?
	3. What is known about the history of the situation?
	4. Is there disagreement about whether this is a condition or a problem? What are the implications of your answer?
	5. Are there persons, theories, literature, records or other sources of information that might be useful in the analysis?

Focusing and Prioritizing	Questions to Ask
Determining Focus	6. Is this an issue among individual volunteers? 7. Is this an issue for a group of volunteers who are part of the program? 8. Is this an issue for the volunteer program as a whole? 9. Is this an issue that is broader than the program? Organization? Community? 10. Is it all of the above?
Assessing Feasibility	11. Within this culture, what can I control as the manager of volunteers? 12. What adjustments can I make if I work with others? 13. What do I have no control over (at least in the immediate future)?

The example of Louis and the art museum volunteers illustrates the importance of focusing and priorizing. Two additional examples are now provided to illustrate different cultural contexts and how volunteer administrators focus and prioritize in different ways. In Case # 2 Juanita coordinates volunteers in a hospice program within a large healthcare system. In Case # 3 Monroe is a sole manager of volunteers, working for a city-wide coalition. Both have to constantly focus and prioritize.

Case # 2: Juanita and the Coordination of Hospice Volunteers

Juanita was hired by a large healthcare system as the manager of hospice volunteers. The hospice program was buried deeply within a mega system with a very traditional culture. It was imperative for this larger system to adhere to strict protocols and procedures in an environment dominated by medicine. The hospice program, on the other hand, had a very clan-like culture in which an interdisciplinary staff of nurses, social workers, chaplains, aides, and volunteers worked in teams. The administrator of hospice was careful to buffer her program, as a subculture, so that the atmosphere of collegiality and friendliness was reinforced. Juanita's role was immediately embraced by team members because they realized how important volunteers are to the families they served, and many of the volunteers were actually family members who had recently lost loved ones. Juanita discovered that volunteer recruitment was not difficult, that in fact there were always people seeking meaningful volunteer roles with hospice. The problem was that some volunteers were still very actively grieving over their loss and unable to focus on the family to whom they were assigned. Volunteers were telling families about their own losses and essentially using them as their support system, when in fact they were there to listen to the families. The clan-like culture of the hospice program actually reinforced this norm because volunteers were embraced by paid staff and families alike. But Juanita realized that some families, who were already overwhelmed with caring for their loved ones, were becoming surrogate therapists to grieving volunteers. These families were actually becoming more overwhelmed as they tried to support their volunteers. Juanita asked herself, "Where do I start?"

One way to begin is to ask what can I control as the volunteer administrator? What adjustments can I make if I work with others? What do I have no control over (at least in the immediate future)? Controllable variables will likely be artifacts — changes in one's own behaviour and interactions, how one recruits volunteers, volunteer assignments, and a host of other things within one's immediate oversight. Contingencies may be artifacts and even values that can shift if others join with you in making changes. For example, if the social workers who work with bereaved families will join with you, together it may be important to establish a policy that potential volunteers wait a year before being placed with families but including them as active participants in grief and support groups during that year. Another contingency might be to work with other departments within the large healthcare system to identify alternative volunteer roles for persons who want to find meaningful things to do, but may not yet be ready to work directly with families. Constraints (that cannot be changed) may be policies about liability to which all volunteers and staff must conform, such as not transporting families in their own cars.

In a clan-type culture, a sensitivity to difference is pervasive. There is high tolerance of emotions and process, and volunteers who come into that culture may be seeking a place to deal with their personal emotions and process their grief-work. Recognizing this, Juanita focused on the problem of having grief-ridden volunteers without boundaries and figured out ways to delineate what she could control (and not) within her program.

While Juanita was figuring out how to refocus and prioritize her efforts, Monroe was working in a completely different environment — that of child advocacy. Case # 3 illustrates how this strategic manager had to rethink his program.

Case # 3: Monroe, Manager of Child Advocates

Monroe has been the manager of child advocates for over a decade. The child advocates program is under the wing of a coalition of city agencies dedicated to protecting children from abuse and neglect. Formed in the early 1980s by a group of concerned professionals, the advocates are volunteers with a cause — to prevent abuse and protect children. Monroe works for the coalition and is the only full-time paid staff person, responsible to a 12-member board of directors representing each of the agencies that formed the coalition. Each agency contributes an annual amount of funds to the effort. This coalition has a social change culture with the goal of raising consciousness about the needs of children.

Over the years Monroe has had an average of 30 active advocates who come to the coalition as a form of civic engagement. These are not shrinking violet volunteers, but volunteers with a cause. They have engaged in systemic change, helping to rewrite the child protective service laws in the state. They have engaged in activities designed to raise consciousness about the inadequate staffing in child protective service (CPS) units within the city and the state, even mounting protests when the state budget did not include additional allocations for CPS. Because they are very cause-oriented, they have consistently remained tied to the coalition over the years and can be counted on to testify before a legislative session or release information to the media. With all these years of experience, Monroe has learned that he needs a special kind of volunteer who is not afraid of contention … but who seeks conflict and visibility. Volunteers who thrive on change and want to make a difference come to see Monroe.

The small size of Monroe's operation makes it manageable. He knows his volunteers extremely well and a third of them have been with him for the decade since Child Advocates was started. Recently, the board has begun asking questions about the coalition's viability, given that the city agencies that fund the program are all suffering from the economic downturn. Monroe recognizes that he may have a problem in that high visibility and conflict may not be high priorities in a time of retrenchment. He begins to analyze the power dynamics of the situation and the fit of a social change culture in an era of economic conservatism.

In conducting his power analysis, Monroe realizes that as long as the coalition agencies had sufficient funds and were geared up for change, that his role was to find volunteers who could be leaders for the cause of child protection. But when agencies that had long supported the coalition began experiencing funding reductions, they became more traditional, tightening their belts and no longer able to afford to play a broader advocacy role that might antagonize potential donors. Earlier volunteers who pushed for change were seen as exactly what the coalition wanted, but now the same type volunteers were seen as problematic. As a strategic manager, Monroe had to refocus on the type of volunteer he recruited, had to re-orient current volunteers to work a bit below the radar screen in changing economic times, and refocus his priorities so that he could weather the transition from a social change to a traditional volunteer program. Perhaps this was a temporary transition until the economy shifted, but it required Monroe to think differently.

STRATEGIZING

Earlier in this chapter, strategic management was defined as approaches, used by persons responsible for volunteer program implementation, to enhance capacity and move programs toward sustainability (survival). Typically strategies are broadly defined, whereas tactics or activities are the smaller steps taken to achieve the broader strategy.

Types of Strategy

Mintzberg, Ahlstrand, and Lampel (1998) broaden the concept of strategy in what they call the "Five Ps for Strategy" (p. 9) — plan, pattern, position, perspective, and ploy. Strategy is often described as a *plan* that guides a course of action. It is also seen as a *pattern* that reflects action over time. The difference between a plan and a pattern is that a plan is theoretical, whereas a pattern is what has been repeatedly done (hopefully with success). A plan is intended direction, whereas a pattern has been realized and one can look back on what happened. This is the difference between "intended strategy" and "realized strategy" (p. 10). Asked if one's intended strategy manifested into a realized strategy, most people will say that some of their intentions were realized, but not exactly as they had anticipated. Mintzberg and his colleagues point out that few strategies are "purely deliberate, just as few are purely emergent" (p. 11), and that broad intentions may be pursued by details that emerge in process. In other words, tactics and activities you use may not be as prescriptive as your strategy might imply, otherwise managers would trade the opportunity to learn for a feeling of being in control and knowing exactly what next steps are going to happen. Thus, there are emergent strategies and deliberate strategies that may lead to what is actually realized.

In some ways, strategy can be perceived as *position* in which one designs their volunteer program to capture a particular type of volunteer or to mobilize existing volunteers on the wave of civic engagement. Thus, a strategy may be to position one's program so that it is moving with the trends in service learning or boomer engagement or whatever happens to be timely. Another way to view strategy is to see it as *perspective* in which a volunteer program is aligned with the larger organizational culture within which it fits. Perspective means using strategy to see the program and its volunteers in context, how they fit within the program, within the organization, and how everything fits within the larger environment. And last, strategy may be seen as a *ploy* — a way to maneuver around obstacles or compete with others for volunteers. In other words, strategy may be seen as a plan, pattern, position, perspective, ploy, or combinations of them all.

Advantages to having strategies are that they set direction, focus one's effort, help define the program (particularly when there are patterns), and provide consistency in a rather uncertain world. On the other hand, strategies can serve as blinders if used too rigidly, can perpetuate groupthink, over simplify complexity, and limit creativity. Thus, strategic management is like walking a tightrope between stability and flexibility in that one wants to encourage enough stability that keeps things moving without losing the flexibility to know when things need to change (Mintzberg *et al.*, 1998).

Strategy Formation

Just as there are different types of strategies as well as advantages and disadvantages to their use, there are different ways in which strategies are formulated. Mintzberg (1998) and his colleagues identify ten schools of thought about strategic management and how strategy formation occurs:

- The design school — strategy is a conceptual process.

- The planning school — strategy is formalized.

- The positioning school — strategy is analytical.

- The environmental school — strategy is a reactive process.

- The configuration school — strategy is transformational.

- The power school — strategy is negotiated.

- The cognitive school — strategy is a mental process.

- The learning school — strategy is emergent.

- The cultural school — strategy is a collective process.

- The entrepreneurial school — strategy is visionary.

Note that these differences reinforce material presented earlier in this chapter — that who determines a program or organization's strategies will vary by what is acceptable within a particular culture. For example, the design, planning and positioning schools tend to be very compatible with a hierarchical culture in a traditional program in which prescribed, directive, and controlled strategies are formulated and carried out in a formal manner. A manager of volunteers within a traditional culture that seeks consistency and wants to sustain an existing program will find these approaches to strategizing to be compatible with what has been established in their organization.

The environmental, configuration, and power schools are heavily focused on responding to the changing larger environment, figuring out how to be more transformative than reinforcing of the status quo, and negotiating new directions. A manager of volunteers within a market culture in which there is competition for volunteers may benefit from thinking about strategy in these ways, and using these approaches to strategy will reinforce the goal of a social change orientation that seeks to raise collective consciousness.

The cognitive, learning, and cultural schools of strategy formation fit well with those clan-like cultures in which serendipity is encouraged and in which emergence of new ideas is greeted as part of an ongoing learning process. Strategy is viewed here as a mental process in which different minds come together in a collective, consensus-building process to identify community building ways to come together as a group. A manager of volunteers committed to these ways of strategy formation will be highly participatory and engaging, coordinating more than managing because volunteer input will be valued and used in an emergent process.

And last, the entrepreneurial school of thought about strategy formation fits well with a culture that is empowering of the individual and has a vision that goes beyond processing what is, but wants to be transformative in a very individualistic manner. Volunteer administrators who subscribe to the entrepreneurial school are visionary leaders who leave the door open for flexibility. "That vision serves as both an inspiration and a sense of what needs to be done — a guiding idea" (Mintzberg *et al.*, 1998, p. 124).

Fit Between Program Culture and Strategy

If we recognize that there are multiple schools of thought and that strategy can take different forms, then almost limitless possibilities are open to the manager of volunteers. Depending on the culture of the organization in which a volunteer program is housed, and the nature of that program's subculture, strategy may be formulated in similar or different ways. For example, a volunteer program with a clan-like culture will use strategies that are more emergent (not pre-determined). This does not mean that the program does not have strategies, it means that the strategy may be to remain open to possibilities. Actions that logically flow from this strategy might be to hold meetings with volunteers so that their input is obtained, to keep communication open among volunteers through a chat room or Facebook, to conduct periodic focus groups of volunteers, to engage volunteers in orientation of new volunteers, and other ways to keep active participation a high priority. If this program is housed in a hierarchical culture, in which structure and control are paramount, then strategies used within the larger organization may lean toward prescriptive, formalized plans. The manager of volunteers must then be bi-cultural, able to move between the larger organization's more rigid approach to strategizing and carefully buffering and protecting the volunteer program so that its subculture can be sustained.

What is important to strategic management is that the manager understands the culture in which they operate so that there is a fit between strategies and cultural norms. This requires skill and flexibility (Cameron & Quinn, 2006), reinforcing Schein's (2004) premise that leadership and culture are intertwined. If the manager of volunteers is aware of the culture in which they are operating, then strategies flow logically based on the assumptions of that culture. Table 7 provides examples of cultural fit.

Table 7: Examples of Fit between Program Culture, Strategies, and Actions

Program Culture	Strategies (Examples)	Possible Actions (Examples)
Traditional	➤ Maintain stability ➤ Formalize program ➤ Sustain program	• Design flow charts to designate what needs to happen • Develop clear job descriptions of set volunteer tasks • Collect and maintain quantitative program data • Supervise volunteers in a formal manner • Evaluate your program based on prescribed outcomes
Social Change	➤ Advocate for change ➤ Be competitive ➤ Focus on a cause	• Mobilize groups of volunteers for collective action • Develop focused job descriptions on cause-related tasks • Manage and lead volunteers in a strong, directive way • Recruit motivated volunteers who can deal with conflict

Program Culture	Strategies (Examples)	Possible Actions (Examples)
Serendipitous	➢ Create meaningful opportunities ➢ Diversify the program ➢ Build community	• Engage volunteers in all aspects of the program • Outreach to and recruit diverse groups of volunteers • Coordinate in a flexible manner • Meet regularly in order to process what is happening
Entrepreneurial	➢ Empower individuals ➢ Transform structure	• Articulate your vision in a comprehensive way • Recognize volunteers for innovation and change • Work with individuals and emphasize their uniqueness • Encourage radical change

Fit between program culture, strategy and actions will not always be possible. And even if there is a fit within the program, those programs embedded within umbrella organizations may find that incompatibility can occur. For example, a program that is focused on social change and is recruiting volunteers who are highly motivated to pursue a cause may find that this type of advocacy is no longer feasible within a large organization that is suffering budgetary cuts. Funders may not appreciate or even agree with the cause that a group of volunteers are pursuing and the larger organization cannot afford to support a volunteer program that "stirs the pot" within the community. Thus, the manager of volunteers may find herself in a difficult situation in which her strategy to recruit outspoken volunteers to influence changes in the long-term care of elders has become a source of tension within the organization that is seeking traditional funding sources. Or a manager of volunteers in a traditional program is evaluated as being too rigid and lacking in creativity in a serendipitous organization that prides itself on thinking outside the box. Strategic management, then, must be considered within context and different contexts may be nested within one another. The effective manager of volunteers will recognize this complexity and adjust accordingly.

Survival Strategies

In addition to programmatic strategies that focus on how to manage human resources (volunteers in this case) and find ways to match volunteers with appropriate tasks, volunteer administrators often find themselves trying to strategize about how to keep their program alive or in smaller organizations how to keep the entire organization surviving. A number of managers have used and built on the now classic work of James Thompson (1967) to explore what strategies might be used to deal with survivability, particularly in times of retrenchment (McMurtry, Netting, & Kettner, 1990, 1992; Packard, 2008). Four umbrella strategies have been identified in order to deal with survivability: 1) maintain services, 2) insure capacity to remain within budget, 3) acquire power over the environment, and 4) alter organizational domain. The first two strategies move from attempting to continue what a program or organization can do internally, to more aggressive externally directed strategies, such as finding ways to acquire power in the environment, to literally joining with other programs and organizations to change the nature of how they are structured. Table 8 provides examples of the type of actions one might take if one wanted to pursue these strategies.

Table 8: Strategies and Possible Actions Used for Survival

Maintain Services	Insure Capacity to Remain within Budget	Acquire Power over the Task Environment	Alter Organizational Domain
Expand the range of funding sources	Freeze hiring	Develop cooperative agreements with other programs/ agencies	Franchise programs
Explore new grant-writing options	Lay off staff		Add new services to meet client demands
	Restrict travel		
Develop new fundraising methods	Make across-the-board cuts in funding	Restructure board composition	Develop a for-profit arm
Invest resources in marketing, advertising, and PR	Realign programs	Increase networking	Become a franchise of a larger organization
	Shrink programs	Increase lobbying	
	Rely more heavily upon volunteers	Seek media attention	Consolidate programs

Maintain Services	Insure Capacity to Remain within Budget	Acquire Power over the Task Environment	Alter Organizational Domain
Computerize/ streamline recordkeeping		Increase fundraising activities	Merge with other organizations/ programs
			Consider terminating program or organization

For volunteer administrators, it is important to recognize that relying more heavily upon volunteers is an action that is frequently being used by organizations that are facing funding reductions. Sometimes this action becomes an overriding strategy — with the assumption that somehow as paid staff members are laid off or staff are not replaced when they leave, that volunteers can assume their roles. This can pose problems for the manager of volunteers who oversees a cadre of volunteers and is being asked to step up recruitment and expand the program. In addition, the roles these newly recruited volunteers may be asked to play are those formerly held by staff, or even simultaneously held by staff, raising questions of competency and creating tensions between paid staff and volunteers (Macduff & Netting, 2005; Netting, 2007; Netting, Nelson, Borders, & Huber, 2004). Thus, an organization's push for increasing volunteers in times of budgetary retrenchment or even in times of expansion, can have an impact on the management of a volunteer program and potentially override programmatic strategies that are already in place.

Change Strategies

In the management of volunteers as human resources and in the consideration of survival strategies to keep programs and organizations going, volunteer administrators will encounter situations that they would like to change. Previously we examined the importance of analyzing situations and focusing on what needs to happen. But once an issue or problem has been identified and analyzed, there are strategies you can use to begin the change process. These type strategies are relationally oriented, heavily focused on interpersonal and power dynamics. They may be internally (program or organization) or externally (community) targeted.

Netting, Kettner, & McMurtry (2008) examine three strategies and sets of tactics used to change programs, organizations, and communities: collaboration, campaign, and contest. Deciding which of these three strategies to use is based on the relationship you have with the person or persons you are targeting for change. A *collaborative strategy* is used if you have good communication and a reasonably strong relationship, a situation in which those persons targeted for change are in agreement that something needs to happen. In these instances, collaboration just needs to be facilitated and the expectation is that parties will work together to make the change happen, once everyone is read in. An example is when a volunteer board of directors is unaware that there needs to be a policy about the transportation of clients. Volunteers need to be covered in terms of their liability and the agency needs to know what risks are associated with transporting. Your volunteers are eager to have a clear policy in place so that they can be consistent in what they tell clients who ask them for a ride. Once the board becomes aware of the situation, they want to do what is best to protect the agency and its volunteers. No one is in disagreement that something should happen, but there is uncertainty as to how the policy should be worded and whom it should cover. Using a collaborative strategy, the manager of volunteers can educate the board to understand the issues associated with transportation and a viable policy can be formulated and approved. In this process, the tactics (or actions) used in this strategy include education to empower the board members and capacity building in the volunteer program.

A *campaign strategy* is somewhat different in that its determination is based on there not being consensus that change needs to happen. Although communication may be open between parties, there may be disagreement about what action to take (or not to take). Educational tactics are very helpful, but a good deal of persuasion may have to accompany that education. Persuasion may include behaviours such as co-optation in which a compromise is reached as to what form the change will take or active lobbying for a cause. Depending on how broad-based the change is, volunteer administrators and others within the organization may appeal to the mass media for support, perhaps running ads or human interest stories to reach a broader audience. The use of campaign strategies may actually engage large numbers of volunteers to promote the change. For example, a manager of volunteers may recruit persons who are interested in "going green." The environmental movement for which the manager works is dependent on volunteers who are highly committed to the cause and who are willing to hand out leaflets in public places, get the word out through a wide-reaching website, and serve as speakers for various community groups on the subject of global warming. Knowing that everyone does not buy into the concept, a campaign strategy is needed in order to state the facts and get the word out.

The third strategy is contest. A *contest strategy* is needed when there is opposition to the change or allocation of resources that you wish to change. Not only is there opposition but communication is not ideal, in fact it may have broken down. More assertive tactics have to be used in this situation such as bargaining and negotiating, leading large scale collective action to demonstrate or highlight injustices, or even participating in a class action lawsuit. The manager of volunteers who uses this type of strategy is typically in a social change program or organization that seeks to make a transformative difference in what they do. For example, a manager of volunteers for a no-kill shelter may recruit volunteers to take on the cause of closing down puppy mills in the state. Volunteers attracted to the program are radically opposed to the practices of some breeders who are seen as putting productivity and profitability above animal rights. These animal rights volunteers are angry and ready for action, and communication between breeders and volunteers has totally broken down. Volunteers have picketed known puppy mills, called in reporters to document what they have found there, and basically antagonized the owners. They are considering breaking into the mills and freeing the dogs, essentially using a civil disobedience tactic that would result in legal prosecution of the volunteers. The manager of volunteers is liable if the volunteers do not restrain themselves. The manager must figure out how to use this contest strategy in a way to expose what is happening without becoming involved in illegal activity.

All three strategies (collaboration, campaign, and contest) concern relationships between various parties. In collaboration, there is agreement that something needs to happen and people work together to figure out how to address the identified need. A campaign strategy is used when people have to be convinced that something needs to happen. Communication is open, but some persuasion needs to occur before everyone is on board. And last, a contest strategy is needed when communication has broken down and you need to get someone's attention in order to leverage change. Table 9 provides an overview of change strategies and possible actions.

Table 9: Strategies and Possible Actions to Leverage Change

Collaboration	Campaign	Content
Used when there is good communication Action needs to be facilitated so that everyone can work together Education of all parties may be all that is needed for change to occur	Used when communication is open but people have to be convinced or may disagree Action needs to be taken to deal with disagreements or misunderstandings about the potential change Active lobbying, media support, and human interest stories are helpful tactics	Used when communication has broken down and you need to get attention Action needs to gain (or regain) attention from parties that are not listening Very assertive tactics may need to be used, ranging from heavy bargaining to class action suits

SUMMARY

Strategic management comes in various forms. There will be variation in the locus of control along a continuum from top-down to bottom-up approaches. Top-down approaches have often dominated, leaving volunteer administrators in decision-making positions without a great deal of input from volunteers. Bottom-up approaches are more participatory in which volunteer input is included in planning and implementation activities. And there is a good deal of variation along the continuum.

In order to think strategically, managers of volunteer programs need at least four skill sets: understanding and assessing program context; planning; focusing and prioritizing; and strategizing. Understanding can be enhanced by recognizing the culture in which you operate, attending to the artifacts, values, and underlying assumptions that are held at the program level and within the larger umbrella in which the program is housed. This understanding is helpful in recognizing paradoxes between the program and the organization, as well as within the program itself.

Volunteer administrators need strong planning skills, and there are multiple ways of planning. It is helpful to envision planning as a second skill set along a continuum that is very prescriptive (structured) and highly emergent (flexible). Most programs will vacillate along this continuum during their implementation, as needs change. Each volunteer and paid staff person will have their own psychological contract with the program, often not stated but incredibly powerful in terms of commitments and expectations. The major thing to realize is that there is no one best way to plan or psychologically contract, there are multiple ways.

A third skill set is focusing and prioritizing. In order to focus and prioritize, volunteer administrators must have analytical skills. This includes the ability to know the difference between a condition and a problem, as well as figuring out how broad the focus needs to be. Even with focusing, it is important to assess feasibility because even the best priority setting will not work if one is trying to change something that is totally constrained. Thus, it is helpful to think in terms of controllable variables, contingencies, and constraints.

The fourth skill set is ability to strategize. There are different kinds of strategies to consider, making strategic management multi-layered. Examining the fit between culture and strategy is important as well as recognizing when you are in a subculture that requires different strategies from the larger organization. Survival strategies include: maintaining services; insuring capacity to remain within budget; acquiring power over the environment; and altering organizational domain. Change strategies include: collaboration, campaign, and contest. Each strategy has a set of actions that fit with its intent, and some actions pertain to multiple strategies. The strategic manager has options from which to select in guiding volunteer programs.

REFERENCES

Bolman, L. G., & Deal, T. E. (2005). *Reframing organizations: Artistry, choice, and leadership* (3rd ed.). San Francisco, CA: Jossey-Bass.

Brody, R. (2000). *Effectively managing human service organizations* (2nd ed.). Thousand Oaks, CA: Sage.

Cameron, K. S., & Quinn, R. E. (2006). *Diagnosing and changing organizational culture* (rev. ed.). San Francisco, CA: Jossey-Bass.

Dunphy, D. (2000). Embracing paradox: Top down versus participative management of organizational change. In M. Beer & N. Nohria (Eds.), *Breaking the code of change* (pp. 123-135). Boston, MA: Harvard Business School Press.

Ellis, S. J. (1996). *The Volunteer recruitment book.* Philadelphia, PA: Energize, Inc.

Farmer, J. D. (1998). *Papers on the art of anti-administration.* Burke, VA: Chatelaine, Press.

Kettner, P. M. (2002). *Achieving excellence in the management of human service organizations.* Boston: Allyn and Bacon.

Kettner, Peter M., Moroney, Robert M., & Martin, Lawrence L. (2008). *Designing and managing programs: An effectiveness-based approach* (3rd ed.). Newbury Park, CA: Sage Publications.

Lindblom, C. (1959). The science of muddling through. *Public Administrative Review, 19*(2), 79-88.

Macduff, N. (1996). *Volunteer recruiting and retention: A marketing approach.* Walla Walla, WA: MBA Publishing.

Macduff, N., & Merrill, M. (2005). *Choices in volunteerism: Social glue or individual toy.* Paper presented at the Annual Meeting of the Association for Research on Nonprofit Organizations and Voluntary Action, Washington, DC. November 2005.

Macduff, N., & Netting, F. E. (2005). The volunteer and staff team: How do we get them to get along? *The Journal of Volunteer Administration, 23*(1), 21-25.

Macduff, N., Netting, F. E., & O'Connor, M.K. (2006). *Rethinking the nature of volunteerism: A multi-paradigmatic approach to volunteer management.* Paper presented at the annual meeting of the Association for Research on Nonprofit Organizations and Voluntary Action (ARNOVA). Chicago, IL.

McCurley, S., & Lynch, R. (2006). *Volunteer management: Mobilizing all the resources of the community* (2nd ed). Ottawa, Ontario: Johnstone Training and Consultation, Inc.

McMurtry, S. L., Netting, F. E., & Kettner, P. M. (1990). Critical inputs and strategic choice in non-profit human service agencies. *Administration in Social Work, 14*(3), 67-82.

McMurtry, S. L., Netting, F. E., & Kettner, P. M. (1991). How nonprofits adapt to a stringent environment. *Nonprofit Management and Leadership, 1*(3), 235-252.

Mintzberg, H., Ahlstrand, B., & Lampel, J. (1998). *Strategy safari: A guided tour through the wilds of strategic management.* New York: Free Press.

Netting, F. E. (2007). Including and excluding volunteers: Challenges of managing groups that depend on donated talent. In R. A. Cnaan & C. Milofsky (Eds.), *Handbook on community movements and local organizations* (pp. 410-425). New York: Springer.

Netting, F. E., Nelson, H. W., Borders, K., & Huber, R. (2004). Volunteer and paid staff relationships: Implications for social work administration. *Administration in Social Work, 28*(3/4), 69-89.

Netting, F. E., Kettner, P. K., & McMurtry, S. (2008). *Social work macro practice* (4th ed). Boston: Allyn & Bacon.

Netting, F. E., O'Connor, M. K., & Fauri, D. P. (2008). *Comparative approaches to program planning.* Hobokin, NJ: Wiley.

O'Connor, M. K., & Netting, F. E. (2008). *Organization practice: A guide to understanding human service organizations.* Hobokin, NJ: Wiley.

O'Connor, M. K., Netting, F. E., & Fabelo, H. (Jan-Mar 2009). A Multiparadigmatic survey of field agencies. *Administration in Social Work, 33*(1), 81-104.

Packard, T., Patti, R., Daly, D., Tucker-Tatlow, & Farrell, C. (2008). Cutback management strategies: Experiences in nine county human service agencies. *Administration in Social Work, 32*(1), 55-75.

Pawlak, E. J., & Vinter, R. (2004). *Designing and planning programs for nonprofit and government organizations.* San Francisco: John Wiley & Sons, Inc.

Schein, E. A. (2004). *Organizational culture and leadership.* San Francisco: Jossey-Bass.

Thompson, J. D. (1967). *Organizations in action.* New York: McGraw Hill.

Weick, K. E. (2000). Emergent change as a universal in organizations. In M. Beer & N. Nohria (Eds.), *Breaking the code of change.* Boston, MA: Harvard Business School Press.

Wilson, M. (1976). *The effective management of volunteer programs.* Boulder, CO: Volunteer Management Associates.

Chapter 5

OPERATIONAL MANAGEMENT

Allan B. Serafino, Ph.D.(c)
University of Calgary

OPERATIONAL MANAGEMENT

The Council for Certification in Volunteer Administration's Body of Knowledge and Job Analysis defines operational management as "the ability to design and implement policies, processes and structures to align volunteer involvement with the mission and vision of the organization" (2008, p. 1). Having a well-designed operational plan that can address these issues is an effective starting place for the volunteer administrator.

The volunteer administrator might assume that planning is a relatively simple matter of sketching out a few simple activities and then putting the volunteers to work, or, of choosing a popular operational planning model and carrying out its steps. Yet, planning is a complex activity, perhaps made more complex by the involvement of volunteers, and requires consideration of a wide variety of design elements. Its process is not linear but is one of going back and forth between the elements to establish consistency and accuracy. The plan will change shape and direction because of this constant checking, but will be better for it.

PLANNING DESIGN ELEMENTS

This chapter will follow operational planning through its design elements from defining the need for the plan to monitoring or evaluating progress in planning. The design elements are:

- Planning design — planning terms, defining the need for the plan, benefits and limitations of planning, and policies and procedures in planning.

- Planning framework — Strategic and operational planning concepts — strategic, operational and project planning. The Logic or Outcomes Model and project planning will be discussed separately.

- Approaches to planning.

- Alignment or "fit" of the plan with mission and vision.

- Program considerations for planning — including scope, purpose and life cycle of the plan, who is involved, risk management in planning, targets, goals and outcomes, and the environment or context of operational planning. Several specific types of plans to be addressed are the marketing, financial, advertising and promotions, sales, service and delivery, resources management, and monitoring and evaluating progress plans.

Planning Terms

Let us clarify a few planning terms. First, "operational planning" and "operational management" are often used without distinction yet "planning" or "designing" is the initial task of the volunteer administrator within the role "management". Second, "operational plan" and "program plan" will refer specifically to the plans that direct and lead to a program or set of activities to distinguish them from the implementation actions themselves. The third term, "organizational plan," is a subset of a larger organizational plan though often used incorrectly to mean operational plan. Finally, "project plan" is a specific application of an operational plan with a fixed set of parameters.

Defining the Need for the Plan

Defining the need for the plan involves answering why a plan is necessary at all. For the volunteer administrator, it may also involve some justification as to why volunteers are a necessary and valuable asset for accomplishing the plan.

Planning is essential to operations, programs, projects, and activities. The key to it is to define what "need" is driving the effort. Hence, a community assessment is a critical starting point for any operational plan. The assessment studies the clients in a given area, their needs, the resources available to them or ones that are missing, and then considers who delivers them and the means of delivery to meet those needs. It will set the stage for determining targets for the plan, the objectives, the resources required including volunteers, and the time-frame. In short, it determines all the elements of the plan. Most important, the plan must match or align with the strategic objectives of the organization, its policies, and its mission and its vision.

Justification for the use of volunteers to carry out the plan is an important issue. Volunteerism is a mainstay of most nonprofit organizations but it may take several years for volunteers to develop and prove their worth. In a world that demands instant results the volunteer administrator needs to ensure that the volunteers' key role is to support the mission and objectives already in place. He or she can do this by first creating a set of policies and procedures that will govern recruitment, training, supervision, and monitoring of volunteers. The next step will be to recruit a team of volunteers whose skill, enthusiasm and experience can become a resource to existing staff (*i.e.*, one that will take some of the pressure off staff time and effort). The final step is to develop a series of specific activities that will be able to prove to clients that the work meets their needs as effectively as when done by staff. The plan to use volunteers must demonstrate to stakeholders that they represent significant community support for the organization. Failure to plan for the effective use of volunteers may result in creating a group of un-wieldy, if good-intentioned, individuals whose effort undermines organizational mission and vision. The volunteer administrator (sometimes called manager, coordinator, or director) may also need to justify his or her own job. He or she alone can "devote the time and attention required for fitting together a complex system matching the needs of the agency with the needs of the community" [through volunteer effort] (McCurley and Lynch, 1989, p. 14). He or she therefore needs to understand the complexity of planning for motivating and supervising volunteers to bring the plan to fruition. The CEO or executive director should design a set of policies and procedures to govern the administrator's work.

Benefits and Limitations of Planning

A well-designed plan gives the organization, staff, and volunteers a sense of direction, rhythm and pace. It provides benchmarks to monitor accomplishments over time. It is, in the case of volunteers, a locus of activity where individuals can "make a difference" in a real way. It is helpful to remember that the plan is also an experiment in social change. In more pragmatic terms, it specifies what needs to be accomplished within a given period, identifies what can be done within it, guides the activities of everyone toward accomplishment of the goals, links strategic plans to daily operations, requires that the organization be realistic about the scope of work, provides assessment of progress and identification of barriers, and is a basis for accountability.

An operational plan is, however, limited. It is not the panacea for all social ills as only finite resources will be available for its implementation, nor is it the only means an organization has of organizing and achieving its goals. Unexpected events can derail it quickly. It is a plan and nothing more — even the best of plans require effective implementation and evaluation. Adjustments and changes will be necessary to its ensuring success. Plans involving volunteers are subject to their motivations, whims, and abilities, but also their availability. Because volunteers are limited in their authority and expertise, the plan needs to account for the means of their supervision. The plan is not "owned" by the volunteer team but belongs to the organization and is therefore subject to the changes that take place within it. Finally, planning conceived as fixed or unchanging solutions to problems is limited and prone to error. It must be an approach that is fluid, capable of sudden change and direction, open to discarding its assumed methods and assumptions, and ready to be creative and generative.

Policies and Procedures

Operational plans do not exist by themselves. As shown below in Figure 1, they are nestled within larger strategic plans and governed by a set of policies and procedures. The board of directors sets overall planning policy and gives intent, scope, direction and limitation to the content, time-frame, and method of the plan. All policy falls within the embrace of mission and vision. Overarching policies are called governing policies; that is, they govern the whole organization. Operational policies, however, govern specific operations. In organizations with policy governing boards, the volunteer administrator may write operational policies but they require approval of the board. Operational policies "ensure uniformity and consistency in operational procedures" and "enable the board to evaluate the management of the organization ..." (Board Development Program, 2001, HO #9).

While planning policy might answer the questions, "*Why* is there a need for the plan?" and "*What* has to be done to meet this need?" procedures often answer, "*How* will the plan be conducted? *When? Who* will plan the plan?" Thus, clear policy statements guide the volunteer administrator's planning process and, later, implementation of the plan. A separate set of personnel policies such as the screening, hiring and dismissal of volunteers govern the management of volunteers.

FRAMEWORK: STRATEGIC AND OPERATIONAL PLANNING CONCEPTS

Framework concepts in planning will involve discussion of the differences between planning and plan, and, the differences between strategic, operational and project planning.

Planning and Plan

Planning is a process. Its product is a plan. As a process, it is the act of creating or designing objectives and methods, but also the rate and shape of accomplishment of goals. It is the alignment of resources such as people, materials and money to achieve those goals. It is a psychological process of thinking that combines forecasting with preparation and adjustment of plans. It is a series of formal activities such as meetings, reporting, developing, changing, and evaluating. It is also an informal and often tacit or internal series of adjustments, responses, and, creations that are sometimes difficult to observe and understand.

As a product, a plan is typically a written series of activities, a blueprint from which people choose their work. However, it is useful here to think of it as a procedure or set of intended actions to achieve an objective. Plans are structured or unstructured, anticipations or expectations, as much as they are also "seat-of-the pants" responses. Whatever the type of plan is — although we will deal here with the more formalized and structured type — it should be a realistic view of the organizations' expectations. For the volunteer administrator the plan is the most important operational management document and key to success for it is the guide by which he or she structures volunteer work, manages volunteer processes, and aligns volunteer involvement with the mission and vision of the organization. This old adage is true: "While designing a comprehensive plan will not guarantee success, lack of a sound plan will almost certainly ensure failure." Overarching plans are widest in scope ever decreasing in focus and detail. We will look at three of the most common ranges of plans: strategic, operational, and project planning.

Strategic, Operational and Project Planning

The interrelationship between the strategic plan, the operational or program plan, and the project plan is demonstrated in Figure 1 below as a series of nested boxes.

Figure 1: Co-relation of Strategic, Operational or Program, and Project Plans

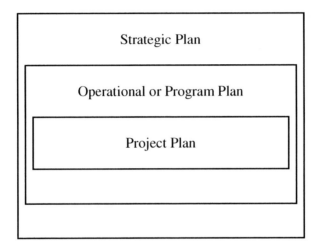

The Strategic Plan

The strategic plan is largest in scope specifying the purpose, goals and programs of the organization. It includes clarifying the mission or purpose, identifying the desired status or vision over a period of time (often three to five years), analyzing the external and internal environments, establishing large-scale goals and action plans, identifying resources to achieve them and ensuring there is a monitoring or evaluation process (McNamara, 2006, p. 33). In short, it answers where you are, where you want to be, and how to get there (Bryson, 2004, p. 7).

The Operational Plan

The operational plan is a series of systematic activities designed to help the organization achieve its goals. It serves to help management to clarify, focus, and research its various strategies, to provide a recognizable framework in which the work will take place, and to offer a benchmark for measurement, especially a benchmark for success in the client community. A plan can therefore play a vital role in helping to avoid mistakes or recognize hidden opportunities. As stated above a well-prepared and implemented volunteer plan demonstrates that the volunteer is a well-situated means for carrying out the organizations' activities, finances and resources in the community.

The operational plan is the day-to-day plan; it is usually a one-year plan that rolls into a subsequent annual plan to achieve specific, targeted goals. Since its purpose is to implement and support the long-range and mission-oriented goals, it is part of the strategic plan. Often, each "operation" has its own plan; for example, the Business Plan, Financial Plan, and Marketing Plan, but they have no life of their own as the same strategic imperatives govern them.

Volunteer administrators should be cautious, however, in developing business, financial and marketing plans and the like from business or other workplace models without testing to see that their assumptions, vocabulary, and goals are compatible with those of the nonprofit environment.

The Project Plan

The project plan focuses on time-related or constrained variables but does have a life of its own. It has clear measurable objectives to achieve a one-of-a-kind effort with quick response time and involves coordinating and managing several independent elements. Cook applies the simple stratagem of "just enough management" to set boundaries for the project and transform its objectives into results instead of creating more projects or work (2005, pp. 2 and 16). A fundraising plan, for example, can be a project when it is limited in its life cycle, parameters and objectives. An operational plan, by comparison, is a creative trigger that expands and continues the vision of the initial operation. The time-specific and goal-specific nature of projects can appeal to volunteers who only have limited time to offer a volunteer agency.

The details of project planning are discussed further below.

LOGIC OR OUTCOMES MODEL

Plans are systems. As a system, a plan involves component parts that interconnect to make a sustainable and effective whole. The Logic Model, a systematic outcomes-based planning tool promoted by the

United Way of America in *Measuring Program Outcomes: A Practical Approach* (1996), is such a system. It involves four components each of which focuses on goals that assist the organization to achieve its mission and vision. The "logic" or flow of the components answers the increased demand for accountability many nonprofits must provide to their funders. It also gives an overview of the planning process as well as a summary of its results. The components of the logic model are:

- Inputs — "resources dedicated to or consumed by the program" such as money, staff, time, equipment, supplies.

- Activities (also called processes) — "what the program does with the inputs to fulfill its mission" including strategies, techniques and methods. The larger organization could consider the volunteer program, in fact, to be one of its activities.

- Outputs — "the direct products of program activities ... usually measured in terms of the volume of work accomplished." Hence, outputs are tangible results that can be measured in numbers — for example, the numbers of program attendees, the number of persons trained, the number of meals delivered, *etc.*

- Outcomes — "the benefits or changes for individuals or populations during or after participating in program activities." They may relate to "behavior, skills, knowledge, attitudes, value, conditions, status or other attributes." (United Way, 1996, pp. 1-3)

Outcomes become an important way of measuring whether the plan has real value or real impact on society. Analyzing only the numbers of attendees at second language classes (output), for example, do little to understand progress compared with demonstrating that the clients actually improved skills in learning a new language (outcome). There are several good computer programs which can help the volunteer administrator to implement the outcomes or logic model. However, the process can be time-consuming, call for an in-depth review of all of the success indicators, involve a complicated computer program, and require some serious training. Not everyone can and should use the model without technical help. Nevertheless, the results can be extremely beneficial for getting a strategic view of the plan that relates to its outcomes.

APPROACHES TO PLANNING

An approach refers to the perspective the administrator takes toward the nature of the work to be done and the organization's ability to do it. The way he or she approaches planning will depend upon the nature and complexity of the organization's programs and services, its resources and stability, and his or her expertise and experience with developing programs. It may be advisable to obtain planning help from formal courses, books or experienced practitioners but one should beware of prescriptive answers or fads. What works in one organization may not transfer easily to another.

Some common approaches to planning include trial and error, building as you go along, making adjustments to current programs, and careful analysis of each of the elements needed. McNamara outlines four basic approaches:

- *Build it and they will come.* The founder builds a program based solely on his or her conviction that there is an unmet need to be met through his or her perceptions of the right methods.

- *Seat of the pants.* This approach also depends upon what the founder does to meet community needs but as time goes by more and more people become involved there will be little to distinguish between the program services and the organization's services.

- *Incremental planning.* The clients are well-known as are their needs, the methods are familiar, and the cost and risk quite low compared to the two former approaches.

- *Business planning.* Business planning involves careful scrutiny of the needs, methods, targets, processes, goals and outcomes before implementation takes place. (2006, pp. 27-30)

These approaches progress from those that are risky because they involve little forethought about clients' needs to approaches that are safer because they analyze the needs first. Small, founder-driven organizations often begin with the first two approaches until more and more people join and strive to make the organization more efficient.

An educational approach to planning in schools ("Five Orientations to Learning" in Merriam and Caffarella, 1999) can be adapted by the volunteer administrator to work with nonprofit clients. Its value is the focus for planning on client outcomes, namely the desired changes the plan will have on the clients' status or well-being. These range from the behaviourist approach involving purely behavioural changes in the client to the humanist approach involving changes in the client's self-esteem and personal development. The latter is intended to aid the client to become more self-autonomous and the administrator's, and volunteers', role is to help facilitate the development of the whole person. This approach resonates strongly with outcomes perspectives on planning.

ALIGNMENT OR "FIT" WITH THE MISSION AND VISION

The problem or gap that an operational plan addresses is how to enact the vision and mission developed in the strategic plan. Essentially, it is about shortening the gap between where the organization is and where it wants to go. The role of the operational plan is to bring momentum and shape to the organization's potential to achieve its mission and vision. With most organizations, this is an ongoing process and rarely, it seems, is the mission ever fully achieved. Unlike a project plan, an operational plan does not exist on its own, nor is it totally measured by its own parameters. Its role is to fit or support the overarching goals of the organization. The role of the volunteer administrator is to bring to the fit the resources and power of volunteer work.

The operational plan, in the ideal world, arises out of the mission and vision of the organization. However, it also responds to unanticipated circumstances such as change in fiscal policy, crises, accountability, and technology. It also arises within and because of the existing structure of the organization, which may be mechanistic or organic, hierarchically controlled or locally controlled. The results of the plan can in turn, have an effect on changing the strategy of the organization and its structure. More recently, some hierarchically dominated organizations have changed to flatter, leaner organizations to become more effective (Senge, 1990; Dixon, 1994). One of the benefits of the flatter organization is the potential for the sharing of information and decision-making across all units of the organization (Dixon, 1994, p. 97). The volunteer administrator, for example, should consider involving volunteers as much as possible in the planning process. Therefore, there is a reciprocal relationship, a fluid and changing relationship, between mission, strategy, structure and operations. The plan is approved by the governors of the organization and directed by its policies based upon the organization's mission and goals.

PROJECT PLANNING

The remainder of this chapter will focus on operational planning specifics (Program Considerations for Operational Planning), so it is useful to outline project planning now. Project management refers to the planning, organizing and managing of resources for specific goals and objectives. It has a start and completion date unlike the ongoing work that occurs in permanent or semi-permanent operational programs. Its purpose is to produce a specific product or service during this period rather than to sustain the ongoing offering of products and services, which is the aim of the operational plan. Hence, a major difference is the constraints that are on project plans — constraints of scope, time and budget. Operational plans are ongoing, stable, and serve larger needs. Project plans, however, are episodic, often one-time events, and serve immediate needs. Projects can be linked to operational plans or be independent of them. Operational planning involves the traditional approaches of initiation, planning and design, execution, monitoring and control, and closing. Project planning includes the life cycle and stages or phases of conception, prioritization, mobilization, execution, completion, and realization.

Project plans include nine components:

1. a feasibility study;

2. building a business case;

3. risk management analysis;

4. creating terms of reference;

5. determining the scope of the project;

6. identifying a sponsor, often someone in the organization;

7. developing a communication plan;

8. doing an impact analysis; and

9. completing a post-project review (Kor and Wijnen cited in Vakil, 2006, pp. 292-93).

A common model for project planning is the Project Evaluation and Review Technique (PERT), designed to analyze and represent the tasks involved in completing a given project, driven by the minimum time needed to complete the total project. It is used to "estimate overall project duration when there is uncertainty in the individual duration estimates" (Cook, 2005, p. 125). Another key feature of the project is that one can schedule its activity without knowing or depending on all the other activities of the organization. Project control systems are also tighter and more demanding than process systems, and this makes them valuable for term-certain outcomes but not as flexible as process systems that can take into account changes and shifts in human temperament. Project fundamentals are project, size, duration, cost, purpose, product, number and types of people, boundaries (time, cost, performance), and priorities.

Project work teams, while they may have links to the organization's structure, can be stand-alone work teams operating under a different set of rules if necessary. The skills required are teamwork, communication, organization, scheduling, cost accounting, appraising and estimating, and, particularly, problem-solving and time management. Accountability and reporting is often stricter and tighter than process accountability where flexibility is critical. Progress reports are more common as are audits and there is a greater emphasis on reducing risk. Yet a common mistake is to assess a project's risk in isolation from other projects and from the organization itself. Volunteers who are constrained for time may prefer to work on projects.

PROGRAM CONSIDERATIONS FOR OPERATIONAL PLANNING

In undertaking the design of an operational plan, the volunteer administrator will need to consider some of the key aspects of operational planning such as its scope, purpose and life cycle, who needs to be involved, and management of potential risk. He or she will also need to determine specific targets, goals, and outcomes and examine the environment or context in which the plan is to take place. Finally, he or she will need to review specific aspects of planning that address marketing, financial matters, advertising and promotion, sales, service and delivery and resources, and determine how to monitor and evaluate progress in planning. Figure 2 below outlines these elements. The most common consequence of planning is the creation of a program or programs designed to achieve specific goals. In this section, we will therefore examine the program consequences of planning.

Figure 2: Program Considerations for Planning

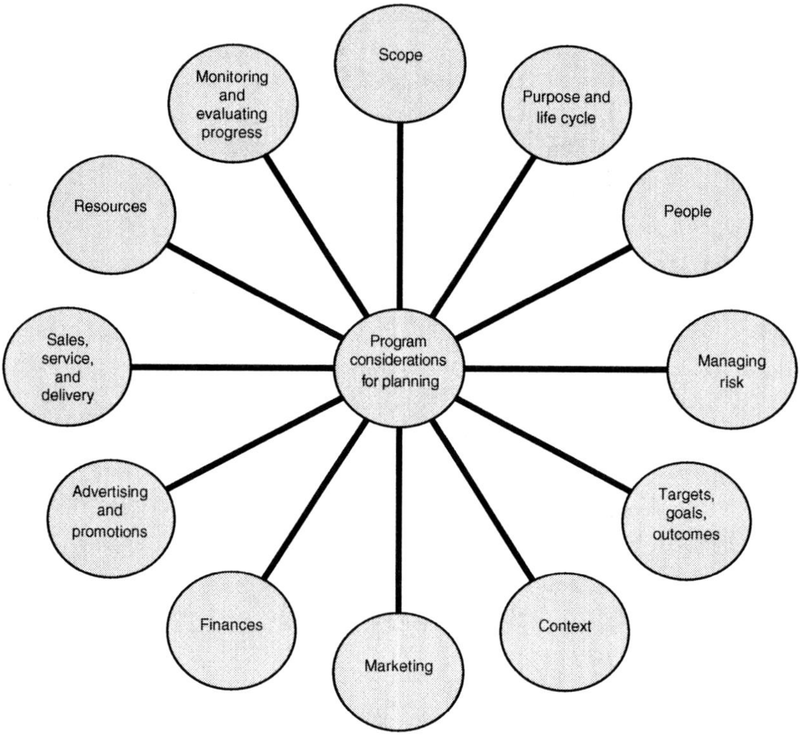

Scope

Operational plans can be designed for short-term, ad hoc, or long-standing applications. Short-term applications may be, for example, seasonal programs, special events, or events that occur regularly at specific times of the year. Ad hoc plans are made in response to an unexpected opportunity or crisis. Long-term plans tend to be designed with the expectation that their applications will follow the annual cycle of the organization or cover an even more extensive period. Plans can be made for stand-alone or freestanding applications, for example, "where the services are delivered completely within the context of the program" (McNamara, 2006, p. 9), or they can occur within the context of one organization or more. In a multi-program effort, "two or more programs are tightly integrated to provide a common set of services to meet one major, unmet need in the community" (McNamara, 2006, p. 9). The advantage of integrating the programs internally is the ability to share the same resources and budget or to increase the effect. Sometimes the nonprofit organization exists as a single, freestanding program; that is, it exists to provide only the services of that particular program to one client base, for example, to a membership. In the initial planning phase, the volunteer administrator must therefore have a sense of the time-frame and type of application that will determine its scope. The scope of the plan is often annual, so it continues or turns over at the end of a planning or fiscal year. However, the plan may change purpose or even cease to exist if and when the strategic direction changes. Ad hoc plans that begin and end as the need dictates are more flexible in scope. Finally, programs are usually distinguished from "activities" in that they have formal goals and timetables within an organization and more rigid definition. The volunteer administrator will need to determine the type of plan and its scope very early in the planning process. It will influence the type of volunteers required, their availability, expertise and commitment and any special training that may be required for a longer-term plan.

Purpose and Life Cycle

Planning typically addresses three purposes:

*   sustaining current operations;

*   improving upon them; and

*   embarking on new ventures or initiative.

The plan's parameters are addressed by the strategic direction but thereafter the plan takes one of these three options. Most plans are designed for the long-term. They exist to sustain the services of the organization for its clients year after year, thus their resources — people and materials — and money require constant maintenance. Planning will address improvements when the client base or need changes, when the resources fail, when new opportunities arise to deliver the service in a better way, and, when external or internal issues threaten the stability of that base. New ventures or initiatives call for a complete new operational plan driven by a new strategic directive. It comes about because of the previously mentioned reasons for improvement, crisis, or because the organization has an opportunity to expand its mandate. Multi-organizational efforts may improve existing community services or combine resources and potential to bring upgraded levels of service to it.

The life cycle of the organization can pre-determine what knowledge, experience and resources are available to the administrator. It is likely that a new organization will need to create all of its resources, marketing initiatives and delivery systems, whereas an experienced or mature organization may be able to depend upon those it has worked to build. However, the mature organization may stand in need of new plans. One of the biggest dangers is to assume that the plan will be sufficient when it has already outlived its usefulness upon reaching the mature phase. For this reason, a new community assessment and program evaluation are necessary. Planners cannot rest on their laurels.

Most plans coincide with the fiscal year, so planning will need to be done and approved before it begins. It should not be left to the end of the current year as it may take several months to complete. In fact, organizations usually have a specific planning period during which this will occur. In terms of structure, the plan will therefore have an initial year, a process year(s), and a concluding year. Strategic plans also undergo life cycles. Thus, a three-year funding plan that is coming to the end of its life cycle will require renewal or change and this will certainly influence the life of the operational plan. The availability of other resources such as venues, equipment, contract personnel, operating budgets, and, of course, availability of volunteers are other contributing factors in life cycle planning. Like scope, the life cycle and purpose will influence the type of volunteers and other personnel required, their availability, expertise, commitment, and training needed.

People: Who Is Involved in Planning?

The operational plan depends upon the interaction of many individuals and it depends on whether they support or conflict with each other. The key individuals of groups include the board of directors, the executive director or CEO (Chief Executive Officer), staff, and volunteers.

Board Members and the Executive Director or CEO

Although the individuals on the board may not be directly involved in the workings of the operational plan, they hold the power to stop or change it. In a "policy governing" board, the board's role, as an entity, is to approve policy, not to operate programs. It hires and directs the executive director or CEO to implement the policy and carry out the plans it makes for the organization. Only in an "administrative governing" board may the board assign implementation to itself, the executive of the board, or to a standing committee (Board Development Program, 2001, HO #18). Thus, one board member or committee chairperson, perhaps in lieu of an executive director, will oversee the work of the volunteer administrator. Administrative boards are very common in small organizations (Gill, 2005).

In most organizations that operate a volunteer program in addition to its other programs, the executive director or CEO hires the volunteer administrator to carry out the work of managing the volunteers and is their direct link or line of accountability. The CEO should do no more than to give general direction such as ensuring that the plan is on track with the strategic directive. The volunteer administrator is accountable for the design and day-to-day implementation of the plan. The plan should clearly state this line of accountability to the executive director or CEO.

Staff

Working with staff can be an invigorating and enjoyable experience or a disagreeable and stressful one for the volunteer administrator. One particular issue is that other staff may not consider her or him to be an equal or professional colleague. This is because not all staff understands or easily accepts the involvement of volunteers in the organization — an ironic twist since most nonprofits began as wholly volunteer-driven organizations with no staff at all. They may view the work of volunteers as problematic and the administrator as unnecessary. Therefore, it is the administrator's job to justify his or her own existence as a professional, to prove his or her capability, and show that the plan and volunteer team are valuable assets to the organization. If successful, the other staff will be not only agreeable but also thankful for the volunteer team's efforts.

It is a peculiarity of the nonprofit sector that the authority of staff and volunteers differs among nonprofit organizations. McManus distinguishes between volunteer-led/staff-supported and staff-led/volunteer-supported roles and responsibilities. In the former, staff are likely an addition to the founding work of a volunteer-created organization. In the latter, staff are "responsible for program growth, vision, development and policies" (2006, p. 264). The design plan must make this distinction clear.

Volunteers

The particular arena of activity for the volunteer administrator is the interaction between volunteers and between volunteers and staff. His or her relationship with volunteers will either make or break the volunteer plan. Volunteers, in the staff supported model referred to above, can also be part of the planning process bringing their experience and expertise to the table but it is the volunteer administrator who takes the lead. The planning design must make clear what the role of the volunteer is to be through directives, job descriptions, and operational policies. The plan must account for everything from a volunteer's orientation, screening and initial training through their supervision, motivation and evaluation. Finally, it should ensure that good volunteers are recognized as an essential part of an integrated team. A relatively new and significant planning task for the volunteer administrator is the management of risk related to using volunteers.

Risk Management in Planning

The volunteer administrator has to plan to manage risk. Therefore, the plan must take into consideration the potential types of risk that can be incurred, the scope of the risk, and the methods to prevent it or work with risky elements. The degree of risk determines the scope, depth, and rate of its management efforts. Indeed, it is so critical that it may sometimes be the deciding factor in deciding whether a plan is worth the effort of an organization at all. Funders and other community stakeholders will look for well-designed risk management procedures to be in place before they offer financial or other support for the plan. Risk needs to be managed to prevent accidents, injury, and harm including abuse, to prevent damage to or loss of property and assets, to protect integrity, reputation, image, credibility and trust, and to ensure the ability of the organization to operate to mission. In the design, the volunteer administrator will need to ask, "What is the risk and why? Why must it be managed? What is the level of risk (high/low)? Why? Who is affected? How? What steps will be carried out? Why?" The steps to carry out or implement a risk management process are detailed in Chapter 12: Risk Management and the related issue of screening in Chapter 6: Volunteer Staffing and Development.

The planning role of the volunteer administrator is not only to determine ahead of time the potential level of risk but to ensure that his or her staff and volunteers fully understand the implications of risk before programs are conducted. Volunteers may refuse, for example, to have a nonprofit organization carry out a criminal record check on them. An astute board will direct the volunteer administrator through policy to ensure a risk management process is in place prior to volunteer recruitment.

In planning risk management, the steps the volunteer administrator will need to take into account include identifying risks, evaluating risks, controlling risks, and reviewing the risk management process (Table 2).

Targets, Goals, and Outcomes

The plan is a design for a targeted group of clients in the community who have a specific need. Targeting focuses on specific criteria such as age, gender, social level, income level, education, health, language, and demographic location. For example, targets could be at-risk women ages 35 to 45 who suffer from spousal abuse, low income seniors without transportation, or new immigrant children without literacy skills in the English language. In the design phase they can be defined by "numbers of" some desired result. Therefore, a well-defined target statement might be:

> "200 boys and girls aged 14-16 in the Greenwood Community (25% of the 14-16 year-olds) participate in one Teens Drop-in Centre activity weekly for six months after the initial promotion of the Centre's programs."

In the design phase, the volunteer administrator estimates the numbers required and adjusts them after the first evaluation. It is a mistake, however, to set goals at this stage that are too improbable. Setting lower, achievable goals is the place to begin since there are many unknown or unanticipated factors that could affect the results poorly. Plan for a slow start with fewer or lower results, a peak in the middle, and a gradual sloping off until, perhaps, the service no longer meets the needs or attracts insufficient numbers to warrant its continuance. Along the way, the volunteer administrator should plan to measure some success indicators or "milestones" such as the estimated numbers of teens in the first month, third month and sixth month.

Measurable goals are, however, not outcomes. In the language of the logic model the goals above are "outputs" or results from the service whereas an "outcome" describes the impact on the clients from participating in the program. Let us say that the community assessment has indicated a need for teen activity based on damage caused by them to public property because they had no other meaningful sustained activity in their free time. The outcome will therefore measure the effects of the plan on meeting this need such as:

"As a result of the Teen Drop-in Centre program, vandalism has been reduced by 30 per cent."

"25 per cent of teens 14-16 describe a higher sense of ability to manage their free time."

"10 per cent of teens 14-16 attribute a greater sense of community pride to their involvement in the Teens Centre program."

Note that the plan writes the outcome as if the outcome has been achieved. This format makes the visualization of planning results easier. Goals, however, tend to be written as if the result has yet to be achieved and lead with the word "to". For example,

"The goal (output) is to reduce vandalism by 30 per cent as a result of creating a Teen Drop-in Centre program."

"The goal is to increase program membership by 10 per cent as a result of the Spring Getting to Know You barbecue."

"The goal is to recruit one new financial sponsor for the Breast Cancer Awareness Run July 13, 2012 as a result of the May Fundraising Dinner."

"The goal is to raise $50,000 for the Diabetes Association as the result of door-to-door canvassing during the annual May Flowers campaign."

The Environment or Context of Operational Planning

The volunteer administrator will need to assess the environment or context in which the plan is to operate. This process is the *environmental scan*. We have already started with a scan in the form of the community assessment. Initially, its results were used to define the need for a plan. Now the details can be used to clarify the dynamics of that environment. The factors that affect the environment are social, economic, political, historical, *etc*. The administrator will need to ask various levels of question prior to planning: "What factors are at work? What factors will affect the target client base? What effect will the factors have on the plan? What data can be used to create the plan?" Let us say the community assessment indicated a need for a lending library for home-ridden seniors aged 75. A few typical questions might include:

- What are the demographics of the geographical area in which the plan will be implemented (data about a population such as age, gender, and race)? For example, How many seniors aged 70-75 are there?

- What affect will economic levels and other economic factors (income, revenue sources, and taxes) have on the target clients? What is the median income of the seniors above? Can seniors afford a fee for the service? How much?

- What resources will be needed to deliver the services of the plan such as a bus or van, drivers, and books?

The volunteer administrator might check to see if the organization has already done some environmental scanning and how long ago. A very popular form of scan is the S.W.O.T. Analysis (strengths, weaknesses, opportunities and threats) used in strategic planning. Other nonprofit organizations may have done scans as well, and, very often, free data is available from town or city census planners. However, it may be a few years out-of-date.

The environment for nonprofit operational planning is constantly changing. It is difficult to plan outcomes with a high degree of certainty given the current economic, social, and political environment, especially if the plan covers a long period. Organization structures may no longer be traditional and mechanistic but organic and fluid, and, leadership may be less hierarchical or top-down. Accountability has sharply increased at all organizational levels. Accountability for public funding dollars is noticeably more demanding. Results are expected faster by boards, by funders, and even by clients. "Bad press" in one nonprofit organization may inadvertently affect another organization's work. Many traditional long-term volunteers are on the wane. Younger volunteers in particular want nonprofit organizations to produce results faster and more effectively but their participation is more "episodic," that is irregular and short-term (Macduff, 1995), and reflective or self-serving (Hustinx and Lammertyn, 2003). Clients are more demanding, too. With more options for them to choose they are apt to seek assistance from organizations that will meet their needs faster, cheaper, and more effectively, but only if the quality of the service is not compromised. The delivery of quality still ranks as the key factor in people making decisions to join an organization, volunteer for it, donate to it, and make use of its services.

As shown above, the planning design begins with a creating a framework such as that of a house. It sets out purpose, targets and their characteristics, time-frame, objectives (sometimes-called deliverables) for their tangible characteristics, outcomes, and an idea of the staffing and resource requirements. Now the plan needs adding or filling in additional structures or elements — the walls, floors, windows, and doors if you will — that could not have been considered before. They are the following program considerations:

- marketing;

- financial matters including budgets, pricing and costs;

- advertising and promotions;

- sales, service and delivery;

- resources management including personnel and materials; and

- monitoring or evaluating progress.

Plans That Address Marketing

Marketing is defined by the American Marketing Association as "the activity, set of institutions, and processes for creating, communicating, delivering, and exchanging offerings that have value for customers, clients, partners, and society at large" (2007, p. 1). It is easier to think of it as an arrangement that allows buyers and sellers to exchange things. In the nonprofit context, however, the exchange is more difficult to envision since many nonprofits appear to deliver products or services without recompense or exchange. The volunteer administrator will need to know about marketing issues to ensure that the plan will communicate, deliver, sell or exchange the right services to the right clients in the most effective way to meet clients' needs.

The first step is market research or analysis. The planner needs to identify opportunities to serve various groups of clients in need of services or products. A community assessment will examine the market to determine how many persons need the service, and to determine the best methods of delivery. The targets must be specific. It is best to consider that each plan is designed to meet the needs of a very specific group of people or targets bounded by specific needs and a specific time-frame. The resulting program is the most precise means to deliver products or services to them to meet their needs (hereafter, for the sake of simplicity, the term service will include both products and services). Critical planning questions include:

- What will the targets be like?

- What will be their age, location, physical ability, *etc.*?

- What service do they need?

- When will they need it?

- How accessible will the service be to them?

- Can they afford it?

- Will they be capable of using it?

- What will they do with it?

- What impediments or challenges will there be in the delivery of it?

The planner needs to consider the configuration or "packaging" of the service as this is what clients will see. It is how they will determine whether the service is useful for or attractive to them and whether they can afford it. There will be competition for this service. Nonprofit administrators may not immediately think about competition, assuming perhaps that it only occurs in business circles. However, other deliverers of services can appeal to the client — they include business competitors and other nonprofit organizations. It is beneficial to think about what will make the service stand out from the rest, that is, its "unique value" or "value added" dimension. It may be the service itself, its quality, access to it, ease of use, cost, delivery, or the customer or client service after delivery. For a house-bound senior the home delivery and pick up of a lending library may be its most valuable asset. One way of standing out from the rest is to "brand" the service, that is, to give it familiarity, recognition, reputation and a memorable name. Branding may include recognizable colours, logos, such as the immediately recognizable red cross of the International Red Cross Society, and any associated music images and slogan. A slogan is a mnemonic device to help customers remember or have recall of a service's key selling characteristic. "Head, heart, hands, health," for example, brand the now familiar 4-H Clubs. Some nonprofits, however, are not often successful at the naming and branding game. Phrases such as "bridging the gap" and "making a difference" may be so overused that they could disappear in a barrage of other communication statements. Planners must be thoughtful and creative and remember the make-up and needs of the client. The Women in Need Shelter (Calgary) uses the appealing slogan "Helping Women Helping Themselves" which describes precisely the humanistic view of how it perceives its clients think of themselves.

A key aspect of marketing is precisely how the organization wants its clients to respond to its marketing communications. The planner must consider how the client will purchase, access and use the service. He or she must think about how he or she will change or add to the service when something goes wrong, or even, how he or she will end the service. Let us look at some examples. The communication may simply be a matter of an easily accessed phone number to request the service, but in some cases such as distressed callers, clients may be reluctant or afraid to call. A distress hot line is only good to the person in need if he or she makes the call. Reliance on e-mail alone will surely limit the response. A computer and the appropriate technical skill is required as well as manual dexterity. Clients who have dial-up operating systems rather than high-speed Internet systems will find it difficult to download information. Thus, a variety of means of access should be available. Some factors to consider are the age of the audience, reading level, health problems or disabilities, language restrictions, location, race or ethnicity, religion and interests. The "Communications Planning Outline," in the advertising and promotions section below, is a useful ten-step checklist with which to design and implement a targeted message. Above all, marketing goals must be specific and measurable.

To market spousal abuse services the goal might read:

"Place 500 brochures with local medical offices over the two-month period January – February, 2012."

To market to the Teen Drop-In Centre:

"Deliver a short invitation to 25 middle and high school classes during September and October, 2012."

Plans That Address Financial Matters

A volunteer administrator will need to consider financial matters such as budgets, revenue, cost, and pricing in order to ensure that his or her plan is financially feasible for the organization and capable of successful delivery to its clients.

Budgets

Budgets are a key element in the operational planning process. A budget, it should be remembered, is only estimation. It can and often is changed throughout a fiscal year. Types of budgets are:

- operating — for annual revenue and expenses;

- capital — for equipment, furniture, even property;

- cash — for payment of immediate expenses; and

- function — for specific programs; separately tracked.

The operational planner of a large organization will often submit the operating budget as one of many separate budgets to a treasurer or accountant who will create an overall organizational budget in turn. Some typical budgeting steps are:

- select the budget period/timeline;

- identify revenue;

- identify expenses;

- balance the budget;

- audit notes and comments;

- review and obtain approval of budget;

- implement, monitor, adjust budget;

- obtain approval for non-budgeted items; and

- identify items for upcoming year.

However, the unexpected will happen. Revenue will be less than expected, expenses more. If cash flow is not too tight, adding a 10 per cent contingency is a reasonable way to prepare for unanticipated financial problems.

Revenue

An operation may receive its operating revenue from the organization or sustain itself by generating its own. Most nonprofits, however, rely on a combination of revenue from earned income and government funding. Traditional sources include operating fees for services, membership dues, government, corporation and foundation grants, investment income, individual donations, sales of products, and fundraising. Government funding often predominates among services, health, hospitals, universities and colleges, earned income among sports and recreation, arts and cultural groups, and, private giving among religious organizations. While some organizations earn millions of dollars, "63% of nonprofits in Canada operate on revenues under $10,000" (Murray, 2006, p. 40). Comparatively, 24.2 per cent of

American nonprofits operate on revenues of US$50,000 (Urban Institute, 2007). A recent innovation is the concept of social entrepreneurship, which "occurs when nonprofit organizations establish or enter into profit-making ventures to finance their nonprofit operations" (Hall, 2006, p. 294). They sell their services such as the rental of their facilities, the selling of their labour, or the catering of special events. Larger nonprofits such as hospitals and universities have even created holding companies and joint ventures while "remaining true to [their] mission" (Hall, 2006, p. 295). However, the volunteer administrator is more likely to finance his or her operations with less exotic and more traditional means. The organizational plan must be clear that it is, nevertheless, true to the definition of nonprofit; that is, that profits are turned back to the organization for the express purpose of delivering its services. All revenues must be explicitly controlled and tracked.

Pricing and Cost

Pricing and cost is a critical planning issue whether the plan operates through a grant or donation or from an operational budget of the organization. In tight economic times when organizations cannot depend upon funding, the volunteer administrator will have to attend to the ways that cost can affect the client's ability to use the service provided. The planner should therefore ask:

- What can the client afford for the service?

- Should there be a fee? How much?

- Should costs be recoverable? Should only a portion of costs be recoverable?

- Can there be a sliding scale for fees or a variable fee based on pre-set criteria such as age and income?

- Should there be discounts?

- What will the effect on the clients be?

- What is the competitor's price?

- How will fees for services be collected and accounted?

There are two traditionally recognized ways of setting a fee or price. *Cost-based pricing*, as the name implies, involves adding the total price of the production and delivery of the service and setting the price to offset those costs. The other is *value-based pricing* or identifying what the client perceives as the value of the service and charging accordingly (McNamara, 2006, p. 62). To ensure that the price is fair, however, surveys should be taken to determine how clients feel about the price, what competitors' prices are, what the market can bear, and what other revenues will continue to support the costs. Last, there is the issue of perceived value. It is a common assumption that the larger the fee the better the service or product. An organization need not undersell itself unless its image will be negatively affected. Yet, fees for products are valuable asset if they make buyers more aware of the organization's work.

Keeping costs or expenses down or at a break-even point are critical for the operation of a plan. This is not the place to detail all types of costs but several key points need to be uppermost in the planner's mind:

- Are the costs "real" or offset in some other way such as a donation?

- Are the expenses a regular annual cost or a special one-time cost?

- Can the reduced cost be expected to be the same in the following year's budget?

- Will costs be offset by "in-kind" donations?

- Will costs be direct or indirect?

"In-kind" donations are helpful, but they may also set a false expectation about the real expense of an item. For example, let us say that an organization was to host a special event. If the event venue is donated or food or prizes donated for it one should ask if they would be donated the following year. A cautious volunteer administrator should assume they will not and plan to treat the item as an expense in the ensuing year's budget.

Costs are either direct or indirect. Direct costs include facilities, personnel salaries, tools and equipment, maintenance, advertising, *etc*. Yet expenses come in many unexpected, hidden, or indirect forms such as:

- insurance fees, taxes, licences or permits and inspections;

- replacement of damaged items;

- monthly fees such as phone and Internet services;

- parking, office staff and contracted help;

- rent and maintenance;

- memberships and dues;

- travel, gas, and auto repair; and

- increases in gas, parking, and meals.

Costs of personnel involve salaries and compensation including those for full-time, part-time and overtime work; benefits such as medical, life and dental insurance, disability and worker's compensation, vacation and holiday pay; more recently maternity (and partner) leave; pension contribution, bonuses and taxes. Recognition for new staff, staff leaving, birthdays, and for special occasions such as parties, volunteer appreciation, banquets, and honours or special awards may all be additional. Other costs can be the contracting of specialized help, consultant fees, one-time event-related help, and repair and maintenance help.

Plans That Address Advertising and Promotions

A volunteer administrator will need to know about advertising and promotions to plan for the ways in which he or she can put forward the best possible message and image to get the desired response from potential clients to his or her program, product, or services. *Advertising* is a form of communication that typically attempts to persuade potential customers to purchase or to consume more of a particular brand of product or service. *Promotion* involves disseminating information about a product, product line, brand, or company. It is one of the four key aspects of the marketing mix, the other three being product marketing, pricing, and distribution. *Promotion* is generally overt ("above the line") in media such as television, radio, newspapers, the Internet and mobile phones where the advertiser pays a third party agency to place the ad, and a more indirect ("below the line") type that includes sponsorship, product placement, endorsements, sales promotion, merchandising, direct mail, personal selling, public relations, and trade shows. Nonprofits have used both advertising and promotion to sell their products or services. Notwithstanding, the less costly approaches of using brochures, neighbourhood signs, posters, newsletters, special events and word-of-mouth can be very effective.

Whatever media is chosen there are some basic communication considerations. The "Communications Planning Outline" (Anonymous, 1992) is a useful tool. The steps include:

1. Know the target audience.

2. Know the targets' context — backgrounds, languages, capabilities, interests.

3. Plan the communication objective or net impression such as sincerity.

4. Craft the key message, usually in one sentence for the specific audience.

5. Eliminate or work around "noise", the external factors that may disrupt the intent or delivery of the message such as competing promotions, complex messages.

6. Determine the appropriate tone of the message; E.g. celebratory, serious.

7. Choose media such as TV, radio, posters etc appropriate to the audience and issue.

8. Determine in advance the response as a result of receiving the message.

9. Decide who the best spokesperson will be. E.g. CEO? client? celebrity?

10. Measure to find out how the response was received by the target audience.

The Communications Planning Outline tool for the volunteer administrator is a planning tool that helps to keep communications focused on the "audience" or client. Of course, it is also useful as a checklist to keep the plan on track as it works through the implementation phase.

Plans That Address Sales, Service and Delivery

A volunteer administrator will need to know about sales, services and delivery to design a plan that can be easily understood by others and therefore implemented in the intended way to provide services to the target clients. He or she also needs to anticipate the blocks (noise) that will prevent successful delivery. One such block is the potential reluctance by some administrators to "sell" their services when they see their work as an extension of doing good for needy clients or communities. Regardless, the service or product will have to be presented to a potential client (customer) and an exchange (sale) will have to take place for it to be successful. Sales service and delivery planning will involve how to find and build potential clients (buyers), convey program features and benefits, and complete the exchange (closing the sale). It requires skills in forecasting, questioning and listening, training a sales force, and connecting sales to mission (McNamara, 2006, p. 75). Solid marketing goals are a form of forecasting that will set the direction for sales efforts. Advertising and promotions vehicles will be some of the tools with which sales will be made. Ultimately, sales will be made by people. The volunteer administrator's sales force is mostly his or her volunteers so plans to train them in questioning and listening, working with difficult people, and conflict management are important. Planning for training includes explaining the mission and vision of the organization, its other services, and its benefits to the community. Volunteers must be knowledgeable about the services and the benefits to the client. It is not surprising that business relates its success in sales to good customer service, so knowing the customer and his or her needs is akin to knowing the nonprofit client. They must know what to do when a problem occurs or if the client is dissatisfied.

Sales, service and delivery are interconnected aspects of the same activity. Once the sale or exchange occurs or the organization representative and the client agree upon the exchange, the plan immediately becomes service delivery and re-delivery. Thus, the volunteer administrator needs to plan for having:

- trained personnel;

- supplies and equipment;

- financial tracking;

- administration;

- delivery methods; and

- tracking and evaluation of the delivery methods.

He or she requires a continuous understanding of what will be delivered, how it will be used, and how effective it will be in meeting clients' needs. In the example of the Teen Drop-in Centre above, an evening's activity can be seen as deliverable to its teenage client. The plan must include how to monitor the service to provide continuous effective operation and improvement of it. The adage "Bring it and they will come" is not enough. They will not come again if the delivery has not lived up to its promises and effected a desired change in the teens.

Nonprofit organizations that have been finding it difficult to survive in hard economic times have, perhaps, been resting on their good reputations to sell their services, but the process is never-ending. Plans must be capable of adaptation or complete turnaround in a short time. Robert Putnam's book *Bowling Alone* (2000) points to numerous traditional nonprofit organizations that failed because they have not found new ways of selling themselves to a jaded clientele. The same old sales pitch that worked for the last 50 years or even 10 years will not invigorate new clientele. Volunteer administrators need to examine continually the way they plan their work and do it.

Plans That Address Resource Management

A volunteer administrator will need to know about what personnel and materials will be required to successfully carry out his or her plan. Good people need good tools and good tools are of no use without good people to use them.

People

The skills required of the administrator who implements an operational plan are the same skills required of anyone who works with people as a resource: good listening, rapport, and openness tempered with a focus on the objectives both are aiming to achieve. In addition, the planner needs an overview or vision of how his people will work together as a team, how they will effectively use their time, the ability to anticipate roadblocks and difficulties, and to see opportunities for motivation and recognition of well-deserved efforts. In addition, the planner needs flexibility. Working with a diverse range of people including stakeholders, clients, staff and volunteers he or she must constantly attempt to balance conflicting or widening views, abilities, temperaments, interests, and, today more than ever, be aware of the potential tensions involved in issues of gender and race.

The people the planner will work with span the breadth and depth of the organization and even outside of it. They include:

- members of the board;
- the executive director or CEO;
- other organization, team or department personnel;
- clerical staff;
- board members who volunteer;
- volunteers;
- staff and colleagues;
- professionals such as contracted consultants or fundraisers; and
- clients.

A good operational plan is the starting place for building harmonious relationships among volunteers and developing their growth. This involves staffing various roles with compatible persons who can share resources, parcelling out tasks appropriate to their expertise, changing their roles, and, adding responsibilities or re-assigning tasks to them. Even clients can be involved at both the design and implementation phase as valuable sources of feedback about the way to provide and improve the service. Since not all staff work full-time, the volunteer administrator needs to consider how to use contract or part-time workers, how they will report, and how they will be paid and recognized.

He or she will need to: create job placement ads; write job descriptions; interview and hire; determine methods of compensation and benefits and termination; and account for day care, sick leave, and holidays. The administrator in a larger organization may not need to be concerned with these if the organization has a separate Human Resources department, but the plan will still need to account for and structure in these elements. He or she will also need to train, supervise, and motivate people. Volunteers may be reluctant to accept training or supervision so the job role needs to specify precisely what expectations there are of them. It is better not to recruit a volunteer who will not follow rules. If necessary, a volunteer can be fired. In that case, a board policy to direct the management of this process and a written procedure is an absolute necessity. A helpful and current Canadian website to assist in people management is the HRVS (HR Council for the Nonprofit Sector).

The operational plan will need to spell out succinctly an individual's role and expectations of them not only to manage their work but also to clarify conflicts that may arise. Issues of risk management should always be present in the administrator's mind. These will be addressed in Chapter 12: Risk Management.

Materials

A volunteer administrator will need to determine how to manage material resources such as facilities, equipment and supplies. This will call for a detailed system of recordkeeping, tracking, and possibly hiring staff or volunteers to manage the materials. He or she may be able to share resources from other programs or from the organization such as housing the work in an office of the organization and using some of its existing clerical staff, computers, and telephones. He or she will need to: select new materials; replace or update others; estimate their costs, sources, and distribution; and plan how volunteers will use them outside of the office. Materials range from buildings and land that is owned, leased, or rented, to office supplies such as computers, telephones, and faxes. Volunteers will need specialized training if they will be responsible for managing the equipment or supplies.

Plans That Address Monitoring or Evaluating Progress

Finally, an operational plan without monitoring or evaluation process is an incomplete plan. Monitoring and evaluation are the threads that weave together the plan for it is the constant checking and subsequent adjustments to the plan that make it viable. A volunteer administrator will need to know about monitoring or evaluating the progress of the plan for the obvious reason that the plan will need to be adjusted to keep it on track and meaningful. He or she will also need to discuss with stakeholders their expectations and those of the organization regarding the plan and lay the grounds for a successful follow-up plan the following year. Monitoring is the constant or ongoing check on the state of affairs of the plan — the direction, pace, rhythm and perceptions about its value. Thus, evaluation, which is usually thought of as occurring at the end of the process, is the check on the impact of services on the client target and in the community. It will help to improve delivery, re-examine the purpose, produce data for advertisers, funders and for the board, prevent duplication, and act as a monitor for the value of the operational staff and volunteers and even the clients.

Designing evaluation is an art in itself. There is, as suggested above, a tendency, to leave evaluation to the end of the project. By then it is too late. To be most effective, the process should begin in the design phase of the plan and continue throughout the life of its subordinate program(s).

The process will include thinking about a vast range of questions that include two categories: questions to plan the evaluation process; and questions to plan how to deal with the results.

- Questions to plan the evaluation process:
  - What data is needed? What questions will need to be asked?
  - Where and how will the data be collected?
  - How will the information be analyzed, interpreted and reported?
  - Will specific data collection and analysis instruments or tools be used?
  - Who will be doing the collection and the analysis and the presentation?

- • How will they be managed? Trained?
- • What role will clients play?
- • Will the administrator or volunteers have the experience to use them effectively?
- • Will expert help such as consultants have to be used?

• Questions to plan how to deal with the results when they are revealed:

   - • What worked well and what did not? What had to be changed?
   - • Was the change effective, costly, or difficult to implement in mid-stream?
   - • What was the client's opinion of the service, its delivery, and its products?
   - • Were the people delivering it knowledgeable and helpful?
   - • Were they good representatives of the organization?
   - • Did the plan achieve the organization's goals and outcomes?
   - • What impact did the plan have on the clients and how did their behaviours change?
   - • Were there sufficient resources of the right type to effect a desired change?
   - • Were advertising plans appropriate, well funded and well communicated?
   - • What has to change about the plan to improve its impact?
   - • Were staff and volunteers adequately trained in outcomes?
   - • Should the board continue with or discard the plan?

A key decision to be made in planning is how the evaluation will be carried out, specifically determining the purpose of the evaluation, and deciding how the data will be collected, analyzed and interpreted. Regarding collection, the plan needs to ask what information is wanted from it. This can range from practical information such as statistics or outputs (number of attendees, days the program was conducted, volunteers required), materials used, timelines met, financial records including revenues and costs, to wider issues such as how the operation was carried out (processes), effectiveness with or impact upon clients (outcomes), and ease of use by staff and volunteers. All evaluations are due shortly after the close of the planning year or operation deadline, but also at specific times such as board meetings, quarterly reviews and annual reporting deadlines.

Collection may be a job for experts but volunteers and staff may participate or carry it out themselves. So it is necessary to decide how they will collect evaluation information and what instruments or methods they will use (Table 1). Surveys and questionnaires are valuable for quick scans of large numbers of users of services and because they are easily quantifiable ("How many times did you use our service?"). Qualitative research methods such as interviews, focus groups, and written responses are better when seeking opinion of a more subjective nature ("How did you feel about our service?"). The "mixed methods" approach, which uses both quantitative and qualitative research methods, helps to balance or clarify, support or question analysis that is too uncritical. Administrators should keep and document as much evidence about the operation as possible from its design phase to its completion. The final phase of evaluation is reporting. While evaluation is an ongoing process requiring interim reports along the way, the volunteer administrator will write a final year-end or program-end report. He or she should plan to involve a team of people to obtain a true evaluation of the operation. In the planning phase, it is useful to consider what content will be required; what presentation format will be wanted (everything from PowerPoint® to brochures); when it will be needed; who will vet it; who will receive it; and what the report is expected to accomplish. Planning at this stage will allow the administrator to manage the collection of what is essential.

Table 1: Comparing Some Common Nonprofit Evaluation Methods

Research method	Purpose	Advantages/ disadvantages
Questionnaire	Obtain large amounts of information quickly and often in quantifiable terms. *E.g.*, need information on what teens do in after-school activities.	Easy to administer, collect, and analyze, inexpensive but results are impersonal; only reflect a narrow range of response.

Research method	Purpose	Advantages/ disadvantages
Survey	Very similar to the above.	Scans a large number of people but difficult to write. An expert may be required.
Interviews	To get in-depth responses based on experience. *E.g.*, need opinions from teens about preferred after school activities.	Data is richer and deeper than above and personal but time-consuming, costly and difficult to analyze. Writing interview questions requires precision.
Focus groups	Through discussion with small targeted groups to obtain a common understanding of a topic or issue. *E.g.*, need opinions of 6-8 teens about the draft of the planned Teen Centre.	Data can be rich and deep, be reflective of a wider range of people than the individuals above but is prone to "groupthink" and difficult to schedule.

Table 2: Steps in Planning Risk Management

Step 1:   Identify risks: ask what kind there are such as people, property, income, and goodwill; review past and present operations including risk-related occurrences; review policies and procedures; and consider what might go wrong.

Step 2:   Evaluate risks: determine a tolerance zone, create a master list of risks, and determine priorities.

Step 3:   Control risks: stop the risky activity, eliminate the risk, minimize the harm, and transfer the liability.

Step 4:   Review the risk management process: make it part of the annual evaluation system; watch for legislation changes; communicate changes in process; and review risk situations/change process.

SUMMARY

Designing an operational plan can be a lengthy and complex process. If the volunteer administrator is attentive toward planning, his or her plan will likely succeed and have good results. For the volunteer administrator the key considerations in planning are defining the need for the plan, linking the plan to the strategic goals of the organization, and aligning it with the mission and vision of the organization. Whether it is to be an operational or project plan attention must first go into framework ideas: scope, purpose, players, risks, targets, goals and outcomes. The environment in which it is to occur must be scanned for their potential influence on the plan's success. Some program considerations will be what needs to be planned in the areas of marketing, financial matters, advertising and promotions, sales, service and delivery and resources. Finally, a clear and well-planned monitoring and evaluation process must be planned to track the plan's progress and to make necessary adjustments or large-scale changes along the way. Working with volunteers is a special consideration. Volunteers need to be motivated, trained, consoled, and even pampered but they also need to be driven, stretched and made to feel valuable whether new or experienced. It is easy to get lost in this plethora of detail. Finally, the volunteer administrator needs to keep in mind that the plan is a means to an end and the end or outcome of the plan is the well-being of the client.

REFERENCES

American Marketing Association. (2007). About AMA: Definition of marketing. Retrieved May 10, 2009, from http://www.marketing power.com/AboutAMA/Pages/DefinitionofMarketing.aspx.

Anonymous. (1992). Communications planning outline. *Planning for Special Events Course. Certificate in Nonprofit Management.* Calgary, Alberta: Mount Royal College, Faculty of Continuing Education and Extension.

Board Development Program. (2001). Policy governance: Handouts (HO) 1-19. In *Content, concepts, and principles guide.* Alberta Community Development. Government of Alberta.

Bryson, J.M. (2004). *Strategic planning for public and nonprofit organizations: A guide to strengthening and sustaining organizational achievement.* San Francisco: Jossey Bass.

CCVA. (2008). CCVA Body of Knowledge for Volunteer Administration. *Council for Certification in Volunteer Administration.* Retrieved May 2009 from http://www.cvacert.org/certification.htm.

Cook, C.R. (2005). *Just enough project management.* New York: McGraw-Hill.

Dixon, N. (1994). *The organizational learning cycle: How we can learn collectively.* New York: McGraw-Hill Book Company.

Gill, M. (2005). *Governing for results: A director's guide to good governance.* Victoria: Trafford Publications.

HR Council for the Voluntary and Non-profit Sector (HVRS). Retrieved June 1, 2009, from http://www.hrvs.ca/home.cfm.

Hall, M.H. (2006). The Canadian nonprofit and voluntary sector in perspective. In V. Murray (Ed.), *Management of nonprofit and charitable organizations in Canada* (pp. 25-51). Markham, ON: LexisNexis Butterworths.

Hustinx, L., & Lemmertyn, F. (2003). Collective and reflective styles of volunteering. A sociological and modernization perspective. *Voluntas: International Journal of Voluntary and Nonprofit Organizations, 14*(2), 167-187.

Macduff, N. (1995b). Episodic volunteering. In T. Connors (Ed.), *The volunteer management handbook* (pp. 187-205). New York: John Wiley and Sons.

McCurley, S., & Lynch, R. (1989). *Essential volunteer management.* Downers Grove, IL: VMSystems and Heritage Arts Publishing.

McManus, A. (2006). Resource development basics. In V. Murray (Ed.), *Management of nonprofit and charitable organizations in Canada* (pp. 215-273). Markham, ON: LexisNexis Butterworths.

McNamara, C. (2006). *Field guide to nonprofit program design, marketing and evaluation* (4th ed.). Minneapolis, MN: Authenticity Consulting, LLC.

Merriam, S.B., & Caffarella, R.S. (1996). *Learning in adulthood: A comprehensive guide* (2nd ed.). San Francisco: Jossey Bass.

Murray, V. (Ed.). (2006). Introduction: What's so special about managing nonprofit organizations? In V. Murray (Ed.), *Management of nonprofit and charitable organizations in Canada* (pp. 3-24). Markham, ON: LexisNexis Butterworths.

Putnam, R.D. (2000). *Bowling alone: The collapse and revival of American community.* New York: Simon & Schuster.

Senge, P. (1990). *The fifth discipline. The art and practice of the learning organization.* New York: Doubleday.

United Way of America. (1996). *Measuring programs outcomes: A practical approach.* Alexandria, Vermont: United Way of America.

Urban Institute. (2007). The nonprofit sector in brief: Facts and figures from the nonprofit almanac. Retrieved June 1, 2009, from http://www.urban.org. Urban Institute Press: Washington, D.C.

Vakil, Thea. (2006). Planning and organizing for results. In V. Murray (Ed.), *Management of nonprofit and charitable organizations in Canada* (pp. 275-306). Markham, ON: LexisNexis Butterworths.

Chapter 6

VOLUNTEER STAFFING AND DEVELOPMENT

Diana L. Kyrwood, MA, CVA

Milena M. Meneghetti, M.Sc., CHRP
Registered Provisional Psychologist, M4i Consulting

INTRODUCTION

The management of human resources, including volunteers, is very central to the role of the volunteer administrator. The Council for the

Certification in Voluntary Administration includes *Human Resource Management* as a Core Competency for volunteer administration (Canadian Council for Volunteer Administration, 2008). They define this area as, "The ability to successfully engage, train and support volunteers in a systematic and intentional way" (p. 3). The Canadian Code for Voluntary Involvement (Volunteer Canada, 2006) (a roadmap for voluntary organizations for effective volunteer involvement) states that the main responsibility of the volunteer administrator, whether paid or unpaid, "is to ensure that volunteers are recruited and engaged effectively, and that volunteer involvement standards are consistently applied within the organization. Increasingly, management of volunteer resources is viewed as a function of human resource management" (p. 7)

The profession of volunteer administration sees the adoption of standards in volunteer management as important. Others have also noted the importance of standards. A 2006 study by the Urban Institute (Hager & Brudney, 2006) surveyed and documented the adoption of various volunteer management practices. A key conclusion of this study was that "the adoption of volunteer management practices is important to the operations of most charities. By investing in these practices and by supporting volunteer involvement in other ways, charities enhance their volunteer management capacity and their ability to retain volunteers" (p. 1). More specifically, this study found that, while volunteer management principles were partially adopted by most organizations surveyed, the complete adoption of volunteer management principles was not widespread. Adoption of volunteer management practices depended on a variety of variables: "The likelihood that a charity adopts a particular management practice depends on its specific needs and characteristics, such as its size, level of volunteer involvement, predominant role for volunteers, and industry" (p. 1). As this chapter will highlight, a well considered volunteer management approach takes into the account the diversity of requirements of voluntary organizations, builds flexibility within each component, and is continuously reviewed and revised.

The following chapter provides information and examples of these foundational elements of effective volunteer management practices related to staffing and development. These elements build on one another, and all part of a continuous Staffing and Development Cycle (please see Figure 1).

Figure 1: The Staffing and Development Cycle

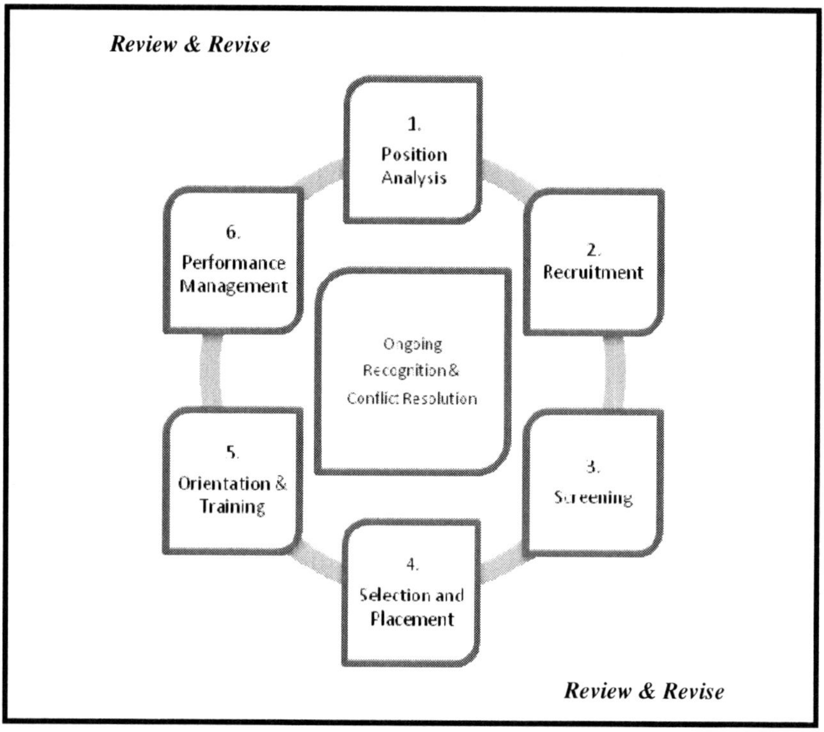

As the diagram shows, staffing begins with clear, realistic and well-defined roles. Once positions have been analyzed and job descriptions developed, recruitment proceeds more effectively. Recruitment leads to screening, selection, and placement of volunteers into appropriate roles. Volunteers are then provided with appropriate orientation and training at the beginning of a proactive volunteer supervision and performance management system. Performance management provides information that is useful for all aspects of the staffing cycle. All of these activities occur in the context of a human resources development approach that includes support, recognition and conflict resolution strategies. More importantly, each of these activities inform the other, and integrate organically to become more than the sum of the parts of the cycle.

Fahri (2009), in an excellent article surveying the newest paradigms in organization development, highlighted the shift that is required in our thinking in today's global community. He very aptly says: "We are moving toward greater appreciation of intuitive, systemic, nonlinear ways of knowing, feeling and doing, as well as the values of cooperation, quality, integration, partnership, and connection" (p. 16). At each stage in the Staffing and Development Cycle the volunteer administrator will increasingly draw on integrative thinking, perspective-taking, holistic thinking, self-awareness, inspiration and passion to accomplish their goals.

VOLUNTEER ROLES: POSITION DEVELOPMENT AND DESIGN

"We need volunteers!" This is a common demand heard by volunteer administrators. A colleague at the last minute realizes that she needs support to complete a project or staff an event and hopes that the volunteer administrator will reach into her pool of loyal supporters and pull out the needed staffing. Responding to last minute requests rarely results in success. An organization must have a thought-out philosophy on volunteerism, a plan for the utilization of volunteers and the integration of volunteers into the staffing structure, and well-designed volunteer positions. These are the foundation blocks for the work of the volunteer administrator. Without them, the administrator cannot effectively recruit, place, train, supervise, or evaluate volunteers.

Philosophy on Volunteerism

The first step to creating a plan for volunteer participation and developing meaningful volunteer positions is for the agency to write a philosophy on volunteerism. This is a clear statement of the rationale for the involvement of volunteers and how they will fit into the organizational structure. A good example of such a statement is the National Multiple Sclerosis Society Vision for Volunteerism (2009):

> Volunteers are integral partners in the fight against multiple sclerosis. Volunteers across the country contribute resources — time, knowledge, skills and leadership — that infuse the organization with energy and passion that will help us move toward a world free of MS. The National Multiple Sclerosis Society strives to be known and respected for excellence in volunteerism among the country's voluntary health agencies. We see an organization where volunteers work as partners at all levels, and where their contributions are embraced, valued and recognized. Volunteer involvement will be expanded and enhanced through exemplary training programs and tools. Our organization will welcome the diversity that volunteers bring to our work and is committed to providing growth and development for those who choose to contribute their resources. The National Multiple Sclerosis Society is enriched by a large network of volunteers who are excited by their work and empowered to achieve the mission of the organization.

Developing a Plan for Volunteer Participation

The ideal for any organization working with volunteers is to create volunteer positions that satisfy the needs of the organization (including the staff and clients) as well as suit the motivations and desires of the volunteers offering their service. The organization must identify those needs staff are not meeting or areas where the efforts of volunteers will enhance services provided by staff. Once administrators understand these needs, they can begin to develop new jobs for volunteers.

It is best to include all parties who will be involved with and affected by the introduction of volunteers into the workplace in the job development process, including staff, clients, customers, and any current volunteers. The introduction of volunteers has the potential to change the responsibilities of staff (*e.g.*, they may be asked to supervise a volunteer), or the work environment (*e.g.*, they may have to share office space and equipment), or otherwise influence the work experience in ways that could make the transition to working with volunteers a challenge. Providing staff with an active role in designing the positions of the volunteers, and thereby giving them some ownership over the process, may help offset any tension that could arise.

Ellis (1996, p. 11) suggests that when querying individuals about their needs, administrators should avoid asking, "What can volunteers do to help you?" This leaves open the space for responses based on stereotypes of what volunteers are capable of doing. Instead, ask, "What needs to get done?" In this way, respondents are free to list all of the unmet needs without projecting whether they are appropriate for volunteers. Below are additional questions a volunteer administrator might ask the job development team.

Questions appropriate for staff, clients, and volunteers:

1. Where do you feel the organization could do more?

2. What needs of clients are going unmet?

3. What projects do you wish the organization could accomplish if there was more time or money?

Questions appropriate for staff only, as these will help determine how volunteers can best enhance or support the work of particular paid employees:

1. Are there aspects of your jobs where you lack sufficient time or experience?

2. Are there areas where, if offered support, you could do more?

Once the administrator has compiled a list of the unmet needs and desired projects, she can go about developing a plan for how best to involve volunteers.

Defining Roles Based on Identified Needs

The next step is to evaluate the projects listed and sort them into role categories, based predominantly on the length of commitment required to complete the task:

1. Long-term, ongoing, or continuous: These volunteers provide service at regular intervals and often for a year or more of time. Often their positions have an indefinite commitment period. These volunteer roles may require extensive training, making a commitment shorter than a year not effective for the organization.

2. Short-term: These volunteers provide a service for a shorter duration than the long-term volunteer does and there is typically a set period of not more than six months to complete the assignment.

3. Episodic: These volunteers may provide service once or on a recurring basis (Macduff, 1995, p. 188), but typically do not commit to an assignment that requires a time commitment longer than a few days. These volunteer roles generally require little or no training. Note that it is possible to have an episodic volunteer who is involved with an organization over a long term (*e.g.*, a volunteer that serves every year at the registration desk for the annual fundraiser), but does not commit to a regular long-term assignment.

In conjunction with duration of time commitment, the location of the volunteer assignment contributes to the role categorization. The commonly accepted definitions here include:

1. Onsite: Those volunteers who report to the organization offices to complete the task.

2. Offsite volunteers: These volunteers can complete their tasks without reporting to the organization's offices. Offsite volunteers would include virtual volunteers who may or may not be located in the same geographic area as the organization and who complete their assignment entirely via the use of technology such as the Internet, video connection technologies, or even postal mail.

Finally, the volunteer administrator must consider if one individual, a series of individuals, or a team is best suited to complete the job.

The volunteer role does not indicate the nature of the work (*e.g.*, direct service, secretarial, advocacy). However, the job responsibilities will guide how the volunteer administrator categorizes the role. Using the categorizations above will help the volunteer administrator write an appropriate position description, design a viable recruitment strategy, and determine the necessary level of training and supervision. Administrators have some flexibility when deciding how to define a particular volunteer assignment. Some assignments can easily fall into more than one role definition. For example, it is possible to categorize an assignment as both a long-term and an episodic role, as either an individual or a team project. Taking into consideration the resources that are available at the time that the assignment must be filled, it is up to the volunteer administrator to determine how she wants to assign the position. For example, if an administrator is aware that a national day of volunteering is approaching she may decide to take advantage of this public awareness. In this situation, rather than recruiting an ongoing volunteer to complete this project over the course of a few months, she may choose to recruit a group or team to complete a project in a day. See Table 1 below for an example of how a few assignments might overlap the various volunteer role categorizations, and others more appropriately belong in one category.

Table 1: Categorizing Volunteer Roles

Example of Volunteer Assignment	Location of Volunteer Work	Role Definition	Individual or Team Project?
Annual shelving of new acquisition and reorganization of elementary school library	Onsite	Episodic	Individual or team
Kitchen help at a homeless shelter	Onsite	Episodic OR short-term OR long-term	Series of individuals OR one individual OR a team

Example of Volunteer Assignment	Location of Volunteer Work	Role Definition	Individual or Team Project?
Producer of a quarterly newsletter	Onsite or Offsite (possible virtual volunteer opportunity)	Short-term OR long-term	Series of individuals OR one individual
E-mentor with a child in another country (Virtual Volunteer)	Offsite	Long-term	Individual

Who Best to Fill These Roles: Volunteer or Staff?

The volunteer administrator and leaders of the organization determine if volunteers should or should not execute the roles and projects identified. Volunteer administrators must diplomatically balance the fears of staff around replacement of their positions by unpaid workers with the often-conflicting need to garner staff support for the volunteer program. For a long time, the golden standard in volunteer administration to achieve this was the belief that, "Volunteers should supplement and not replace staff" (Points of Light Foundation, 2002; McCurley and Ellis, 2002). However, there is an ongoing discussion worldwide as to the extent to which volunteer administrators in practice follow this guideline (Keyboard Roundtable, 2005).

Given the right circumstances, volunteers can and do provide all levels of skill and service and participate in all areas of work. Volunteer administrators often spend a large portion of their time working with staff to generate new and creative ways to involve volunteers. They serve as advocates for the greatest potential of volunteerism and work against negative stereotypes (*e.g.*, volunteers are unreliable and of low skill level).

The delicate decision to assign a job to a volunteer versus a staff member is organization specific. There is no universal determinant that indicates whether a volunteer should or should not hold any given position. What one organization decides may not match another. It is best to consider each position individually and ensure that all the parameters of successful volunteer involvement are in place before assigning any position to a volunteer.

Writing Position Descriptions

All volunteer positions within an organization should have written job descriptions. Written job descriptions are a sign that the organization is running a professional volunteer program that respects the time and contribution of volunteers and that the organization takes the placement of volunteers seriously. This is true regardless of the level of responsibility assumed by the volunteer. A position description for an event coat-check volunteer may differ in length or level of detail from that of a volunteer working on an ongoing public relations campaign. Nevertheless, both require a position description. In every case, the organization must understand why they are involving volunteers. Writing a position description helps to clarify this in the minds of those recruiting and supervising volunteers. Additionally, a position description is required regardless of the number of volunteers serving in a specific role. So for example, if a museum uses docents in their galleries, there can be one description for the position of Docent regardless of the number of docents volunteering at the institution.

Much like job descriptions for paid staff, volunteer position descriptions make clear the volunteer's responsibilities to everyone — staff, co-volunteers, and the volunteer administrator. Each volunteer should have a copy of his or her position description, as should any staff member who works with the volunteer. In this way, the volunteer and the members of the organization are clear on what is expected and there is a standard for supervision, training, performance appraisals and resolutions of conflict over responsibilities should they arise (Points of Light Foundation, 2002; Ellis, 1996).

Typically, paid job descriptions serve as the model for volunteer position descriptions. But, if it has already been determined which roles will be filled by volunteers and those to be filled by staff, the volunteer administrator can create position descriptions tailored to volunteer recruitment and management, utilizing such factors as volunteer motivations, the length of the assignment, flexibility of hours, and benefits to volunteering.

Figure 2: Essential Components of a Position Description

Job Title: Be specific and clearly indicate the degree of responsibility. Examples include Tutor, Firefighter, Assistant to the Customer Services Manager, Friendly Visitor.

Mission of the organization and how this position helps to further the mission.

Supervision and Support Plan: Indicate to whom the volunteer will report, requirements for progress reports and supervisory meetings and any support the volunteer will receive, including training, readings, in-house mentoring or other guidance.

Outcomes/Goals: What are the measurable tasks? Measurable outcomes can serve as one indicator for performance appraisals, recognition, and completion of the job.

Responsibilities/Duties: What exactly is the volunteer going to do? Clearly outlined duties will minimize misunderstandings about the organization's expectations for the volunteer.

Expected Hours of Service: What is the schedule? Will the volunteer be coming to the main office for two hours on the same day each week, or will the volunteer be working from home on a flexible schedule, but expected to provide two hours of service per week.

Start and end date for assignment: Even if the assignment is ongoing, it is helpful to put an end date so that the position description can be re-evaluated and all parties given an opportunity to evaluate the success of the arrangement.

Desired abilities, skills and/or experience: Include here the minimum qualifications needed.

Benefits: Include here any items that may tap into a volunteer's motivation to fill this position. Examples include reimbursement for expenses, training in a specific skill, or something less tangible like the opportunity to brighten the day of a homebound senior.

The job development process and design of position descriptions should be the same regardless of the responsibility assumed by the volunteer or the duration of the commitment. It is important to convey to the short-term or virtual volunteer that their service is valued as much as the service provided by the continuous volunteer. One way to do this is to create position descriptions specific to their roles. Job design for episodic or virtual volunteers requires the same level of detail, flexibility and creativity as does planning for long-term volunteers (Macduff, 1995, p. 193). In some cases, job design for the short-term or episodic volunteer may require more creativity as it can be challenging for an organization to develop complete, meaningful projects for volunteers who may not be available for training and who have limited time to give.

Something to Consider: Recruitment Before Position Design

Although the ideal approach is to create volunteer positions before recruiting volunteers (which guarantees that the needs of the organization drive the position), there are situations when the reverse may be true. Volunteer administrators sometimes must create positions to meet the demands of certain volunteer populations, volunteer trends, funding organizations, or organization directors. For example, your organization receives a grant from a corporation. As requirement of that funding, the organization must create a day of volunteering for the corporations' employees. In this situation, there may not have been a one-day group project designated in the needs assessment process, yet the volunteer administrator must work with staff to develop a project to suit the demands of the funding organization. The goal here is to find work that is meaningful and necessary to the organization and for the volunteers as well. In another case, a graphic designer approaches the volunteer administrator and offers to design a new brochure. New promotional materials were not on the list of projects the organization had designated for volunteers, yet they are using a brochure that is more than ten years old. The volunteer administrator has the opportunity to accept the offer, but first must make sure that all the necessary requirements for success are in place. For instance, is there someone in the agency available to work with the volunteer around issues of concept, branding, content, and editing? Does the agency have the money to produce new promotional materials or will the design sit unused for years to come? If the answers are "yes" then the administrator can enthusiastically accept, if "no" then she must graciously decline what is otherwise a wonderful offer.

Finally, there are trends that can influence volunteer position design. For example, in the United States in the last decade there has been a shift in the prevailing paradigm from the use of long-term volunteers, who had dominated volunteering in the twentieth century (McCurley & Ellis, 2002), to volunteers who seek short-term assignments with defined timelines and fewer hours. Interest in open-ended commitments is on the decline (Independent Sector, 1999). McCurley and Ellis advocate a new paradigm, one that moves away from likening volunteers to unpaid staff who may provide similar or even the same services as staff for an indefinite amount of time, that volunteer administrators consider "volunteers as analogous to consultants — paid specialists who are trained to perform short term projects, event or activities" (McCurley & Ellis, 2002). As fewer individuals volunteer for long-term assignments, volunteer administrators in the United States may be forced to meet the demands of this paradigm shift.

Each of these examples demonstrates that there is a dynamic relationship between meeting the needs of the agency and responding to the demands and motivations of the volunteers available at any given time. (For further reading on designing jobs based on identified volunteer skills and interests see Scheier, 1981.)

EXTERNAL MARKETING AND RECRUITMENT

Knowing what you have to offer potential volunteers makes it more likely that potential volunteers will be interested in your organization and your volunteer opportunities. Once you have developed volunteer roles and position descriptions, and you have established the necessary support from colleagues within the organization, it becomes much easier to market volunteer opportunities externally and recruit volunteers.

Promoting the Organization's Mission

Fundamentally, the process of attracting volunteers begins with the reputation and profile of your organization as a whole. Any recruitment message should emphasize the importance and relevance of the organization's mission. Also helpful is to include information that conveys the positive effects that the organization and its volunteers have on the issue. This can be accomplished using statistics or personal testimonials. Including such indicators of positive outcomes communicates that the cause is worth supporting, and that the organization is effective at addressing the problem (Wymer & Starnes, 2001, p. 83).

Competition for volunteers can be intense between organizations. As opportunities to volunteer increase, organizations must demonstrate their comparative advantage to entice volunteers to join their program rather than a similar related program. Organizations with a positive image and that provide meaningful, effective, well-coordinated services to its client base will be more likely to attract potential volunteers. This is even more the case for volunteers who are highly motivated by the cause of your organization, or who have a personal connection to the clients it serves in some way.

General Appeal Versus Targeted Recruitment Messages

There are two broad approaches to marketing a volunteer program and its opportunities outside of the organization, or externally. We can frame the two approaches as messages intended to generate general mass appeal and messages intended for the targeted recruitment of individuals.

General appeal campaigns utilize mechanisms that aim to increase public awareness about the organization, cause, or volunteer program. They disseminate broad messages, such as the organization's mission, population served, longevity of service in a particular neighbourhood, or other overarching message. For example, a small Dominican Women's Development Centre might post flyers with attractive woman-centred iconography, and their slogan that they offer an open window to the development of the Latina woman, along with contact information. Some individuals may be attracted to an organization based solely on the cause, in this case, helping Latina or specifically Dominican women develop individually or as a community. Such volunteers may not yet have clearly defined needs or expectations surrounding volunteer work. Rather, they simply want to make a difference with some of their free time. In fact, they may even not be actively seeking out a volunteer opportunity, but after exposure to a marketing message (*e.g.*, through a flyer, editorial in a paper or public service announcement on the radio), they may approach the organization to learn more. General appeal campaigns can also be effective when an organization requires a large number of volunteers for opportunities that require little or no training, minimal commitment, and can be accomplished by a diverse group of individuals with a range of abilities (*e.g.*, water cup holders for runners at a local marathon).

In contrast to general appeal messages, targeted recruitment campaigns aim to fill particular volunteer opportunities and are directed at individuals who already have an idea of what they are looking for in a volunteer opportunity. Rather than attract a large number of volunteers, the goal is to attract a limited number of applicants, all who possess specified qualifications for a given opportunity. Targeted recruitment messages are more effective than general appeal campaigns at attracting individuals who already have a sense of what they are looking for in a volunteer opportunity, such as: what skills they would like to offer; what scheduling they require; what benefits they hope to obtain; and other specific needs and desires. Returning to the example above, the Dominican Women's Centre might instead post a flyer stating that they are looking for volunteers to provide childcare for the children of single Latina mothers, while these women work with career counsellors on their résumés. The flyer would include specific information about the volunteer opportunity such as volunteers are needed five days a week in the evenings from 5 to 8 p.m., single evening shifts are possible, dinner is provided, and the relevant contact information.

Using both methods in conjunction will help guarantee that the overall marketing and recruitment campaigns reach a wide array of potential volunteers, all with different desires, needs, interests, and motivations for volunteering.

A 2004 survey of nearly 1,000 volunteer administrators indicated that administrators utilized certain marketing techniques more than others (O'Rourke & Baldwin, 2004, p. 17). The results of the study indicated that the top five preferred methods of recruitment were, in order of preference, (1) word-of-mouth, (2) some form of Internet recruitment, (3) live presentations to groups, (4) events, and (5) newspaper advertisements. Other less frequently utilized strategies included working with a local volunteer centre or corporation, direct mail campaigns, and radio or TV advertisements.

It is important to note that a high degree of preference does not necessarily indicate that the method is more effective than any other. Each technique has strengths and weaknesses. The resources available, timeline of the project, and the desired target audience will determine the appropriate method. While it is typically the job of the volunteer administrator to oversee recruitment for all volunteer opportunities in the organization, it is wise for the administrator to consult and even seek the cooperation of other departments who may have valuable ideas, information, and contacts that may increase the success of the recruitment appeal. For example, the Development Department may already have a list of supporters who have offered to assist in fundraising. Since these volunteers will likely be assisting in their department, it is even more crucial to have their support during the recruitment campaign. The marketing techniques mentioned above, as well as a few others, are discussed in more detail below.

Word-of-Mouth

Most people become volunteers because someone they know asks them to volunteer. In its 2001 national survey, Independent Sector found that 50 per cent of all people were asked to volunteer. Individuals who were asked to volunteer were much more likely to volunteer (71%) than were those volunteers who had not been asked (29%). In 2008, the United States Department of Labor supported these data. Their survey found that 44 per cent of the respondents indicated that they became involved with the organization for which they performed volunteer activities after an employer, friend, relative, co-worker, or someone in the organization asked them to participate in a project (U.S. Department of Labor, Bureau of Statistics, 2008).

Family, friends, and co-workers are credible sources of information. During a personal appeal to friends and family, current volunteers are available to provide first-hand positive descriptions of the volunteer experience, respond to concerns or objections and to provide detailed information. They are also able to provide support as the new volunteers begin their experience. This is especially true when attempting to recruit for a potentially difficult situation (*e.g.*, working with children in a cancer ward) or an opportunity perceived as dangerous (*e.g.*, working with an HIV infected population or within a low income neighbourhood with elevated crime statistics). Using current volunteers to attest to the fact that the work is both safe and rewarding, or how they have adapted to unique situations will often overcome barriers of fear and resistance (McCurley, 1994, p. 520).

Internet Technologies

Organizations now have the option of recruiting volunteers through their own website or through the many online recruiting sites available. Assuming that the organization has a website, it should have at minimum information about who to contact should someone viewing the site be interested in volunteering. Beyond that, depending on the level of resources available for web development, the website could post current opportunities, reports from current volunteers, features on successful volunteer events or activities, and even include and online application.

Volunteer managers can also seek out relevant websites on which to post their opportunities. Some of these sites include: Volunteer-Match (U.S.); Idealist (International); VolunteerSolutions (U.S.); GoVolunteer (Australia); Charity Village Volunteer Bulletin Board (Canada); Do-It (U.K.); as well as many local volunteer centre websites. These sites provide an easy and accessible way for potential volunteers to search for opportunities by cause, location, skills required, schedule, ongoing or episodic opportunities, and many other characteristics. Often these sites are free or have minimal membership costs. They offer an effective way for organizations to reach a diverse pool. However, whenever possible, administrators should learn the demographic of the users of any given site. For example, the same 2004 study cited earlier showed that the user profile of VolunteerMatch is overwhelmingly female (84%) and under the age of 30 (50%) (O'Rouke & Baldwin, 2004, p. 19). This may not present a problem, unless you are attempting to target specific groups such as males or seniors for your opportunities. In this case, an administrator may opt to use the site along with other more male focused sites or senior-friendly locations.

With the increased proliferation of these types of websites, there are many options for the volunteer administrator. An excellent online resource is E-Volunteerism: The Electronic Journal of the Volunteer Community. Members have access to an ongoing feature called "Along the Web" that regularly provides current guidance on the use and development of Internet tools for volunteer administrators.

Finally, if an organization uses Internet technologies effectively, with well-defined and enticing postings, the organization can expect an increased response rate as opposed to those organizations not using Internet technologies (Wymer & Starnes, 2001, p. 87). This may be a mixed blessing. While administrators may welcome an abundance of potential volunteers from which to choose, administrators must be prepared and able to respond to this increased inquiry rate: to respond to inquiries in a reasonable time-frame; to spend staff time answering questions and reviewing applications; and to turn away volunteers as needed in a professional and respectful manner.

Live Presentations

Utilizing members of your organization such as clients, board members, or current volunteers to make public presentations carries the strength of first-hand experience, much like the word-of-mouth approach. A strong message delivered by a committed supporter is invaluable to any organization. Options for presentation locales include: community centers, churches, schools and universities, professional association meetings, and other community or civic groups. Speakers clearly need to have good public speaking skills and should focus on the organization and its mission, not just on volunteer opportunities. The goal of presentations, much like print or online media, or any other attempt at recruitment, is to be provocative and enticing to the audience. One way to do this is to get the audience excited about the cause and the clients so that they become excited about joining the volunteer team.

Recruitment Events and Volunteer Fairs

Table-top exhibits presented in a public arena offer possible exposure to a large audience. However, a large audience does not guarantee recruitment success. For example, if you participate in a community-wide event at a street fair or shopping mall, you may get increased visibility but you must also take into account that the majority of people in that locale did not come to learn about volunteering. The best strategy is to find an event targeted to your organization's cause. For example, an HIV Testing Clinic would do better at a community health fair than at the local library book fair. Another excellent strategy is to exhibit at a fair sponsored by a university, city council, or volunteer centre focused exclusively on volunteer recruitment. Visitors to such an event will go with a mind toward learning about volunteer opportunities. Because creating the booth materials (*e.g.*, display boards, videos, handouts, *etc.*) and staffing the booth take a substantial investment of time and money, an organization must always decide whether the potential benefits outweigh the costs.

Paid Advertising

Organizations can develop advertising for magazines or newspapers, bus stops, local radio, television and cable stations, and other high-traffic locales. Of course, such a recruitment method requires the allocation of funding. A key benefit to this method is that the organization has full control over the delivery timeline and distribution method of the message content. It also allows a single message to reach either a large audience or a very specific audience.

Local Volunteer Centre

These non-profit organizations or groups are dedicated to fostering and developing volunteerism in the community as a whole (Volunteer Canada, 2009). Over the years, they have developed significant volunteerism expertise through the development of programs, research, and training. As part of their offerings, most volunteer centres provide recruitment posting and referral services for member organizations.

Relationship with Local Corporation

Corporate volunteering, also referred to as employee volunteering or employer supported volunteering, is a feature of many corporations large and small. Businesses of all kinds have statements of corporate social responsibility as part of their mission statements. As an instrument of corporate philanthropy and corporate community involvement, volunteering fits under this umbrella of corporate social responsibility. Typically, corporate volunteers provide service to nonprofit organizations through their workplace or with the assistance of their employer (Mejis *et al.*, 2009, pp. 23-32). A company may simply encourage its employees to offer time and expertise or may even go so far as to permit work-release time to allow for the volunteer activities. Others may wish to use volunteering as a means of team building and so will look for group volunteering activities. Companies will also use such group volunteering activities as opportunities to generate positive public relations images.

Corporations will typically choose to support specific causes such as youth services, environmental education, or literacy. Nonprofits are wise to research and seek out corporations whose corporate philanthropy programs align with their cause. Nonprofits can also use other links. For example, a business may support your nonprofit if they serve the same population demographic, are located in the same neighbourhood, or if their customers are also your clients. If an organization can determine a clear connection in advance, the recruitment message will be stronger. If the agency is successful, the corporation will help recruit volunteers from within their employee pool, utilizing internal websites, newsletters, corporate team building programs, and other mechanisms. Ultimately, if the relationship benefits both the corporation and the nonprofit, the company could become a fertile ground for volunteers (and sometimes financial support) for years to come.

Corporate volunteering is one example of recruiting from a targeted group. Any time an administrator targets a specific group, such as families, students, seniors, or corporate employees, she will have to think about how best to devise and market the volunteer opportunity. Return to the questions outlined in the section on creating volunteer positions to think about how to create opportunities that meet the needs of specific groups.

Direct Mail

Ellis (1996, p. 71) identifies three types of direct mail volunteer recruiting. Administrators can (1) send a mass mailing to a targeted mailing list, (2) include an insert in another organization's mailing, or (3) send personalized letters to select individuals. Mass mailings can be expensive and their efficacy is largely related to the quality of the list of recipients (*e.g.*, accurate mailing addresses, expressed interest in the organization or in volunteering, recipients possess the appropriate skills for the opportunity, or recipients have some personal investment in the organization or the cause).

Program-Specific Associations

Organizations may have the opportunity to join local partnerships or associations with similar missions. Individuals turn to these umbrella organizations to learn more about a cause (*e.g.*, tutoring, mentoring, domestic violence). By having your information as part of the umbrella organizations list of resources, you may not only increase referrals to the agency but also inquiries about volunteer efforts.

Free Publicity

Public Service Announcements (PSAs) on the television or radio and press releases distributed to newspapers about upcoming events, successful past events, and organizational, volunteer, and client achievements all provide positive free publicity for an organization (for further reading on the successful creation of PSAs and press releases see, McCurley, 2004 and Foster, 2004). Regardless of the specific topic of the press release, there should always be a tagline at the end (included with the description of the organization) that indicates that the organization welcomes and values volunteer support for its programs. Additionally, there should be contact information for anyone who wishes to inquire about more information on volunteer opportunities. The main disadvantage with such media releases is that the organization cannot guarantee that the news story will be picked up or the editing and portrayal of the information provided.

Designing a Targeted Recruitment Campaign

The key messages in any volunteer recruitment campaign should focus on the potential motivators and the necessary skills/attitudes needed for successful volunteer involvement. McCurley suggests working through a series of three questions about the volunteer position (McCurley, 1994, pp. 518-19). Answering these questions will target the dissemination sites, marketing techniques, and message-type best used to fill the open opportunity.

1. What are the skills/attitudes needed to do this job?

The answer to this question should be easily identifiable from the position description. Does the position require someone who can make a year-long commitment, someone with knowledge of local tax codes, or someone with a degree in art education? Refer to the position description for the key qualifications needed to fill the position.

2. Based on this picture, where can we find these types of people?

Given the kind of applicant you seek, determine where recruitment efforts would be most effective. Think about work settings, professional organizations they might belong to, publications they might read, where they might buy their morning coffee, or parts of the surrounding areas they might live in. Endeavour to hit as many locales as possible with your recruitment message. For example, if you are looking for volunteers to run an after school athletics program, consider posting information at local gyms, with sports leagues, along jogging/cycling/skating routes, at universities with physical education programs, and so on.

3. What motivations for volunteering can we appeal to in our recruitment effort?

Some volunteers will have an overarching altruistic motivation for volunteering (Meneghetti, 1995, pp. 12-35). For such volunteers, the mission and mandate of your organization are critical to attraction, providing a cause to believe in. Other volunteers will be motivated by some of the intrinsic aspects of the role (such as contact with others, or opportunities to use unused skills), which requires the recruitment message to be linked in some way to these. Much research has been conducted on the motivations of different sectors of volunteerism. What motivates a hospice volunteer will likely not be the same as the motivations for a spring clean-up volunteer at a local park. Whatever the volunteer focus of the organization, it is wise for the administrator to research the motivations that drive volunteer participation in that area and then specifically craft the recruitment message to target these motivations.

As an example, Omoto and Synder (1995, pp. 671-86), in their study of AIDS volunteers, used the following constructs to categorize what motivates individuals to continue volunteering: Global motivation, Values, Understanding, Personal Development, Community Concern, and Esteem Enhancement. Please refer to Table 2 for examples of recruitment messages that would target some of these particular volunteer motivators.

Table 2: Matching Recruitment Messages with Volunteer Motivation

	Possible Volunteer Motivators				
	Values	Under-standing	Personal Development	Community Concern	Esteem Enhancement
Sample Recruit-ment Message	"If you love the feeling that comes from making a difference in someone's life, this might be an opportunity for you."	"If you'd like to learn more about our organization and what we do, this is one way to do it."	"We provide valuable training, and can provide the opportunity you need to develop your skills further."	"If making our community a better place is a priority for you, this opportunity could interest you."	"We need the skills and talents you can share with us, so please apply now."

Special Considerations in Recruitment

Recruiting for Diversity

Whether or not an organization may wish to expand the diversity represented in their volunteer pool is a decision specific to each organization. Diversity may enhance the program operation to better serve its clientele. For example, if an organization in a metropolitan area operates a suicide hotline and aims to provide services to *all* residents of the area; it may benefit them to have volunteers on their team who speak a variety of languages to be able to respond to the needs of all callers. In this case, designing recruitment campaigns, materials, and activities that are inclusive and that speak to all potential volunteers is one way of increasing your pool of volunteer resources. Translating recruitment materials into a variety of languages and posting them in areas where certain ethnic groups are concentrated might be one way to attract the needed diversity. Another practice, although not currently widely accepted, is that of including a proactive statement about diversity in recruitment brochures or posters. Such a statement could read, *"Our organization is committed to diversity, and the inclusion and representation of all members of our community as volunteers."* The practice of including a similar statement is common when recruiting employees (although typically makes references to being an "equal opportunity employer" or "committed to employment equity"), and could be transferred to volunteer recruitment in the same way that other accepted human resource management practices have been. Such a message would signal to all potential volunteers, including individuals with disabilities, with varying levels of education, or of diverse religion, race, and sexual orientation for example, that your organization will consider all volunteer applicants.

As a rule, before recruiting any volunteers, the organization should be ready to support them. In the situation presented above, if the organization recruited applicants for their ability to speak another language, but who speak minimal or no English, the organization must consider if they can meet the training needs of these volunteers. Is there someone on staff who can communicate effectively with them to be able to support them in their volunteer role should a crisis arise? If the organization cannot support a diverse pool of volunteers, the recruitment plan should be adjusted to target only applicants who can be appropriately supported. It is also important to remember that diversity is not a universal goal. Using the example above once again: If the suicide hotline were instead intended to serve *only one community* (*e.g.*, Polish women living in a specific neighbourhood), rather than all residents of a city, then diversity of language representation would not be a recruitment goal. In this case, the organization may wish to recruit primarily Polish or Polish-speaking women who would relate most closely to the callers.

Members and Clients as Volunteers

An organization's clients or members are one natural pool of potential volunteers from which you may wish to draw. It is natural to encourage those who have received services to give back to the organization. In addition, given that they have benefitted from the programs of the agency, they presumably understand the operations of the organization and view it favourably. For example, small to medium sized not-for-profits often select board members from existing members, who know the organization's services from direct experience. Clients are also often helpful in assisting with a fundraising activity or may want to assist new clients enrolled in the organization.

There can, however, be some issues worth thinking about in regards to engaging members as volunteers. First, it can sometimes be difficult for members to separate their roles as *members* from their roles as *volunteers* who represent the organization. How will you ensure that the volunteer member understands the distinction between these two roles and acts accordingly? Are there differences between how "internal" and "outside" volunteers are placed, supervised, and rewarded? Second, when members with professional or technical areas of expertise serve as volunteers, it can sometimes create difficulties. Most professional codes of ethics have stipulations or guidelines related to pro bono work, conflict of interest and/or avoidance of dual roles. An open discussion of these is important and will serve to prevent issues that could arise. Third, the administrator of volunteers is wise to remember that clients and/or members are expecting to receive value for their membership fee, and resentments can begin to build when member volunteers feel that they are giving more than they are receiving. Similarly, administrators must be careful not to appear as though they are utilizing or coercing clients into free labour. It must be clearly defined that clients have chosen to participate voluntarily and can withdraw services at anytime without punishment or loss of services or membership.

VOLUNTEER SCREENING AND PLACEMENT

The Role of Screening and Interviewing in Your Selection Process

Once you have attracted individuals to your organization, the next step is to determine the fit between the organization and the potential volunteers (McCurley, 1996). The foundation of effective volunteer placement is alignment between what the organization requires and what the volunteer is seeking from a volunteer opportunity.

Volunteer placement begins with screening and interviewing. Screening and interviewing taken together are the key processes by which the manager of volunteers comes to understand the motivations, needs, talents, skills, experience, background and availability of the potential volunteer. The purpose of this is to match applicants with the volunteer opportunities in the organization. The most effective volunteer placement process allows individuals to choose volunteer roles that appeal to them, while also allowing the organization to identify and approach individuals whose interests, talents and motivations align with other opportunities not initially considered by the individual. Taken together, volunteer screening and interviewing must allow this to occur. It is usually fruitful to have a conversation about the best possible opportunity for the individual within the organization, whether or not it is the opportunity the individual originally sought out. For example, an individual may initially be attracted to the organization as a special events volunteer. The astute manager of volunteers remains aware of the skills and abilities of returning special events volunteers, who may well be best suited to a more regular, ongoing, volunteer opportunity within the organization.

The degree of formality of the screening and interviewing process varies according to the type and risk level associated with a given role. For example, the volunteer administrator on a more informal basis, at a more basic level, will screen one-time volunteers attending to low-risk activities (*e.g.*, stuffing envelopes for a newsletter mailout). On the other hand, program volunteers working with vulnerable persons (*e.g.*, volunteer childcare attendants for persons with disabilities) should be screened more formally, and include a more thorough process. Regardless of the level of detail undertaken during the screening and interviewing process, volunteer placement that omits these steps prior to placing a volunteer results in two potential problems. First, you could place the volunteer in a role for which they are not suited or in which they are posing a risk to themselves or others. Second, and just as importantly, the organization could lose a potentially excellent volunteer due to a poor placement decision into the wrong role.

Screening of Volunteers

Screening refers to that part of the recruitment process that begins after the expression of interest by a volunteer applicant (either a formal application form, or some other less formal means). It includes the vital component of security screening, to ensure that the volunteer does not pose a risk to him, herself, or others in a given volunteer role. However, screening does not begin or stop there. Volunteer screening includes review of the applicant's experience and background as it relates to the volunteer opportunity that you are filling. The outcome of this part of the screening process is a short-list of applicants from which to choose individuals for interviews.

The volunteer administration profession has borrowed the term "short-list", along with the general lexicon for volunteer recruitment, from that used in the recruitment for paid staff. In both paid and nonpaid positions, this term can be a misnomer. For example, there are cases where the need for volunteers outstrips the ability of an organization to find individuals to fill the roles they have available. In such cases, the idea of reducing the pool of initial applicants from many people to only a few seems like a dream, rather than a practical reality of a volunteer manager's job. That being said, the volunteer manager is well advised to remember that harm can be done when "warm body" recruiting becomes a matter of course, without any consideration for the quality or appropriateness of an individual applicant. For many reasons, an organization's placement efforts really are typically most successful if they allow for choice on the part of the organization and the potential volunteer.

Police Records Checks and Other Reference Checking

Volunteer screening includes police records checks as well as reference checks that are suited to the type and nature of the role you are filling. For example, for some roles you may wish to consider the following checks: credit, driving records, sex offender registries and child abuse registries. It is the responsibility of the organization to determine the level of clearance required for a given role. For example, you may still offer an individual with speeding or other serious traffic violations a volunteer role, where one's driving record is not related to the role being considered. However, such an individual may not be suitable for the position of volunteer driver.

Police records searches — also known as criminal record checks — are generally conducted by the police and include a search of several police records databases. For example, in Canada, a Police Records Check will identify if an individual: (1) has a criminal record for any *Criminal Code* or other federal statute offence, and/or (2) has been judged not criminally responsible for an offence because of mental disorder, and/or (3) has federal and/or provincial charges pending and/or (4) is on probation or subject to a Prohibition Order. In addition, such a records check will identify any records of: (1) local disturbances, (2) offences contrary to provincial statutes (such as traffic violations or liquor-related violations), (3) abuse of children, and (4) allegations of offences where charges were not laid (Volunteer Canada, 2009). The specific details disclosed, and the exact searches conducted, will vary according to local and provincial policies, so it is always a good idea for the volunteer manager to become fully informed about police records checks in their jurisdiction.

There are two methods for ensuring that a police records search is completed. The simplest and most efficient method for most organizations is to request that applicants provide one themselves, as part of the application process. In most cases, individuals can acquire such a clearance by visiting their local police station and providing your organization's contact information. The information uncovered during the records check will then be forwarded directly to your organization. Another approach is to request permission from applicants to conduct the police records checks before making an offer. You may choose to do this on the application form for reasons of efficiency. As a preferred professional practice, a volunteer administrator should not conduct background checks of this nature on an individual without their prior permission in writing. If an individual chooses not to provide such permission it would be wise to take this into consideration when making the selection decision.

Reference checks are most often telephone conversations conducted with individuals who know the volunteer applicant. However, if time is limited you may request written references directly from the sources provided by the applicant. References typically come from previous employers, or from agencies where the applicant has previously volunteered. The volunteer administrator should base reference checks on questions that are directly related to the role. A well-planned reference check, which involves asking for behavioural examples of a volunteer's performance, can prove to be invaluable. Even when a volunteer selects their references carefully, the skillful volunteer administrator can often obtain information about an applicant's challenges and shortcomings. One can also use information from reference checks to understand what motivates a potential volunteer. Please refer to Form 1 for a sample reference check.

Form 1: Sample Reference Check

(For use in a telephone interview with a Reference)

1. Introduce yourself and the purpose for your call. Do not yet describe the role you are filling.

2. Let the referee know how long the call might take. Ask whether now is a good time for them, or if they would prefer you called back.

3. Begin to ask open-ended questions. Some questions you may ask at this point include:

   • How do you know _____?

   • How long have you known _____? How long did ____ work/volunteer for you?

   • What did _____ do for you?

   • How would you describe _____?

   • Tell me about a time you were particularly impressed with how ____ did their job.

   • We all have areas that we need to improve on. What do you think ___ could use help or training with?

   • Why is ___ no longer working for you?

4. Describe the job/ role/ opportunity you have available, including the nature of the schedule and the work environment.

5. Ask some additional questions at this point that relate to the role such as:

   • Based on your experiences with ___ how do you think s/he would do in this role?

   • What areas would ___ be best at?

   • Where would ___ require training?

   • What concerns would you have about ____ ability to do this job?

6. Ask the referee:

   • Is there anything else you think is important for me to know about _____?

7. Thank the referee for their time and let them know that the information they provided was very useful.

Volunteer Expression of Interest and the Application Process

The volunteer application process is a combination of (1) the process by which volunteers learn about an organization's volunteer needs, and (2) the informal or formal expression of interest by a potential volunteer. Screening typically begins with an expression of interest by an individual who wants to become involved as a volunteer with the organization. Informally, individuals may express an interest in being involved as a volunteer in an organization by talking to a personal contact inside the organization. In most cases, however, volunteer applicants are best introduced to the organization through a more formal application of some sort.

The volunteer application form is the formal expression of interest by a potential volunteer in an organization or in a particular volunteer opportunity within an organization. The volunteer administrator can design the application form to be role-specific, or more general, depending on the needs of the organization and the ways in which volunteers are involved in that organization. Role-specific application forms help a volunteer target one or more specific roles that interest them, providing information that is particularly relevant for the role. For example, the application form used when volunteers express interest in an advisory committee contain very specific questions designed to gather information about an individual's experience in leadership roles, particularly as it relates to the mandate of that committee. More general application forms gather applicant information that could be useful for a wide variety of roles within the organization, and can be used to short-list for a range of volunteer types. Please refer to Forms 2 and 3 for a sample of these types of application forms.

Form 2: Parent Advisory Committee Application Form

Calgary and Area
Child and Family Services Authority

Calgary and Area Family Support for Children with Disabilities (FSCD) Regional Parent Advisory Committee

Application for Committee Membership

Date of Application: _____

Name: _____

Address: _____

Home phone: _____

Work phone: _____

Cell Phone: _____

E-mail: _____

What is the date of your latest FSCD contract? _____

What is the nature of your child's disability and what is his/her age? (If more than one child in your family has a disability, please describe as well.)

Please provide a brief history of your family's experience with the FSCD program.

Why are you interested in becoming a member of the Parent Advisory Committee? What do you hope to contribute/learn?

We are interested in your experience with disability-related programs. For example, describe any connections with support groups or with other organizations supporting families and children with disabilities.

If you have other volunteer experience, past or current, please provide a brief description of the organization and your role.

Briefly describe the vision you have for your child.

Are you able to commit to meeting 6 – 8 meetings per year, for 3 hours during the day time?

Yes / No, please comment

We thank you for taking the time to complete this application. We will be completing a full review of all applications received. We will contact you directly should we be interested in pursuing your application further. Short-listed candidates will participate in a telephone interview.

Form 3: Sample General Volunteer Application Form

Thank you so much for your interest in volunteering with our organization.

We rely on volunteers in a variety of roles, based on your interests and our requirements.

We keep applications on file for six months.

Name:_____

Address: _____postal/ zip code:_____

Telelphone Numbers (h) _____ (w) _____ (c) _____

Availability: (check all that apply) __ Days __ Evenings __Weekends
_____ other: _____

Do you have a vehicle and are you willing to drive as part of your volunteer assignment? ___ no _____ yes

Education (please list certificates, diploma's, degrees and note specific program)

_____
_____
_____
_____

Languages: Spoken: _____

Written: _____

Technical Skills and Abilities

Please list/describe any skills or abilities you have which may be useful in a volunteer role with our organization (for example, first aid, computer proficiency, carpentry, public speaking, sewing, project management).

_____

Volunteer Experience

Please list current and previous volunteer roles. Please include any Board or other leadership experience, if relevant.

Position   *Dates*   *Reason for Leaving*

_____

_____

_____

Work Experience

Please list current and previous paid work experience.

_____

_____

_____

References

Please provide the names of three individuals who can comment about your abilities as a volunteer.

_____

_____

_____

Other Comments

Please comment briefly on why you are interested in our organization, the type of role you are seeking and what you hope to contribute and gain from your involvement.

_____

_____

Pease note: A recent Police Records Check may be required prior to final placement in a suitable volunteer role. By signing below, you indicate your agreement to provide such a Check on request.

_____   _____
name   *signature*

In general, your volunteer job descriptions should guide the development of your application forms. For example, if your job descriptions state a specific scheduling requirement such as working evenings and weekends, your application form should include a question about evening and weekend availability. If your job descriptions refer to certain credentials such as an up to date CPR (Cardio-pulmonary Resuscitation) certificate, your application forms should request information about completed safety courses. This compatibility between volunteer position descriptions and your application form(s) will make the other steps in the screening and selection process much more efficient and effective.

Internet-based Applications

Online Internet-based application methods are becoming increasingly common. Not many years ago, the creation and maintenance of websites by not-for-profits was difficult and costly. Now, many feasible and reasonably cost-effective options exist, even for small organizations. The result is that more and more organizations looking for volunteers are using Internet-based application methods. The same guidelines provided above for developing application forms apply to online forms. However, some specific things should be considered when moving from a paper-only system to an Internet-based system. Some questions to ask yourself include:

1. Will your organization continue to accept applications in paper form? It is generally advisable to continue to have a paper-based system for individuals who have problems or limited experience accessing the Internet. However, organizations are now favouring online application methods, when they are available, and they are encouraging potential applicants to apply online.

2. How secure is your website? It is beyond the scope of this chapter to discuss the technical details of website development. However, it is important that due diligence is taken in ensuring that private information is safe and secure. One can easily accomplish this by consulting with an Information Technology professional who can advise you accordingly.

3. Will your organization take advantage of technology to make the application process more role-specific? Technology makes it simple to tailor application forms and questions to the specific position being sought. Instead of a single application form for all applicants, online methods often allow for variations based on the

position description. You will need to make a decision about how far you will take this customization.

4. Who will be responsible for the maintenance and monitoring of online systems? It is sometimes the case that an organization eagerly moves forward with automating their processes, only to discover they do not have the resources required to respond and deal with the information involved. The volunteer manager should ensure that any automated processes are also maintained and monitored regularly and professionally.

Whether candidates complete an application online via a secure website, or in paper format, having the basic particulars about a volunteer is usually useful. For example, an individual's full name, address, e-mail address, and telephone numbers, along with information about a volunteer's particular areas of talent, passion and/or expertise should always be kept on file. In some cases, requesting an up-to-date résumé may make sense, although keep in mind that adding such a request may delay or curtail applications.

Interviewing

Interviewing is a two-way communication process between the volunteer candidate and the volunteer manager and/or other representative(s) of the organization. Interviewing can take place in person, by telephone or by conference call, but it is better practice in most cases for the interview to take place in person. Non-verbal cues that are critical to the overall selection process are missed when other methods are used.

Interview Questions

Interview questions that can be used in the context of volunteer recruitment can be divided into four broad categories, based on the information they are designed to explore. These are:

1. *Experience and background questions.* These relate to things that you can verify through other means, such as through reference checks or by asking for documentation. Questions falling in this category include: "What is your educational background?" and "What experience do you have working with children?" In general, there are better ways to gather this type of information.

Face-to-face interviews should serve mostly to confirm this information rather than focus on it.

2. *Situational questions* are future-oriented, hypothetical questions. Examples of these types of questions include: "What would you do if you were not able to fulfill a shift due to personal responsibilities?"; or "Tell me what you *would* do if you were not getting along with another volunteer." In general, such questions are of limited value, since most people would know what might be considered the correct answer, but may not actually do the correct thing when put in that situation (Janz, Hellervick & Gilmore, 1986). These questions are best for you to use with volunteers who have very little to no experience doing the type of work associated with the volunteer role.

3. *Behaviour Descriptions.* The key feature of these questions is that they are actually not questions at all, but rather requests for descriptions of actual behaviour in specific circumstances (Janz *et al.*, 1986). Research has shown that these types of questions are the most valid in predicting future behaviour, particularly when they relate to the key tasks or competencies involved in the role. Examples of behaviour description questions include: "Tell me about a time you were able to work through a difference of opinion with someone."; and "Describe your most creative idea for a children's activity." When you ask these types of questions in an interview, you will find you get a rather detailed accounting of something the potential volunteer actually did in a real situation. This information can be invaluable.

4. *Motivation questions* are those that focus on the needs and drives of an individual, and the things that sustain their volunteer involvement. These are foundational to understanding which roles would maintain the interest and fulfill the needs of the volunteer. Examples of motivation questions include: "Aside from the role itself, what is it about volunteering that appeals to you?"; or "Where does volunteering fit for you at this stage in your life?" These types of questions attempt to address the underlying motivations for an individual's involvement, whether these be to attain a desired outcome (such as prestige), to meet a basic need (such as belonging), or to develop certain skills (such as leadership skills). An understanding of volunteer motivation is critical to designing and interpreting these questions. For a more detailed discussion of this, please refer to Meneghetti's detailed consideration of volunteer motivation (Meneghetti, 1995).

In general, every volunteer role in an organization should have a role description and an accompanying interview guide used to interview individuals for that role. The majority of the interview should be based on Behaviour Description-type questions and Motivation questions. Part of such an interview guide should be a generic portion that allows the interviewer to determine if other types of roles may interest the applicant.

Legal Considerations

When designing an application form or an interview guide, use only questions that are directly related to an individual's ability to do the volunteer role at hand. As with the recruitment of paid staff, the process used to recruit volunteers must adhere to local Human Rights legislation. For example, in Canada, the *Canadian Human Rights Act* prohibits discrimination based on race, national or ethnic origin, colour, religion, age, sex, marital status, family status, disability and conviction for which a pardon has been granted (Canadian Human Rights Commission). Most countries have similar human rights legislation. This means that questions related to these areas on the application form, or at other stages in the recruitment process, are generally not appropriate. There are exceptions to this general guideline. The manager of volunteers is wise to seek legal advice in the following circumstances:

1. Legal advice should be sought when there is a *bona fide* occupational requirement that relates to the volunteer role that is considered a protected area under Human Rights legislation. For example, when recruiting a volunteer in the role of personal care attendant for a person with a disability, you may consider a directly related job requirement that the volunteer be of a certain gender for more intimate personal assistance (such as bathing). As a result, you could use gender as a *bona fide* occupational requirement. It can sometimes be difficult to determine how *bona fide* a requirement is, and so legal counsel is advised in most cases.

2. Legal advice should be sought when an organization is seeking to increase the diversity of its volunteers in order to be more representative of the population they serve. In these cases, an organization may wish to be proactive in recruiting members of designated groups. For example, an agency that serves immigrants may wish to increase the representation of volunteers

from various ethnic backgrounds. However, it may not be appropriate for an organization to seek information about ethnic background on application forms.

As a general rule of thumb, focus on the requirements of the volunteer roles you have in your organization, and whenever feasible and practicable, tailor the application form to the type of volunteer role. The more your screening and interviewing processes relate to the volunteer opportunities, the more effective, and legally defensible your selection process will be.

Selection

The ultimate goal of volunteer screening and interviewing is to acquire sufficient information about a potential applicant in order to make a selection decision. It is also to make sure the applicant has enough information on which to base his or her own decision about whether to take on a volunteer role. In some cases, applicants will choose not to do so. This is not necessarily a negative thing. Such "self-selection" at the beginning of the process generally saves a great deal of time and resources that you will otherwise spend on responding to an unmotivated or poorly committed volunteer.

You should always base your selection decisions on how closely the potential volunteer's motivation and competencies fit the requirements of the specific volunteer role. The relative importance (or weighting) of these two core areas depends on the type of role. Where behaviour, knowledge and skill requirements are low, volunteer motivation becomes the key.

Regrets to an Applicant

Individuals who express an interest in becoming involved in your organization may not always be suited to what your organization has to offer them. As noted earlier, it is also important to remember that if there is a poor fit between the organization's current need and the potential volunteer's abilities and interests, this does not mean that the volunteer might not be suited to some other opportunity in the future.

It is critical for you to treat all applicants with respect, regardless of whether or not a volunteer opportunity exists for them now. These individuals may also be current or future clients of your organization, and they will take away an overall impression that will last for years into the future. As a volunteer administrator, you have the responsibility to ensure that their impressions of your organization are positive, even when they have not been selected for a role within your organization.

Ideally, an individual who is not a good fit for a volunteer role becomes aware of that themselves, as the screening and interview process unfolds. It should not come as a surprise when a volunteer is not offered a role. In most cases, the regrets to the applicant can take the form of saying: "We were able to find someone whose background and needs better suited the opportunity that is available. Please stay in touch, because something may become available in the future!" It is rare that a final "no" is required, making the commonly used phrase "rejecting an applicant" inappropriate and negative.

VOLUNTEER ORIENTATION AND TRAINING

Volunteer orientation and training are the first line of support after placing volunteers in their positions. Volunteers are most likely to be comfortable and successful in their assignments if they feel supported by staff and prepared with the skills and knowledge necessary for their new role. Thorough and well-planned orientation and training sessions help to insure that this is so. Orientation and training are also important parts of the screening process. Potential volunteers often self-screen out of a program after fully realizing the extent of commitment, experience and service expectations required by the organization. In addition, since orientation and training sessions may be the first opportunity for a volunteer manager to spend significant time with the volunteers, observation of the participants' responses within these sessions helps to determine their strengths, weaknesses, and personalities, and thereby to gauge whether particular volunteers have been appropriately placed. The reassignment of volunteers to different positions after their participation in orientation and training sessions is not uncommon. Trainings that offer new learning experiences and professional development contribute to a positive volunteer experience and therefore to volunteer retention. Research shows that one of the most frequent reasons for discontinuing volunteer service is inadequate training (Wymer & Starnes, 2001), while volunteers who receive high-quality orientation and training are more likely to succeed in their role and remain with the organization (Skoglund, 2006, pp. 217-20). Providing training to volunteers demonstrates investment in, and value of, the volunteer, which encourages volunteer commitment and reduces volunteer turnover. Orientation and training build connections within the community of volunteers and between volunteers and staff.

Volunteers often work individually and lack opportunities to interact with other volunteers and staff. Orientation and training provide opportunities for sharing experiences and bonding with each other and with the supervisory staff. If group work is involved, orientation and training can be the first step to building the sense of team, which is essential to any group volunteering project. Finally, training establishes and publicly acknowledges the minimum level of competence expected of all volunteers. In so doing, the organization signifies that it is professional, capable, and aims to high standards of service delivery (KU Work Group for Community Health and Development, 2009).

The Orientation

Regardless of their assigned position, *all volunteers* should receive a standard orientation to the organization for which they are volunteering. Orientation differs from training in that it focuses on information about the organization, rather than on the specific knowledge, skills, or attitudes that a volunteer will need to be successful. The orientation provides an overview of the organization and will typically cover the following topics (Lulewicz, 1995, p. 96; Noble, Rogers, & Fryar, 2003, pp. 103-108; U.S. Department of Health and Human Services/Substance Abuse and Mental Health Services Administration, 2005):

- A tour of the offices or location where the volunteers will be working (Note: If the volunteers will be working offsite, for example in clients' homes, at recovery sites, a call centre or at various locations, a tour of the main office is still valuable in connecting them to the larger organization.)

- The history of the organization

- The mission and vision of the organization

- The organization's programs and services

- The staffing and departmental structure within the organization, including the Board of Directors, Junior Board, or other working committees

- The organization's funding sources and annual budget

- The organization's philosophy on volunteerism and volunteers, including a detailed review of the Volunteer Program Policies and Procedures, along with any internal procedures such as reporting volunteer hours, dress codes, volunteer space allocations, use of phones, lunch facilities, parking, *etc*.

An agency may also determine that its volunteers need additional information. For example, if there are clients with infectious diseases such as HIV (human immunodeficiency virus) or Hepatitis, it may be important for all volunteers to learn the organization's policies on protecting client confidentiality. The volunteer manager should work in conjunction with staff to determine which information is needed by all volunteers, and thus should be included in the orientation, and which is better suited for specific trainings catered to individual volunteer positions.

As mentioned in the Recruitment and Marketing section, volunteers often provide the best form of promotion, marketing and advocacy for an organization (U.S. Department of Health and Human Services/Substance Abuse and Mental Health Services Administration, 2005). They are likely to talk about their volunteer experience as they network within their local communities, families and places of employment. With this in mind, use the orientation to provide your volunteer pool with a bank of reliable and up-to-date information that will enable them to speak knowledgeably about the organization (Lulewicz, 1995, p. 96).

Designing the Volunteer Training

This section is geared toward the volunteer manager who will be training volunteers who *do not* have the specific skills or knowledge needed to succeed in their volunteer position. The skills needed for volunteer assignments can vary over a wide range. Some activities, such as checking coats at a fundraising event, stuffing envelopes for a direct mail campaign, or participating in annual park clean-up day, do not require extensive training, If specific skills are required, managers may be able to recruit volunteers who already possess them. For example, an elementary art educator might run a weekend art program at a homeless shelter or a police officer could speak with neighbourhood associations about how to protect their homes from burglary.

The best way to determine the level of training required to ensure the success of your volunteers is to conduct a needs assessment. The assessment need not be extensive but should, in its most basic form, answer the following three questions: (1) what do the volunteers *need* to know (as determined by the organization); (2) what do the volunteers *already* know; and (3) what do volunteers *want* to know (KU Work Group for Community Health and Development, 2009; Lubertozzi, 1989, pp. 26-30)? Staff and volunteers alike must participate in the assessment. Current volunteers along with staff can help determine the knowledge and skills needed by the incoming or soon-to-be-trained volunteers. The incoming volunteers can participate in the assessment by describing their strengths and requesting the information they think they need in order to perform successfully. Involving the incoming volunteers serves the dual purposes of alerting the trainer to the range of skills, values and life experiences the volunteers already possess so that the training can be tailored appropriately, and of keeping the volunteers engaged and interested. The answers to the needs assessment questions will guide the learning objectives for the training (Lubertozzi, 1989, pp. 26-30). The learning objectives are what the volunteers should know or be able to do at the conclusion of the training. Learning objectives will often address (KU Work Group for Community Health and Development, 2009):

1. what is expected of the volunteer and what are the responsibilities of the position;

2. guidance on the recommended approach for executing their responsibilities;

3. activities prohibited for volunteers and actions falling beyond their outlined responsibilities; and

4. what to do in an emergency.

Once the learning objectives have been determined, write them down clearly and succinctly. Present them to the volunteers at the outset of the training. This insures that everyone has a good understanding of the material to be covered and the goals of the program, and makes the trainers *and* the volunteers accountable for covering the specified curriculum.

The next step is to select the resources and learning activities. In order to do this effectively, it is important to understand a little bit about the principles of adult learning. Martin Cowling (2006), international consultant and trainer in volunteer engagement, sums up the work of Martin Knowles, pioneer of adult education:

• Adults are autonomous and self-directed: Facilitators need to understand the subjects their participants wish to cover and then allow them to work on topics that reflect their interests. Participants should also help establish their own personal goals. Finally, participants need to assume responsibility for presentations, group leadership and facilitation.

- Adults want learning which capitalizes on their experiences: Adults have accumulated a reservoir of ideas from previous education, employment and interpersonal relationships. Trainers need to draw out this experience and knowledge and link it to new learning. As people can accumulate a lifetime of prejudices and myths, this will sometimes entail guidance toward understanding, unravelling and challenging those previously unquestioned beliefs.

- Adults believe learning must be goal-oriented: Adult students usually know at the outset the goal they wish to attain, so they appreciate an early and clear presentation of the training objectives.

- Adults seek relevancy: To be of most value, learning must be applicable to their work and other responsibilities.

- Adults are practical: The training content should be useful and immediately applicable.

- Adults seek respect: Treat participants as equals in experience and knowledge and, within reason, allow them to voice opinions and beliefs.

When selecting your resources and learning activities, it is important to return to your training objectives. Will the training transfer knowledge, teach a skill, modify attitudes, or do all three? Let us consider the possible training needs of new mentors for at-risk youth living in poverty to illustrate the differences between knowledge, skill, and attitude. Here, a trainer may want to convey knowledge (information) about the characteristics of children raised in homes with domestic abuse, the approved activities to do with the children, or what to do if a child is injured when under the care of the mentor and away from the parent. A trainer may also wish to help new mentors develop the ability or skill to respond to sensitive questions posed by the youngsters or to troubleshoot potential conflicts with parents. Finally, the trainer may want volunteers to evaluate their beliefs and attitudes about poverty, domestic abuse, and class and race issues before working with families where these issues are prevalent and where the volunteers' values may differ from those of their clients. Each of these objectives requires one or more appropriate training methods.

Learning methods that are most appropriate for increasing knowledge include lectures, readings, expert questioning, group discussions, films or videos, attending field trips or making observations. Methods most suitable for acquiring skills include role-playing, shadowing or job-sharing with a current volunteer, simulations and on-the-job practice. When training volunteers in a new skill, remember that the facilitator tries to simulate as closely as possible the situations in which the volunteers may find themselves. Demonstrations of skills, combined with practice sessions, not only help establish baselines of acceptable performance, but also help build the volunteers' confidence (Lulewicz, 1995, p. 87). This also goes a long way toward solidifying the manager's trust in the volunteers' potential performance. When attempting to modify attitudes, the facilitator should avoid embarking on a mission of attitude reversal, as this is almost never possible. For example, if a volunteer believes that poor people deserve their plight, everyone might be better served by the recruitment of a different volunteer. However, consciousness raising (developing or strengthening an attitude that is already or potentially there) (Lynch, 1980, p. 35) is possible and is increasingly becoming a significant part of volunteer training as cultural competence and respect for diversity is expected of all organizations. Exploring attitudes through group activities or games that encourage participants to reflect on their own experiences and perspectives are best. Reflections on such exercises are then shared with others in the group and followed up with a well-facilitated discussion. Exploring values through role-playing or by presentation of case studies for reaction and analysis is another possibility. In this type of scenario it is crucial that the participants feel safe enough to explore their honest reactions to the exercises and not to feel vulnerable to judgement for sharing their beliefs.

Evaluation, a two-way measure to determine if the learning objectives have been met, is the last and necessary step. Equally important, the trainees should have the opportunity to evaluate the program. The participants' reactions to the materials, methods, trainers, and the space, as well as their suggestions for improvement of the program, provide valuable information for use in designing future training workshops.

The above information is only a general guide to help managers think about the process of developing training programs. It is understood that volunteers in crisis call centres, mentor programs, hospices and hospitals, offices, museums, and fire departments will all require very different knowledge and skills. Given the breadth and diversity of the work accomplished by volunteers, it is beyond the scope of this text to outline detailed volunteer training modules. Each volunteer resource manager, with support from the supervisory staff, must determine the level and type of training needed for their particular program.

Remember to utilize colleagues in the field. Regardless of the type of work your volunteers are doing, there is likely to be an organization that has trained volunteers for this same kind of work. Seek out these organizations and ask them to share their protocols, policies, training modules and materials, which you can then adapt for your specific needs. Also, involve staff and seasoned volunteers in your training design and implementation. From the staff's perspective, this may help alleviate any skepticism or doubt about involving volunteers in their work, and they may feel a greater commitment to volunteers whom they helped to train. For the volunteer, ongoing involvement maintains interest and investment in the program, allows them to refresh their skills, and minimizes any competition they may feel from new recruits.

New Trends: Distance Training

Developments in technology are changing and improving the administration of volunteer programs across all industries. We have already discussed the increase in online volunteer recruitment and the growth of the virtual volunteer sector. volunteer resource managers are using computer technology to track and communicate with volunteers, and increasingly are using distance learning technologies to train volunteers. Distance learning is any approach to education that replaces the traditional face-to-face learning environment, and may include one or a combination of web resources, e-mail, video and audio presentations, satellite broadcasts, teleconferencing, streaming video or Internet workgroups.

There will always be strong arguments for the benefits of in-person training. For many, distance trainings will never sufficiently replace the value of personal connections made in face-to-face work-shops. Volunteers and staff alike may also present a certain level of resistance to learning new technologies. Many distance-based technologies share advantages and disadvantages (Trottier, 2001; Reach and Train Someone, 2002), and it is important to consider both when deciding whether these technologies are appropriate for your volunteer population and for the training content you plan to provide.

Some of the common advantages of most distance learning technologies include:

- allows for a small number of instructors;
- increases flexibility in training schedules;
- makes available interactive tools to help facilitate learning;

- enhances options for people to learn through a variety of methods;

- allows for self-pacing and self-scheduling by the volunteer;

- allows for a potentially wider audience reach;

- connects volunteers over a wide geographic area;

- provides the opportunity for volunteers to easily revisit the training materials in the future;

- eliminates the need for volunteers to travel and therefore increases access to volunteers who may not be able to travel to a workshop due to disability, lack of funding, or scheduling conflict;

- minimizes stress on facilitators to find and fund appropriate training spaces; and

- increases access to experts who might otherwise require stipends for travel and accommodation in addition to honorariums.

Despite these and other advantages, some common disadvantages to consider include:

- participants need appropriate computer hardware and software or other audio/video equipment;

- participants need a certain level of computer literacy;

- delivery has the potential to be impersonal and therefore threaten participant engagement with the material;

- decreases or eliminates the use of group dynamics and group learning techniques as well as the use of body language and other visual cues often used in workshops;

- unfamiliar or distasteful to those accustomed to more traditional learning styles; and

- technology can be unreliable and at times frustrating.

Before moving toward a distance-based format, consider the following questions:

1. *Is the training primarily knowledge, skill or attitude-based?*

    If the training is largely knowledge-based, distance training may be appropriate. If it is primarily skill-based, a training technology that does not allow for simulation or practice and repetition of valuable skills is not likely to be successful. If the training addresses values and beliefs, where active discussion is most suitable, *some* distance-based training that allow for discussion, such as online chats, may be appropriate. However, this type of training is generally better suited to a more traditional, in-person learning environment.

2. *Where are the volunteers located?*

    If you are attempting to train a large number of volunteers across a large geographic area (*e.g.*, in several branch locations), then distance training will help you reach this audience and provide a consistent training. If there is a small pool of local volunteers, distance training may not only be unnecessary, but also will not capitalize on the opportunity to gather volunteers together, create a sense of team, and utilize group learning techniques.

3. *Who are the volunteers?*

    As discussed earlier, consider the audience before developing a training module. What are the motivations and skills of the volunteers? If they are motivated to volunteer as a means of access to a new community and are interested in building personal connections, or if they are not computer literate, or do not prefer computers as a means of communication, distance-based training is probably not the best approach. If, however, the program engages primarily with virtual volunteers who prefer to work individually and are proficient with computer technology, then such an approach is appropriate.

4. *What are the facilitator's skills and access to resources?*

    It is the responsibility of the training facilitator to provide an engaging workshop. If the skills of the trainer are such that this can be better accomplished in person, consider whether the advantages of distance training are worth the sacrifice of the face-to-face workshop connection. Finally, do the organization, and volunteers, have the resources to support the required technology? Is there someone on staff who has the skills to troubleshoot problems, as well as to guide new volunteers in the use of the technology? If the answer is "No," then technology-based training is not advisable.

Form 4: Volunteer Training Content Guide for a Volunteer in a Direct Service Agency

The following is a list of training topics that are either *required* or *recommended* for new volunteers. Please refer to this list when assigned a volunteer to supervise. The staff member who provides the training should initial and date the blank space next to each topic. Once training is complete, keep this form in the volunteer's file.

VOLUNTEER NAME _____ DATE: _____

VOLUNTEER ASSIGNMENT _____

VOLUNTEER'S SUPERVISOR _____

1st Tier Mandatory Volunteer Orientation
Administered by Volunteer Program Coordinator or Senior Volunteer

- _____ Organization overview: including tour of office, mission, programs and services, staff organizational structure, funding sources, dress code.

- _____ Volunteer Program Policies and Procedures — Collect Signed Agreement

- _____ Emergency Protocols and Reporting

- _____ Confidentiality Policies

- _____ Reporting Volunteer time

- _____ If a non-one-time event volunteer, Welcome to Organization including desk assignment, job description, work schedule, performance evaluations, office culture, holidays, supervision and reporting.

2nd Tier Potentially Mandatory Topics (To be determined by the Supervisor of the volunteer)
Administered by Supervisor or other appropriate staff member at Supervisor's request

- _____ Computer and Network orientation, with MIS associate or Supervisor (Mandatory if using computers in the office)

- _____ Diversity, with Co-Chairs of the Diversity Committee (Mandatory if to have any contact with clients)

- _____ Field Safety (Mandatory if volunteer will be completing home visits)

- _____ Family Case Presentation, with Social Worker (Recommended for most ongoing volunteers)

- _____ Organization educational video viewing (Recommended for most ongoing volunteers)

3rd Tier Optional Topics to be considered based on volunteer assignment

- _____ Legal Services overview, with Director of Legal Department

- _____ Social Services overview, with Director of Social Services

- _____ Satellite Office Tour and Introduction, with Satellite Site Director

- _____ Teen Services, with teen group Social Worker

- _____ Development and Fundraising, with Development Associate

- _____ Research and Evaluation, with Dir. of Research and Evaluation

- _____ Job Specific Training TBD by the Volunteers Supervisor

(Kyrwood, 2005)

Tips to Remember

Regardless of the training topic, number of volunteers in the program, duration or format of the training, there are some golden rules that if followed will help guarantee volunteers receive a complete and successful orientation and training.

1. **Create a training guide (see Form 4)**: Provide this to all staff who supervise volunteers and document who provided each portion of the orientation/training. This will help ensure that volunteers receive all the training requirements. Maintain this document in the volunteer's file.

2. **Make all orientation and training materials available to volunteers**: Create a manual with relevant readings, handouts, policies and procedures, and/or put all these documents online for volunteers and staff to access at any time. Having training materials, policies, and procedures written and made public

serves the dual purpose of backing up the orientation and training content as well as protecting the organization against liability.

3. **Encourage volunteer community building**: Volunteers should be able to seek support not only from the volunteer manager or their supervisor, but also from each other. Ask participants to share their contact information with the other volunteers or the greater volunteer pool, and then create and distribute a contact sheet. This is one of the first steps to nurturing a sense of community and support from within the volunteer pool.

4. **Provide ongoing training**: Ongoing training not only keeps your volunteers engaged and educated, it also highlights their value. Look for opportunities within your organization or in similar organizations. Offer to pay for a continuing education workshop offered by a professional association or offer annual refresher courses or workshops for those who are currently volunteering. When appropriate, invite volunteers to attend in-house staff trainings.

5. **Schedule trainings at times that are convenient for your volunteers, not your staff.**

6. **Start and end ON TIME**. Respect your volunteers' and trainers' investment of time.

PERFORMANCE MANAGEMENT AND SUPERVISION

Performance Management of volunteers is a critical part of the overall management of volunteer resources. *Volunteer performance management* is the process that includes: job clarification and goal-setting; ongoing monitoring and supervision; and performance review and evaluation. It is ultimately what ensures a good placement decision has been made and it informs many of the other human resource activities in your organization. The basis for performance management is the job description, which clearly states the roles and responsibilities of the volunteer.

The Need for Managing Volunteer Performance

Performance management is an essential part of volunteer man-agement. There was a time when it was believed that we could not justly place expectations on the performance of volunteers. Some thought: "How can we expect a volunteer to be on time, or to show up for a shift, for example, when they are volunteering their time?" With the increasing involvement of volunteers in a wider range of sensitive and high-risk areas, this attitude has shifted quite dramatically. This is so much the case that the government of Canada has established practice guidelines in the supervision and evaluation of volunteers (Government of Canada, 2009). Written from a risk management perspective, these guidelines note the following key purposes for performance management:

- to ensure a certain standard of service is maintained;

- to improve the job performance of volunteers and staff;

- to obtain the volunteer's input on what the organization could do better to support them in their role within the organization; and

- to protect all participants.

There are other key reasons to engage in the ongoing and proactive review of volunteer performance. First, performance management is another way of understanding the skills, abilities and motivators for a particular volunteer. The more frequent and regular the communication between volunteers and their supervisors, the more effectively you can manage the volunteer pool. Second, ongoing and regular performance management of volunteers allows you to remain proactive, rather than reactive. The early identification of missed training needs, for example, can save hours of time and seriously improve the effectiveness of a volunteer. Finally, any trends noticed during the active management of volunteers helps you with the development, coordination and planning of future recruitment and placement activities. Therefore, while time and other constraints (including geographic distance) can sometimes create challenges in this area, it is usually worthwhile to find ways to include performance management as a priority activity.

Performance Management Process

Some novice managers of volunteers view performance management as a form that has to be filled out. However, at its broadest level, performance management of volunteers is a *process*, and it begins and ends with the mandate of the organization. The tasks and responsibilities of any given volunteer should always relate back to the organization's missions and goals. Similarly, the management and evaluation of volunteers should be based on their contribution to these. The line of sight between what a volunteer does, and how they contribute to the overall vision of the organization will vary. Board governance volunteers can be expected to have a direct impact, as can front-line service volunteers, for example. On the other hand, episodic special event volunteers are more likely to contribute indirectly, by providing the support necessary for a fundraising effort that allows the organization to fulfill one or more of its goals. The ideal performance management system always comes back to the question: "How have you helped the organization do what it is set-up to do?"

The job description forms the foundation of any performance management tool and system. If job descriptions have been developed, designed and maintained properly, as noted in previous sections of this chapter, the process of managing performance becomes much easier. Based on this job description, in some cases the volunteer may wish to consider some goals for him or herself. For example, a volunteer who has taken on the task of canvasser for a fundraising effort may wish to set a monetary target they would like to reach. A volunteer who delivers programs to high-risk youth may wish to help improve the course content or materials.

Figure 3: Strategic Performance Management

E. Process Improvement and links to other Human Resource Processes

Conversations

A. Organizational Goal Setting based on Mission and Goals

Conversations

Conversations

The Full Performance Management Cycle

D. Performance Review based on Job Description, Goals & Developmental Needs

B. Individual Goal Setting based on Job Description (Possible 360 Feedback)

Conversations

C. Regular Ongoing Supervision and Monitoring

Conversations

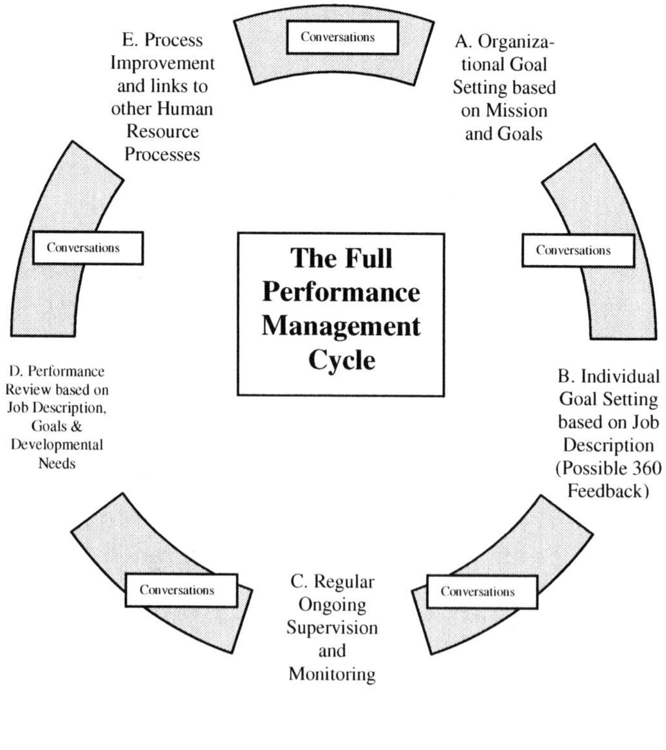

Performance Management Conversations

At a fundamental level, performance management takes the form of conversations between a volunteer and whoever is responsible for managing that volunteer. These discussions occur throughout the performance management cycle, and should be considered a two-way conversation. Open-ended questions and opportunities for volunteer input are essential. At the beginning of the performance management cycle, this conversation is about the job itself and any related goals for the volunteer. As the individual carries out his or her job, the conversation is about the day-to-day needs and issues that arise for the volunteer. As the volunteer nears completion of their assignment, or at any other appropriate end-point or interval based on the role, the two-way discussion should be about how effectively the volunteer carried out the job, and met his or her goals. Also at this stage, some consideration of the future development and/or training needs of the volunteer can take place. Finally, forward-thinking performance management involves a consideration of the volunteer's motivations, interest and abilities and how they can best be contributed in the organization.

Approaches to Performance Management

Managing the performance of volunteers is not optional, as we have noted above. However, the nature and scope of the performance management system will rightly depend upon three factors: the nature of the volunteer role; the risk level inherent in that role to self or others; and the skill level required to perform that role well. Please see Table 3, which summarizes how these variables affect your approach to performance management. In general, the following questions should be considered in determining the approach to performance management:

1. What is the type of volunteer role? Is it episodic and short-term, program-related and longer-term, or governance-related and longer-term?

2. What level of potential risk to self or others is inherent in the role? Risk is assessed in a variety of ways, including the potential to physically or emotionally harm, to adversely affect the organization's reputation, or to cost the organization financially. For example, a low-risk role may be something like stuffing envelopes for a membership mail-out. A higher risk role would be work with vulnerable populations, such as persons with disabilities.

3.   What degree of skill and or knowledge that is required for the role? Skills and knowledge can be both technical (*e.g.*, computer proficiency) and professional (*e.g.*, legal knowledge). Roles requiring a high level of organizational wisdom and experience (such as being the president of the board) are also higher knowledge roles.

Table 3: Focus of Volunteer Performance Management According to Type and Risk Level of Role

Type of Volunteer Role	Lower Risk		Higher Risk	
	And Lower Skill/ Knowledge	*And Higher Skill/ Knowledge*	*And Lower Skill/ Knowledge*	And Higher Skill/ Knowledge
Episodic/ Short Term	Task-oriented supervision (Stages B, C & E)	Task-oriented supervision and review (Stages B & C & E)	Task-oriented Supervision and Review (Stages B, C and E)	Task & Development-oriented Performance Management (Stages B, C and D)
Program/ Longer Term	Task and Development-oriented Performance Management (Stages B, C and D)	Task and Development-oriented Performance Management (Stages B, C and D)	Strategic Performance Management (All Stages)	Strategic Performance Management (All Stages)
Board/ Governance		Strategic Performance Management (All Stages)		Strategic Performance Management (All Stages)

The most basic and minimal level of performance management could be called *task-oriented.* At this fundamental level, the supervisor ensures that duties as set out in the job description are understood and carried out effectively by the volunteer. The supervisor also ensures that the volunteer has all the necessary resources available to do this. This level of performance management can easily be accomplished at a distance, by telephone or electronic means. An enhanced level of task-oriented performance management adds the component of performance review, after the completion of an assignment or at any natural break (for example, the end of a program session). Here, the supervisor provides and requests feedback from the volunteer regarding the duties of the role.

The next level of performance management could be called *Task and Development-Oriented Performance Management*. At this level, the supervisor of volunteers not only ensures that the role and responsibilities are understood and carried out effectively, but focuses to a varying extent on the development of the volunteer. This development focus allows for ongoing improvement and learning on the part of the volunteer, and as such is considered developmental. This level of performance management occurs in person and generally takes a minimum of an hour to complete.

The highest level of performance management could be called *Strategic Performance Management*. This level of performance management is the most forward-looking and the most linked to the organization's overall mission and goals. At this level, typically more than just the volunteer administrator is involved. This conversation includes a discussion of the duties and responsibilities of the role, the ongoing development requirements of the volunteer, as well as a discussion of potential other volunteer opportunities suited to this volunteer. It is at this level that a consideration of 360-degree feedback should be considered at the beginning of the performance review process, when goals are being set (see below for a more detailed description of this).

This three-level classification of performance management is presented in order to emphasize that performance management varies according to several variables. In the end, the volunteer administrator in conjunction with the staff supervising the volunteer will determine the best approach based on the needs of the organization and the volunteer. Regardless of the approach, performance management should be proactive rather than reactive whenever possible, and always be a constructive two-way conversation.

Performance Management and Volunteer Retention

Effective performance management can have a positive impact on volunteer retention. We know from research that some key motivators for volunteer involvement are understanding, personal development, and esteem enhancement (Omoto and Snyder, 1995). Performance management conversations allow the manager of volunteers or volunteer supervisors to contribute directly to these motivators. For example, asking a volunteer what other roles and opportunities interest them, and providing the related training, fulfills the motivation for personal development. Giving a volunteer positive and specific feedback about their performance helps to enhance their self-esteem. Not surprisingly, ineffective performance management that is reactive and focuses on issues and problems can have exactly the reverse impact and drive volunteers out of your organization.

360-Degree Feedback and Performance Management

360-Degree Feedback is the process of gathering feedback from supervisors, clients and co-worker as one part of a performance management process. Rather than relying solely on input from the volunteer's supervisor, this approach to understanding a volunteer's performance recognizes the value of considering other points of view. It is beyond the scope of this textbook to provide a detailed description of how to do 360-degree feedback. However, some important issues to consider prior to implementation are listed below. For a more detailed treatment of the use of 360-degree feedback, please see Meneghetti (1999).

1. How will 360-degree feedback fit in with the existing performance management process? 360-degree feedback is *not* a substitute for a complete performance management process. It is a tool that can be used as part of the performance management process.

2. At what point in the performance management cycle will it be used? This type of feedback is best used for developmental, rather than evaluative purposes, at the beginning of the performance management cycle. This allows the volunteer to respond to the feedback and set goals for themselves based on it. Often, problems can arise when 360-degree feedback is introduced as an evaluation tool at the end of the cycle.

3. How will the results of the 360-degree feedback process be communicated? The usefulness of 360-degree feedback data is directly related to how that feedback is communicated to the volunteer. The approach should be non-judgemental, and provide opportunities for the volunteer to have a dialogue about the results.

4. How will the tool that is being used for 360-degree feedback be developed? It is very important that the questionnaire, which forms the basis of the 360 tool, is based on valid competencies

that relate well to the volunteer role. It is strongly advised that you engage the services of a Human Resources professional if you are considering developing your own tool. There are issues related to confidentiality and ownership of the results that need to be discussed with the volunteer beforehand.

Inappropriate Placement or Selection: Corrective Action and Dismissal

The management of performance is a proactive approach that attempts to ensure the volunteer has the necessary tools and resources to do their job in a strategic way. In the majority of cases, issues that might arise can be resolved through an active consideration and elimination of barriers to success. For example, the organization may be required to change a process that is creating problems, or a volunteer may need to develop better skills in a certain area. This approach sees "corrective action" as an integral part of the performance management system where everyone involved can play a part in creating a solution. It is not something separate from performance management that looks to place blame or transfer responsibility to the volunteer.

There are cases when the outcome of performance management is the recognition that an individual is not a fit for the role. Even less frequently, it is possible that someone is not a fit for the organization all together, regardless of the role. These situations of inappropriate placement or selection require a decision and action on the part of the volunteer administrator. With a well-designed performance management system, the administrator's job at this "end stage" for the volunteer is not that difficult. Rather, it is the culmination of a series of events and is not a surprise to either the volunteer or the organization's representatives.

When it has been determined (through proactive performance management) that individual is not able to perform successfully the duties of the job, there are two possible courses of action. The first is consideration of other jobs or volunteer opportunities that may be a better fit for that particular individual. Just because a volunteer is unsuccessful as a board member, for example, does not meant that same volunteer is unable to contribute as a special events volunteer, for example. Given the investment of time and resources to recruit, orient and train a new volunteer, finding another role for the volunteer is really the best possible outcome for everyone involved if that is possible. The other course of action is to dismiss the volunteer. Although this is a sensitive task that requires professionalism and skill on the part of the volunteer administrator (or other staff member), it need not necessarily be an overly negative experience. Often, a discussion with the volunteer of other ways they might contribute in other types of organization is enough to send the volunteer off into something that better fits their needs at this time. When a volunteer has been inappropriately placed or selected, they are sometimes very ready to move on to something else. Providing a referral to other agencies that you believe would be a better fit can help the volunteer leave your organization with a sense of direction and confidence in their ability to continue volunteering.

It is critical to remember that any individual who interacts with your organization, including a volunteer who has been dismissed, will carry the message of your organization. The more constructive and positive the parting of ways, the more likely that the message a volunteer will carry will be one that maintains the good reputation of your organization.

Impact of Volunteer Performance Management

In a general way, the information obtained during the performance management process feeds into all of the other human resource management activities undertaken by the organization. You may wish to consider enhancements or revisions to the staffing and selection process, the training and orientation programs, and the job design process using feedback and information gleaned during the performance management cycle. There truly is a far-reaching impact of effective and proactive performance management.

CONFLICT RESOLUTION

Whenever people work together, misunderstandings and differing points of view are always a possibility. As a result, conflict resolution can become a necessary and important aspect of a volunteer administrator's role.

The word *conflict* is defined as (1) a competitive or opposing action of incompatibles: antagonistic state or action (as of divergent ideas, interests, or persons), (2) a mental struggle resulting from incompatible or opposing needs, drives, wishes, or external or internal demands (Merriam Webster, 2009). In the case of volunteers, it can be helpful to think of conflict as being either interpersonal or task-related. As noted by DeChurch and Marks (2001) task-related conflicts occur when group members argue over alternatives related to the group's task, whereas relationship conflicts result over interpersonal clashes not directly related to achieving the group's function. Research has shown that task-related conflicts can actually improve the quality of outcomes, especially when such conflicts are managed proactively and positively with agreeable behaviour.

Once a volunteer administrator becomes involved in helping to resolve conflict, whether it be task or interpersonal conflict, it is often true that the conflict has significantly affected either the volunteer and/or client or staff member. In other words, there is often a perceived crisis which the volunteer administrator is being asked to help resolve. A key strategy for managing conflict is to create a climate that limits how much conflict escalates to a more serious level.

Prevention of Serious Conflict

Ideally, volunteer administrators avoid the need to become involved in conflict resolution by establishing an environment where people feel safe to express concerns and differing opinions on an ongoing basis. It is common for a small misunderstanding to become a significant issue simply because the misunderstanding was not addressed in the early stages. For example, in a situation where volunteers are working as a team and have regular team meetings, time can be set aside on the agenda for people to raise concerns or issues at an early stage, rather than waiting for them to have a more significant impact. At an early stage, it can be sufficient to use a brainstorming approach to issue resolution. Brainstorming involves the free expression of ideas, without other team members judging or responding to any ideas presented. Once ideas have been offered, the team selects the best option according to group consensus.

Another key way to prevent serious conflicts is for volunteer administrators to operate in a style that is conducive to a positive climate and to resolution of difficulties. Interestingly, some novice volunteer administrators respond to situations of conflict by becoming rule-bound and looking to policies and procedures to solve the issues. However, an interesting study that considered volunteer perspectives on effective volunteer management found that use of what they called a *managerial* style in managing volunteers was viewed very negatively by women volunteers (Leonard, Onyx and Hayward-Brown, 2004). Among other things, such a style (as opposed to a nurturing style, for example) was characterized by strict adherence to policies and procedures; reliance on processes that are formalized; promotion of hierarchy; a view that decision-making is better done by professionals; and where close relationships of volunteers with clients or coordinators are discouraged. This does not mean that policies and procedures are not helpful in the management of volunteers. They are a critical component of any volunteer program. However, such policies should be background information for the volunteer administrator, guiding decisions, rather than foundational elements of the volunteer administrator's style in responding to conflict. In other words, quoting chapter and verse of a policy manual is unlikely to lead to a healthy resolution of conflict.

Approaches to Conflict Resolution

When efforts to avert or limit conflict are unsuccessful, then sometimes the volunteer administrator must step in to help. Whether the conflict is between a volunteer and another volunteer, a volunteer and a staff member, or a volunteer and a client, the basic principles are the same. Foundational work in the area of conflict management included Blake and Mouton's five-style typology of conflict management (1964). This typology identified five styles used in conflict situations: competing, avoiding, collaborating, accommodating, and compromising. This typology was useful in that it helped identify the individual differences in the way people might respond to situations of conflict. However, it had only limited ability to help us act meaningfully in the resolution of conflict.

Research that is more recent helps us understand that conflict resolution is a process that involves the use of significant interpersonal and managerial skills. For our purposes, we could say that conflict resolution approaches could be grouped into two general categories. One approach is to provide volunteers and staff with the necessary support and skills to resolve conflicts on their own. This approach is particularly relevant in the case of intact work teams, especially those that will have a longer-term common purpose and task (*e.g.*, a board of directors, a team working on a year-long project). An interesting study with 57 autonomous work teams found that "groups that improve or maintain top performance over time share 3 conflict resolution tendencies: (a) focusing on the content of interpersonal interactions rather than delivery style, (b) explicitly discussing reasons behind any decisions reached in accepting and distributing work assignments, and (c) assigning work to members who have the relevant task expertise rather than assigning by other common means such as volunteering, default, or convenience" (Behfar, Peterson, Mannix and Trochim,

2008, p. 170). In cases where the conflict is related to "who does what", these guidelines are beneficial.

Another approach to conflict resolution involves the volunteer administrator, or some other party, in the role of mediator. This approach is best suited in cases when conflicts are more interpersonal in nature, but can also be employed with task-related conflict. The mediation literature has shown that the success of efforts to resolve disputes between individuals is largely dependent on the process, rather than the content, of such interventions (Jorgensen, 2000). Helpful processes focus on helping each individual understand the other's point of view and show compassion, while still allowing each individual to continue to feel empowered and self-directed. For example, a question like "What ideas do you have about why Susan might have done things this way?" helps the other volunteer consider Susan's motivations more directly. A question like "What are some ways you can make improvements, so that you're not relying on someone else to change?" may serve to empower an individual.

Regardless of the specific approach to conflict resolution, the process of conflict resolution always begins with the volunteer administrator understanding each person's point of view and moving from there. Rather than jumping to action or providing advice, the volunteer administrator listens and tries to understand the volunteer using a non-judgemental perspective. Depending on the situation at hand, and the nature of the concerns, the process of understanding the points of view involved can take various forms. Such a process can occur during one on one meeting with the individuals involved, or in a joint meeting between the parties. It can occur in one session on one day, or it can take up several sessions over a longer period.

Appreciative Inquiry and a Focus on Solutions

Recently, there has been an evolution in approaches to helping individuals navigate difficulties both in personal and organizational life. It draws on work in business management and psychology, and applies it to the management of human resources. In organizations, this evolution which has been called Positive Organizational Scholarship (Karakas, 2009) and includes such lenses as *Appreciate Inquiry* (see Cooperrider, 1986). In psychology, an example is *Solution Focused* therapy or counselling (see de Shazer *et al.*, 2007). Fundamentally, these perspectives rest at least partially on the assumption that we are all resilient and capable human beings who can learn from what has worked for us in the past. Rather than focusing on past problems and issues, these approaches value what has been effective and allows us to develop creative, sometimes organic (naturally occurring) solutions for the future. Such an approach would use questions like: "Think about the last time something like this happened, but things worked out okay. What did you do? What worked? When you did that, what did you notice about other people?" Incorporating such an approach to conflict resolution is consistent with the notion of personal empowerment, and holds a great deal of promise for new ways to respond to conflict.

This section has provided a basic overview of the area of conflict resolution. A volunteer administrator is strongly advised to educate him or herself about conflict resolution and seek additional training. Such an investment will help ensure a smooth-running and effective volunteer program. The skills learned transfer to many different human resource interactions.

VOLUNTEER RECOGNITION

The most successful recognition systems are those that use a variety of techniques, both formal and informal, to convey to volunteers that they are valued by the organization. They also provide year-round acknowledgement that are sensitive to the motivations and needs of the volunteers. Recognition is not just the job of the volunteer administrator. All members of the organization who benefit from volunteer support, including staff and clients, should be trained and encouraged to participate in recognizing the contributions of volunteers.

Volunteers might be likely to say that they do not desire any recognition for their service. Yet, it is generally accepted that volunteer recognition is crucial to keeping volunteers motivated and therefore closely connected to volunteer retention. Many administrators of volunteers believe that volunteers who go unacknowledged for their contributions may feel unvalued and unsatisfied and ultimately lose interest in donating their time and talents to an organization.

Recognition Is Respect in Daily Practice

Recognition is not only acknowledging a job well done or saying thank you; it starts with literally recognizing volunteers for their talents and that they are a part of the team working toward the organization's mission and goals. It is respecting all volunteers on a daily basis. Consider how you might do this for paid colleagues and apply these techniques to volunteers. Greet them with a smile. Learn and address them by their names and ask others to do the same. Ask their opinions about newly proposed projects. Do not waste their time. Allow them ownership of their projects. Give them credit for the work that they have accomplished and when possible provide opportunities for them to present to staff or the community the results of their efforts. Provide growth and development opportunities. These and other practices demonstrate that basic respect for volunteers is at the foundation of the volunteer program and at the core of any volunteer recognition system.

Matching Motivation with Recognition Efforts

Recognition efforts are typically thought of in terms of informal and formal. Informal recognition commonly takes place on a day-to-day basis and costs little or no money. Examples include remembering a volunteer's birthday and sending a note, celebrating the volunteer's anniversary with a small gift, simply saying "thank you" at the end of the volunteer's shift, and being available and supportive if the volunteer is having personal issues outside of their volunteer commitment. Such informal activities provide a consistent feeling of appreciation and belonging. Formal recognition generally requires advanced planning, coordination, and can require a large commitment of organizational funds. Examples include award ceremonies, plaques presented and publicly displayed for all to see, dinners or luncheons, annual recreational events for all volunteers, highlighting the volunteer in the organization's annual report/newsletter and nominating volunteers for local, state, or national awards.

Recognition systems that focus on the individual, that are matched to the personality of the volunteer, and are appropriate to the level of the individual's contribution tend to be the most successful. It is important to acknowledge that all volunteers are individuals and motivated by different needs. Understanding what motivates a volunteer or more simply put, what a volunteer thinks is important, will guide the volunteer administrator in determining the best way to recognize that volunteer.

It can be a challenge for the volunteer administrator to determine (often without direct indication from the volunteer) how each particular volunteer or specific volunteer population wishes to be thanked and acknowledged. Ideally, the volunteer administrator will adapt the overall recognition system to one that accommodates the needs of all.

One way to achieve this is to strive to implement a recognition system that utilizes all levels and varieties of volunteer recognition activities.

There are many theories regarding the motivations of volunteers that help administrators to understand why their volunteers are participating in their programs. We already discussed one use of such motivational theories in the section on Marketing and Recruitment. Another example is a functional approach to volunteer motivations put forth by Clary *et al.* (1998, pp. 1516-30), who suggest that although acts of volunteerism may appear quite similar in terms of the roles assumed or work accomplished, for each volunteer there are very different underlying motivations that compel the volunteer to contribute their time. They identified six functional motives for volunteering: (1) using volunteerism as a way to express personal values, or simply to help others; (2) understanding or having the desire to use volunteerism as an opportunity to gain new learning experiences; (3) seeing volunteerism as a way to be a part of a group or to be with one's friends; (4) utilizing volunteerism as a means to career enhancement; (5) believing that volunteerism provides an escape from day-to-day life challenges and reduces guilt around being more fortunate than others; and (6) deriving a sense of personal importance from volunteering.[*]

See Table 4 for some examples of matching this construct of volunteer motivations with volunteer recognition efforts.

Table 4: Matching Motivational Needs with Recognition Efforts

MOTIVATIONAL NEED	POSSIBLE RECOGNITION ACTIVITY
Values	Personal thank you letter from a client who benefitted from services
Understanding	Pay for attendance at a relevant conference
Social	Grant an award and present it in front of peers
Career Enhancement	Provide a promotion indicating more challenging tasks and responsibility, with associated trainings

---

[*] See also Independent Sector 2001, p. 75, for national survey results on volunteer motivations.

Protective	Provide concrete evidence of the volunteer's contribution to the cause
Self-Enhancement	Provide special commendation letter signed by the Board of Directors or other noted organizational leader

In addition to matching the motivation of the volunteer, recognition should match the level of contribution. It would not make sense to provide a volunteer who has given only a few hours of service the same level of recognition as a volunteer who has dedicated years of service.

For example, consider a group of 100 episodic volunteers who help to set up and run an annual auction. They might receive a standard letter of thanks and a team photo placed in the newsletter. However, an appropriate form of recognition for a long-term volunteer who mentored a child for a year or more is a personal handwritten note of thanks from the executive director and the child, and a gift card to offset costs incurred by the volunteer.

In all cases, the volunteer administrator should keep the volunteer as the primary motivation for any plan, not the organization. An organization may think that holding a fancy award dinner with staff and volunteers will provide an opportunity to acquire some new photos for their website, to offer volunteers a spotlight to celebrate their successes, or for staff to become better acquainted with the agency volunteers. Such an event will only be successful if volunteers are motivated to attend. If they do not attend, much time, effort, and money will be spent without any of the organizational goals being met and the recognition attempt will have failed. These events may appeal to volunteers who are motivated by community notoriety or affiliation, but may hold little interest for those volunteers who have demanding schedules, or are primarily focused on helping the clients. Such volunteers may prefer that money not be spent on them but rather on services provided by the organization. Before planning such an event, the administrator should learn and understand the desires and motivations of the volunteers on the proposed invitation list.

Budgeting for and Justifying Recognition Activities

Recognition activities must be included in the volunteer program's budget. As discussed, volunteer recognition need not be extravagant or expensive to be effective. Nevertheless, even some of the simplest efforts (*e.g.*, thank you or birthday notes, copies of event photographs, or a page added into the quarterly newsletter) have financial implications. If your organization intends to provide more substantial rewards such as luncheons, plaques, movie tickets, or retail gift cards, the financial costs will be greater.

Sincere appreciation and the desire to acknowledge the contributions of volunteers should be the basis of any volunteer program's recognition system. However, when justifying expenses associated with volunteer recognition there are other reasons to support these activities:

1. the money spent on recognition efforts will ultimately save funds associated with staff time and resources spent on managing unmotivated and unappreciated volunteers;

2. a lack of recognition and appreciation of volunteers ultimately creates turnover. The investment in volunteer recognition reduces turnover, and the associated recruitment costs;

3. funding organizations often factor in the level of volunteer support in organizations in their decision-making. Publicly acknowledging the number of volunteer hours contributed by volunteers (and the dollar equivalent of this service) in annual reports or other official organization literature can be instrumental in the Development Department's acquisition of funding for the entire organization;

4. local, state/provincial, and national recognition awards granted to volunteers provide the organization with a positive image and marketing opportunities to wide audiences; and

5. volunteers often become financial donors. If they have a positive perspective on their volunteer experience and on the organization, they will be more likely to participate in fundraising campaigns.

The volunteer administrator can use such rationale to advocate to his directors and the Development Department that the costs associated with volunteer recognition require ongoing funding and support. They are necessary expenditures vital to a well-managed volunteer program and fiscally responsible organization.

SUMMARY

This chapter gives a solid foundation for the development, staffing, and management of a thriving volunteer program. Volunteers are valuable resources. A UPS Foundation study (1998) revealed that two-fifths of volunteers stopped volunteering because of one or more poor volunteer management practices such as wasting volunteer time and talents, or not clearly defining volunteer positions. Organizations cannot afford to jeopardize their volunteer support in this way. Good ongoing management is essential for the successful involvement and retention of volunteers. Success is at least partly based on carefully moving through the staffing and development cycle we have outlined here. Careful planning and development, maintaining sensitivity to the needs of the organization, the staff and the volunteers, thoughtful screening and placement, providing appropriate training, support, and supervision, and recognizing the good work of all involved in making the program a success is the foundation of a responsive, reputable program.

The staffing cycle depends on continuous improvement. Given that the needs of the organization, the funding and resources available for programming, and the trends in volunteer interests, requirements, and availability is always in flux, the volunteer administrator must constantly review and revise all the processes in the staffing cycle. There lies an opportunity to improve the process with every volunteer (new or veteran) and every organizational need (ongoing or newly identified). Along every step of the staffing cycle, the volunteer administrator can promote growth and renewal by viewing the Staffing and Development Cycle holistically, evaluating the successes and challenges encountered, and making changes as necessary. Like anything else in life, lack of maintenance leads to deterioration. Ongoing attention is required to insure that your program infrastructure is strong and running smoothly, is responding to the current needs of all parties involved, and does so in a way that creates a supportive and welcoming environment that will encourage volunteer participation for years to come.

REFERENCES

Behfar, K.J., Peterson, R.S., Mannix, E.A., & Trochim, W. (2008). The critical role of conflict resolution in teams: A close look at the links between conflict type, conflict management strategies, and team outcomes. *Journal of Applied Psychology American Psychological Association, 93*(1), 170-188.

Blake, R.R, & Mouton, J.S. (1964). *The managerial grid*. Houston, TX: Gulf.

Canadian Human Rights Commission. *Canadian Human Rights Act*. Retrieved May 14, 2009, from http://www.chrc-ccdp.ca/default-en.asp.

Clary, E.G, Snyder, M., Ridge, R.D., Copeland, J., Stukas, A., Haugen, J. *et al.* (1998). Understanding and assessing the motivations of volunteers: A functional approach. *Journal of Personality and Social Psychology, 74,* 1516-1530.

Cooperrider, D. L., & Srivastva, S. (1987). Appreciative inquiry in organizational life. *Research in Organizational Change and Development, 1,* 129-169.

Council for Certification in Volunteer Administration (2008). Body of Knowledge for Volunteer Administration page. Retrieved June 3, 2009, from http://www.cvacert.org/documents/CCVABOK2008-Final_000.pdf.

Cowling, M. (2006). Why I learnt to hate icebreakers. *E-Volunteerism: The Electronic Journal of the Volunteer Community, 6*(4).

de Shazer, S., Dolan, Y., *et al.* (2007). *More than miracles: The state of the art of solution-focused brief therapy*. New York: The Haworth Press.

DeChurch, L.A., & Marks, M.A. (2001). Maximizing the benefit of task conflict: The role of conflict management. *International Journal of Conflict Management, 12*(1), 4-23.

Ellis, S.J. (1996). *The volunteer recruitment (and membership development) book*. Philadelphia, PA: Energize Inc.

Foster, I. (2004). Getting the attention you want from the media. *Volunteerism: The Electronic Journal of the Volunteer Community: Featured Articles, IV*(2).

Government of Canada Website: Safety Canada. Retrieved June 3, 2009, from http://www.publicsafety.gc.ca/prg/sc/vol/vol-ben-eng.aspx#a12.

Hager, M., & Brudney, J. (2004). *Volunteer management practices and retention of volunteers*. Washington, DC: The Urban Institute. Retrieved May 18, 2009, from http://www.urban.org/publications/411005.html.

Independent Sector. (1999). Giving and volunteering executive summary. Retrieved from http://www.independentsector.org/GandV/default.htm.

Independent Sector. (2000). Volunteering: Volunteering levels and numbers of hours recorded.

Independent Sector. (2001). Giving and volunteering in the United States: Key findings. Retrieved from http://www.independentsector.org/uploads/Resources/GV01keyfind.pdf. For the complete report, visit http://www.cpanda.org/pdfs/gv/GV01Report.pdf.

Janz, T., Hellervick, L., & Gilmore, David C. (1986). *Behavior description interviewing: New, accurate, cost effective.* Englewood Cliffs, NJ: Prentice Hall.

Jorgensen, E.O. (2000). Relational transformation in mediation: Following constitutive and regulative rules. *Mediation Quarterly, 17*(3), 295-312.

Karakas, Fahri. (2009). New paradigms in organization development: Positivity, spirituality, and complexity. *Organization Development Journal, 27*(1), 11-26.

Keyboard Roundtable: When should we not involve volunteers? (2005). *E-Volunteerism: The Electronic Journal of the Volunteer Community, V*(3).

KU Work Group for Community Health and Development. (2009). Developing training programs for colunteers (Chapter 11, Section 4). Lawrence, KS: University of Kansas. Available at http://ctb.ku.edu/en/tablecontents/section_1109.htm.

Kyrwood, D.L. (2005). Volunteer training content guide for a volunteer in a direct service agency. Unpublished form.

Leonard, R., Onyx, J., & Hayward-Brown, H. (2004). Volunteer and coordinator perspectives on managing women volunteers. *Nonprofit Management & Leadership, 15*(2), 205-219.

Lubertozzi, M. (1989). Help! I have to plan a training program. *The Journal of Volunteer Administration* (Spring), 26-30.

Lulewicz, S. J. (1995). Training and development of volunteers. In T.D. Connors (Ed.), *The volunteer management handbook* (pp. 82-102). New York: John Wiley and Sons, Inc.

Lynch, R. (1980). Training volunteers: Choosing the right methods. *Voluntary Action Leadership* (Fall), 35.

McCurley, S. (1994). Recruiting and retaining volunteers. In Robert D. Herman & Associates (Eds.), *The Jossey-Bass handbook of nonprofit leadership and management* (pp. 511-534). San Francisco: Jossey-Bass Publishers.

McCurley, S. (2004). PSA and volunteer recruitment campaigns. *e-Volunteerism: The Electronic Journal of the Volunteer Community: Along the Web, IV*(4).

McCurley, S., & Ellis, S.J. (2002). Supplementing or supplanting? The mystery of "volunteer" versus "paid employee" right to work. *E-Volunteerism: The Electronic Journal of the Volunteer Community, III*(2).

McCurley, S., & Ellis, S.J. (2003). Thinking the unthinkable: Are we using the wrong model for volunteer work? *E-Volunteerism: The Electronic Journal of the Volunteer Community, III*(3).

McCurley, S., & Lynch, R. (1996). *Volunteer management.* Illinois: Heritage Arts Publishing.

Macduff, N. (1995). Preparing the organization for episodic volunteering. In T.D. Connors (Ed.), *The volunteer management handbook* (pp. 187-205). New York: John Wiley and Sons, Inc.

Meneghetti, M. (1995). Motivating people to volunteer their services. In T.D. Connors (Ed.), *The volunteer management handbook* (pp. 12-35). New York: John Wiley and Sons, Inc.

Meneghetti, M. (1999). Using multi-source feedback to improve performance. In Tracy D. Connor & J.M. Greenfield (Eds.), *The nonprofit management handbook*. New York: John Wiley & Sons.

Mejis, L.C.P.M., Tschirhart, M., Ten Hoorn, E.M., & Brudney, J.L. (2009). Effect of design elements for corporate volunteer programs on volunteerability. *The International Journal of Volunteer Administration, XXVI*(1), 23-32.

Merriam Webster Online. Retrieved June 5, 2009, from http://www.merriam-webster.com/dictionary/conflict.

National Multiple Sclerosis Society. (Updated January, 23 2009). Volunteering Vision and Philosophy. Retrieved from http://www.nationalmssociety.org/chapters/ORC/volunteer/volunteering-vision-and-philosophy/index.aspx.

Noble, J., Rogers, L., & Fryar, A. (2003). *Volunteer management: An essential guide* (2nd ed.). Volunteering SA Inc.

Nonprofit World. (2002). Reach out and train someone: The many faces of distance learning. *Nonprofit World, 20*(2), 24.

O'Rourke, M., & Baldwin, G. (2004). How the Internet has changed volunteering: Findings from a VolunteerMatch user study. *The Journal of Volunteer Administration, 22*(3), 16-22.

Omoto, A., & Snyder, M. (1995). Sustained helping without obligation: Motivation, longevity of service, and perceived attitude change among AIDS volunteers. *Journal of Personality and Social Psychology, 68*(4), 671-686.

Points of Light Foundation and Volunteer Center National Network. (December 2002). Working solutions: Volunteers versus paid employees. Available at training@handsonnetwork.org upon request.

Scheier, I. (1981). *The people approach handbook.* Denver: Yellowfire Press. (Out of print but available at http://academic.regis.edu/volunteer/ivan/sect01/sect01c1.htm.)

Skoglund, A.G. (2006). Do not forget about your volunteers: A qualitative analysis of factors influencing volunteer turnover. *Health & Social Work, 31*(3), 217-220.

Trottier, V. (2001). Workshops the wired way. *E-Volunteerism: The Electronic Journal of the Volunteer Community, 1*(3).

U.S. Department of Health and Human Services/Substance Abuse and Mental Health Services Administration. (2005). *Successful strategies for recruiting, training, and utilizing volunteers.* Retrieved from http://www.samhsa.gov/fbci/Volunteer_handbook.pdf.

U.S. Department of Labor, Bureau of Labor Statistics. (2008). Volunteering in the United States, 2008. Table 6: Volunteers by how they became involved with main organization for which volunteer activities were performed and selected characteristics, September 2008. Retrieved from http://www.bls.gov/news.release/volun.t06.htm.

Volunteer Canada. Understanding Police Reference Checks page. Retrieved May 14, 2009 from http://volunteer.ca/files/PRCBrochureEng.pdf.

Volunteer Canada. (2006). The Canadian Code for Voluntary Involvement page. Retrieved May 18, 2009, from http://volunteer.ca.

Volunteer Canada. (2009). Volunteer Centres in Canada. Retrieved from http://volunteer.ca/en/about/volunteer/centres.

Wymer, Jr., W.W., & Starnes, B. (2001). *Conceptual foundations and practical guideline for recruiting volunteers to serve in local nonprofit organizations: Part I.* Haworth Press Inc.

Wymer, Jr., W.W., & Starnes, B.J. (2001). Conceptual foundations and practical guidelines for retaining volunteers who serve in local nonprofit organizations: Part II. *Journal of Nonprofit and Public Sector Marketing, 9*(1/2).

Chapter 7

SUSTAINING VOLUNTEER INVOLVEMENT

Mark A. Hager, Ph.D.[*]
Arizona State University

Jeffrey L. Brudney, Ph.D.[*]
Cleveland State University

[*] The authors thank Kimberly Cooper for her dedicated research assistance and Maria Kipfstuhl and Vinola Vincent for their excellent editorial assistance. Portions of this chapter draw on research conducted with support from the Corporation for National and Community Service, the UPS Foundation, and the Urban Institute.

SUSTAINING VOLUNTEER INVOLVEMENT

Once upon a time, people spent their days working and talking with people in their communities. They knew what was going on because of their regular conversations with their neighbours. When they had a common need or wanted to solve an issue that arose in the community, they banded together and created groups to meet those needs. They and their neighbours volunteered their time and attention to these groups, because spending time with these organizations was all part of the commons and the betterment of their community. When time allowed, the people would ride their unicorns and chase elves and pixies through the fields, laughing and wanting for nothing. Everything was perfect, just like you expect at the beginning of any fairy tale.

Whatever is past, we do not live in that fairy tale now. The world as we know it does not always match up with that idyllic past, although we often hear versions of it when we talk about ways to build our communities and the organizations we use to serve ourselves and our common needs. Communities really do work best when people know and talk with each other, and when we all work together for the benefit of others. However, modern community is fragmented in ways that make togetherness difficult.

For one thing, people are as busy now as ever. Even our leisure time makes us busy, with television and the Internet cutting into opportunities for people to talk with their friends and neighbours, or otherwise interact with their community. Facebook changes the way we keep up with the people we know. Amazon changes the way we shop for goods. People do not have to leave their houses any more, and many do not. Even as the Internet creates new kinds of communities, we have to come to grips with the fact that people do not talk much with their neighbours, and they are often too preoccupied to see the needs and desires of the people around them. The world has changed, and the idyllic conception is hard to recognize in contemporary times. We have to take these factors into account when we build our modern community organizations.

At the same time, a second source of fragmentation is the growth in the number and concentration of organizations that compete for our money and attention. The desire to do good and be involved is as strong as ever, but people do not always know how best to channel those helping impulses. The founding of multiple and varied versions of similar organizations is itself an example of the lack of connection to community. Social entrepreneurs *build* rather than *build on*. Even where one strong organization serves community needs, several more crop up to compete. Each needs a mix of qualified staff, a committed board, grants, contracts, contributions and volunteers. A baffled public gives a little, volunteers a little, and cares a little about each new enterprise that touches them. However, unless people give a lot, volunteer a lot, and care a lot, they will not fully connect with their community, and their organizations will be fragile and similarly disconnected.

Thirdly, nonprofits and their volunteer administrators have to realize that people bring a complex range of motivations in their decisions to volunteer their time and effort with community organizations. Some are moved by a cause, others are fulfilling a vague sense of obligation, others are looking for job skills, and still others are looking for human connections, just to name a few. Sustaining volunteer involvement means recognizing the needs of volunteers and trying to find a way to make sure those needs are met.

This chapter is about both people and their organizations. The first part of the chapter focuses on the variety of reasons why people choose to become involved or not in community organizations: *the reasons why people work*. Our approach is to outline major theories of workplace motivation from the past 70 years or so, and then to consider what they can teach us about the motivations of volunteers and what we can do to keep them satisfied and active in our community organizations. The second part of the chapter focuses on what organizations do to entice a fragmented public to keep dedicating time and attention to their cause: *retention of volunteers*.

WHY PEOPLE WORK (OR VOLUNTEER)

Theories of workplace motivation are divided into two categories: content theories and process theories. Content theories are so named because they describe the "content" of the forces that motivate people to carry out various tasks. These theories examine the needs and incentives that influence workplace motivation, although we believe that they can be fruitfully applied to volunteers. Because of the great variety of human motivations, the range of needs to be met varies widely across individuals. Whereas some people are highly motivated by such things as money or fame, others prefer accomplishment and emotional fulfillment. Still others crave social belonging and approval. For others, meeting basic security and safety needs is the highest priority.

By contrast, process theories are not concerned with particular individual needs. Rather, they deal with the means or process through which any need can galvanize action. Process theories assume that regardless of the "content" of particular motivations, the same processes move people from motive to action. In this first half of the chapter, we describe the major content and process theories of motivation and then consider what they mean for volunteer administrators. Our discussion is based on examination of the major theories of workplace motivation provided by Rainey (2003) and Halachmi and van der Krogt (2005).

Content Theories

Content theories focus on the factors that produce motivation to carry out a particular task. The factors are traditionally divided into two groups: intrinsic and extrinsic. A factor is labelled "intrinsic" when it satisfies some internal need or desire. An example is *challenging work*, which might motivate us because it provides an opportunity to showcase skills in a meaningful way, or to feel good about a job well done. In contrast, monotony or busy-work might hold less promise for motivating people to do their best. An intrinsically motivated worker might say: "I do this job well because it gives me a sense of achievement."

The other sources of motivation are "extrinsic," which refers to external forces. The prime example of an extrinsic motivation is *money*, especially when cash is tied to performance. A promise of money, or more of it, can be a powerful motivator in certain circumstances, regardless of how the task makes us feel inside. An extrinsically motivated worker might say: "I do this job well because it allows me to earn money to buy things that I need."

All of the content theories presume that an unmet need provides motivation. That is, if a person craves interaction with others, a task that addresses that need should prove motivating to that individual and stimulate positive work activity. The content theories are similar, although each takes a somewhat different approach to clarify the needs that lead to motivation.

Hierarchy of Needs

You have probably heard of Abraham Maslow's Hierarchy of Needs, perhaps the best example of a content theory. In the midst of World War II, Maslow identified five categories of human needs: physiological, safety, social, self-esteem, and self-actualization. The needs are ranked by increasing order of importance and are often displayed as a pyramid with the primary needs (physiological) at the base. For Maslow, physiological needs (primarily food, clothing, and shelter) are the base needs upon which all others follow, from primarily extrinsic to primarily intrinsic. Safety needs, which include meeting threats of harm and unpredictability, come next. The remaining needs are often termed "higher order." Social needs involve earning people's admiration or acceptance into different social units. Self-esteem needs include a sense of personal achievement and the desire to be recognized and appreciated by others. Finally, self-actualization, the need to become all that one is capable of becoming, is at the top of the pyramid. To some people, self-actualization means becoming a musician or doctor; for others it means seeing the world or giving oneself to serve humanity.

As one moves up Maslow's Hierarchy from the base, needs become both more personal and more difficult to satisfy. Providing an employee with physiological needs is relatively easy because such a need is extrinsic and easily identified, and can normally be met by a fair paycheck. Self-actualization, by contrast, is much more difficult to accomplish since it is not "content-specific." Intrinsic needs are specific to individuals, and self-actualization needs can therefore vary greatly from one person to the next. This element complicates the ability of managers to know how to motivate a particular individual, once base extrinsic needs have been met. Maslow's Hierarchy was highly influential to later theorists. Many aspects of this model can be seen, indirectly and directly, in the other content theories we describe below.

Two-Factor Theory

A good example is Herzberg's Two-Factor Theory. This model treats factors related to job-related satisfaction as separate from factors that lead to dissatisfaction at work. Rather than conceiving a single line from dissatisfaction to satisfaction, Herzberg proposed two separate dimensions that he named *hygiene factors* and *motivator factors*. Hygiene factors include salary, personal life, and one's status — extrinsic factors that can lead to dissatisfaction when they are not present. These external factors cannot, in themselves, motivate workers; however, unless they are met, Herzberg maintains that the motivator factors will not come into play. Motivator factors include challenging work, additional responsibility, and advancement — intrinsic factors that yield satisfaction for workers. The two sets of factors must work together, one to prevent dissatisfaction (hygiene) and the other to provide satisfaction (motivator). Both factors must be addressed to provide a satisfactory work experience for workers. For example, even the most challenging job (motivator) will be lost on the worker if she or he feels greatly underpaid (hygiene). Tending to both hygiene and motivation can increase worker productivity. Consistent with Maslow, Herzberg's theory proposes that extrinsic needs must be satisfied before intrinsic needs become relevant, even if intrinsic motivations ultimately provide the greater satisfaction.

Needs Theory

Adding nuance to the debate, McClelland advanced his Needs Theory. McClelland identified three important non-physiological needs that define workplace motivation. The theory proposes that individuals' behaviours can be explained by examining their needs for *achievement*, *affiliation*, and *power*. Needs for achievement involve the aspiration to have control over one's situation by one's own work and effort, coupled with acceptance of risk if it will facilitate goal achievement, and a desire for feedback and personal responsibility. Employees who have a strong need for achievement set difficult (but achievable) goals for themselves and work hard to see that they are met. The need for achievement contributes to an entrepreneurial spirit and a desire to learn through constructive feedback. The need for power includes the condition that one be the master of oneself, exert some control over others, or gain authority over peers. Power needs are characteristic of effective managers, whereas achievement needs lead to entrepreneurship. The desire to have positive and meaningful relationships with others is seen in the need for affiliation. Social settings at work, home, and elsewhere may be fulfilling to those with strong affiliation needs.

Although McClelland believed that motivation could be categorized by a dominant need for affiliation, power, or achievement, worker motivations often stem from a combination of competing needs. Maslow's Hierarchy of Needs has the same limitation. Expecting workers to have only one need is usually unrealistic. Viewing needs as simple categories carries the risk of forcing individuals into groups they do not neatly fit. Nevertheless, *awareness of a worker's dominant need can be useful in tailoring tasks and situations that cater to her or his strengths and motivations.* This advice is central to effective application of psychological content theories.

Theory X/Theory Y

Influenced by Maslow, McGregor's Theory X/Theory Y views workers' needs from the perspective of the manager. McGregor felt that American industrial management literature prior to 1960 had been dominated by Theory X: the idea that workers lacked the ability for self-motivation and self-direction. Because workers were assumed to need extrinsic motivation and direction, the role of managers was to maintain and exert control and authority over them. By contrast, McGregor's Theory Y is founded on the idea that workers have their own higher-order (intrinsic) needs that can be addressed at the workplace through joint decision-making, participative performance evaluation, and on-the-job improvement, factors that keep employees involved in critical organizational processes. McGregor's higher-order needs include the need for growth, interesting work, and self-actualization and development. Including employees in organizational processes, rather than allowing them to be only the recipients of mandated change, empowers them and helps to fulfill these needs. Lumping workers into a stereotyped group of unmotivated employees who need constant direction and extrinsic rewards (Theory X) contributes to a self-fulfilling prophecy — little is expected of lazy and inefficient workers, which leads to lowered performance and decreased productivity, thus justifying management's lowered expectations. According to McGregor, including workers in processes and treating them as capable workers (Theory Y) is the key to building and maintaining a motivated workforce. Intrinsic motivations are key.

Equity Theory

Proposed by J. Stacy Adams, Equity Theory advanced the idea that people's work behaviours are heavily influenced by the desire for equity. The absence of equity (or the presence of inequity) leads to uneasiness and discomfort. In return, people adjust their behaviours to reduce those feelings of inequity. Adams suggested that employees weigh what they contribute to an organization (such as effort or loyalty) against what they receive from it (such as pay or challenging work), and then seek a balance between them in comparison to a referent person or group in the organization. For example, if two program directors in the same organization work an equal number of hours per week and complete the same number of tasks of equivalent difficulty, equity is present. However, if one of the workers feels that the other worker receives greater recognition or compensation for the same work, inequity arises. Adams' theory predicts that the first worker will adjust her or his behaviours to bring effort and reward into balance. In this case, she or he might withdraw effort to balance the perceived imbalance of rewards. So, intrinsic motivations depend on one's internal calculations of satisfaction, balanced by perceptions of how fairly work and resources are distributed.

Process Theories

Whereas content theories are primarily concerned with the specific factors that stimulate workplace motivation, process theories deal with the manner by which a need or motivation is translated into positive action. Process theories explain the mechanisms that translate needs into productive work behaviour, or how "goals, values, needs, or rewards operate in conjunction with other factors to determine motivation" (Rainey, 2003, p. 258). The primary process theories related to worker motivation follow.

Expectancy Theory

This perspective is primarily about risk and rewards. The main idea contributed by Expectancy Theory is that of choosing a path that presents minimal risks. The theory proposes that two types of expectancies exist. "Expectancy I" expectancies are those that help to convince a person that she or he is actually capable of performing a given task. "Expectancy II" expectancies are concerned with the perceived rewards (such as qualifying for a promotion) that come from carrying out a particular task. To be motivated, the person must find both sets of expectancies to be credible.

Expectancy Theory proposes that individuals consider all possible outcomes of an action and act in a way that maximizes the opportunity for desired outcomes and minimizes unwanted outcomes. For example, in deciding whether or not to take on an optional work assignment, Expectancy Theory holds that an individual will evaluate the likelihood of preferred results (such as higher pay, promotion, increased respect) against the probability of negative outcomes (such as more time on the job, time away from family, less workplace flexibility) and act accordingly.

Operant Conditioning

Expectancy Theory was extended by a focus on operant conditioning. Operant Conditioning Theory and Behaviour Modification are heavily influenced by B.F. Skinner and psychologists of the Behaviourist School. Behaviourists believe that human conduct can be understood by direct observation and analysis of observed behaviours rather than inner states such as attitudes. Operant conditioning grew from previous psychological research that showed that human behaviour develops not only from reactions to external stimuli but also by anticipating consequences of actions. Learned behaviours are also contingent upon environmental factors such as family structure, socioeconomic status, education, and income. The severity of consequences of actions determines if certain behaviours will be repeated or stopped. Following the Behaviourist School, the theory proposes that consequences are based only on visible behaviours, not on inner states such as intent.

Operant conditioning theory specifies four types of reinforcement: positive reinforcement, negative reinforcement, operant extinction and punishment. Positive reinforcement is that which leads to an increase in desired and beneficial behaviours by giving positive stimuli, whereas negative reinforcement looks to decrease adverse behaviour by removing aversive stimuli. For example, if a nonprofit CEO wanted to decrease or eliminate a treasurer's money-counting mistakes, she or he can provide rewards for keeping an accurate account of cash, a positive reinforcement. If strong punishments for counting violations already exist, removing them each time good behaviour is exhibited would be negative reinforcement. Operant extinction is the product of eliminating a positive reinforcement, and punishment is simply applying a penalty to a behaviour to reduce or eliminate it. In regard to the effectiveness of reward or punishment in inducing desired behaviours, positive reinforcements are found to work better than negative. In the long-run, intermittent reinforcement is superior to punishment (Rainey, 2003, p. 262).

Social Learning Theory

This psychological perspective embraces many of the concepts of Operant Conditioning Theory, adding recognition of internal cognitive processes. Social Learning Theory proposes that people learn most often through copying of observed behaviours, experiences, and social context. People see what others have done and experienced and learn behaviours purely through observation, interaction and awareness of the outcomes of the behaviour. New workers, for example, often learn what acceptable water-cooler talk is, exceptions to dress code policies, and appropriate ways to address others through observation of current workers. The behaviour is then reinforced (or discouraged) by others in the organization.

Learning through observation could also lead to no change in behaviour. Workers can learn proper protocol, but with no incentive or reinforcement their behaviour may go unchanged. If, for example, a newly hired social worker observes co-workers wearing nametags on their shoes but continues to wear her or his badge on the shirt because she or he has not been reprimanded for the deviant behaviour, the new hire has learned how people in the organization behave but has no incentive to adjust her or his behaviour accordingly.

Goal Setting Theory

The Goal Setting perspective holds that difficult and precise goals lead to increased performance, in contrast to ambiguous, easy, or non-existent goals. Those goals deemed difficult to achieve enhance performance by "directing attention and action, mobilizing effort, increasing persistence, and motivating the search for effective performance strategies" (Rainey, 2003, p. 266). Vague goals are incapable of such motivation because people are unsure of the target to which their effort is focused. Goals must be limited, manageable, achievable, and realistic in order to keep workers motivated toward goal-attainment. Managers should not overwhelm workers with goals that are overly ambitious. For example, although an ultimate, long-term and certainly difficult goal would be to re-organize the workplace to achieve higher productivity, creating a series of more specific, lesser goals to serve as steps toward this larger goal will maintain a level of practicality to keep workers motivated.

The Challenge of Work Motivation

An example drawn from paid employment helps to illustrate the challenge of engaging workers. Karen Farkas (2009, p. B1) describes Bari Lambert, who has worked full-time as a toll collector in the same small toll booth on the Ohio turnpike since it opened for business in 1993. Lambert chooses not to listen to the radio or read on the job; she prefers to look out at the (same) scenery and wildlife day after day. Although traffic has declined at Lambert's toll booth to 25 vehicles per hour, Lambert insists, "I'm fortunate I have a job I enjoy." The only downside to the job that she can identify "is getting sprayed with rain or snow from windshield wipers when she leans out to collect the toll."

Although nearly every theory of workplace motivation would predict that employees (or volunteers) in this situation would opt for more stimulating, responsible, and/or highly paid work as quickly as possible, Lambert has turned down opportunities to become a supervisor or to move to a busier interchange. "The part of the job I enjoy working in the lane is talking to people. Being happy in my job is more important than money." If a job that would seem to offer so little in the way of excitement, creativity, leadership, or remuneration can nevertheless provide enduring motivation to a paid worker, imagine how much more difficult it can be to discern and present factors in the volunteer workplace that will engage and sustain those who donate their time.

Implications of Content Theories for Volunteer Administrators

The theories described above were either developed to describe workplace motivation, or have generally been applied to paid workers. Figure 1 describes the implications of the workplace motivation theories for volunteer involvement.

Figure 1: Theories of Motivation:
Implications for Administrators of Volunteers

Motivation Theories	Brief Summary of Theory	Implications of Theory for Volunteer Administrators
Content Theories		
Maslow, Hierarchy of Needs	People are motivated by five basic needs that they are thought to pursue in order from the most basic needs, physiological and safety, to the most ambitious, social, self-esteem, and self-actualization.	Physiological and safety needs are met outside of volunteering, for example, through paid work. Administrators of volunteers need to appeal to the social, self-esteem, and self-actualization needs of volunteers by offering work assignments that reflect these needs.
Herzberg, Two-Factor Theory	Worker dissatisfaction and satisfaction are two independent dimensions, both of which must be pursued to stimulate motivation. Hygiene factors are concerned with job dissatisfaction; motivator factors address job satisfaction.	Hygiene needs are important but not motivating: organizations sometimes overlook that volunteers need a place to work and an acceptable job environment. Once hygiene needs are met, motivator factors such as achievement, recognition, and the work itself can engage volunteers. Administrators of volunteers must attend to both hygiene and motivator factors.
McGregor, Theory X and Theory Y	Managers' beliefs and stereotypes regarding workers affect the level and quality of effort that will be elicited from them.	The power of the self-fulfilling prophecy: Volunteers will live up — or down — to the expectations of the administrator of volunteers. If the administrator presumes and manages as if volunteers are "lazy" (Theory X) they will tend to act in that manner. Conversely, if the administrator assumes that volunteers are capable of self-directed effort and want to excel (Theory Y) and treats them accordingly, volunteers will strive to justify that belief.

Motivation Theories	Brief Summary of Theory	Implications of Theory for Volunteer Administrators
McClelland, Needs for Achievement, Power, and Affiliation	People have a predominant need for achievement, power, or affiliation that can be applied to motivate them at the workplace.	Volunteers have particular needs, for achievement, power, and affiliation. Knowing the driving need is important to motivating volunteers. The volunteer administrator should allow volunteers with power needs in leadership positions, give those with achievement needs challenging tasks, and place those with affiliation needs in healthy social settings.
Adams, the Need for Equity	Workers seek balance in their contributions to the organization and the rewards they receive from it and will redress imbalances. They judge equity/inequity in relation to the referent person(s) in the organization.	Volunteer administrators need to make sure that volunteers feel appreciated or rewarded for their efforts, especially in relation to other volunteers. Administrators should actively seek out imbalance (inequity) and work to eliminate it.
Process Theories		
Expectancy Theory	Motivation is a product of a worker's expectation that she or he is capable of greater effort and the expectation that the greater effort will yield rewards valued by the employee.	Volunteers will be motivated to the degree that they believe that they can accomplish tasks, and that accomplishing those tasks is rewarding to them. Volunteer administrators should coach or mentor volunteers to build confidence in performance and should follow through with their commitment to reward positive volunteer behaviour.
Operant Conditioning Theory and Behaviour Modification Theory	Motivation results from reinforcing positive work behaviours and removing sanctions to deter negative work behaviours.	Volunteer administrators should use rewards to reinforce desirable behaviour in volunteers, such as timeliness, reliability, and high work productivity, and remove rewards to reduce undesirable behaviours. Applying reinforcement

Motivation Theories	Brief Summary of Theory	Implications of Theory for Volunteer Administrators
		intermittenetly rather than at regular time intervals yields the best long-term results.
Social Learning Theory	Workers learn acceptable and unacceptable work behaviours from the culture and activities prevalent in the workplace.	Volunteer administrators should work with volunteers to help them see that other volunteers perform at a high level, and that they can realize the same results. Administrators should strive to establish a volunteer culture that is welcoming and sets high expectations for behaviour and performance.
Goal Setting Theory	Worker motivation can be achieved by setting specific, difficult, and realistic goals; generating commitment among employees to the goals, and giving feedback regarding goal attainment.	Administrators of volunteers should set difficult, specific, and attainable goals. They should also encourage commitment to the goals and give feedback concerning their attainment. Administrators should support a series of smaller intermediate objectives leading to a grand goal. By contrast, vague, unclear, or non-existent goals are not motivating (for example, "Give it your best").

Maslow's Hierarchy of Needs has a clear application to volunteers. The two most basic (lower order) needs, physiological and safety, must be met through paid employment or other sources of income rather than through volunteering. What paid employment cannot guarantee, however, is engagement with Maslow's higher order needs. By contrast, common motives for volunteering pertain directly to needs for social acceptance and involvement, self-esteem, and self-actualization. An effective volunteer administrator must identify these needs in volunteers and work to satisfy them.

Because individual volunteers are at different stages of the need hierarchy, volunteer administrators should communicate with those prepared to donate time to assess their skills, desires and expectations for volunteer service in order to best meet the volunteer's needs in relation to the organization's tasks and assignments. For example, volunteers seeking to meet social needs might be placed in assignments in which they work with other volunteers rather than individually or alone. Volunteers seeking self-esteem might be placed in positions where successful accomplishment of tasks is evident, such as on a host committee for a regional conference. Jobs that appeal to the highest aspirations of volunteers are suitable for those motivated by self-actualization. Those aspirations vary from volunteer to volunteer (for example, from helping a single child to creating a new department at the free clinic), thus reinforcing the need for the volunteer administrator to keep in close contact. Placements will fail if a volunteer's needs do not reasonably match the characteristics of a particular assignment. The consequence is unmotivated volunteers who are prone to turnover.

Herzberg's Two-Factor Theory describes motivator factors leading to job satisfaction and hygiene factors preventing dissatisfaction. Herzberg's motivators are comparable to Maslow's higher order needs and can be met through soliciting and heeding volunteers' input with respect to preferred task assignment. Hygiene factors offer a useful reminder to volunteer administrators that appealing to higher order needs may not be sufficient to motivate volunteers if hygiene factors are not met. That is, volunteers also require a work situation conducive to task accomplishment: adequate space, necessary supplies, requisite training, proper supervision, and so forth. Although not motivating in themselves, these factors should be present so that volunteers are able to meet their higher order needs through the tasks assigned to them, which can provide (intrinsic) motivation. Satisfying hygiene factors requires additional preparation on the part of the volunteer administrator. For example, prior to a volunteer's shift, the administrator will need to have a schedule, supplies, and instructions for the volunteer. The volunteer is unlikely to find these preparations a source of satisfaction. However, unless they are present to prevent dissatisfaction, engaging volunteers in meeting higher order needs will prove difficult or even futile.

McGregor's Theory X/Theory Y pertains more to administrators' perceptions of volunteers than to the volunteers themselves. This theory reminds us to set high expectations for volunteers and to treat them as if they were fully capable and interested in meeting these expectations. By contrast, if the administrator of volunteers presumes that volunteers are lazy, unreliable, and incompetent and establishes management procedures and controls with these stereotypes in mind, volunteers will "live down" to the expectations of lowered performance.

By contrast, when administrators act with an expectation that profes-sional conduct of volunteers is the norm and reinforces these expecta-tions through careful selection, orientation, training, placement and supervision of volunteers, she or he is likely to be rewarded with high levels of volunteer engagement and achievement. They would "live up" to expectations. As applied to volunteer administration, the implication of McGregor's view is that managers are likely to get the behaviour they expect (and influence) from volunteers.

McClelland's theory focuses on the needs of people for achieve-ment, power, and affiliation. With respect to volunteering, the theory advises that the volunteer administrator recognize these different needs and place volunteers in roles where they are likely to be met. The varying needs require administrators to be familiar with the range of organizational tasks so that both volunteers and the organization benefit through careful work assignment. As Helen Little states: "It is important to recognize these differences and match the tasks, work environment, and rewards to the individual's own reasons for volun-teering" (p. 29). Volunteers motivated by the need for achievement should have task assignments that offer the chance for responsibility and clear indicators of success (for example, staffing a fundraising event). Those motivated by a need for power should have the opportu-nity to occupy leadership positions, after they have demonstrated ability and interest. Finally, where affiliation is the predominant need, the theory calls for working with other people, possible in a great many volunteer opportunities.

Equity Theory concentrates on maintaining a balance between one's contributions to the organization and returns from it, judged in relation to others in the organization. The theory suggests that people seek fairness or equity in relation to the perceived treatment of their organizational counterparts. When they perceive inequity, people alter their work behaviour to bring their contributions into balance with organizational rewards. For volunteer administrators, the implication is to try to make sure that volunteers are rewarded equally for the same work. Although the principle seems straightforward, it is much more difficult in practice because equity is largely determined through the volunteer's perceptions, which can be highly sensitive to imagined personal slights as well as praise from others. In sum, the volunteer administrator must not only do her or his best to treat volunteers fairly but also be prepared to mediate volunteer complaints.

In all of the content theories of motivation, the role of the volun-teer administrator is the satisfier or fulfiller of needs. She or he works with volunteers to identify their needs and to meet them through appropriate management practices and organizational work assignments. As we show below, in each of the process theories of motivation the volunteer administrator plays a different role in engaging and sustaining volunteer involvement.

Implications of Process Theories for Volunteer Administrators

The process theories of motivation explain how the needs of volunteers can be translated into positive work activity. Expectancy Theory holds that action is a function of satisfying two types of expectancies. With respect to volunteers, Expectation I expectancies reinforce the belief that the volunteer is capable of performing a given activity. Expectation II expectancies tie desirable rewards to successful completion of the activity, such as valuable work experience or networking opportunities. Consistent with other process theories, in Expectancy Theory the content of the needs to be met through volunteering is variable. The theory does not presume that every volunteer seeks self-actualization or the other higher-order needs in Maslow's Hierarchy, and the "rewards" of the activity are not assumed to be equally motivating to all. Not everyone wants job experience or networking from volunteering, even though these forces are motivating to a certain segment of the volunteer community.

According to Expectancy Theory, volunteers will prefer those work assignments that offer the greatest rewards as they perceive them and ignore or leave tasks with lesser-perceived benefits. For volunteer administrators, the implications for management are that they learn about the needs and rewards that animate different volunteers and the positions that are most likely to confer these benefits. Since potency of rewards can change over time, effective administrators must stay in touch with volunteers. In addition, Expectancy Theory puts a premium on coaching volunteers to develop skills and confidence to perform organizational assignments (*i.e.*, building Expectancy I expectations). No matter how captivating the rewards to a volunteer, if she or he feels incapable of performing a given task, motivation will decrease. The volunteer administrator must therefore see to training, developing, and coaching volunteers, where appropriate. In this theory the volunteer administrator is a developer of volunteer beliefs, self-confidence, and talents.

Operant Conditioning Theory and Behaviour Modification applies to observable behaviour rather than unobservable inner states of volunteers. The theory suggests that behaviour can be directed through application of positive and negative reinforcements. The volunteer administrator might use positive reinforcement to praise or reward desired behaviour to make its recurrence more likely. Following successful completion of a demanding task by a volunteer, for example, the administrator might thank the volunteer, publicize the accomplishment in the organization, or offer another desirable work assignment. The positive reinforcement will depend on the individual volunteer. The administrator might also reward more mundane achievements of volunteers (for example, handling their work shifts in a professional manner) by acknowledging and thanking them.

By contrast, subpar behaviour or performance on the part of volunteers should not go overlooked and implicitly condoned. Ignoring lapses such as tardiness, lack of preparation, absenteeism, and violation of rules by volunteers, especially if they recur, sends the wrong message that "anything goes." Ignoring such behaviour is de-motivating to the higher performers, and the volunteer administrator must address it through sanctions and penalties. In Operant Conditioning Theory, the volunteer administrator is a builder of a work environment that reinforces desirable volunteer work behaviour.

According to Social Learning Theory, people learn acceptable and unacceptable behaviours from observing actions and their consequences in the workplace. They mimic or copy behaviour that is prevalent and rewarded in the organization. Accordingly, volunteer administrators can build a culture that is welcoming to new, diverse volunteers, and where (high) performance matters and is valued and rewarded. The administrator should work with volunteers to raise their self-efficacy so that they come to appreciate that they belong to a quality organization and can succeed in their work tasks. From the perspective of Social Learning Theory the administrator of volunteers is a creator and maintainer of organizational culture.

Goal Setting Theory tells us that motivation can be achieved by setting specific, difficult, and attainable goals. Personal motivation is enhanced by commitment to a goal and by feedback from supervisors regarding its achievement. Vague goals lack motivating force. Whenever possible, volunteer administrators should engage volunteers in setting goals, ensuring that the goals are challenging but within reach, and in monitoring progress toward goal achievement. Suppose that the nonprofit organization places the volunteer administrator in charge of the annual fundraising event. Who should be involved in making the relevant decisions? From the standpoint of Goal Setting Theory, volunteers should not only carry out the activity but also participate in determining the goals of the event and in evaluating progress. The volunteer administrator should start by including volunteers in setting a reasonable goal for the fundraising event, one that is difficult but not unmanageable, such as increasing the amount donated over the previous year by 5 per cent.

Others may also participate in goal setting, including paid staff and organizational leadership. The volunteer administrator might then break the overall task into meaningful segments, such as theme, publicity, and invitations, and work with volunteers interested in each of the areas to set the sub-goals for the segment. As the event draws closer, the administrator and the lead volunteers might provide feedback on goal attainment in each segment and help the volunteers coordinate the overall event. Absent such measures to define goals and encourage participation, the fundraising event is more likely to be a source of anxiety than positive work motivation and commitment for the volunteers. In Goal Setting Theory, the volunteer administrator is a facilitator of the participation and performance of volunteers.

ORGANIZATIONAL STRATEGIES FOR RETENTION OF VOLUNTEERS

Now we turn our attention to a second, but related, topic: strategies that organizations use to keep their volunteers. If recruiting volunteers were not difficult enough, organizations interested in their service must also sustain their involvement. Sustaining volunteer involvement may be even more important, for in its absence continual recruitment is a waste of organizational resources and dispiriting to everyone involved. Sustaining volunteer involvement, moreover, is likely more daunting. Recruitment might be conceived as a "mass market" activity: regardless of the characteristics of prospective volunteers, organizations that seek their involvement tend to use a fairly standard set of practices that entice them into service. By contrast, sustaining and retaining volunteers is a "micro market," or individually based activity, intended to meet the needs of volunteers and those of the host organization at the same time.

Knowing *why* people volunteer is the most important dimension of retention, and the reason we spent the first half of the chapter exploring the topic. Like most aspects of the management of a non-profit organization, retention of volunteers is rarely a matter of implementing the one, two, three things you learn in a book. Instead, retention of volunteers is the result of knowing your volunteers and ensuring that their needs are met, two dimensions that are more about creativity and attention than they are about studies and book learning.

That said, studies and book learning can help volunteer administrators hone in on the things that deserve their attention. Knowing what other organizations do, and how successful they have been, can be valuable in making your own decisions about what you need to do to retain volunteers. They can also be important allies when you have to explain to your supervisor, executive director, or board members why you need to increase volunteer management capacity in order to do your job better.

Retention Is Not Always Job One

Before we consider what organizations can do to retain volunteers, we should begin by saying that retention is more important to some people than others, and more important to some organizations than others. In short, even if retention of volunteers is a priority, you should know that keeping some of your volunteers may be outside of your control.

The Corporation for National and Community Service (2007a, 2008b; Eisner, Grimm, Maynard & Washburn, 2009) provides several snapshots of volunteer retention by comparing two years of Current Population Survey data. In September 2005, the Corporation collected one round of survey data on volunteerism across the United States. In September 2006, half of the 2005 respondents were tapped by the survey again, allowing for a comparison across the two years. The headline finding was that one out of three people who volunteer one year do not volunteer the next year. That is, of the estimated 65.4 million people that the Corporation for National and Community Service counted as volunteers in 2005, approximately 20.9 million did not do *any* kind of formal volunteering in 2006 (CNCS, 2007a).

If you assumed that much the same people volunteer from year to year, this finding is an eye-opener. Further, it reflects the proportion of people who go from volunteering to *no* volunteering, and does not capture the additional proportion of individuals who hop from one volunteer opportunity to the next. What should we make of this finding? The Corporation's response to this high level of churn was to attribute the loss of volunteers to poor management, and to count their exit as "lost labour" that cost nonprofit organizations an estimated $38 billion (Eisner *et al.*, 2009).

Surely, some people do leave their volunteer duties, and perhaps leave volunteering altogether, because of bad experiences at their sites. A decade ago, the UPS Foundation (1998) published an oft-cited study that reported that two-fifths of volunteers who had stopped volunteering for an organization had done so because of poor volunteer management practices. We also know from our own national study (more on that study below) that a large majority of nonprofits have not adopted volunteer management practices that might be helpful to their efforts to attract, serve, and retain volunteers (Hager & Brudney, 2004, 2008).

However, we believe that the Current Population Survey numbers tell us something more, and that the Corporation's "lost labour" interpretation can be understood differently. Labour is not lost: it is constantly replaced as community members cycle through. So, an estimated 65.4 million people volunteered in 2005, with 20.9 million not volunteering the following year. Does this mean that the estimate of Americans who volunteered fell to 44.5 million in 2006? No, the estimate for 2006 was 61.2 million (Bureau of Labor Statistics, 2007). As people cycled out of their volunteer duties, nearly just as many cycled in who had not volunteered the year before. The message, we believe, is *not* necessarily that labour is lost: the message is that people are on the move. You can impact that somewhat with best practices, but the churn is a social force that operates somewhat beyond our control. Some change and churn is natural and to be expected.

The second point is less dramatic: some tasks and missions do not lend themselves to retention. The value of retention of volunteers for some organizations is very important — recruiting and training cost time and money, so retaining happy volunteers minimizes the need to find and train their replacements. This picture is particularly true for organizations that employ volunteers for regular service assignments, such as line workers in a soup kitchen. However, organization missions and their needs for volunteers come in all shapes and sizes. Some use volunteers primarily in episodic events, such as infrequent service projects or events. Retention of booth volunteers at a bike-a-thon may not be a primary goal. Retention of volunteers who sign on for a month-long service assignment in Costa Rica may not be a primary goal. Instead, these organizations may be more interested in engaging volunteers as a means of educating them about a cause, or developing a relationship that might lead to long-term financial support. However, even where such things as education and fundraising are more important than retention, having satisfied and productive volunteers is still a central concern.

Management Practices and Volunteer Retention

In 2003, with collaboration and backing from the Corporation for National and Community Service, we undertook what is still the only national study of volunteer management capacity in the United States. We began with a representative list of nearly 3,000 public charities large enough to have a recent Form 990 filed with the Internal Revenue Service. The project completed telephone interviews with representatives from 1,753 nonprofit organizations across the United States, although only 1,354 told us that they used volunteers in their operations. The conversations with these 1,354 nonprofit executives formed the basis for our study.

One basic question that we asked in the national nonprofit survey was whether organizations had adopted certain management practices for volunteers, as shown in Figure 2. The individual practices may look familiar to you since they are drawn from prevailing lists of "best practices" in the field of volunteer administration. As with retention, not all practices are important or necessary to every kind of organization that involves volunteers in its operations. The critical question is whether nonprofits that can and should be adopting a particular practice have the resources, support, and know-how to put it in place. The main conclusion emanating from Figure 2 is how few nonprofits (and these are the ones that use volunteers in their operations) have adopted most of the "best" practices to a large degree. Others have "dabbled," but not adopted. A second conclusion is that these practices vary from organization to organization: some are more prevalent or necessary in particular places.

Figure 2: Management Practices That Charities Say They Practice to a Large or Some Degree

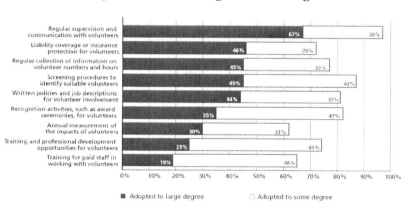

Adapted from Hager and Brudney, 2008.

We learned about retention by asking the nonprofit respondents, "Of the volunteers that worked with your organization one year ago, approximately what percentage would you say are still involved as volunteers?" Nearly 3 per cent said "zero," calling to mind those organizations that have episodic needs or event-based volunteers who are not expected on a regular basis. However, 17 per cent said that "100 per cent" were retained, illustrating those nonprofits that have tapped into the secret of how to keep people involved. The remaining 80 per cent of organizations fell somewhere in between, retaining some volunteers and losing others. The median charity reported an 80 per cent retention rate, with half reporting a higher rate and half a lower rate.

Recognizing the Contributions of Volunteers

If we might boil the theory from the first part of the chapter down to its essence, we could say that volunteers will be most satisfied and productive when the characteristics of a job are matched with their motivations. However, perhaps nothing is more universal in touching the intrinsic needs of volunteers than recognizing their contributions to the cause. This practice may be as simple as a private, heartfelt "thank you," but our study asked about formal recognition activities such as award ceremonies. The practice is common enough, with over 80 per cent of charities at least dabbling in the practice, and one in three practising it to a large degree. Recall how Equity Theory concentrates on the balance between contributions to the organization and returns from it, while also considering how others are treated in comparison. Recognition is an important intrinsic reward for many people, and it is a way to show volunteers that their contributions are valued in equal measure in comparison to the work of others in the organization. Failure to recognize volunteers is not only a failure in personal relationship, but also a failure to reinforce the motivations that come with equity.

We grouped organizations by size depending on how much they spend in a year, ranging from a low category of under $100,000 to a high category of more than $5 million. We learned that award ceremonies and other recognition activities is more dependent on the size of the nonprofit than any other volunteer management practice studied. Those organizations with a budget of under $100,000 a year do not differ from organizations spending upwards of $500,000, but in larger organizations the likelihood of awards ceremonies is very high. Smaller organizations may rely more on personal relationships, and small group recognition including a simple "thank you," whereas larger organizations have both the need and wherewithal to organize special events for their volunteers.

The type of volunteer involvement makes a big difference, too. Irrespective of size, nonprofits with few volunteers who average few contact hours with the nonprofit are considerably less likely to host formal recognition activities. In contrast, and not surprisingly, nonprofits with many volunteers who collectively contribute many contact hours (at least 50 total hours in a typical week) are substantially more likely to host such activities. Falling in between are organizations with few volunteers who contribute many hours and organizations with many volunteers who contribute few hours, with the latter being somewhat more likely to host recognition ceremonies. These findings reinforce the notion that recognition ceremonies are most popular among organizations that need an official way to show appreciation for their volunteers when the size of the volunteer base makes personal thank yous impractical.

Do recognition activities help to retain volunteers? Yes, absolutely. When we take into account such things as the size of the nonprofit and the amount of funds it has for support of volunteers, we found that recognition activities have the largest positive effect on retention of any of the volunteer management practices we asked about in the survey.

Training and Professional Development for Volunteers

Volunteers conduct a vast array of activities in North America's nonprofit sector. The range of direct service volunteer activities is most visible and almost too numerous to count. Less obvious to the casual observer, volunteers also work in service rolls that do not bring them into contact with clients, members, or the general public. Others work in internal administration, sometimes copying and filing, sometimes keeping the computers or financial systems running, and sometimes running the whole show. Others work in an external administrative role, raising funds and serving as the public face of the organization, including board members, who merit a whole different book on volunteer management. Whether volunteers are working in one or another area of service or administration, their duties can range from simple and ancillary to complex and central to the organization's operations. Complex, central involvement taps into McGregor's Theory Y motivations to be involved in higher-order organizational tasks and decision-making. However, involving volunteers in higher-order organizational tasks requires the time, effort, and resources required to adequately train and provide for their professional development.

Figure 2 reveals that training and professional development is fairly common among America's nonprofits, with nearly three in four at least dabbling in the practice. However, only one-quarter of nonprofits that employ volunteers in their operations say that they have adopted the practice to a large degree, suggesting either that a minority are tapping into Theory Y motivations, or that too few are adequately preparing their higher-order volunteers for their organizational tasks. Those dabbling "to some degree" possibly have a haphazard approach to the preparation of their volunteers for their assignments, some of which may not require much sophisticated training. Professional development may be rare in those cases, too, which might explain why so many nonprofits say they have only adopted the practice to some degree.

The likelihood of providing training and professional development for volunteers is only loosely connected with the size of organizations. Only when budgets exceed $1 million does volunteer training become more prevalent. A deciding factor appears to be the number of hours that volunteers spend with the organization. Regardless of the number of volunteers the nonprofit has, it is less likely to provide training when the number of volunteer hours is low overall. Conversely, training is more likely where volunteering represents a critical mass of at least 50 hours in a typical week, making it a more worthwhile investment for the nonprofit.

Does training and professional development lead to retention of volunteers? Yes. As with recognition activities, the adoption of training and professional development practices yields a positive influence on retention, independent of the influence of other practices and organizational characteristics. This finding reinforces the value of Theory Y approaches to motivation, in contrast to the Theory X approach of keeping volunteers away from vital organizational tasks and decisions.

Screening Volunteers and Matching to Assignments

If the prevailing wisdom is to be believed, too many volunteers are matched to tasks that do not hold their attention: too little or too much personal interaction, too little or too much responsibility, too little or too much time involved. As suggested by both Maslow's Hierarchy of Needs and Herzberg's motivator and hygiene factors, different people are motivated by different things, depending on where they are in life. Assigning a volunteer to a necessary organizational task might resonate with the volunteer, or it might not. Assigning a volunteer to her or his ideal task might meet the needs of the organization, or it might not. Volunteer retention is a delicate dance: a savvy volunteer administrator is able to cultivate a portfolio of organizational tasks, discern the needs and motivations of individual volunteers, assign people to appropriate tasks, and maintain an atmosphere of equity. No wonder volunteer retention is so difficult!

According to Figure 2, screening is among the most prevalent volunteer management practices, with 45 per cent of charities adopting the practice to some degree, and nearly that many again dabbling in the practice to some extent. The survey item actually read, "screening procedures to identify suitable volunteers, and to match them with appropriate tasks or jobs," so both screening and matching are covered here. Dabbling may indicate screening without matching, or matching without screening, or simply an as-needed approach to both. Whatever the situation, volunteer administrators across the country at least recognize that a match of skills and aspirations with organizational tasks is a best practice.

Except for being more common, the practice of screening and matching volunteers to appropriate assignments varies similarly with training and professional development opportunities for volunteers. That is, larger organizations are more likely to engage in screening and matching, although smaller organizations are hard to differentiate from medium-sized ones. Screening is more common among organizations with a critical mass of volunteer hours, and thereby less frequent among organizations where volunteer hours are thin. Interestingly, screening and matching is most prevalent among organizations with both a lot of volunteers (at least 50 over the course of the year) and at least 50 collective volunteer hours over the course of a typical week. Whereas we might expect that screening and matching might be most challenging among organizations that must cater to the needs of a large number of volunteers, it is precisely among this class of nonprofits where screening and matching returns the greatest dividends. In these cases, volunteer administrators have a lot of volunteers that they can screen into specific jobs, satisfying either the task needs of the organization or the motivational needs of the volunteer, and hopefully both.

Does the practice of screening and matching with appropriate tasks lead to retention of volunteers? Yes. Screening and matching has an equal positive influence when compared with the practice of training and providing professional development for volunteers, all else equal.

This finding both reflects the earliest content theories of motivation (for example, Maslow, Herzberg) and suggests that some volunteer administrators have been able to use this practice to their advantage. When volunteer administrators can meet both organizational task needs and individual volunteer motivation needs, we all win.

Regular Supervision and Communication with Volunteers

Far and away, the most common volunteer management practice is supervision and communication. Two out of three nonprofits that use volunteers in their operations lay claim to a "great degree" of supervision and communication with their volunteers, with almost all the rest saying that they have adopted the practice to some degree. The practice seems important in light of popular accounts of volunteers leaving their positions and organizations because they feel out of the loop. Properly executed, supervision and communication should at least cater to those volunteers who are motivated by clear and simple tasks.

Because the practice of supervision and communication is so common, we observe little variation across types of organizations. Size does not matter — small and large organizations are equally likely to report adoption of this practice. However, consistent with the three practices described previously, supervision and communication is more common among nonprofits with volunteers that collectively work at least 50 hours in a typical week. Regardless of the number of volunteers, nonprofits with less reliance on volunteer labour (in terms of number of hours) are also less likely to report the need for regular supervision and communication. Conceivably, where contact with volunteers is thin, less formal supervision and communication is required for carrying out tasks.

Does regular supervision and communication with volunteers lead to retention? We were surprised to find that it does not. In fact, those nonprofits that adopted the practice to a large degree tended to have *lower* volunteer retention rates. Higher retention rates are found when supervision and communication is adopted only to some degree or not at all. Though surprising, the finding is consistent with both Maslow's and Herzberg's recognition that motivations can range from physiological to self-actualization, or from hygiene to motivator. Whereas supervision and communication might appeal to basic and extrinsic motivations, it may be off-putting to volunteers who seek higher-order work, responsibility, and advancement. When supervision is too tight, volunteers seeking to meet these higher-order ("motivator") needs may look for another opportunity to use their skills. We do not suggest that charities stop supervising and communicating with their volunteers. Nonetheless, we believe that a good volunteer administrator must be aware and recognize when supervision and communication may be stifling the contributions of their most valuable assets.

Other Volunteer Management Practices

Figure 2 notes the prevalence of adoption of other best practices in volunteer administration, namely the provision of liability coverage or insurance protection for volunteers, the regular collection of information on volunteer numbers and hours, written policies and job descriptions for volunteers, annual measurement of the impacts of volunteers, and training for paid staff in working with volunteers. Adoption of these practices varies, but is more or less in line with the variation in the other practices described above. One thing that sets them apart is that none of them are statistically associated with retention of volunteers. That is, whether or not or how much a non-profit has adopted one of these volunteer management practices has no influence on whether it retained all, some, or none of its volunteers the following year.

Another thing that sets them apart is that none of these practices are related to the motivations of volunteers. Rather, these "other" volunteer management practices are primarily concerned with the managerial or communications functions of the nonprofit. If volunteers are concerned about these things at all, they are nonetheless not motivating forces for whether they stay committed to an organization or not. The nonprofit organization may need to carry out these tasks for liability, financial, accountability, and other reasons. To the extent that volunteer motivation and retention are critical issues in your organization, you should devote time and resources to the best practices we have discussed previously.

Investment in Volunteer Resources and Retention of Volunteers

Organizational *capacity* is a term that gets thrown around a lot, but the meaning is not always clear. We think of *volunteer management capacity* as not only the ability and willingness to adopt appropriate management strategies like the ones we described in the previous section, but also the ability and willingness of the nonprofit organization to invest in volunteer management personnel (Hager and Brudney, 2008). Too often, volunteer administration gets short shrift when money is tight. Even when resources are available, too many directors and board members do not recognize the importance of making proper investments in the people and processes necessary to recruit, engage, and retain volunteers.

We asked our nonprofit survey respondents if the lack of adequate funds for supporting volunteer involvement was a big problem, small problem, or not a problem at all. Most (40 per cent) reported "not a problem," which is either good news or an indication that many nonprofits are comfortable with their low levels of support for management of volunteers. Fewer (32 per cent) reported a small problem with adequate funds, and fewer again (28 per cent) reported a big problem. The kicker is that organizations that report a lack of adequate funds for supporting volunteer involvement have a significantly lower volunteer retention rate. Conversely, retention is higher in those organizations where funding is not a problem. Investment in volunteer management capacity pays tangible dividends in terms of sustaining volunteers.

Hiring a full-time volunteer administrator is crucial for big organizations with a large and varied volunteer base. However, our study revealed that only 62 per cent of charities that engage volunteers have a paid staff volunteer administrator. Of those, the typical volunteer administrator spends only 30 per cent of her or his time on the job on volunteer administration, suggesting that volunteer management is not the primary duty for many who are charged with the task. That said, our study revealed that the amount of time that a paid volunteer administrator spends on volunteer management is unrelated to retention.

By contrast, we also learned that many nonprofits were successfully carrying out their volunteer management tasks *with* volunteers. As nonprofits become more bureaucratized, staff members sometimes get isolated from the passion of the cause. Volunteers, however, can be effective spokespersons, conveying passion and encouraging trust among other volunteers. We asked nonprofits about the extent to which they use volunteers to recruit other volunteers. We learned that employing volunteers this way has one of the greatest positive impacts on retention of all the factors we studied. So, while we believe that investment in paid staff is an important dimension of volunteer management capacity, we also emphasize the value that volunteers bring to an effective recruitment and management effort.

Organizational Factors: Beyond Our Control?

What kind of organization fares better in volunteer retention, smaller ones or bigger ones? Bigger organizations tend to have more volunteer management capacity and a greater variety of placement options, so maybe we should expect that they would do better on retention. However, this turns out not to be the case. Our study indicates that retention of volunteers is negatively related to size, meaning that retention tends to fall as total organizational expenditures rise. The survey cannot tell us exactly why this is the case, but we can imagine several possibilities, especially in light of the motivation theories we discussed in the first half of this chapter. Smaller charities tend to have fewer volunteers, which means that volunteer administrators can spend more time on individual relationships. Volunteers in smaller nonprofits may tend to be more involved in the operations of the organization, especially when the organization has very few or even no paid staff. That kind of involvement and responsibility is exactly the kind of motivation that some volunteers seek. Small organizations can use this aspect to their advantage. Larger organizations cannot get small, but they can pursue innovations that allow volunteers to feel like they are valued and involved. When volunteers feel like they are just one more number being counted for a grant report, they will find something else to occupy their time.

Nonprofits also have marginal control over the kinds of people who choose to volunteer with them. Hospitals tend to attract older volunteers, and they sometimes struggle to attract younger people. Younger people flock to environmental causes, but organizations in this domain often struggle in their appeals to older people. Most nonprofits recognize that their cause resonates with a particular group of people, so they build their messages and systems to appeal to those particular donors and volunteers. We learned from our study that retention can be a special struggle for nonprofits that rely on young volunteers. We asked our survey respondents what proportion of their volunteers were under age 24. Far and away, this factor proved to be the strongest predictor of retention and loss of volunteers; as the percentage of young volunteers increased in an organization, the retention rate tended to plummet. Conversely, nonprofits that rely more on older volunteers (well, in our study, over 24-years-old) reported higher retention rates. Why might this be? We suspect that the strength of this finding has to do with the fact that younger people are newer to work life, their life circumstances often change season-ally, and their roots in the community are less deep than older volunteers. Consequently, they are less likely to maintain relationships with the charities with which they volunteer. Volunteer administrators might not be able to change the character of their volunteer base, but knowing how their volunteer base tends to approach volunteering can help them to devise better strategies for recruitment and retention.

Lastly, we return to the central concept of volunteer management capacity. Adoption of relevant management practices and support for the volunteer administrator come only when the board and top management team of any nonprofit organization recognize the value that volunteers bring to their organization. They then vote with their budget decisions; nonprofits that value volunteers also tend to understand the need to invest in volunteer management capacity. Nonprofits that do not value their volunteers do not invest in volunteer administration and the management support necessary to insure that volunteers have a good experience.

In a way this process reinforces the self-fulfilling prophecy expressed in McGregor's Theory Y and Theory X that we discussed in the first half of the chapter. When organizations appreciate the self-motivation and self-direction of volunteers to do good work for the agency as in Theory Y, they take steps to support them through building volunteer management capacity. As a result, these organizations are able to elicit and sustain stronger volunteer involvement, which in turn encourages them to continue to provide a sound foundation for volunteer management. By contrast, when nonprofit organizations do not value volunteers but consider them an add-on or do not trust them to take on central work activities as in McGregor's Theory X, they fail to build volunteer management capacity. As a consequence, these organizations are unable to successfully recruit, serve, and retain volunteers, an unfortunate result that further (and falsely) persuades them that volunteers are not worth the effort.

We asked our study respondents about a variety of limitations that they might have encountered in the development of their volunteer programs. Among these questions, we asked if indifference or resistance on the part of paid staff or board members toward volunteers was a big problem, small problem, or not a problem at all. The good news is that only one in six of the nonprofit organizations witnessed such behaviour: 3 per cent reported a big attitude problem in their organization, and another 14 per cent reported a small problem. The rest of the news is that the organizations with indifference or resistance toward volunteers also tended to be the ones with lower volunteer retention rates. On one hand, we expect that volunteers pick up on that resistance and do not stick around where they are not appreciated. On the other hand, we know from the study data that the nonprofits that resist volunteers are the same ones that do not invest in volunteer management practices or volunteer administrators. With little support, no wonder volunteers leave.

Figure 3 depicts what we call the "benefit circle" of volunteer involvement. When nonprofits recognize benefits emanating from volunteer involvement, they invest in volunteer management capacity. Investments in volunteer management capacity lead to greater benefits from volunteers. The circle continues around and around. The circle can be reinforcing when organizations recognize and appreciate what volunteers can do for them, with appropriate support in volunteer management capacity. It can also cycle in the opposite direction when organizations cut back on volunteer management capacity or begin to question the value of volunteer involvement. Part of your job as a volunteer administrator is to keep the benefit circle positive and reinforcing.

**Figure 3: The Reinforcing Cycle of Investments
in and Benefits from Volunteers**

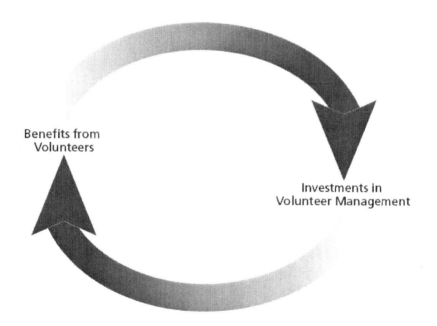

Benefits from
Volunteers

Investments in
Volunteer Management

CONCLUSION

This chapter considered why people are motivated in the workplace and what strategies nonprofits can take to tap into those motivations for purposes of working with and retaining volunteers. Psychologists provide us with a long list of ideas and explanations about why people do what they do, and these sources of motivation apply to volunteers. However, knowing that volunteer motivations range from intrinsic to extrinsic is only a beginning to understanding your volunteers. Knowing that some volunteers want to relax while others want and need to be more involved with higher-order planning and management functions provides only an educated first step. The next practical step is to use your understanding of human workplace motivations as a basis for considering the needs of your volunteers and the tasks of the organization, to plan and think strategically about your recruitment activities, administrative processes, and retention practices.

True, not every volunteer is interested in a long-term relationship, and not every nonprofit is geared toward retention of volunteers. However, if sustaining volunteer involvement is a priority for your organization, there is no substitute for your best efforts to match a volunteer's motivations with the tasks available. Remember that the volunteer has a thousand other options about how to spend his or her time. If you cannot match motivations with tasks, the volunteer will keep looking for other ways to connect to the fragmented society. When you do make a match, you take one very real step toward reconnecting people to a civil society.

REFERENCES

Bureau of Labor Statistics. Press Release: January 10, 2007. *Volunteering in the United States, 2006.* Washington, DC: United States Department of Labor.

Corporation for National and Community Service. (2007a). *Issue brief: Volunteer retention.* CNCS: Washington, DC.

Corporation for National and Community Service. (2007b). *Keeping baby boomers volunteering: A research brief on volunteer retention and turnover.* CNCS: Washington, DC.

Eisner, David, Grimm, Jr., Robert T, Maynard, Shannon, & Washburn, Susannah. (2009). The new volunteer workforce. *Stanford Social Innovation Review, Winter*, 32-37.

Farkas, Karen. (2009, June 21). Plant closing takes toll: Ramp traffic slows to a crawl. *Plain Dealer*, pp. B1, B3.

Hager, Mark A., & Brudney, Jeffrey L. (2004). *Volunteer management practices and retention of volunteers*. Washington, DC: The Urban Institute.

Hager, Mark A., & Brudney, Jeffrey L. (2008). Management capacity and retention of volunteers (chapter 1). In M. Liao-Troth (Ed.), *Challenges in volunteer management* (pp. 9-27). Charlotte, NC: Information Age Publishing.

Halachmi, Arie, & van der Krogt, Theo. (2005). The role of the manager in employee motivation. In Stephen E. Condrey (Ed.), *Handbook of human resource management in government* (2nd ed.) (pp. 469-498). San Francisco: Jossey-Bass.

Little, Helen. (1999). *Volunteers: How to get them. How to keep them.* Naperville, IL: Panacea Press.

McCurley, Steve, & Lynch, Rick. (2005). *Keeping volunteers: A guide to retention*. Olympia, WA: Fat Cat Publications.

Rainey, Hal G. (2003). *Understanding and managing public organizations* (3rd ed.). San Francisco: Jossey-Bass.

UPS Foundation. (1998). *Managing volunteers: A report from United Parcel Service*. Atlanta, GA: UPS Foundation.

Chapter 8

MEETING MANAGEMENT

Melissa Eystad
World Spirit Consulting

Meetings are indispensable when you don't want to do anything.

~John Kenneth Galbraith

INTRODUCTION

Seldom does a work day pass without a Volunteer Administrator attending an organizational or community meeting, planning a committee meeting or focus group, or leading a meeting as a chairperson. Most action in voluntary efforts, as well as business and government and other social settings, occurs as a result of a group of people working together to solve problems, make decisions and determine acts to be carried out. Why then does the average person dislike going to meetings? Why do so many people declare meetings a waste of their time? Why is there such a lack of preparation for and participation in the meeting by those in attendance?

There are approximately 11 million meetings held in the United States every week. Many reviews and surveys reveal that meetings dominate workers' and managers' time and yet are considered to be costly, unproductive and dissatisfying. Studies show that meetings are essential and that the number of meetings and their duration has been steadily increasing. Surveys of managers and knowledge workers reveal that they spend between 25 per cent and 80 per cent of their time in meetings, suggesting that meetings are an important part of one's working life. Estimates of meeting expenses range from costs of $30 million to over $100 million per year to losses between $54 million and $3.7 billion annually! (Romano and Nunamaker, 2001, p. 13). Estimate a meeting's cost by taking the average hourly rate of participating staff and volunteers, and multiplying it by the number of people at the meeting and the length of the meeting. It becomes evident how costly an ineffective meeting is to a nonprofit. Voluntary organizations must ensure the time spent in meetings by staff and volunteers directly contributes to their ability to achieve their mission.

This chapter will describe ways in which the volunteer administrator can design and lead effective meetings and be a more productive participant in meetings.

CONSIDERATIONS WHEN PLANNING A MEETING

Characteristics of an Effective Meeting

There are basic characteristics of an effective meeting that lead to dynamic and productive results. They include:

- clear purpose and goals for the meeting;

- the appropriate participants;

- timed agenda is distributed in advance;

- key background information is shared in advance, with assignments as appropriate or needed;

- meeting is effectively facilitated;

- meeting concludes with summary, action steps, assignments and deadlines; and

- written meeting minutes or notes are disseminated as soon as possible.

A study measuring meeting effectiveness suggests the following are important processes leading to effective meetings: open communication, focus on tasks, thorough exploration of options, analysis of decision consequences, action planning, adherence to the agenda and time schedule, and leader impartiality (Nixon and Littlepage, 1992, p. 367).

Determining the Need for a Meeting

Why a meeting? Too often people call a meeting without a clear idea about what needs to be accomplished. Perhaps a meeting is not necessary.

> Avoid a meeting if the same information could be covered in a memo, e-mail or brief report. One of the keys to having more effective meetings is differentiating between the need for one-way information dissemination and two-way information sharing. To disseminate information you can use a variety of other communication media, such as sending an e-mail or posting the information on your company's intranet. By remembering to ask yourself, "Is a meeting the best way to handle this?" you'll cut down on wasted meeting time and restore your group's belief that the meetings they attend are necessary.

(SMART Technologies ULC, 2004.)

Good reasons to hold a meeting can include:

• the need for a variety of opinions and perspectives to creatively develop a plan, project or solution to a problem;

• the stakeholder group interaction is key to accomplishing the goals;

• it is the most time-effective option;

• the topic is complex and there is a need for information and explanation; and/or

• superiors require the meeting.

Choosing the Right Meeting Type and Format

There are a number of ways people get together to discuss topics and make decisions. The type of meeting and format follows what is considered to be the most effective and efficient use of time as well as the most appropriate process through which to achieve the meeting's goals. The following are some familiar meeting types and their purpose:

1. **Briefing** — a meeting at which detailed information or instructions are given, with possibly some time for questions.

2. **Business meeting** — traditional business model of eight to ten people sitting around a table with a chairperson or facilitator at the head leading the meeting.

3. **Retreat** — usually a multi-day meeting of a department or work team for the purpose of long-range planning, team-building or renewal. Often held offsite in non-work surroundings.

4. **Consultation meeting** — the act of consulting or conferring; deliberation of two or more persons on some matter, with the goal a decision.

5. **Review and Evaluation meeting** — purpose is to present results, collect information and exchange knowledge and experiences for future efforts.

6. **Stand Up Meeting** — a team, department or other small group agrees to gather at a certain time in a certain place each day to quickly discuss and agree on specific actions to move their work forward.

7.   **Staff Meeting** — one type of meeting that tends to be very ineffective and dreaded by attendees is the staff meeting. Typically, they are for check-in and information-sharing, are held on a regular schedule and not called when there is a need. If you want to have staff meetings that are effective in meeting the goals of building team, solving problems and generating ideas, you should keep them short (an hour or less), focused positively, have reports be no longer than five to ten minutes, and have them include time for skill development, information from an outside speaker, and/or brainstorming.

Selecting and Inviting Meeting Attendees

Charlie Hawkins pointed out in *Public Relations Quarterly* (Fall 1997, p. 33) that the most important personnel to invite are those people who can best achieve the objective of the meeting.

The success of any meeting depends on who is there. There is a saying often used that illustrates this important point — "the world is run by those who show up." Here are some suggestions from meeting expert Steve Kaye for The Effective Admin website that will help you decide who best to include:

1.   Invite only people who can contribute to the meeting. Observers who have nothing to add can disrupt the process.

2.   Avoid filling the meeting with allies as a show of force. This intimidates your "opponent," which can result in counter attacks, retaliation, or false cooperation.

3.   Avoid inviting people because they would feel offended if left out. A meeting is a business activity, not a party. You can always ask the person to choose between watching others work in a meeting or being left to work on tasks that contribute to raises and promotions.

4.   Be sure to invite the stakeholder (the person who owns the issue). This person is a valuable resource in finding solutions.

5.   Make sure the opponents to issues attend your meetings. They can help you find equitable solutions that they will support. Without them, any results that you develop are likely to prove useless.

6.   Invite key participants with minor roles to only the part of the meeting where they can contribute. Schedule these parts of the agenda at the beginning of the meeting or when you resume after a break.

7.   Invite spectators only for good reasons. For example, you may invite a new employee to learn about an issue; you may include members

of other organizations to win empathy for your needs, you may invite
an outsider to catalyze creative thinking.

8. In general, meetings that are held to make plans, seek solutions, or
reach agreements work best when eight to twelve people attend.

9. Any number of people can attend parties, social meetings, lectures,
or demonstrations.

In "The Training Clipboard" e-newsletter, Morris Taylor says
there are also a number of strategies to get people to attend your
meetings on time. They include: scheduling meetings to begin at odd
times; always starting on time, no matter who is missing; closing the
door when the meeting begins; sending out the meeting agenda in
advance and beginning with your most important business; placing
topics that are of particular interest to potential latecomers at the top of
the agenda; and speaking privately to frequent offenders.

Finding the Appropriate Setting and Logistics

For an in-person meeting, a successful event requires the appropriate length, location, space, environment, room set-up and other
details. The wrong approach to any of these can derail the most well-
crafted agenda and meeting process. How do you determine the right
setting and time for your meeting? The following partial list of
questions includes some of the key elements that should be considered
when setting up your meeting:

- Meeting location — Where will attendees be coming from? Is the
location convenient and easy to find? Parking easily available? Is
there a logical place to hold the meeting given the nature of the
topic?

- Time of day — Will you get better attendance in an early
morning meeting? Does the group typically prefer the lunch time-
slot? If you schedule the meeting for later in the day, will people
have difficulty getting away from their responsibilities to attend?
Will they be more mentally fatigued than earlier in the day?

- Length of meeting — The agenda drives the time needed for the
meeting, but in general shorter is better (one to one-and-a-half
hours). If the meeting goes longer than two hours, be sure to
build in breaks periodically.

- Space needs and room set-up — Do you have adequate table
space and comfortable chairs? Are participants able to easily see
and hear each other? Is there wall space for flipchart pages if

needed? A white board? Are there AV capabilities in the space? Is the room relatively quiet so outside sounds won't disrupt the meeting? Are restroom facilities available? Will any of the attendees need special accommodations for physical challenges?

- Lights and temperature — Does the room have good lighting? Is it adjustable for presentations and speakers? While it is difficult to account for everyone's room temperature preferences, if necessary does the room have a thermostat that can be adjusted if the majority of attendees are not comfortable?

- Food and refreshments — Does the group typically provide refreshments at meetings? Will there minimally be water, coffee and tea? Who will be responsible for ensuring refreshments are available? Is there a budget for food? How much should be provided?

- Technology needs — Will there be any presentations requiring equipment such as projectors, laptops, screens, microphones, *etc*.? Will a speakerphone be required?

A note about using technology to conduct meetings: Today there are a number of technology-based options for having real-time meetings with people who cannot be physically present in the room. The most commonly used is likely the teleconference or audio-conference, which is the live exchange and interaction among several persons remote from one another but linked by a telecommunications system. There are also other web-based meeting formats and tools in which people can interact in real time using e-mail programs such as Live Meeting, or Skype™, which lets you make calls over the internet to anyone else who also has the service anywhere in the world, and has video and instant chat functions.

If you will need to conduct the meeting using technology to connect with remote participants, additional planning time will be needed to ensure those participants can fully contribute to the meeting.

DESIGNING THE AGENDA

An effective agenda is at the heart of a good meeting. The agenda guides the group through a natural flow of information, discussion, decision-making and determination of future action. In the tipsheet "The Organized Agenda: A Vital Tool for Efficient Meetings" published by the University of Illinois Extension Service, author Ruby Lingle says:

A well-prepared and organized agenda is an important tool for helping groups hold orderly, efficient meetings. An organized agenda is not thrown together in a few minutes. Thought and planning are necessary to develop an agenda that provides meaningful information but does not become a lengthy narrative document. In addition, a carefully prepared agenda can influence the outcome of a meeting.

If you are responsible for planning the meeting, develop the agenda together with key participants in the meeting. Think of what overall outcome you want from the meeting and what activities need to occur to reach that outcome. The agenda should be organized so that these activities are conducted during the meeting and the goals are accomplished. For a successful meeting:

- Design the agenda so that participants get involved early by having something for them to do right away and so they arrive on time.

- Next to each major topic, include the type of action needed, the type of output expected (decision, vote, action assigned to someone), and time estimates for addressing each topic.

- Ask participants if they will commit to the agenda.

- Keep the agenda posted at all times.

- Unless it is a public meeting (where agendas are typically set and cannot be altered later), do not be rigid; be willing to adapt the meeting agenda if members are making progress in the planning process.

- Think about how you label and describe an event, so people come in with that mindset; it may pay to have a short dialogue around the table to develop a common mindset among attendees, particularly if they include representatives from various cultures.

Identifying and Clearly Stating Meeting Objectives

Writing out the objectives for a meeting helps everyone understand its purpose. It should be included prominently on the agenda and in any communications with attendees prior to the meeting. When the objectives are also posted where they can be seen during the meeting, they keep the group focused. It is helpful to think of a meeting objective as having three ingredients: an action, an outcome, and qualifiers. (Rees, 1991, pp. 93-95). An example of a meeting objective would be, "The purpose of our meeting is to decide what changes should be made to our volunteer screening process."

The more concrete your meeting objectives, the more focused your agenda will be. A second important benefit of having specific objectives for each meeting is that you have a clear measure against which you can evaluate that meeting. Were you successful in meeting the objectives? Why or why not? Is another meeting required? Setting meeting objectives allows you to continuously improve your effective meeting process.

Types of Agendas

An agenda is simply a list of meeting activities in the order in which they are to be taken up, beginning with a call to order and ending with adjournment. It is usually headed with the date, time and location of the meeting, followed by a series of topics outlining the order of the meeting.

Points on a typical agenda may include:

* welcome/open meeting;

* noting absences if needed;

* approving minutes of the previous meeting;

* continuing business from previous meeting if needed;

* a list of specific points to be discussed — this section is where the bulk of the discussion as well as *decisions* in the meeting usually takes place;

* any other new business;

* arranging/announcing details of next meeting; and

* adjourning meeting.

There are a number of agenda formats to consider depending on the goals for the meeting. The two most common formats are described below.

General Basic Agenda

There are many variations of the basic agenda. The agendas below (McLaughlin, 1998) show different approaches to structuring the same board meeting.

Table 1: Comparison of Typical and Strategic Agendas

Exhibit 1 **Typical Board of Directors' Agenda**	Exhibit 2 **Strategic Board of Directors' Agenda**

I.   Executive Director's Report
 	
  A. Information technology plan update
 	
II. Finance Committee Report
 	
  A. Analysis of overall agency profitability
 	
  B. Analysis of new program profitability
 	
  C. Cash flow and investment needed for new program
 	
  D. Consideration of next phase of technology capital investment
 	
  E. Proposed change in insurance agency
 	
III. Nominating Committee Report
 	
  A. New candidates report
 	
IV. Program Committee Report
 	
  A. Documentation of need for new program
	I. Expand Educational Program into East Side
	
	  A. Documentation of need *(Program Committee)*
	
	  B. Analysis of program profitability *(Finance Committee)*
	
	  C. Cash flow and investment needed *(Finance Committee)*
	
	  D. Potential Board member from East Side *(Nominating Committee)*
	
	II. Increase Profitability
	
	  A. Analysis of overall agency profitability *(Finance Committee)*
	
	  B. Proposed change in insurance agency *(Finance Committee)*
	
	III. Develop Information Systems
	
	  A. Discussion of five-year information technology plan *(Executive Director)*
	
	  B. Consideration of next phase of capital investment *(Finance Committee)*

Used with permission, Thomas A. McLaughlin is Vice President of Consulting Services, Nonprofit Finance Fund, and a member of the faculty at the Heller School for Social Policy and Management at Brandeis University. His email address is tom.mclaughlin@nffusa.org.

Consent Agenda

Organizations having a large number of routine matters to approve often save time by use of a *consent agenda*, also called a *consent calendar* or *unanimous consent agenda*. This is a portion of the printed agenda listing matters that are expected to be non-controversial and on which there are likely to be no questions.

Before taking the vote, the chair allows time for the members to read the list to determine if it includes any matters on which they may have a question, or which they would like to discuss or oppose. Any member has a right to remove any item from the consent agenda, in which case it is transferred to the regular agenda so that it may be considered and voted on separately. The remaining items are then unanimously approved *en bloc* without discussion, saving the time that would be required for individual votes (The Standard Code of Parliamentary Procedure, 2000). Examples of items that could be grouped within the consent agenda include committee reports, minor changes in a procedure, routine revisions of a policy, *etc.*

Developing Agenda Topics

The format for an agenda is like an outline, with main topics being listed as main outline headings, and the smaller issues or concerns within a topic forming the sub-headings. Each major heading should have an estimated time-frame so the facilitator and the group have an idea of how long to spend talking about that topic. If a topic is taking longer, the facilitator can ask the group if they want to just work through that one issue and defer the other topics, or set the challenging issue aside for further discussion at the next meeting.

Time-Frame

Meetings expand to fill their space — however long you've set the meeting or a topic for is as long as it will take. Many agenda items do not require the length of time assigned to them, but you must allow adequate time for discussion on more important items. The more you can accomplish ahead of the meeting (providing background, soliciting questions, *etc.*) the more efficiently you can accomplish your meeting goals. Try experimenting with meeting times to see if you can cut two-hour meetings to 90 minutes and still accomplish the objectives.

Distributing the Agenda and Background Information

Typically, the meeting planner will circulate a draft agenda to participants before sending out the final meeting agenda and background materials. This helps to minimize any surprise additions during the meeting that might affect the agenda and length of the meeting and ensures all participants have the opportunity to share any important information that could be key to the meeting's success. At minimum, participants should receive the agenda 24 to 48 hours prior to the meeting.

MEETING FACILITATION

What Makes a Good Meeting Facilitator?

The meeting facilitator's primary role is to achieve the objectives of the meeting by following the agenda and ensuring participants have the opportunity to contribute. An effective meeting leader will:

- Get to know individual participants.
- Follow the agenda — and guide others to do so.
- Actively listen, paraphrase and restate opinions & ideas expressed.
- Summarize key points and discussion.
- Encourage participation and contributions from all.
- Share the spotlight — invite others to lead specific topics/ discussions.
- Be honest about his or her own limitations — and mistakes.
- Control body language.

Setting the Tone and Ground Rules

Meetings that will involve discussion and interaction require ground rules. They ensure that people understand the "terms of engagement" during a meeting. Here is an example of ground rules frequently used by Head Start program teams (HHS/ACF/ACYF/HSB, 1998), but each group and situation may require additions or changes:

- Make decisions by consensus.
- Share all relevant information.

- Explain the reasons behind your statements, questions, and actions.

- Publicly test assumptions and inferences.

- Make statements, then invite questions. Stay focused.

- Discuss the topic thoroughly so everyone has a common understanding.

- Focus on interests, not positions.

- Be specific. Use examples to illustrate key ideas.

- All members are expected to identify and solve problems.

- Challenge opinions you do not agree with without attacking the individual who expresses them.

- Together, design ways of testing disagreements and solutions.

- Maintain a sense of humour.

When to Use Formal Meeting Procedures

Meeting rules simply are prescribed guides for conduct or action during the meeting. Having some kind of rules ensures the wishes of the majority are respected, the interests of the minority acknowledged, and that the meeting is conducted in a fair and equitable manner. You will need to decide which of the following options will work best for your meeting:

1. No rules.

2. Participants review and agree on basic principles or ground rules.

3. Comply with by-laws (or change them).

4. "Roberta's Rules of Order" by Alice Collier Cochran.

5. "Robert's Rules of Order Newly Revised."

6. "The Standard Code of Parliamentary Procedure."

Dealing with Common Challenges and Disruptions

A good meeting manager is adept at minimizing disruptions that interfere with the goals of the meeting. Some common challenges meeting leaders face and tips for handling them include:

- Latecomers — welcome and introduce them briefly, and ask them to connect with another participant at a break or after the meeting for an update on what they missed.

- Early leavers — at the meeting opening, ask if any participants need to leave before the meeting concludes. If so, and they are important to some of the agenda items, you may want to rearrange the agenda to accommodate them (although ideally you would have gotten that information from them when the agenda was circulated for review and comment). Also ask that they check with other meeting participants following the meeting to see what happened in the rest of the meeting.

- Side "meetings" — these are simply rude behaviour. Ask those conversing if they have any questions or information to share with the group so the meeting can stay on schedule.

- Cell phones and Personal Digital Assistants (PDAs) — at the beginning of the meeting, request that participants either turn them off, or if they must be available for a call or e-mail, to set them on vibrate.

- Domineering personalities — these can be dealt with by establishing ground rules about disagreement, giving the domineering person a specific role in the meeting, requesting a separate time to deal with issues that are not specifically related to the goals of the meeting, *etc*.

Being an Effective Meeting Participant

While much attention is given to being a meeting leader or facilitator, it is equally crucial to be an effective meeting participant. Careers have been made and broken by how well a person is perceived to not only lead, but participate, in meetings. To make the best contribution and impression as a meeting participant, adhere to these good practices (Lindsay, 2009):

- Be on time

- Avoid using mobile phones — if you must take a call or send an e-mail, leave the room

- Come prepared — read materials ahead of time

- Listen

- Take effective notes — do not try to record everything that is said; stick to key points

- Make it effective — stay on topic and contribute

CREATING A MEETING RECORD

Types of Meeting Records

Whether you call it the meeting record, minutes, or notes, there should be a written record for every meeting that documents at minimum what was decided and actions taken. While a written record of nonprofit board and committee meetings procedures is legally required, it is advisable to have some documentation of any meeting where work is being done. There are really just two types of meeting minutes: (1) verbatim, and (2) summary. The differences between the two are in the amount of detail recorded from the meeting.

What should be included in the meeting record or minutes? In the PTO Today website article "Meeting Minutes: Just the Facts," author Sandra Pfau Englund describes the four basic types of information that should be included in minutes:

1. Time, date, and location of the meeting.

2. The fact that proper prior notice of the meeting was given or that notice was waived by those attending the meeting.

3. Who was in attendance (names of board members or the approximate number of people attending) and whether a quorum was present.

4. The official actions taken by the meeting participants (motions made and approved or defeated).

Not required in minutes are:

- Names of those who make and second motions.

- The vote (number voting for and against) for each motion.

- Detail of the debate that occurred regarding each motion.

A common practice in contemporary meetings is to also include action items, person assigned, and completion or reporting date.

The minutes recorder is ideally someone who is not actively involved in the meeting; however, that is not always possible. He or she should come prepared with attendee list, and an agenda with space to make bullet notes.

Dissemination

All too frequently, meeting minutes are sent far after the meeting or just prior to a subsequent meeting with the agenda. Minutes should be completed as quickly as possible following the meeting (within a day or two), reviewed by the meeting chair for accuracy and then disseminated either by mail or electronically to meeting attendees. This will help ensure an accurate record of the meeting and serve as a reminder to participants of assignments they may have received during the meeting.

ASSESSING MEETING EFFECTIVENESS

When, Why and How to Evaluate Your Meeting

When and why should you bother to evaluate a meeting? In the online Free Management Library's "Basic Guide to Effective Meetings," Carter McNamara notes how often people will complain about a meeting being a complete waste of time, but after the meeting. He advises facilitators to get feedback during the meeting so you can adjust during the meeting.

Evaluating a meeting only at the end of the meeting is usually too late to do anything about participants' feedback. Try this:

- Every couple of hours, conduct 5-10 minutes "satisfaction checks". In a round-table approach, quickly have each participant indicate how they think the meeting is going.

- Leave 5-10 minutes at the end of the meeting to evaluate the meeting; don't skip this portion of the meeting.

- Have each member rank the meeting from 1-5, with 5 as the highest, and have each member explain their ranking.

- Have the chief executive rank the meeting last.

You might also want to do an oral or written evaluation post-meeting depending on the importance of the meeting. The following is an example of the kind of information you could gather:

1.   Did the meeting achieve its objective(s)?

2.   Was the meeting time managed effectively?

3.   How well did the meeting leader manage interpersonal relationships? What could be improved?

4.   What aspects of the meeting could have been better?

5.   Was everyone encouraged to actively participate in the meeting?

RESOURCES FOR EFFECTIVE MEETINGS

There are many publications and online tools and resources available on the topic of meeting management. A sampling of helpful resources is listed here as a starting place:

*   **Free Management Library** <www.managementhelp.org> — comprehensive resources regarding the leadership and management of for-profit or nonprofit organizations.

*   **Meeting Wizard** — free web-based meeting scheduler <www.meeting-wizard.com>.

*   **National Association of Parliamentarians** — <http://www.parliamentarians.org>.

*   **MyCommittee** — <www.mycommittee.com> is a free tool to manage committees and/or meetings. Allows users to create meeting agendas and minutes, share and work together on documents and other committee tasks, add and reply to comments, communicate with members and other contacts.

*   **Suite 101 – Nonprofit Management** — <http://nonprofitmanagement.suite101.com/general>.

*   **Skype™** — <www.skype.com> is a free software application that allows users to make voice calls, instant messaging and video-conferencing over the Internet.

CONCLUSION

As a volunteer administrator, your skill in planning and facilitating effective meetings will be critical not only to how you are perceived by your superiors, work peers, volunteers and professional colleagues, but also will reflect your own confidence, professionalism and competence in your getting important work accomplished for your organization and its mission. Continuous practice, skill-building and constructive feedback will help you achieve excellence in meeting management. The key to planning effective meetings is to be intentional and clear about your purpose and goals and to design the best process to reach those goals. Make the most of your time investment in meetings.

REFERENCES

Cochran, Alice Collier. (2004). *Roberta's rules of order: Sail through meetings for stellar results without the gavel.* New York: Jossey-Bass.

Englund, Sandra Pfau. (2008). Meeting minutes: Just the facts. Available at http://www.PTOToday.com.

Hawkins, Charlie. (1997). First aid for meetings. *Public Relations Quarterly, 42*(33).

Kaye, Steve. (2010). Whom do you invite to a meeting? *The Effective Admin.* Available at http://www.admin-ezine.com/meeting-attendance.htm.

Lindsay, Peter. (2009). *Meeting basics: Attending a meeting.* [Slideshare presentation]. Retrieved from http://www.slideshare.net/triviality/attend-a-meeting-1003127.

Lingle, Ruby. (2002). The organized agenda: A vital tool for efficient meetings. *Local Government Information and Education Network Fact Sheet.* University of Illinois Extension Service.

McLaughlin, Thomas A. (1998, March). The strategic agenda. *The Nonprofit Times.*

McNamara, Carter. (2010). Basic guide to conducting effective meetings. Retrieved from http://managementhelp.org/misc/mtgmgmnt.htm.

Microsoft® Office Live Meeting is one of a number of commercial subscription-based web conferencing services available.

Nixon, Carol T., & Littlepage, G. (1991). Impact of meeting procedures on meeting effectiveness. *Journal of Business and Psychology, 6*(3).

Rees, Fran. (1991). *How to lead work teams: Facilitation skills* (pp. 93-95). San Francisco: Pfeiffer & Company.

Robert, III, H. M., Evans, W.J., Honemann, D.H., & Balch, T.J. (2000). *Robert's rules of order* (newly rev., 10th ed.). Cambridge, MA: Da Capo Press.

Romano, Jr., N.C., & Nunamaker, Jr., J.F. (2001). Meeting analysis: findings from research and practice. *Proceedings of the 34th Annual Hawaii International Conference on System Sciences*, p. 13.

Skype© is a free software application that allows users to make voice calls, instant messaging and videoconferencing over the Internet.

SMART Technologies ULC. (1998). *Six tips for more effective meetings.* Available at http://www.EffectiveMeetings.com.

Sturgis, Alice. (2001). *The standard code of parliamentary procedure* (4th ed. rev. by American Institute of Parliamentarians). New York: McGraw-Hill.

Taylor, Morris. (2007). Eight strategies to get people to attend meetings on time. *The Training Clipboard.* Available at www.talisman-training.com.

U.S. Department of Health and Human Services (DHHS). (1998). Meeting ground rules. *Job Performance Situations 3-C: Building Essential Skills in Facilitation, Decision-Making, and Communication.* Head Start Moving Ahead Competency-Based Training Program.

Chapter 9

FINANCIAL MANAGEMENT

Marianne Kerr, M.Ed., CVA
University of Alaska Fairbanks

INTRODUCTION

Financial recordkeeping is the foundation of any organization, whether for profit or not for profit. An accountant or bookkeeper analyzes and records every financial transaction using accepted accounting practices. These transactions form a picture of a nonprofit organization that can be presented to stakeholders, funding sources, boards of directors and governmental evaluators. An organization that demonstrates good recordkeeping and sound financial planning conveys a message of trustworthiness and good practices to the public and the community it serves.

Financial reports can include budgets; grant proposals and grants received, private and public income anticipated as well as projected and actual expenses. Each employee in an organization that uses agency funds can expect to be asked to track and report on their income and expenditures. Employees can expect to be accountable for using proper expense codes, following an established budget plan as well as operating a program within established budgetary guidelines.

Staff members are expected to be well acquainted with the overall mission and the goals of the organization. Staff members may be required to state how their program and the volunteers who participate contribute to the overall organizational mission. Staff can also be asked to describe in depth the activities performed to accomplish those goals. Financial reporting is one aspect of contributing to the overall mission. A budget and expenditures help create a picture of what impact the organization is having and what staff members are doing with funds to reach the program's goals.

For volunteer administrators, financial management is a central element in running a successful volunteer program of any size. To be an effective staff member as well as a program leader the volunteer administrator needs to understand all aspects of building program budgets as well as knowing how to project spending and expected income. Understanding how a financial system works is crucial for a volunteer administrator who is expected to recruit volunteers to help expand program services. The terms and procedures for understanding a financial system can seem daunting but learning how to use them as well as how to see the "big picture" of an organization's foundation is helpful for program planning and implementation.

This chapter lays out the basic elements of financial management for volunteer administrators who will be creating budgets for program use as well as using budgets to explain the overall mission and foundation to volunteers and potential contributors. Knowing the language of financial management is helpful not only in building a budget but also in working with financial professionals.

FINANCIAL MANAGEMENT AND FISCAL DEVELOPMENT

A professional accountant or bookkeeper is necessary for an organization to keep good controls over the fiscal foundation. A good system is needed that processes all financial transactions by following standard written policies and procedures. The policies and procedures must cover all aspects of financial management of the nonprofit and are frequently updated. A good standard system means that every organization, whether for profit or nonprofit, will be able to demonstrate the financial picture of the organization in a language that is understood by those who evaluate financial performances. The accounting system of nonprofits is constructed based on an accounting equation in which:

$$ASSETS - LIABILITIES = NET\ ASSETS$$

This equation means that the financial value (net worth) of the organization is equal to what the organization owns (assets) minus what the organization owes (liabilities). Financial statements show how or why the assets, liabilities or net assets change during a time period. The best financial practice systems are designed for the future as well as presenting a picture of the present situation.

The agency's financial statement is a clear picture internally and externally of how the organizational mission is being accomplished. The mission of the organization will be reflected in the programs and the services offered. The budget and how the organization operates fiscally, demonstrate the leadership commitment to providing services that meet the goals of the organization. An evaluation of the budget by a grantor, board member, community member, staff member or a volunteer will give a picture of the commitment to meeting the goals and objectives; in other words, is the money being spent on the right things? A budget will show how much is being spent not only on staff but also on the types of services. A shortage in funding can also illuminate where obstacles in delivering programs will arise.

Volunteers and the volunteer program are part of a nonprofit's financial picture. Volunteer participation and involvement in the programs of the nonprofit can demonstrate the extent of support from the community. The level of volunteer support can also demonstrate the support for the nonprofit mission and how the programs reflect the mission. Volunteer time is also an important monetary contribution to a nonprofit. The value of volunteer time can be computed using a standard measure based on the local economy. Volunteer services can also be assigned a monetary value based on the position and the skill level of volunteers who provide the services and the hours worked. Many non-profit clearinghouses and funding sources use the Independent Sector's value of volunteer time: <http://www.independentsector.org/>. In 2008, the value of an individual's time was set at $20.25 per hour. The value of a volunteer's time has risen steadily since 1980 when it was listed as $7.46 per hour. Another demonstration of community and volunteer support can be with an in-kind contribution rate, that is, volunteer time donated to the nonprofit and assigned an overall value. This in-kind contribution is an important figure to present to stake-holders, grantors, board members (often volunteers also), politicians, and the community at large. The number of volunteers can also be a positive reflection of fundraising, again using the computation of time donated. How the volunteer asset is managed is the responsibility of the volunteer program and the volunteer administrator. An increase in volunteer assets demonstrates a level of support and reflects on the values of the organization and how the goals and objectives reflect the mission.

The importance of understanding the financial operating system of the nonprofit is something every staff member must understand. This can mean learning to fill out a timesheet correctly or how to read a budget as well as the income and expense reports for a program. Financial managers for nonprofits are usually required to prepare monthly and/or yearly financial reports for funders, board members and auditors. Learning how to read a financial report and recognizing where volunteers and volunteer programs impact these reports can benefit a program and also be used for future strategic planning within the program and the organization.

Financial Reports

A financial report is a picture or reflection of how the nonprofit is doing. A financial report can be prepared monthly, yearly, quarterly or other time-frame requested by a board of directors. Generally, in a financial report, there is a totalling of income and expenses. Standard practices can demonstrate how these amounts reflect year-to-date, how they reflect on what was projected for the year, or how they compare to past years. A financial report can be an explanation of where the funding came from and where it has been spent. However, a financial statement is not a prediction of future financial status. Instead, a financial statement reflects what has already happened. A financial statement does not show, for instance, if a deficit is caused by a serious cash flow problem or a funding source that has not contributed funding to date. A deficit is cause to question if there is a problem that may exist into the future.

A financial report should be easily understandable so that an interested person will be able to comprehend the organization's financial picture. It should not be heavily detailed and should embrace all aspects and program activities of the organization.

Figure 1

Monthly/Yearly Financial Statement for XYZ Organization As of September 30th, 2009			
Income	Actual to Date	Planned Budget	% of Budget
Special Grants	0	10,000	0%
Foundation/Corporate Members	9,300	55,000	17%
Individual/Sm Business Members	3,788	20,000	19%
University Employee Giving Campaign	0	250	0%
Subtotal	**13,088**	**85,250**	
Other Income			
Fees	225	250	90%
Donations	40	100	40%
Interest Income	128	250	51%
Subtotal	**393**	**600**	
Total Income	**13,481**	**85,850**	
Expenses			
Facility Rent	5,000	20,000	25%
Travel		12,500	0%
Telephone		30,000	0%
Advertising/Promotion		1,000	0%
Utilities	5,085	7,100	72%
Equipment/Supplies	2,000	10,000	20%
Postage	179	3,000	6%
Printing	1,015	1,500	68%
Mileage		1,000	0%
Copier		1,000	0%
Miscellaneous	209	1,000	21%
Total Expenses	**13,489**	**88,100**	

Financial statements are used to provide information about:

- what the organization owns and what is owes;

- the changes over the time period covered in what the organization owns and what it owes; and

- whether the organization operated at a surplus or a deficit over the period.

What the organization owns and what is owing to it are assets. What the organization owes are liabilities. This liability can include amounts owed to others or a cumulative total of operating expenses that will be spent in the future, such as unpaid salaries or vacation time earned but not taken by staff.

The financial report does not show individual budgets for the organization, instead the budgets are totalled together and will be reflected in the staff salary and benefit totals as well as under program supplies, travel and other daily operating items like telephone, postage and office supplies.

Operating Budgets

A nonprofit financial picture consists of administrative and overall costs as well as budgets for programs and services offered through staff activities. Program budgets are the pieces of the overall financial report. The expenses for the volunteer program will not be detailed in a financial report, but will be grouped with other program expenses. Income is handled in the same manner; donations or fees will be grouped under income categories. In order to track programs such as a volunteer program, a financial manager may provide a monthly income and expense picture to a program manager. Understanding the budget report is a responsibility of nonprofit program managers and staff. As with the financial report for the organization, a program budget and report will show if the program is on track, fulfilling the program goals and will reflect what has happened up to the present time. It is important to create a program budget that will reflect the goals, objectives and activities of the organization and the part that the program will play in fulfilling the mission of the organization.

Figure 2: Example of a Project Budget for a Volunteer Program

One-year projection:

Income:

Membership Dues:	500
Annual Fundraiser:	3000
Grant from XYZ International:	1000
Other: Donation	1200

Total Anticipated Income: 5700

Expenses:

Printing:	825
Copying:	
Equipment Rental:	200
Postage:	350
Subscriptions:	75
Volunteer Appreciation:	500
Travel:	600
Mileage:	250
Telephone:	400
Office Supplies:	1000
Program Supplies:	1500

Total Projected Expenses: 5700

Please note that staff salaries and benefits are not included in this budget. If an agency director asks for those amounts, they can be requested from the financial director, the board of directors treasurer or other financial representative. These amounts are usually included in the overall agency budget rather than a program budget.

Also not included in this program budget are items that may be pro-rated throughout the organization such as facility rental, and overhead expenses such as electricity and use of shared items such as copiers or printers.

If these items are to be included in your program budget, request the financial director to notify you what amount(s) you should include.

Creating a Program Budget

A budget is a financial plan. A program budget, like an organizational budget, will have two main parts — income and expense categories. When asked to build a budget, directions can be to include or not include such costs as:

- staff salary and benefit amounts,

- overhead for the office, as well as

- shared office costs like utilities or office equipment.

Some organizations will handle staff and overhead as separate categories and have program budgets reflect the actual operation of the program activities. If program staff members are instructed to have a balanced budget, this means that income and expense will equal each other. If a program does not charge for services, there will be an expense-only budget created.

In *Bookkeeping for Nonprofits,* Murray Dropkin and James Halpin (2005) acknowledge that,

> Budgeting performs a number of important functions. Effective budgeting helps an organization to accomplish the following:
>
> - Adjust plans, activities, and spending as needed
>
> - Spend money cost effectively
>
> - Reach specific financial goals
>
> - Prevent adverse audit findings
>
> - Avoid incurring disallowed costs or other unnecessary expenses
>
> - Act as a foundation for effective cash flow management. (p. 205)

If there are questions, or questionable items, asking the organization's financial representative is the best practice. The financial professional will have the policies and procedures that have been approved and will understand the big picture and what amounts need to be placed in what categories.

Income

When starting a budget creation, the first category is income. Income can be received in many forms. When money is received into income accounts, the amount is debited to the category.

Cash for sales of items will be reflected in income. This would be cash for program items only and in a final financial report would be reflected in overall sales within the organization. Depending on the organizational structure, sales can also include items sold for fundraising such as a bake sale or sale of handmade items.

Revenue is another term for income and can be interpreted as income from sales and/or services. Revenue can be used as a term to include sales and also fees for services. If a program has workshops, events, classes, *etc.*, and charges attendance fees, the amounts can be included in a revenue account or a separate account for fees or registrations. These categories will be named and defined by the organization's financial professionals. When anticipating revenues within a volunteer program, the volunteer administrator should consult with the person responsible for their organization's financial processes and ensure that revenue is properly recorded and tracked according to organizational procedures. Different sources of income will be placed in different categories, this aids not only in tracking grants or contributions, but also in preparing for an audit or a grant review.

Grants from funders are another item to be placed in the income category, as long as the funds are committed and available to be used. In a budget creation, however, it may be possible to identify funds from grants that are anticipated, as long as noted as such. After completing the income category, the total is noted under the amounts. A budget creation may also ask for the amounts to be spread out over the fiscal period, this also aids the financial professional in projecting income over the course of the year.

Expense

Expense categories are used to show a decrease in income or revenue resulting from a withdrawal of funds, usually for purchases or other costs. When an expense is entered in a financial system the amount is credited to the designated expense category. An expense can be noted as a purchase. The type of purchase will determine the expense category; for instance, program supplies, office supplies, postage and printing costs can all be credited to different expense categories. It is important to understand which category an expense will be credited to and note that it is the correct category listed on the program budget.

Categories in a Budget

Staff whose work includes creating a budget must be familiar with the categories necessary to each budget. Financial professionals within an organization can be expected to assign income and expense categories to each department and instruct staff what items belong in each line item.

Income Categories

The following represent common income categories with an explanation:

- Cash: can be from sales, fees, memberships or any other way designated.

- Fees: can be educational, supplies for a program or class, services provided, equipment provided or ongoing program income. Accounts receivable can also be part of fees and services, that is, money billed but not yet collected.

- Membership: can be a subscription to join the organization or other designation.

- Donations: can be anonymous cash donations, for an endowment or any other designated account.

- Events: can be included as fees or designated as one-time events income.

- Grants: grant budgets as usually kept separate from ongoing, daily workings of an organization. Grant funding must be kept with expenses to report to grantors periodically.

- In-kind: contributions that can be a match for other income. In-kind can also be a monetary value placed on goods or services contributed by individuals, businesses or volunteers.

- Miscellaneous: this can be where one-time income items or unique income that does not fit into other categories will be recorded.

- Investments and Interest: income from investments and deposits.

Categories

The following are common expense categories with an explanation:

- Staff: salary and hourly costs will be noted here. Organizational directors will designate who fills in the staff costs in the budgets.

- Benefits: this covers all organizational benefits for staff, filled in as part of personnel costs.

- Vacation and sick leave: this portion of a budget is done at a director's level as an unpaid expense; it is used as staff members take the time allocated.

- Overhead: this can be lined out as rental, utilities and any other recurring monthly or yearly expenses to maintain the organization's facility.

- Equipment: this category can have a cost limit and items above the cost are put into the capital budget for making large equipment or furniture purchases.

- Office supplies: consumable supplies such as paper, pencils and other operational items.

- Program supplies: supplies to run individual programs that are necessary to accomplish objectives and activities of organizational program.

- Travel: automobile mileage, travel to conferences, meetings and workshops.

- Training: cost of educational, workshop, event registration, can be split into categories for staff job descriptions.

- Printing: cost of professional printing and/or copiers and computer printers.

- Postage: can be split into program designations.

- Telephone: may be one total cost with each program assigned an amount.

- Membership: costs of maintaining and recruiting a membership base.

- Volunteer recognition: can be a stand-alone cost or part of a program cost or part of a membership cost.

- Publicity and public relations: costs for promotion of programs and organization.

- Contractor services: costs for hiring non-employee workers such as website designers, consultants and outside evaluators.

- Publications and subscriptions: magazines and educational resource materials.

- Food: costs for food are usually kept separate since many grants and local funding organizations do not allow their funds to pay for food.

BUILDING A BUDGET

Building a program budget reflects the organization's goals and objectives as part of the overall mission. The mission of the organization has been approved by the board of directors and the organization's budget and all the program budgets reflect anticipated steps to accomplish that mission. A budget illustrates that the organization's funds are being spent properly and cost-effectively. Therefore, develop the budget based on a strategic plan set in place for a specified time in the future. A program budget can be continually monitored to see if the activities and objectives are compatible with program costs. Dropkin and Halpin (2005, p. 156) state that:

> Well prepared budgets have other benefits too. They let everyone in the organization know:
>
> - The goals to be achieved
> - The work to be done to reach the goals
> - The resources (people and things) needed to get the work done
> - The resources available for getting the work done
> - The time table and deadlines for getting specific work done
> - The individuals responsible and accountable for doing the required work.

Directions for creating a budget within an organization will be given, usually from the director or the financial professionals. Directions provide answers for categories such as: including or excluding staff salary and benefits; expense and income categories to be used; and account numbers for categories. Some organizations will give a set amount for a budget and ask staff members to explain how it will be used, or a staff member can create a budget based on need and plans and justify the amounts listed. In either case, it is best to have the budget amount be as realistic as possible. If the budget is based on past expenditures, the justification can be easily explained. If there are new amounts being requested, staff members may be asked to justify the amounts and provide a more detailed reasoning for the request. If there is a need for new equipment or furnishings, these are capital expenses and are often included in another portion or the organizational budget. These must be justified and are often kept separate from the operating budget.

Staff who are involved in creating a budget for a department or program are expected to understand the organizational mission and also how it relates to the program activities. Just as an organizational budget involves all departments and programs in the process, a program budget must be a result of collaboration of staff involved in the activities to be carried out. Having a work plan for a time period into the future, or a strategic plan will go hand in hand with a budget. When a yearly work plan is viewed over a time period, for instance, a year, it can become clear what expenses and income are expected to appear during that time. For example, a program that works with school-age children, providing a day camp in the months of school breaks, can expect to have higher income and higher expenses during the months that the day camp program is offered. If the income is higher during these months, it must be illustrated that during other months, the income will be much lower or non-existent. The expenses may be noted all during the year and the overall budget creation will probably show that the income during even the short time period will adequately cover the expenses throughout the year. These types of variances must appear in budgets or explained in a spreadsheet in order for the financial professionals to plan accordingly for the overall funding picture. Clearly illustrating these yearly and monthly variances can help the overall organization budgeting process as well and a clearer picture of the organizational activities will be reflected in the financial reports.

Budgets and budgeting are best viewed as an ongoing process. Once a budget is prepared and approved, either by the organization director or the board of directors, it becomes a document to be monitored, analyzed and evaluated. If a budget is not being used and the program(s) are not being monitored there is a potential that the programs will not meet approved goals. A budget that is used as a tool can also be important in making the case to increase funds or expanding programs. Responsible program managers will see tracking a budget's income and expense as an essential element in ongoing program development.

Volunteer programs have been viewed in the past as not needing budgets because there was (and still is) the perception that volunteer labour is cost-free. There are real costs for volunteer programs. A budget for a volunteer program reflects the value that the organization places on volunteer contributions and recognizes that there is a cost to maintain a quality program. Knowledgeable volunteer program managers will not only use a budget wisely to maintain and increase the volunteer support but will track the contributions that volunteers make of time, in-kind contributions and overall organizational goals that are being reached and expanded because of the support.

Budget Narratives

A budget narrative, while not always requested, can be a useful document providing justifications or background for budget expenses. Many grantors will require a budget narrative to explain the amounts requested in the budget. During budget creation, projections are based upon events that will happen in the future. A narrative allows the budget developer to explain when the expenses will be incurred and why they are being incurred. These expenses can also be tied to the goals and objectives of the organization as well as predicting the outcome based on the activities.

Creation of a budget narrative involves studying the desired program goals and the plans to accomplish them. For example, if a travel budget looks very large, a budget narrative can be an opportunity to explain that the funds are being used, for example, to rent busses to transport youth six times to an event that they would otherwise be unable to attend.

A budget narrative uses the quantitative amounts from a budget, explains the reasoning and transforms the numbers into qualitative reasoning for pursuing an activity. Figure 3 provides an example of a narrative for a volunteer program expense:

Figure 3: Volunteer Program Budget Narrative

Program Supplies amount requested: _1500_

    The funds will be used for volunteer appreciation and volunteer retention.

Volunteer appreciation: _825_

    Volunteer appreciation will consist of tokens created by local schoolchildren using supplies provided by the volunteer program. Certificates will be created for each volunteer. A special event is planned at a location yet to be determined.

Volunteer retention: _675_

    This amount will be used to create binders with information about the program and the organization, and will include personalized nametags, as well as supplies for two in-service educational trainings held in October and April of the fiscal year.

Using a budget narrative is a mixture of a quantitative and qualitative explanation. The amount requested is stated, but the narrative can expand upon the reasoning and justify the request and how the funds will benefit the program.

Ongoing Budget and Fiscal Management

Ongoing budget and fiscal management in an organization is a method to monitor funding as well as goal accomplishment. Steps to be taken before a budget is created will be to involve top management working with direct services staff to ascertain that the budgets are in line with the desired outcomes of the organization's programs. To be effective, objectives must be specific and measurable and agreed upon by all members of the organization. With measurable goals in mind, a budget then becomes a vehicle to contribute to the overall program success. By tracking programs' budgets throughout a fiscal year, staff and management have another evaluation tool to monitor a program's progress. With a budget and accompanying narratives, board members and executives will be able to clarify goals and predict outcomes for future programmatic endeavours.

Figure 4

Volunteer:	January Hours	February Hours	March Hours	April Hours	May Hours...	Yearly Total
John Smith	10	5	15	0	8	38
Mary Jones	5	0	10	10	5	30
Nancy Friend	0	20	12	15	8	55
Total Volunteer Hours	15	25	37	25	21	123

Spreadsheet example for tracking numbers such as hours

The individual yearly totals equal the amount of the total volunteer hours.

Tracking budgeted expenses on a spreadsheet — as of April 30

Expenses	January	February	March	April	Total Spent to Date	Total Yearly Budget
Office Supplies	75	300	100	600	1075	1200
Printing	0	0	375	100	475	750
Program Supplies	500	100	100	225	925	1500

Spreading costs over a year to track expenses and how budgeted amount reflects spending throughout the year.

A bookkeeping form will have the rows numbered down the left-hand side, the columns across the top are lettered or named and the point where the row and column meet is called the cell.

A spreadsheet is a useful tool for financial professionals as well as programmatic staff. For example, spreadsheets can be used for monthly expenditures as well as making projections for future spending. Other uses of a spreadsheet could be tracking hours, percentages, and scores. A spreadsheet can give a clear overall picture of a budget, program or steps in attaining a goal. Once used, the figures can provide clues for future projections. Income and expense projections can be made following trends of previous years. Much like a calendar, a spreadsheet can show a time span at a glance and indicate how resources can be allocated over time.

Dropkin and Halpin (2005, p. 156) state that:

additional functions that budgets serve for well-managed nonprofits include the following:

- Budgets provide the financial and operational guidance needed to successfully implement board policies and directives.

- Budgets allow management to measure and guide the nonprofit's immediate and long-term financial health and operational effectiveness.

- Budgets guide a nonprofit's acquisition and use of resources.

- Budgets anticipate expenses and identify income to pay for those expenses.

- Budgets are tools for controlling spending and avoiding deficits.

- Budgets help integrate all of the organization's activities.

- Budgets enable management to monitor actual income and expenses against those that were budgeted in order to assess the nonprofit's overall financial situation and to alter plans as needed.

- Budgets can serve as the basis for performance reviews and, in some cases, as compensation criteria.

In order to fully understand making budget projections into the future, all staff who work with the programs and the administration must work together. The budget process is not quick but the results can be rewarding. All staff can have input on the budget preparation by stating program goals and the anticipated financial support necessary to obtain those goals. By prioritizing program and organizational needs, the budgeting process then becomes a team effort to create a workable picture that everyone can agree upon. Organizational administrators can then take requests and input into the projected budget. If requests exceed available funds, reductions can be based on criteria that will cause least impact on program functioning. If a budget revision is necessary, either before a fiscal year begins, or during a year based on a surplus or deficit of funds, using the mission, goals and objectives makes decisions less biased. In the same manner, if a program is exceeding a budget allotment, use of the budget, expense report and spreadsheets can pinpoint a problem.

Day-to-day use of organizational funds by program staff can be done through use of purchase orders, credit cards, store accounts, and at times, a reimbursement of personal funds. It is important to create a paper trail for every amount used. These back-up documents are used by financial professionals to compare expenses with actual purchases and to compare income with cash or monies received. Back-up documents are often saved with yearly financial transactions and are made available for evaluators and auditors who analyze an organization's financial system.

Grants in Nonprofit Organizations

Many nonprofits depend on grants to support and expand their programs. A grant is given for a specific activity or program and not as overall support for the organization until it is stated as such. Such grants are known as "restricted" because the use of those funds are restricted by the terms of the grant agreement. Therefore, grant funds must be kept separate and the accounting for these funds kept separate from the general organizational accounting. When applying for a grant, the directions will be specific in what is allowed as a cost and what is not. For instance, some grants do not allow any staff time to be charged to the grant funds, while others will allow staff time to be funded.

Grant Budgeting

When applying for a grant, a budget for the requested funds is a necessity. Many grantors also ask for a narrative to provide additional information about the anticipated expenditures of grant funds. Grant requests address specific program needs or can also be requested for the total organization. Whatever type of grant is being written, a budget will be necessary. The budget request must follow the goals, objectives and activities that are listed in the body of the grant. These goals show the grantor what type of program will be created or continued, the desired outcomes and the activities proposed to reach the outcomes.

A volunteer program manager who is asked to provide input into a grant proposal can be prepared with the number of volunteers and the hours donated by the volunteers. Turning the volunteer hours into how much is being donated can become another method for demonstrating community support, show the value of the programs offered as well as showing the volunteer hours as staff hours and how much father the programs resources can reach with volunteer support. A volunteer program that is requesting grant funds can also use the information above to show what volunteers have done for the organization and what else they could do if given the support and program funds.

A grant budget form can be different for each granting organization. Some grants allow staff salaries and benefits to be requested, others do not allow staff costs at all. It is important to understand the proposal and stay with the guidelines. An organization's financial profession can also provide the figures for the costs based on previous expenses. If a grant request asks for matching funds, this means have additional community support in terms of money to match the grant funds, thereby demonstrating local support. If in kind contributions are requested, this can mean goods and supplies, but also a collaborating organization or volunteers providing program hours. Many grant proposals will allow indirect costs such as facility costs and administrative costs and others will not — this is important to note before writing the budget. When writing the budget, keep in mind the length of time for the grant; for instance, do ask for funding for program supplies only for the length of time of the grant.

Once a grant is received, there will be requirements for reporting back to the funding group. A financial professional will create separate accounting forms for grant funds in order to keep them separate from day-to-day operation costs. If the granting agency requires budget and narrative reports and updates throughout the grant cycle, it is important to have clear, up-to-date information with back-up information for the expenses. A good system can be created to keep track of all expenses using account codes that will note what funds are to be charged for a budget expense. It is vital to keep all back-up for any audit or other evaluation of the grant and it's use by an organization.

FUNDRAISING

Some organizations do fundraising on a regular basis in order to increase funds, support and community recognition. These can be yearly, quarterly or monthly. There are rules and regulations governing the fundraising activities of local nonprofits and it is important to follow all policies and procedures. For instance, some funders do not allow organizations they support to raise funds during certain times of the year. This can be when the funder is also doing community support and awareness campaigns and do not want any confusion or competition. Other locations require legal permits and licences to do fundraising and have legal regulations that must be followed. A good resource for fundraisers is the Association of Fundraising Professionals, an organization that is dedicated to "advancing ethical and effective fundraising worldwide." They offer the over 30,00 worldwide member online resources, audio and videoconferencing as well as in-person conferences to discuss the latest in fundraising rules, regulations and techniques. They can be found online at: <http://www.afpnet.org/>.

If a volunteer program would like to do a fundraising activity for the benefit of volunteer recognition or appreciation, the rules and policies may be different than the overall organization regulations. Fundraising for a volunteer program can involve writing a short grant request to a local business; asking local businesses for support with donations or services; or selling foodstuffs or crafts to support the program. As always, the local organization and legal regulations will govern all activities regarding fund raising for a specific program.

AUDITS

An audit is an examination of records or financial accounts to check their accuracy or to adjust or correct the account. An individual grant or income or expense categories can also be audited. As a result, an audit can be a stressful time for anyone working in a nonprofit organization. Auditors are professionals from outside the organization who are hired to review and evaluate the financial records of the organization and the policies and procedures of the financial practices. The financial professionals are expected to provide auditors with information regarding any expenditure including receipts to prove the cost. Organizations that receive grants or public funds expect to be audited. An audit can occur at any time, after the close of the fiscal year, after a grant has been spent, or at any other interval deemed appropriate. Total organizations can be audited or single programs. To prepare for an audit, financial professionals will accumulate records, financial proceedings, reports and budgets and all parts that will be examined. Timesheets can be included as well as travel costs, equipment costs, and grants received. If staff members are asked to assist in preparing for an audit, it can mean using program narratives to explain an expense or justifying an expense based on an activity. Audits can be viewed as an in-depth evaluation of a program's fiscal foundation.

CONCLUSION

An organization operates efficiently when all staff members understand the purpose of financial practices and their part in keeping good records to assist in the overall management. Budgeting is an important process within the overall organizational fiscal picture and all staff, but especially program managers, have an obligation to follow procedures when creating and using a budget. Volunteer program managers play a key role in the fiscal picture of an organization. Volunteers provide in-kind donations to staff costs, extend program dollars by their activities and show funders, stakeholders and community members that the organization's program is worthy of support.

Budgets not only keep the programs on track but also keep a program's goals realistic. Knowing how far the budget can be stretched to cover costs is a factor in knowing how far a program can reach. A program director who uses spreadsheets to keep track of program costs and create budgets will be able to explain and justify activities and possibly be able to see areas where activities can be shifted and/or expanded.

Financial reports give a clear picture of the organization and how well funds are used and programs are valued. A sound financial foundation will be the basis for the mission of the organization. Trust is built within boards of directors, funders, stakeholders, program recipients as well as staff when the finances of an organization are managed well and exhibit the value that is placed in that trust.

REFERENCES

Cowperthwaite Mehta Chartered Accountants: Not-for-profit Administration. Available at http://www.187gerrard.com/home.htm.

Dropkin, Murray, & Halpin, James. (2005). *Bookkeeping for nonprofits. A step-by-step guide to nonprofit accounting*. San Francisco, CA: Jossey-Bass.

Chapter 10

DATA MANAGEMENT

Norman A. Dolch and Pamela J. Sybert
University of North Texas

INTRODUCTION

Collecting and maintaining information or data about volunteers and their engagement with your organization and, subsequently, the analysis of the overall volunteer program are, of course, necessary components of an accountable, transparent, and well managed volunteer program. While few would doubt its importance, knowing what data to collect, how to collect it, and what to do with it once collected docs present various challenges.

This chapter takes a look at some of the questions that must be answered in terms of deciding what data to collect; what methods can be employed to collect the data; how the data can be used; the importance of keeping the data current and safe; and the evolution of data collection and maintenance with particular regard to the technological advances of the last several decades.

DATA AND VOLUNTEER PROGRAM MANAGEMENT

Why collect data? A simple answer might be how else can a volunteer administrator communicate with prospective and current volunteers without certain information about them? Thinking more broadly, however, without tracking volunteer involvement how can a volunteer administrator measure the impact of the volunteers in carrying out the mission of the organization (Brinkerhoff, 2008, pp. 35-49; Grobman, 2004, p. 99)? What documentable evidence is there that the volunteers are working to accomplish the goals of not only the volunteer program but the overall organization without collecting information and disseminating it to various stakeholders? Stakeholders might include the staff and leadership of the organization, the volunteers, the funders, the donors, the clients, and the community at large (Kettner, Moroney, and Martin, 1999, pp. 215-38; Powell, 1995, pp. 148-49).

Why is maintaining the data important? An obvious answer is that knowledge about program demographics, trends, and other analyses of the volunteer program cannot be accurate without ongoing and current information. It has been said that a report is only as good as the data that it contains. Although entering data may not seem like an important or exciting task for some, it is crucial in order to document a program's status and growth patterns as well as tracking accomplishments and results.

Should paper files or computer software programs be used for recordkeeping? It is safe to say that before computers and software programs were ubiquitous all data about volunteers and programs were kept in paper files. Many small programs or programs without any staff support still use paper files either exclusively or in part. In fact, one volunteer administrator that we spoke with who runs a small volunteer program still likes to have a paper file for every volunteer that contains certain information such as their performance reviews. Also, she noted that nothing is entered into their custom-made database until the volunteer is ready to be placed, meaning that original inquiries, application data, interview information, and training records are not entered until the volunteer is cleared and ready to start work. Other organizations might decide to track all inquiries and steps along the way. These types of decisions must be made at the organizational level or in cases of affiliate chapters of large national organizations at the national office.

What data should you collect? The answer to this question depends in part upon the organization's mission but several basic types of data are collected by all volunteer-based organizations such as the volunteer's contact information, volunteering preferences, skills and experience, and other information from the application. Tracking volunteer screening such as status of background checks and interview results, orientation and training dates, placements, hours, performance, and recognition is standard as well. Other types of data collection will be discussed later in this chapter.

Whether a volunteer administrator has the luxury of starting a new volunteer program, or inheriting or resurrecting an existing one, it is recommended that decisions about what data truly needs to be collected, why, how it will be collected, and plans for safeguarding it be made by a knowledgeable task force or planning group. Ideally, the group should consist of leaders and stakeholders in the organization that have historical and current knowledge about what data has and is being collected throughout the organization. Once the planning group has mapped out its strategy to collect the knowledge about the current system, its objectives are to outline how they will determine what current and future data needs are; how they will investigate what data collection systems are available; what safeguards need to be put in place; and an action plan for implementing and evaluating the system. Deciding how the information will be used and who should have access to it are critical questions that must be answered.

DATA COLLECTION CONCEPTS

The next section looks at the concepts of data collection by following the life cycle of a volunteer in a typical volunteer program. The names of the life cycle phases come from the collaborative volunteer engagement model of Fixler, Eichberg and Lorenz (2008). Specially, they replace the top-down staff-driven language with more inclusive and collaborative terms. Volunteer management becomes volunteer engagement, recruitment becomes cultivation and networking; placement becomes negotiation and agreement; supervision becomes support; performance review becomes performance measurement; recognition becomes acknowledgement; and retention becomes sustainability.

Table 1: Volunteer Life Cycle

Management Terms	Engagement Terms
1. Recruitment	1. Cultivation and Networking
2. Placement	2. Negotiation and Agreement
3. Supervision	3. Support
4. Performance Review	4. Performance Measurement
5. Recognition	5. Acknowledgement
6. Retention	6. Sustainability

Reproduced with permission from *Boomer Volunteer Engagement: Collaborate Today, Thrive Tomorrow* by Jill Friedman Fixler, Sandie Eichberg, and Gail Lorenz.

This is not just a change in semantics but a change in how organizations and volunteers can interact in a more participatory fashion. Although the work of Fixler, *et al.*, looks specifically at plans and strategies for engaging boomer volunteers, we will use the terms of their collaborative volunteer engagement model as a model for the life cycle of a volunteer, and, in particular, to consider the possible areas for data collection and management.

Data Collection Within the Volunteer Life Cycle

Using the previously discussed volunteer life cycle approach to understanding volunteers, a flow scheme for data collection and recordkeeping is developed in this section. The first consideration in establishing data collection and recordkeeping for volunteer management programs is the cultivation and network stage which includes the systems for volunteer utilization. These systems should be in place before the recruitment of any volunteers and any data collection about applicants for volunteer positions or volunteers engaged by the organization. Before data collection and recordkeeping, these systems and closely related considerations should be developed or obtained by an organization:

1. Statements relating volunteers to the organization's mission.

2. Surveys on enhancing paid employee performance or going beyond activities of paid staff with volunteers.

3. A SWOT (Strengths, Weaknesses, Opportunities, and Threats) Analysis of the volunteer program (Maynard, 2007) or a volunteer program audit (Ellis, 2003).

4. Development of volunteer positions within the organization's structure with job descriptions.

5. A written plan for recruitment.

6. Application procedures with written applications.

7. Interview procedures with guiding questions.

8. Form letters or e-mails for acceptance or rejection of volunteers after interviews.

9. Development of an orientation and training program for volunteers.

10. Organizational policies regarding information and data collection that take into account applicable legislation for your geographic location.

11. The selection or development of a software program for electronic volunteer recordkeeping with appropriate back-up data unless maintaining a paper record system in which case the paper record system would be established.

Cultivation and Networking Stage

The Cultivation and Networking stage also concentrates on the contacts that staff and other stakeholders make to reach out to volunteers such as implementing the recruitment plan, getting persons to fill out volunteer applications, and interviewing prospective volunteers. Additional data collection responsibilities during this phase include:

1. Documenting in detail the groups targeted for volunteer recruitment and types of marketing including quantification of responses whenever possible.

2. Having people who are interested in volunteering complete online or paper applications, then entering the application into an online database to track statistics such as ages of applicants, gender, race, previous volunteer experiences, volunteering interests, *etc.*, of the applicants.

3. Interviewing applicants and either keeping interview notes in paper files, in an online system, or possibly both for back-up.

4. Documenting applicants' permission to conduct a background check, executing the background check, and recording its outcome.

5. Documenting the date on which an applicant is invited or declined to be a member of the volunteer staff of the organization.

6. Documenting the date that a person is scheduled to attend an orientation and training session, when they were sent the invitation, and their response.

Consider for a moment the kind of data that fundraisers record after visiting with prospective donors, and you begin to realize how important it is to document outreach efforts. As the language, at least in this collaborative model, is moving toward the language of fundraising with such terms as cultivating so, too, are some of the techniques. Contact information and follow-up notes about prospective volunteers can be entered into your system for future reference. Fundraising books often advise organizations to look upon everyone they meet as a potential donor. The same principle could be applied to volunteers as well. Having accurate data about potential volunteers enables your organization to invite them to your next special event or volunteer project, to add them to your newsletter list, or to include them in a social networking message.

Negotiation and Agreement Stage

Negotiation and agreement is the second stage of the volunteer life cycle. This phase includes considerations such as the newly invited volunteer accepting their job description, and the tracking of data about their volunteering such as hours and accomplishments. Continuing to develop the flow scheme for data collection and recordkeeping, these are the critical, not necessarily the only considerations, for this phase of the cycle:

1. Having the volunteer accept the volunteer position by signing the job description as is or having the volunteer administrator and the volunteer tweak the description to make a better fit between the volunteer and the organization and then sign it.

2. Documenting the completion of the orientation and training session as well as receipt of materials such as the volunteer handbook, confidentiality agreements, conflict of interest disclosures, documents relevant to the acceptance of ethical principles, and others.

Support Stage

Once a volunteer becomes an organization member, they move into the Support stage. As a volunteer continues their tenure with the organization, their needs change, and so should types of support. Once a volunteer understands their work role it is important for the organization to continue to support the volunteer and make sure that the volunteer has ample opportunities to get their questions answered. Fostering openness to the input of volunteers is important in this phase and can be accomplished with questionnaires, telephone calls, online chats, or interactive sessions through online applications such Skype™ in which persons can see and talk with one another. These are the critical, not necessarily the only considerations, for this phase of the cycle:

1. Scheduling and providing coaching, additional training, and mentoring.

2. Assessing and documenting what type of knowledge and experience will continue to enhance the volunteer's ability to perform their agreed upon tasks.

3. Scheduling training as deemed appropriate and using various delivery options ranging from interactive Internet modules, compact discs (CDs), and face-to-face training (these are not necessarily mutually exclusive.)

4. Documenting the hours of service and tasks performed.

Recording the results of the training, coaching, and subsequent support efforts is important to document. Tracking the volunteer's hours and accomplishments round out this stage of the volunteer life cycle.

Performance Measurement Stage

The next stage of the volunteer life cycle is Performance Measurement. Evaluating the work of a volunteer requires having established success indicators and benchmarks embedded in the previously discussed negotiation and agreement stage. The understanding among the volunteer, the staff with whom the volunteer works, and the volunteer administrator on not only what the work is and how it contributes to the mission of the organization but also how the work will be assessed is crucial. These are the two critical, not necessarily the only considerations for this stage:

1. Documenting the results of the performance review.

2. Documenting the newly developed goals and indicators for success.

Acknowledgement Stage

Acknowledgement is the next stage of the volunteer life cycle. A volunteer's contribution must be recognized and acknowledgement should be evident throughout the life cycle. These are some suggestions to consider including and tracking in your system:

1. certificates of volunteer appointment;

2. certificates for hour benchmarks — 100 hours, 250 hours, *etc*;

3. certificates for training completion;

4. special event recognition;

5. outstanding performance recognition; and/or

6. recording all acknowledgements a volunteer is given over time.

McCurley and Lynch (2006) reiterate that a well run volunteer program is some of the best recognition that you can offer a volunteer. At the same time, acknowledging a volunteer's efforts and accomplishments should be as personal as possible and should change and evolve over time.

Sustainability Stage

Sustainability is the final aspect of the volunteer life cycle. The question is how can a valuable volunteer be retained? Part of the answer, of course, is that the volunteer is satisfied with their work in the organization although it may have changed considerably over time. Having an established career path for volunteers in which they can take on more leadership roles is a strategy employed by some organizations. Even if the work of the volunteer remains somewhat constant, the relationships within the organization evolve becoming important links to sustainability. Respecting a volunteer's time and effort through good organization, excellent communication, and continued support is both a recognition of their worth to the organization and also a strategy for sustaining the volunteer. These are critical, but not necessarily all the data collection responsibilities, during this phase:

1. Collecting data on volunteer satisfaction through interviews, questionnaires, and planned conversations.

2. Soliciting information and ideas from the volunteer on how to improve and enhance the work and recording these.

3. Documenting disappointments or joys expressed.

4. Documenting reasons why volunteers leave the organization.

Ongoing efforts to solicit valuable feedback from volunteers are encouraged. When a volunteer does decide to leave the organization, it is important to know and document their reasons. Over time, certain patterns may emerge that can give an organization important feedback on their program.

TOOLS FOR RECORDKEEPING

There are two options for recordkeeping and data gathering. One option is to use a paper system. While one might think that paper systems are antiquated this section argues otherwise. Data collection deals with the gathering of information such as telephone numbers, driver licence numbers, and survey responses. Recordkeeping, on the other hand, is establishing a system for retrieval of data such as completed volunteer applications and performance measurement of volunteers. Obviously, these are two interrelated considerations exemplified by statistics on the age range of volunteers or percentages of applicants who are not accepted due to background checks. While this section focuses on using software packages and paper recordkeeping systems, these are not mutually exclusive. For example, an organization might give a potential volunteer a paper application form to complete but that data may be entered into a computerized system at a later date. This section is not on the interrelationship but rather the establishment of the recordkeeping system.

Software Packages

Numerous software packages exist in the market place, and a few of these will be discussed with no endorsement implied to illustrate some of the features of software programs in general. One software package specifically marketed for volunteer management was titled VolunteerWorks™ and the Red Ridge Software Company who made it has now joined forces with Volgistics to provide the web-based Volgistics system (<http://www.volgistics.com/>). The system is hosted through Volgistics' own servers so that organizations do not have to maintain software. Volgistics offers features such as online application forms, e-mail, scheduling, and even the ability of volunteers to update their own records.

Another software package is VolunteerSoftware which is loaded onto organization computer networks for one price and has a support plan as well as training videos. The company does offer a *Web Assistant* so that volunteers can enter information from home, check schedules, and new applicants can apply. The company reports that it has been in business since 1986 and its software management package is used in 60 per cent of all RSVP Programs in the United States[*] (<www.volsoft.com/faqs/faqs.html>).

The organization Volunteer[2] (or Volunteer Squared) advertises applications specifically for small and large nonprofits (<http://www.volunteer2.com/default.asp>). This package is also web-based and includes features such as creating schedules for volunteers and an online application. It also generates a wide range of reports such as ones based on job categories or even just one particular volunteer.

Trying to make comparisons between software packages like the three briefly discussed quickly becomes rather mind boggling. An excellent source for a listing of various software packages available is Coyote Communications (<http://www.coyotecommunications.com/tech/volmanage.html>). Regardless of the package considered, the Resource Center of the Corporation for National and Community Service (2009) recommends these considerations when purchasing volunteer data management software:

1. How much does it cost, and what is included?

2. Is a demonstration version available so I can try it out first?

3. How simple is the installation process?

4. How will I receive updates, and will there be a separate fee?

5. What kind of support is available, and is there a separate fee?

6. If data needs to be brought over from another system, are conversion services available?

7. Is the software designed for our operating system? (PC, Mac, Linux, etc.)

8. Does the software provide for internal volunteer tracking, external volunteer tracking, or both?

9. Can more than one person use the database at a time?

---

[*] RSVP is a program of the corporation for National and Community Service that "connects volunteers age 55 and over with service opportunities in their communities that match their skills and availability" (<http://www.seniorcorps.gov/about/sc/index.asp>).

10. Can data be entered via the web (e.g., volunteers making entries from the field)?

11. Is there an option for password protection?

12. Can a developer reconfigure the software later to accommodate a change in our organization's needs?

While one might think that commercially available software management packages are definitely the smart way to set up and monitor a volunteer data management, system volunteer administrators tell us that this is not necessarily so. Some mentioned that they had less than optimal experiences and actually wound up creating their own custom software by hiring a programmer. This allowed them to totally control the type of data gathered, the type and format of scheduling reports, and other document produced. These volunteer managers claimed that the cost of producing a customized package was more economical than paying the user fees and consulting fees for the commercially available packages. Volunteer administrators need to carefully consider the options available to them.

Paper File Systems

Although the world seems to increasingly be using more and more computer-based applications, paper data management systems might still make sense for some organizations where the staff lack experience or comfort with technology or the number of volunteers is small. If the staff is not comfortable with computers or struggles to use them then maybe a paper management system makes more sense. Utilizing the classification system for large and small businesses, a small nonprofit would have less than 50 volunteers.

A good paper system will probably necessitate using extra capacity hanging folders and either file guides that are alphabetic or non-alphabetic. The use of non-alphabetic guides might be useful if you want to divide the system into major headings such as the volunteer life cycle. Individual file folders can be created on various topics such as recruitment fliers or volunteer applications, and then an index prepared on a word processing package that lists each major file guide topic, alphabetic or non-alphabetic, and the particular files located under the file guide. This allows quick and easy location of material in the file.

McCurley and Lynch (2006) provide an appendix of forms and worksheets that they suggest one carefully review and then modify to serve the particular needs of their organization. These forms range from "Staff Assessment Survey on Volunteer Involvement" to "Volunteer Position Description," "Volunteer Recruitment Exercise," and "Exit Interview Questionnaire." Similar collections of forms and worksheets may be available in other places but this is one excellent source to use for establishing a paper data management system.

CONFIDENTIALITY AND PRIVACY

Data collection and data management systems inevitably raise questions of confidentiality and privacy. Persons sometimes want to know why certain information on them is necessary. A volunteer may ask, "Why is it necessary for you to know my social security number when I am a volunteer and not paid?" Persons are sometimes concerned about release of information such as telephone numbers, e-mail addresses, and street addresses. For example, a retail store owner may not have their home phone listed by the telephone company in the phone book, and they may not want it released to anyone by an organization for which they volunteer.

Confidentiality means that information is shared with an organization or person but may not be shared with another. This is the common understanding regarding health information shared with a physician or discussion between an attorney and their client. The information shared is privileged and private. It is not openly available to other persons and is to be protected from them. For example, according to guidelines from the U.S. Department of the Interior (2009), "privacy is the right to be left alone and to control the conditions under which information pertaining to you is collected, used, and disseminated." This definition captures the essence of the discussion in this section of the chapter which really cuts across every dimension of the volunteer life cycle. The collection, use, and dissemination of data will be elaborated upon by examining commonly accepted underlying principles and some strategies for implementation.

Applicable Law and Guiding Principles

Lichtblau (2008) points out that neither the U.S. *Freedom of Information Act* nor the *Privacy Act of 1974* applies to private nonprofits; however, there are applicable federal laws regarding disclosure of specific information such as HIPAA (the *Health Insurance Portability and Accountability Act*) which do apply to nonprofit organizations. She points out that state laws are most relevant and should be carefully researched because they vary widely. Lichtblau further points out that disclosure of information to granting agencies and even in response to a subpoena may not be legal under state law without volunteers specifying in writing that the information may be released. State nonprofit associations and local or regional management support organizations should be of assistance in this regard.

Besides applicable state law, the Canadian Standards Association developed a code for protection of personal information which was included in the Canadian *Personal Information Protection and Electronic Documents Act*. Readers are referred to two sources:

1. *Guide for Business and Organizations to Canada's Personal Information Protection and Electronics Documents Act*

2. *The PIPEDA Privacy Principles: A Guide for Associations and Non-profit Organizations.*

The code provides ten principles for the collection, use, and disclosure of personal information that are good guides in establishing a volunteer data management system. In Canada, these principles are required by law, and Canadian volunteer managers should consult legal counsel regarding their implementation.

Principles found in the Canadian *Personal Information Protection and Electronics Documents Act* can be divided into two categories: data collection and data management. Two of the ten principles may be considered to concern data collection. These are the principles of consent and accuracy. Consent entails receiving the written permission of persons to collect information about them. The principle of accuracy deals with ensuring that the information collected on persons is correct. The remaining principles may be considered primarily to concern data management and include the following:

1. Accountability — The policies of the organization regarding confidentiality and privacy as well as designating the responsible officer for the organization.

2. Identify purposes for data collection — Why is it needed and how will the information be used?

3. Limiting Collection — Do not collect what is not needed.

4. Limiting Use, Disclosure, and Retention — The data should be available to only those who need access and should not be retained when no longer needed.

5.   Safeguards — Protect the information and data against loss and theft.

6.   Openness — Be sure to inform persons of policies and practices.

7.   Challenging compliance — Provide methods for complaints and process for their resolution.

Although not binding on nonprofits as already mentioned earlier, U.S. federal laws and guidelines applicable to government organizations may provide useful guides for nonprofit organizations and the protection of confidentiality and privacy just as the Sarbanes-Oxley legislation, while not mandatory, provides good financial management guidelines for nonprofit organizations. In this regard, the U.S. Code Title 5, § 552a is particularly informative and is readily obtainable at the following web address: <http://www.law.cornell.edu/uscode/html/uscode05/usc_sec_05_00000552---a000-.html>.

U.S. Code title 5, § 552a deals with the collection, use, or dissemination of employee information. Keep in mind that volunteers are often equated as being unpaid employees. In many ways it reinforces the principles of confidentiality and privacy already set forth in this discussion. Another excellent guide in this regard comes from the U.S. Justice Department's "Privacy and Civil Liberties Policy Development Guide and Implementation Templates," which can be retrieved at this web address: <it.ojp.gov/documents/Privacy_Guide_Final.pdf>.

To close this discussion on the principles of confidentiality and privacy, one will want to keep in mind these seven steps to privacy protection suggested by Human Services Technologies in their *Nonprofit World* article (2001):

•   Step One — Hire the right people because you cannot teach persons to value someone's confidentiality and privacy.

•   Step Two — Create a confidentiality policy and you can look at those of similar organizations to build one.

•   Step Three — Implement good solid procedures that reduce the improper sharing of information.

•   Step Four — Train everyone in the procedures protecting confidentiality and privacy.

•   Step Five — Be most cautious of sharing personnel and client information via phone and fax because faxed messages may lie around the machine for anyone to see.

- Step Six — Be sure all information is as safe as possible by having it encrypted on computers, password protected on computers, and/or in locked file cabinets.

- Step Seven — Check the laws in your state because privacy and confidentiality is primarily regulated at the state level for nonprofit organizations. Outside the United States, carefully check laws at the national level and regional governing levels like provinces.

The importance of protecting the privacy of information on persons including volunteers is expressed by Posner (2008, p. 2249), who says, "... the degree to which a disclosure of personal information inflicts harm on a person depends less on what information is disclosed than to whom and to how many, and to what use it is put by the persons to whom it is disclosed."

Strategies for Ensuring Privacy

There are various strategies for ensuring privacy and confidentiality regarding data collection and management. The discussion will focus on the use of volunteer handbooks, volunteer service agreements, training, encryption, and the use of background checks to ensure client, staff, and organization safety. There may be other strategies but the discussion will focus on these.

Volunteer Service Agreements are similar to agreements and/or job descriptions for paid employment. Meltzer (1988) points out that volunteer service agreements should emerge from policy statements regarding volunteers such as confidentiality and privacy statements. In addition to spelling out expectations such as amount of work time and attendance at training sessions or accident insurance coverage by the nonprofit, the volunteer service agreement should include expectations about the information provided by a volunteer or the sharing of information about others as a result of a volunteer's involvement with the organization. For example, someone who visits residents for Meals on Wheels should not be sharing with their friends and families information on the residents visited just as they should not be returning to residences to provide personal assistance to persons or doing physical repairs to residences.

An extension of using volunteer service agreements is the Volunteer Handbook. Just like paid employees often receive a printed employee handbook or have access to an electronic handbook, this should be done with volunteers as well. This is an excellent place to share all policies and expectations with volunteers, especially those dealing with confidentiality of information and privacy issues.

Volunteer handbooks are closely related to employee handbooks for which a ready resource is the Society for Human Resource Management. Numerous examples of volunteer handbooks are available on the web, and one from the National Wildlife Federation can be found at this site: <www.nwf.org/volunteer/handbook.cfm>. Volunteer handbooks often give overviews of the volunteer program and discuss volunteerism and the giving of one's time as well as organizational facts, health and safety information, and information on confidentiality and screening including information on volunteer screening such as required background checks.

Background checks are done for a variety for legal and risk management reasons. For example, in the United States organizations are required by the various states to conduct background checks for persons working with children and the elderly, those who are often considered to be unable to care for themselves or defend themselves. State laws vary and should be carefully checked. For example, Ohio law encourages but does not require youth organizations to conduct background checks according to Schweers (2009). He also points out that if a volunteer does harm a child, the Ohio law provides immunity from civil liability for organizations that do fingerprint checks.

From a risk management perspective, background checks may be done to protect co-workers, including volunteer co-workers, and clients from persons with previous criminal records (Harris and Keller, 2005). Background checks may be done to eliminate persons with criminal records from having access to cash and other liquid assets of an organization as well as keeping persons barred by the Securities and Exchange Commission from serving on the board of a nonprofit organization just as the *Sarbanes-Oxley Act* prohibits them from serving on for-profit corporate boards (Greenlee, Fischer, Gordon, and Keating, 2007).

Doing these checks requires obtaining a volunteer applicant's social security number and driver's licence, which is considered private information. These identifiers are then submitted along with the person's name to a law enforcement agency or private screening firm. There is a cost for the check which is sometimes paid by the organization but often by the volunteer as part of the application process and it may be reimbursed or not reimbursed depending on an organization's finances and policies.

Four specific recommendations are made for organizations by the Privacy Rights Clearing House (2008) regarding volunteer background checks:

1. Organizations should adopt a volunteer screening policy with considerations such as those positions requiring screening and the offences or findings that would disqualify a potential volunteer.

2. Organizations should adopt a privacy and data security policy which includes among other considerations openness and security safeguards.

3. Organizations should contact state criminal history depositories and become a "qualified entity" to search not only the state data base but also the FBI's (Federal Bureau of Investigation's) Triple I data files.

4. Organizations should consider a commercial background screening company and it should be one that follows the *Free Credit Reporting Act* because these companies can help the organization with appeals in case of inaccurate information.

Privacy rights may seem especially important as the vulnerability of the client/patient population increases. A common sense approach is that organizations will want to be especially thorough and careful on privacy right issues if they are dealing with clients or patients who have extremely fragile health problems, infants and young children who cannot speak on their own behalf, or individuals with severe mental challenges. Actually, privacy rights are important regardless of the population served, and volunteer administrators should exercise great caution to protect information about their client/patient population.

Diligence and constant care are required to protect the private information of persons. Drawing on 2007 Canadian data, Gonzales (2008, p. 17) indicates one reason that personal information is compromised is because "employees did not follow established company practices, which companies can address by providing ongoing privacy training." Gonzales also points out that breaches of personal information most often occur because organizations have an unsecured electronic format. Securing electronic formats can be done through the use of measures such as firewalls and encryption. Grobman (2005, p. 266) points out that the industry standard for e-commerce is Secure Sockets Layer created by Netscape and referred to as SSL. He references two popular encryption programs which can be found at these two websites: <http://www.pgp.com> and <http://www.gnupg.org>. He also indicates that the website <http://www.hutworld.com/members/file.php?ID=28>

provides a good explanation of encryption. Vigilance, skill, and knowledge are clearly required by the volunteer administrator to protect the private information of volunteers.

SUMMARY AND CONCLUSION

Collecting data about volunteers and their work towards the mission of the organization, and ultimately, compiling and disseminating reports about the entire volunteer program is both a basic, and yet sometimes, a complicated task. It is nonetheless, critical to the success of the volunteer program, and thus, the organization. Meticulous planning on the part of the organization is required. Being able to answer with clarity questions about the purpose of the data collection and how it will be maintained and used is of utmost importance. A prime directive and one that will have to be revisited throughout the planning and implementation process is: don't collect data that you do not currently need just because you have a chance to do so. This is often a mistake that is made in survey design. Even with those that have considerable knowledge in research methods and survey design, there is the temptation to try and ask as much information as possible, thinking that there may be a need for the information later. We caution against this. Not only does this practice usually complicate the survey instrument but it presents an additional problem of safeguarding information. Decide what data needs to be collected and why, how it is to be collected, who will have access to the data and under what circumstances, and how the data will ultimately be used.

In summary, the steps for planning and implementing a data collection and management system are as follows:

1. Form a committee or task force to establish the guidelines and to provide direction for data collection and management.

2. Review the current data collection and management practices, and, if necessary, collect additional information from the leadership and staff to aid in deciding what data is essential to the organization.

3. Know why the data is being collected and how it will be used.

4. Research, and, if possible, try out some of the commercial software packages. Even if the organization decides to have a database designed and customized, previewing commercial systems can help in making decisions about data collection and management. If a paper system is to be used, research some ways to organize and safeguard the data.

5. Know the laws and best practices concerning confidentiality and privacy and ensure that all staff is well versed on these issues.

6. Back up the data often, and keep the back-up copy in a secure location.

7. Review and evaluate the data collection and management system to determine if the organization's needs are being met.

Remember the golden rule of volunteer management from McCurley and Lynch, 2006): "Their niceness will let you recruit a volunteer but only your competence will let you keep them."

REFERENCES

Association Xpertise, Inc. *The PIPEDA privacy principles: A guide for associations and non-profit organizations*. Retrieved October 22, 2009, from http://www.axi.ca/resdocs/privacy_guide.pdf.

Brinckerhoff, P. C. (2009). *Mission-based management: Leading your not-for-profit in the 21st century*. (3rd ed., pp. 35-49). New York: Wiley.

Corporation for National and Community Service (n.d.). *Volunteer management software options*. Retrieved November 1, 2009, from http://www.nationalserviceresources.org/volunteer-management-software-options.

Ellis, S. J. (2003). *Volunteer management audit*. Philadelphia: Energize.

Fixler, J. F., Eichberg, S., & Lorenz, G. (2008). *Boomer volunteer engagement: Collaborate today, thrive tomorrow*. Bloomington, IN: Author House.

Gonzalez, G. (2008, June 9). 'Leaks' of data surge. *Business Insurance, 42*, 17.

Greenlee, J., Fischer, M., Gordon, T., & Keating, E. (2007). An investigation of fraud in nonprofit organizations: Occurrences and deterrents, *Nonprofit and Voluntary Sector Quarterly, 36*(4), 676-694.

Grobman, G. M. (2004). *An introduction to the nonprofit sector: A practical approach for the 21st Century*. Harrisburg, PA: White Hat Communications.

Grobman, G. M. (2005). *The Pennsylvania nonprofit handbook*. (7th ed., pp. 99; 266). Harrisburg, PA: White Hat Communications.

Harris, P. M., & Keller, K. S. (2005). Ex-offenders need not apply: The criminal background check in hiring decisions. *Journal of Contemporary Criminal Justice, 21*(1), 6-30.

Human Services Technologies. Seven steps to privacy protection. (2001). *Nonprofit World, 19*(2), 6-7.

Kettner, P., Moroney, R. M., & Martin, L. L. (1999). *Designing and managing programs: An effectiveness-based approach.* (2nd ed., pp. 215-238). Thousand Oaks, CA: Sage Publications, Inc.

Lichtblau, A. (2009, June). Can I disclose this information? Complying with confidentiality & disclosure requirements. *Caplaw Legal Update.* Retrieved October 22, 2009, from http://www.probonopartner.org/publications/Can%20I%20disclose%20this.htm.

Maynard, S. (2007). *Exploring growth strategies for the volunteer movement.* Retrieved October 22, 2009, from http://www.service learning.org/filemanager/download/2006_grantee_mtg/Growing_to_Scale.pdf.

McCurley, S., & Lynch, R. (2006). *Volunteer management: Mobilizing all the resources of the Community.* Kemptville, ON: Johnstone Training and Consultation, Inc.

Meltzer, P. (1988). *Volunteer service agreements: A new strategy of volunteer management.* A paper presented at the Annual Meeting of the American Society on Aging, San Diego, CA.

Office of the Privacy Commissioner of Canada. (2004). *Guide for business and organizations: Your privacy responsibilities.* Retrieved October 26, 2009, from http://www.priv.gc.ca/information/guide_e.cfm.

Posner, R. A. (2008). Privacy, surveillance, and law. *The University of Chicago Law Review, 75*(1), 245-260.

Powell, J. L. (1995). *Pathways to leadership: How to achieve and sustain success* (pp. 148-149). San Francisco: Jossey-Bass Publishers.

Privacy Rights Clearinghouse (n.d.). *Volunteer background checks: Giving back without giving up on privacy. Fact sheet 16d: Volunteer background checks, 2008.* Retrieved October 22, 2009, from http://www.privacyrights.org/fs/fs16d-VolunteerScreening.htm.

Schweers, J. (2009, November 1). Volunteers screened before working with children, elderly. *USA Today.* Retrieved November 4, 2009, from http://www.usatoday.com/news/nation/2009-11-01-volunteer-background-checks_N.htm.

U.S. Department of Justice (n.d.) *Privacy and civil liberties policy development guide and implementation templates.* Retrieved October 30, 2009, from http://www.it.ojp.gov/documents/Privacy_Guide_Final.pdf.

U.S. Department of the Interior (n.d.) *The Privacy Act, privacy, and you.* Retrieved October 30, 2009, from http://www.doiu.nbc.gov/orientation/privacy_act.html.

Chapter 11

EVALUATION AND OUTCOME MEASUREMENT

R. Dale Safrit, Ed.D.[*]
North Carolina State University, Raleigh, North Carolina

[*] This chapter is based upon a journal article co-authored in 1998 with the late Mary Merrill, an international consultant in volunteer administration, former editor of *The Journal of Volunteer Administration*, and a dear friend and mentor. The author wishes to dedicate the chapter to Mary and her memory in recognition of her selfless lifelong devotion to volunteers worldwide, and those professionals who support them.

IMPACT EVALUATION IN CONTEMPORARY VOLUNTEER PROGRAMS

One of the most challenging demands upon managers and directors of volunteer programs that emerged during the final decade of the twentieth century was that of documenting and dollarizing the impact of the volunteer efforts upon clientele served. No longer were the mere mobilization and management of volunteers adequate to justify the continued existence (much less expansion) of a specific program or agency. Rather, as competition for increasingly scarce public and private resources became more intensive, calls for more extensive and more rigorous accounting of the ultimate impact of these resources became much louder and much more widespread. This intensive demand for greater documentation and accountability initially arose from program funders but quickly expanded to include sponsoring government agencies, professional and accreditation organizations, the taxpaying public, and even the volunteers themselves. As early as 1993, Taylor and Sumariwalla (p. 95) stated:

> Increasing competition for tax as well as contributed dollars and scarce resources prompt donors and funders to ask once again: What good did

the donation produce? What difference did the foundation grant or United Way allocation make in the lives of those affected by the service funded?

Although this phenomenon was not limited to public sector organizations, it quickly became a major issue facing nonprofit organizations that depended upon multiple funding sources and (most often) all-volunteer staffs in order to deliver ever-expanding services and programs to clientele (Kearns, 1996). Volunteer resource managers (also called volunteer administrators or VAs) quickly came to realize that a new and emerging skill set was fast becoming requisite to their profession. No longer were long-standing professional competencies focusing upon program development, volunteer recruitment and supervision, and resource allocation and management adequate in themselves.

In 1968, Creech suggested criteria for evaluating a volunteer program. The earliest writings on the profession of volunteer administration and management either did not address program evaluation at all (Naylor, 1973; Wilson, 1981) or included only tangential information (Naylor, 1976; O'Connell, 1976; Stenzel & Feeney, 1968; Wilson, 1979). Still, in the early 1980s, the former Association for Volunteer Administration (AVA) established "the ability to monitor and evaluate total program results ... [and] demonstrate the ability to document program results" as fundamental competencies of the volunteer administration profession (as cited in Fisher & Cole, 1993, pp. 187, 188).

Early advocates for evaluation and accountability in volunteer programs included Fisher and Cole (1993) who suggested that "volunteer administrators are continually faced with the need to demonstrate the value of their programs" (p. 138) and devoted an entire chapter of their text to evaluating volunteer programs, processes, and impacts. Ellis (1996) agreed, concluding that "just as with employees, it is possible to monitor and measure the accomplishments of volunteers by stating goals and objectives ... and then assessing whether these were achieved" (p. 22). By the end of the twentieth century, new professional competencies had emerged and were becoming prevalent that additionally focused upon evaluation methods, data collection and analysis, and marketing and accountability as related to the volunteer-based programs to which they provided leadership (Merrill & Safrit, 2000; Safrit & Merrill, 1998). In 1999, Medaugh described five criteria for evaluating a volunteer program, including one from the individual volunteer's perspective.

In the National Human Services Assembly's 2004 treatise, *From Research to Action: A Unified National Response to the 2004 Volunteer Management Capacity Study*, a "focus on evaluation and impact measurement" (p. 21) was one of seven transformational strategies identified to further demonstrate volunteerism's value to communities and expand the capacities of nonprofit organizations' capacities to successfully engage volunteers. Empirical research published in the first years of the twenty-first century helped to establish that the evaluation of volunteer program impacts and accountability of funds expended in volunteer-based programs had become entrenched competencies for volunteer resource managers (Culp & Nolan, 2000; Safrit & Merrill, 2001, 2005; Safrit & Schmiesing, 2002, 2004; Schmiesing & Safrit, 2007). Safrit, Schmiesing, Gliem, and Gliem (2005) suggested the P.E.P. model for contemporary volunteer administration that emphasized (personal) Preparation, (volunteer) Engagement, and (program) Perpetuation; P.E.P. included the targeted professional competencies of "Regularly updating stakeholders on the results of evaluations", "Evaluating the training/orientation program," and "Educating others on how to evaluate components of the volunteer program" (p. 15). Subsequent work by Safrit and Schmiesing (2005) found that members of the Association for Volunteer Administration responding to a mailed survey rated program evaluation, impact, and accountability as being important in the daily management of volunteers. In 2008, the Council for Certification in Volunteer Administration (CCVA) identified "Accountability: The ability to collect relevant data and to engage in meaningful monitoring, evaluation and reporting to stakeholder" (p. 3) as one of five core competencies serving as a foundation for the profession of volunteer administration.

The pressure on nonprofit organizations to evaluate the impact of volunteer-based programs has not abated during the first decade of the new century, and if anything has grown stronger. Today, according to Morley, Vinson, and Hatry (2001, p. 5):

> Nonprofit organizations are increasingly being pressed to measure and report their outcomes regularly to funders and other constituents. Service organizations are increasingly recognizing that they need some form of regular feedback on their outcomes to help them improve their services. ... [Still,] Outcome measurement is new to most private nonprofit organizations. Nonprofit organizations are more often familiar with monitoring and reporting such information as the number of clients served, ... [and] the number of volunteers and volunteer hours contributed. These are important data, but they do not help nonprofit managers or constituents understand how well they are helping their clients, that is, such statistics ... about the program's results.

Thus, professional managers and administrators of contemporary volunteer programs must accept the professional challenge to access and develop the knowledge, skills, and attitudes required to effectively and efficiently evaluate the outcome and impacts upon clientele that are the result of volunteer efforts. Furthermore, once they have collected and summarized such impact data, they must become more vocal advocates for the programs they serve through professional and programmatic advocacy and accountability.

Terms and Definitions: Evaluation, Impact, and Accountability

As discussed in the preceding section, impact evaluation is still a relatively new concept for many volunteer resource managers and volunteer-based programs and organizations. As such, there are three closely related (but not synonymous) terms that often are used in dialogues and communications with which volunteer resource managers must become familiar if not proficient. They are (1) evaluation, (2) impact, and (3) accountability.

Evaluation

As early as 1970, Steele believed that evaluation was "the process of judging (or a judgment as to) the value or worth of a program" (p. 5). Thiede (1971) approached evaluation as a process of determining the extent to which a program's objectives had been achieved. Gay (1985, pp. 12-13) defined evaluation as:

> The systematic process of collecting and analyzing data ... [and] with minor variations, ... represents one of two philosophical viewpoints ... : (1) Evaluation is the systematic process of collecting and analyzing data in order to determine whether, and to what degree, objectives have been, or are being, achieved; (2) Evaluation is the systematic process of collecting and analyzing data in order to make decisions.

Boone, Safrit, and Jones (2002) suggested that evaluation involved a broad perspective of decision-making about an educational program including "how program inputs, context, and processes relate to program outcomes; how efficient a program is; how suitable it is [for the targeted clientele]; and its overall importance" (p. 197). Contemporary approaches to this concept build upon these earlier concepts and themes, and include:

- "A form of appraisal, using valid and reliable research methods, that examines the processes or outcomes of an organization that exists to fulfill some social need" (Grinnell & Unrau, 2008, p. 553).

- "Applied research used as part of the managerial process ... conducted to aid those who must make administrative decisions about human service programs" (Royse, Thyer, & Padgett, 2010, p. 12).

- "Providing the information for making data-driven decisions that lead to improved performance of programs and organizations" (Guerra-Lopez, 2008, p. 6).

Thus, for the purposes of this chapter and in the context of volunteer-based programs, evaluation involves measuring a targeted program's inputs, processes, and outcomes so as to assess the program's efficiency of operations and/or effectiveness in impacting the program's targeted clientele group. This definition addresses two long-standing types of overall evaluation: (1) *formative* evaluation involves measuring and assessing the ongoing operations of a program to adjust program operations so as to maximize efficiency. Consequently, formative evaluation focuses more upon a program's inputs and processes; (2) *summative* evaluation involves measuring and assessing a program's outcomes so as to maximize effectiveness. Summative evaluation is more closely aligned with a second term closely related to evaluation (*impact*) to be discussed momentarily.

In closing, I suggest that the easiest day-to-day approach to defining the concept of *evaluation* is to equate it with the concept of *measuring*. Either consciously or unconsciously, each of us routinely *measure* daily aspects of our lives, whether it be how much coffee to put in the coffee-maker to brew eight total cups, how much further we can drive before refilling the gasoline tank in our vehicle, our chances of being excused from the four-hour office meeting that we are supposed to attend, or what training and development opportunities would best help us secure a job promotion. Similarly, as volunteer resource managers we must become proficient so as to routinely *evaluate* how many volunteers are required to reach a certain number of clientele in a new targeted program, how many more volunteer training sessions we may resource with a limited financial budget, our chances of minimizing risks related to a specific volunteer-delivered program, or how much in new resources we would need to expand an existing volunteer program to reach additional clientele.

Impact

In comparison to the concept of evaluation, impact focuses any evaluation upon "whether and to what extent a program causes changes in the desired direction among a target population" (Rossi & Freeman, 1993, p. 12). The W.K. Kellogg Foundation (2000) approached impacts

as changes that occur in a system, community, or organization resulting from an intervention or project. Bamberger, Rugh, and Mabry
(2006) defined impacts as "long-term economic, sociocultural,
institutional, environmental, technological, or other effects on identifiable populations or groups produced by a project, directly or indirectly,
intended or unintended" (p. 39).

Thus, *impact* may be considered the *ultimate effects and changes*
that a volunteer-based program has brought about upon those involved
with the program (*i.e.*, its stakeholders), including the program's
targeted clientele and their surrounding neighborhoods and communities, as well as the volunteer organization itself and its paid and volunteer staff. Impact usually refers to longer-term changes and effects in a
larger target group or system that warrant being evaluated, such as
decreased hunger in a specific neighbourhood, increased levels of
literacy in a targeted school system, or decreased incidences of a chronic
disease in a specific geographic region. In comparison, *outcomes* are
shorter-term, more focused, and more immediate results or changes that
a volunteer-based program has brought about upon the program's
stakeholders, such as the percentage of a neighbourhood's households
that benefitted from a recent food drive, improved reading scores at a
specific elementary school, or the percentage of a city's elderly population who indicated increased knowledge about the causes and symptoms
of Type 2 diabetes. While the two terms (*impacts* and *outcomes*) are
often used interchangeably, they are not synonymous; a program's short-
term *outcomes* contribute to its long-term, ultimate *impacts*, and are
usually easier to grasp conceptually and measure realistically.

While today's program funders and decision-makers may appreciate and welcome knowing about a volunteer program's outcomes,
they usually are more focused upon the program's ultimate impacts
upon the targeted population. In summary, when one *evaluates impacts*
of a volunteer program, one is simply *measuring ultimate effects and
changes* the volunteer program has brought about among those
involved with the program. However, having measured such effects
and changes is increasingly not sufficient to justify a program's
continuation or expansion, and this reality of today's nonprofit sector
brings us to the third and final closely related term.

Accountability

The concept of *accountability* was the most recent of the three
closely related terms to appear in the nonprofit literature. Not until

1985 did Boone first define the term as "the process of reporting efficiency of program operations, primarily to the learners and leaders of the targeted publics, the organization, funding sources, the profession, and (where appropriate) the governance body" (p. 196). Rossi and Freeman (1993) suggested that accountability involves providing concrete evidence to stakeholders and sponsors regarding the operations and impacts of a specific program, and according to Brizus and Campbell (1991), "What sets today's emphasis on public accountability apart is the part of the message involving proof" (p. 1). According to Carman and Fredericks (2008), the demand for improved and expanded accountability among nonprofit organizations is a major need to communicate a program's impacts to targeted stakeholders, both internal (*e.g.*, paid and volunteer staff) and external (*e.g.*, program clientele, funders, government legitimizers, *etc.*) stakeholders.

The key point in this discussion is not the concept of being held responsible for how resources (public or private) are used within a volunteer program. While this approach historically may be considered accountability, it omits a key contemporary responsibility of volunteer resource managers and program administrators to purposefully and proactively communicate the evaluated impacts of a specific volunteer program to a targeted stakeholder group. *Measuring a volunteer program's ultimate effects and changes* upon the program's clientele is commendable, but many volunteer organizations did so very well, yet failed to *purposefully and proactively communicate the information* to targeted important individuals or groups within and/or outside the sponsoring organization. Unfortunately, during times of resource retrenchment and fiscal crisis, such passive volunteer programs were the first to be eliminated to achieve targeted cost-savings and budget reductions. As one former professional colleague and volunteer resource manager told me, she developed a volunteer program at a children's hospital that was "nationally known" among her volunteer resource management peers, yet she was "too silently effective" at the local level. As a direct result, when the hospital board was forced to eliminate specific programs to meet decreased revenue amounts, her program was one of the first to be eliminated. "I only wish I had known then what I know now — you can't wait to be asked — you have to aggressively toot your own horn about how your program helps its clients because trust me, no one else will do it for you."

BASIC PRINCIPLES OF IMPACT EVALUATION DESIGN AND IMPLEMENTATION

Expectations by today's volunteer program funders, paid and volunteer staff, and clientele as well as by organizational administrators and decision-makers have resulted in new demands being placed upon VAs. Many experiences and long-tenured VAs have never before been expected to measure and communicate long-term, holistic effects realized within a volunteer program. While others may be somewhat familiar with the concept of program evaluation, they have applied it mainly to the evaluation of individual volunteer efforts and not the ultimate impacts of a program volunteers helped to deliver. Few formal training and education programs exist focused upon volunteer resource management as a profession, and those that do may not devote adequate time to the importance and process of impact evaluation and accountability.

Myriad descriptions of both conceptual and empirical evaluation models exist in the literature of the past 50 years. Kirkpatrick (1959) approached impact evaluation from the four conceptual hierarchical outcome levels of reactions, learning, behaviour, and results. Stufflebeam (1987) suggested the CIPP process for evaluation involving the evaluation's Context, Inputs, Processes, and Product. Fetterman (1996) suggested a social-consciousness-raising approach that he called "empowerment evaluation: the use of evaluation concepts, techniques, and findings to foster improvement and self-determination" (p. 4) involving the steps of 1. taking stock; 2. setting goals; 3. developing strategies; and 4. documenting progress. Combs and Faletta (2000) described a very pragmatic Targeted Evaluation Process (TEP) involving:

- Step 1 — Partnering with stakeholders;

- Step 2 — Understanding the intervention and organizational context;

- Step 3 — Targeting evaluation questions and identifying evaluation dimensions;

- Step 4 — Designing the tools, technology, and techniques;

- Step 5 — Gathering and analyzing data; and

- Step 6 — Reporting results.

Holden and Zimmerman (2009) proposed the EPIC model (Evaluation Planning Incorporating Context) including the five steps of:

1. assessing context,

2. gathering reconnaissance,

3. engaging stakeholders,

4. describing the program, and

5. focusing the evaluation.

And the list of authors and models goes on.

Consequently, the remainder of this chapter is devoted to describing basic knowledge and skills necessary in order for a volunteer administrator (VA) to effectively design and implement an impact evaluation of a volunteer program, and to be accountable for the evaluation findings. In doing so, I have attempted to discuss only academic ideas and concepts most critical to the chapter topics and to connect them to pragmatic, real-life contexts related to volunteer programs. Too often the concepts of "evaluation," "impact," and "accountability" are assumed to be too esoteric by VAs for them to apply the concepts in every-day situations involving volunteer programs. Too often administrators and decision-makers of volunteer programs immediately conclude that external paid evaluation consultants are required to conduct a valid and reliable evaluation of a volunteer program, and that outsourcing a program evaluation (usually at the considerable expenditure of ever-limited public and private dollars) is the only valid course of action. Too often we ourselves as VA professionals argue that we are simply too busy with the current demands upon our professional time to add another layer of professional competencies that could require expending our personal and professional time and resources in order to become proficient in them.

To address all of these and similar attitudes, arguments, and rationalizations I offer the following ideas and resources that I have developed as a result of 26 years working with volunteer programs at the community, regional, national and international levels. They are intended to challenge the reader to expand his/her perceptions of impact evaluation and accountability, to guide the reader in developing his/her own unique understanding and application of basic ideas and concepts, and to serve the reader as a source of materials and resources to strengthen both the reader as an individual professional VA and as a leader of a volunteer-based program or organization.

The Universal Standards

In 1975, The Joint Committee on Standards for Educational Evaluation was established to develop what have come to be called "universal standards" for conducting education evaluations worldwide. The Committee used an extensive and thorough public process to discuss and identify critical aspects of any educational evaluation that, as responsible professionals and resource stewards, evaluators should recognize and follow in their work. The resulting Program Evaluation Standards (1994) included examples and applications from "schools, universities, law, medicine, nursing, the military business, government, and social service agencies" (p. xvii). During the past 15 years, the Standards have undergone some revision and editing. While the full text of the current Program Evaluation Standards (2009) may easily be accessed online, Figure 1 summarizes the four main areas of utility, feasibility, propriety, and accuracy with examples of their applications to volunteer programs.

Figure 1: Examples of The Program Evaluation Standards in Evaluating Volunteer Programs

Standard	Key Components[*]	Examples in Volunteer Programs
Utility	Evaluation stakeholders should be identified; The evaluator must be trustworthy and competent to conduct the evaluation; Information collected should be pertinent to the program; Evaluation reports should clearly define the program being evaluated and evaluation parameters; Reports should be disseminated in a timely fashion; Evaluations should be conducted to insure that the results are utilized by stakeholders	• All stakeholders in the volunteer program evaluation should be identified before the evaluation is conducted • VAs should seek out formal training in conducting impact evaluations so as to develop requisite knowledge and skills • Evaluation findings should be shared with all identified volunteer program stakeholders in a timely manner

Standard	Key Components[*]	Examples in Volunteer Programs
Feasibility	Evaluation procedures should be practical to minimize participant disruption; Evaluation should be planned and conducted anticipating potential involvement of special interest groups; The evaluation must be efficient and warrant the expenditure of organizational resources	• VAs should devote ample time to planning an evaluation before it is conducted • VAs should consider aspects of both efficiency and effectiveness in planning a volunteer program evaluation • VAs should identify key aspects of targeted volunteer programs that warrant evaluation so as to be stewards of organizational resources
Propriety	Evaluations should serve the needs of the organization and targeted participants; Evaluations should be guided by formal signed agreements between formal parties; Evaluations should protect the rights of human subjects as well as individuals' dignity and worth; Evaluation findings should be made available to persons affected by the evaluation; Conflicts of interest should be dealt with openly and honestly; The evaluator should be fiscally responsible and accountable	• VAs should target evaluations to those volunteer programs, and aspects thereof, that warrant evaluating • VAs must aggressively seek to protect the rights and dignity of all volunteer program evaluation participants • Volunteer program evaluations should be made available to evaluation participants and stakeholders • VAs must demonstrate competence and accountability in conducting volunteer program evaluations

Standard	Key Components*	Examples in Volunteer Programs
Accuracy	The program being evaluated should be clearly described and documented; The context for an evaluation should be examined; The evaluation's purposes and procedures should be monitored and described; Sources of evaluation information should be described; Evaluation information collected should be valid, reliable, and systematically reviewed; Quantitative and/or qualitative information collected should be appropriately and systematically analyzed; Evaluation conclusions reached should be explicitly justified	VAs should describe both the volunteer program being evaluated and its context VAs must clearly describe and justify all methods and procedures used to evaluate a volunteer program VAs should document and justify all data collection and analysis methods used Conclusions from a volunteer program evaluation must be explicitly supported by the evaluation findings

* These key components have been paraphrased and summarized by the author based upon The Program Evaluation Standards (2009).

Anonymity and Confidentiality

In seeking to plan and conduct volunteer program evaluations that seek to follow The Program Evaluation Standards, VAs are often confronted by issues surrounding an evaluation's confidentiality or anonymity. An anonymous evaluation means that no one (including the evaluator) knows exactly who participated in an evaluation (Daponte, 2008). Anonymity in a volunteer program evaluation helps to ensure that participants (*e.g.*, program clientele, paid staff, volunteers, *etc.*) feel free to respond to evaluation questions in a totally honest and frank manner, regardless of the type of response or to whom a response is directed. The assumption is that by ensuring evaluation participants' anonymity, the evaluation data collected will be completely reliable and truly represent participants' feelings, opinions, and ideas.

However, while anonymity may strengthen the reliability of evaluation data collected, it can present the evaluator with methodological challenges. By promising to purposefully not record or track who has responded to an evaluation, the evaluator is left without any idea as to who has *not* responded to the evaluation. This is especially an issue when the evaluation involves large numbers of participants, and after the stated data collection period has ended, only a small number of the participants have actually completed the evaluation. Consequently, the evaluator cannot ascertain with any degree of confidence whether the respondents truly represent the target evaluation population as a whole, or rather only some subset of the total population. As a result, the evaluator may be limited in applying (or inferring) the evaluation findings to the total target population, and the original purpose of the evaluation could be compromised.

A more manageable approach may be to ensure the evaluation participants of the confidentiality of their evaluation responses. Confidentiality means that the evaluation answers will be held in confidence by the evaluator and used appropriately. Specific responses will never be directly linked to an individual respondent, and never presented in a manner that would allow anyone to deduce the identity of an individual respondent. So as to ensure confidentiality, evaluation participants are assigned a random number or other code as a surrogate label for their true identities. The key to such a random code is known only to the evaluator, who is required by professional and ethical standards to respect and honour it.

While traditional logic in evaluation methods argues that ensuring anonymity or confidentiality to evaluation participants helps to increase response rates and encourages participants to respond to evaluation questions more truthfully and honestly, legal issues may also be involved. Consequently, while it is not a required methodological aspect of planning an evaluation, a VA may be well-served to share the proposed evaluation plan with the organization's legal affairs office so as to proactively address issues of anonymity and confidentiality from an organizational risk management perspective.

Four Fundamental Questions

As a whole, I find that VAs are by nature action- and result-focused. I include myself in this stereotype, and recognize that my first professional instinct is usually to assemble a team of my peers so as to get to work addressing a challenge or issue that most often involves volunteers. While such an action-based focus is commendable, it does not always ensure the best use of our time, energies, and resources.

Thus, before any actual impact evaluation initiative is initiated, a VA should first contemplate and respond to four fundamental questions regarding a potential impact evaluation that will guide the VA in structuring the most effective and efficient evaluation for the particular situation. In fact, the remainder of this chapter is organized around these four practical questions to better guide VAs through the impact evaluation process.

QUESTION 1: WHY DO I NEED TO EVALUATE THE VOLUNTEER PROGRAM?

At first glance, this question may seem fundamentally redundant to the reader. However, as Guerra-Lopez (2008, p. 7) stated explicitly:

> In specific terms, before evaluators start to plan [an evaluation], they must determine why they are conducting an evaluation. Is this their initiative, or were they directed to do this work? What is the motivation for the study? What are they looking to accomplish and contribute as a result of the evaluation?

Of course, any impact evaluation within a volunteer organization must be directed toward a specific and identifiable volunteer program. However, a few basic realities must be highlighted at this point. First, not all volunteer programs need to be evaluated. One-time-only volunteer-based programs, or programs that are inherently part of the organization's mission may not warrant the extra resources necessary to evaluate them. Secondly, a VA must ascertain the balance between the potential results and benefits of a specific volunteer program evaluation, and the time, resources and materials that would be required to conduct it. In today's era of increasingly scarce resources, some funders may frown upon too large of an expenditure for a program's evaluation when the resources necessary could have been instead used to expand or strengthen the program's impact upon clientele. And finally, not everyone wants to know everything about every volunteer program. This reality relates to the concept of targeted accountability that will be addressed later in the chapter wherein a VA proactively identifies both key types of volunteer program stakeholders and the specific targeted impacts in which each stakeholder type is most interested.

Regarding Question 1, the author routinely encounters two pervasive types of situations in working with real-life volunteer programs and VAs that make this first question critically fundamental to the three remaining questions. First, as already alluded to, most often when approached with the concept of impact evaluation, VAs immediately begin to discuss evaluating the impacts of a specific volunteer program upon the *volunteers involved with the specific program that they supervise and support*, and not *the targeted clientele group that the volunteers actually work with*. This first type of situation relates directly to the prior discussion of the difference and relationship between the concepts of *outcome* and *impact*. While a program's effects upon its volunteers is an important outcome of the program, most nonprofit programs do not exist and are not funded so as to benefit the volunteers involved in the program; rather, funders give resources to programs, and decision-makers approve and advocate for programs, that support the engagement of volunteers as an effective strategy in making positive differences in the lives of some targeted group of clientele. As such, unless otherwise specified, the focus of an impact evaluation should be upon the program clientele (*i.e.*, a summative approach) rather than upon the program volunteers (*i.e.*, a formative approach).

The second situation is best represented by a small page out of an old children's book that a colleague framed and presented to me as a gift several years ago. It is a page from a 1939 edition of Lewis Carroll's *Through the Looking Glass* and shows Alice's encounter with the Cheshire Cat. Alice has been wandering around lost, and looks up at the Cat in a tree. "Would you tell me, please, which way I ought to go from here?" she asks, to which the Cheshire Cat responds, "That depends a good deal on where you want to get to." Like Alice, I am often asked to help evaluate a volunteer-based program, or provide some ideas about how the VA should go about evaluating such a program. Yet, too many times when I ask, "What exactly do you want to evaluate about the volunteer program?" I am answered by blank stares and something to the effect of, "Well, you know — the volunteer program." The simple yet brutally honest fact about this situation is that one cannot evaluate any aspect of a volunteer program for which a program objective was never written.

Developing Measurable Program Objectives

Impact evaluations in any program (including those involving volunteers) are based upon existing measurable program objectives focused upon the program's clientele.

A measurable program objective includes each of the following five critical elements:

1. the target audience/clientele group;

2. the intervention to be made with the targeted group (*i.e.*, the volunteer program);

3. the desired change/effect upon the targeted learner group as a result of the intervention (*i.e.*, impact);

4. the desired level of success for the intervention upon the targeted audience; and

5. how the intervention's success/failure will be measured (*i.e.*, evaluated).

Thus, a few hypothetical examples of well-written learner-focused measurable program objectives include:

• "As a result of the volunteer-staffed Nutritious-Meals-On-Wheels Program, at least 50 per cent of the identified 450 elderly shut-ins living within the greater metropolitan area served by the program will indicate improved knowledge of proper nutrition and its role in preventing chronic disease each fiscal quarter, as measured by a volunteer-administered follow-up telephone interview."

• "At least 30 per cent of parents of middle-school students participating in the three-week volunteer-delivered Summer Fun Reading Program at the library will report that their child(ren) is/are reading more often on their own, as measured by a mailed follow-up written survey ."

• "As a direct result of the 30-hour (*i.e.*, 10 separate three-hour sessions) corporate volunteer delivered Retool for the Future program, at least 50 per cent of the targeted 100 unemployed participants will demonstrate new workplace skills as observed and recorded during task simulations during the final two session meetings."

In reflecting upon these theoretical examples, consider what their non-measurable counterparts could entail, that are most often currently developed for volunteer-delivered programs:

• "At least 50 volunteers will contribute a total of 1,000 volunteer hours reaching at lcast 450 shut-ins through the Nutritious-Meals-On-Wheels Program."

• "At least 150 middle-school students will participate in the three-week volunteer-delivered Summer Fun Reading program at the library."

- "At least 100 unemployed adults will receive training from a minimum of 25 corporate volunteers contributing more than 150 hours of their personal time."

Tyler (1949) first approached the idea of measurable program objectives focused upon students in a formal school setting, yet they are requisite for the overwhelming majority of both contemporary school-based curriculum development models as well as community-based program development models. (For a more thorough discussion on the history and current use of measurable program objectives, the reader is directed to Boone, Safrit, and Jones, 2002.)

In closing this discussion of the first critical question to be answered in developing an impact evaluation plan, the author wants to point out one very important aspect: if a VA develops well-written measurable program objectives for a volunteer-based program before the program even begins, then his/her work in planning the program's evaluation is 90 per cent completed! The target audience for the impact evaluation has been identified, as well as the proposed method for collecting the impact data. Furthermore, well-written measurable program objectives focus a VA upon the ultimate clientele audience of the volunteer program, and the ultimate impact the program seeks to bring about.

Using Logic Models in Impact Evaluations

During the past decade, a new approach to identifying why an evaluation should be conducted and exactly what should be evaluated has arisen that involves tracking and connecting the inputs, processes, activities, reactions, outcomes, and impacts of the specific program or intervention being evaluated. As early as 1982, Honer was describing the rudimentary beginnings of an input-process-outcomes system for evaluating volunteer programs. Safrit and Merrill (1998) suggested an inputs-process-outcomes-impacts model for evaluating volunteer programs based upon Bennett and Rockwell's (1994) earlier work with the Targeting Outcomes of Programs (TOP) model. Such approaches are termed "logic" models since they seek to follow the logical development and implementation of a program or intervention from its conception to its targeted long-term impact. According to Frechtling (2007), a logic model "has become a powerful and useful tool for scaffolding evaluations, helping to define and clarify what should be measured and when. [A logic model] is a tool that describes the theory of change underlying an intervention, product, or policy" (p. 1). The most prevalent type of logic model used today in program evaluation was first popularized by the W.K. Kellogg Foundation (2000, 2004).

The four basic components of a logic model include:

1. Inputs: actual and in-kind resources and contributions devoted to the project;

2. Activities: all activities and events conducted or undertaken so as to achieve the program's identified goal;

3. Outputs: immediate, short-term services, events, and products that document the implementation of the project; and

4. Outcomes: the desired long-term changes achieved as a result of the project (Frechtling, 2007).

In some approaches to logic models, the components of Outputs and Outcomes are further divided into three distinct components: Outputs: immediate reactions or responses to the program; Outcomes: short-term knowledge, attitude, skills, and/or aspiration changes achieved in the program's target population; and Impacts: long-term, sustained changes brought about in the program's target population and its environment (Dunn et al., 2005). Figure 2 illustrates the use of a typical logic model in a volunteer program focused upon decreasing teen obesity. Note that with the logic model, the Outcomes are really the program's measurable program objectives.

The major strength of using logic modelling in volunteer program impact evaluations is that it forces a VA to focus on the ultimate, long-term outcome (impact) of a specific volunteer program while also identifying the shorter term outputs that are requisite to achieving that outcome/impact. Another strength is that along with identifying targeted outputs and outcomes, the logic model provides the VA with a succinct yet holistic summary of the various resources and activities that are being devoted to the volunteer program being evaluated. The stylized, summarized logic model developed for a specific volunteer program can serve as an excellent resource for reporting and account-ability of the volunteer program in question, and serve as an important basis for potential efforts to translate the volunteer program evaluation into monetary values for purposes of benefits cost analysis (BCA), and/or return on investment (ROI) calculations. These concepts will be discussed later in this chapter.

Figure 2: A Sample Logic Model For a Volunteer Program Focused Upon Decreasing Teen Obesity

Inputs	Activities	Outputs	Outcomes
• $350 in nutrition curricula purchased • $750 for use of the day camp facility (in-kind) • 10 members of the Program Advisory Committee • 12 adult volunteers working with the program	• Program coordinator devoted 3 work weeks (120 hours) to planning and implementing the program • Three, 2-hour meetings conducted of the Program Advisory Committee • Three, 3-hour volunteer training sessions conducted	• At least 30 teens who are clinically obese will participate in the three-day, 21-hour program • At least 10 adult volunteers will serve during the actual day camp • Program Advisory Committee members will volunteer to teach program topics to participants during the day camp	• At least 80% of teen participants will increase their knowledge of proper nutrition and/or the importance of exercise along with diet as evaluated using a pre/post-test survey • At least 70% of teen participants will demonstrate new skills in preparing healthy snacks and meals as evaluated by direct observation by program volunteers • At least 50% of teen participants will aspire to eat more nutritious meals and to exercise daily as indicated by a post-test survey

QUESTION 2: HOW WILL I COLLECT THE REQUIRED IMPACT EVALUATION DATA AND INFORMATION?

Once a VA has identified the purpose of the volunteer program evaluation, and what specific aspects of the program will be evaluated, Question 2 moves a VA forward to thinking about actual methods for collecting (and analyzing) impact evaluation data and information. Basically, two types of data and data collection methods exist: qualitative methods and quantitative methods. According to Thomas (2003, p. 1):

> The simplest way to distinguish between qualitative and quantitative may be to say that qualitative methods involve a researcher describing kinds of characteristics of people and events without comparing events in terms of measurements or amounts. Quantitative methods, on the other hand, focus attention on measurements and amounts (more and less, larger and smaller, often and seldom, similar and different) of the characteristics displayed by the people and events that the researcher studies.

Within non-academic contexts (including volunteer programs), quantitative methods are most commonly used in program evaluations. Quantitative methods allow the evaluator to describe and compare phenomena and observations in numeric terms. Their predominance may largely be due to the increasing demand for "number-based evidence" as accountability within nonprofit programs and organizations. However, qualitative methods may also be used very effectively in volunteer program impact evaluations. Qualitative methods focus upon using words to describe evaluation participants' reactions, beliefs, attitudes, and feelings and are often used to put a "human touch" on impersonal number scores and quantitative statistics.

Before exploring these two equally important data collection and analysis methods in more depth, the author wishes to quickly address two issues that the reader may be questioning. First, for the purposes of this chapter, the terms "evaluation" and "research" may be considered synonymous, and the author has been using both as such. However, in the strictest sense, "research" is defined as "a process of gathering information" (Glanz, 2003) and may involve "basic research" (*i.e.*, gathering information to increase knowledge for the sake of the knowledge itself) or "applied research" (*i.e.*, gathering information to increase knowledge as applied to a specific problem or issue). Consequently, "evaluation" may be considered "applied research used as part of the managerial process" (Royse, Thyer, & Padgett, 2010, p. 12) and is thus used most often in the context of knowledge as applied to improving the management and/or results of a specific program or product. Many times, evaluation methods and data analysis are also referred to as research methods and data analysis.

Second, the author wishes to acknowledge that the following discussion of qualitative and quantitative approaches to impact evaluation is in no means an exhaustive or even survey treatment of the topic. A quick search on the Internet will reveal the enormous numbers of texts, tomes, and other resources devoted to both topics. Entire university courses (and series of courses and even college majors) are devoted to both evaluation/research approaches. The following sections are instead designed to provide a VA with a basic introduction to each method, as well as combining the two methods, so as to provide a conceptual foundation for making basic decisions regarding what type of impact evaluation data to collect, and how to systematically analyze the data once it is collected.

Qualitative Approaches

Qualitative methods are as diverse and varied as the contexts in which they are utilized (Babberger, Rugh, & Mabry, 2006). Examples include case studies, ethnographies, content analysis, participant observation, and experienced narratives (Thomas, 2003). However, by far the most common qualitative method used with volunteer program impact evaluations is the case study approach, using focus groups and/or participant interviews to collect data (Spaulding, 2008).

With this approach, the volunteer program being evaluated is treated as a specific entity and the actions associated with it are explored in depth by collecting qualitative data describing participants' experiences and reactions to the entity (*i.e.*, program). Data may be collected from internal program stakeholders (*e.g.*, paid staff, volunteers, organization/program administrators, *etc.*) and/or external stakeholders (*e.g.*, funders, legitimizers, program clientele, *etc.*). Unlike with quantitative methods (to be discussed shortly), with qualitative methods and the case study approach, the evaluator is not as concerned with pulling a random sample of program participants from whom to collect data. The impact evaluation may be focused specifically upon improving the volunteer program's management, and thus the evaluator may purposefully collect data from paid and/or volunteer staff only. Or, with the usual situation in using the case study approach in a volunteer program impact evaluation, the evaluator seeks to collect data directly from the targeted clientele of the program so as to explore how the program has changed or affected their lives (*i.e.*, impact).

Case study data collection may involve the content analysis of program documents (*e.g.*, progress reports, meeting minutes, volunteer training designs, *etc.*), but most often in an impact evaluation context, it involves interviewing program clientele individually (Creswell, 1994), or collectively in small groups through focus groups (Dean, 1994; Kruger & Casey, 2000). Interviews may be conducted either face-to-face or over the telephone (or even via e-mail or texting!) but focus groups are always conducted face-to-face. With both data collection methods, the evaluator has developed ahead of time a list of questions, or interview schedule, that he/she wishes to ask the participant (Safrit & Lopez, 2001). The interview schedule is based upon the volunteer program's measurable program objectives, focuses the evaluator on the most important questions to be asked about the volunteer program, and keeps the evaluator on track during the limited time for interaction with the evaluation participant. While the interview schedule is organized around major questions, each question may include sub-questions (or probes) to encourage more in-depth and focused responses from participants.

During the interview, the evaluator takes notes regarding the participant's responses and/or tape-records the interview (with the participant's permission) so that it may be reviewed later. With focus groups, the main evaluator is usually supported by an assistant; while the evaluator guides the focus group session and asks the specific interview schedule questions, the assistant is taking notes and/or recording the focus group session (again, with participants' permission). Wells, Safrit, Schmiesing, and Villard (2000) provided practical examples of implementing focus groups in evaluating volunteer programs.

In analyzing both interview and focus group data (Miles & Huberman, 1994), the first step involves transcribing the verbal data into written transcripts, recording date, time, location, and basic participant information for each separate session for each transcript. Each transcript is then assigned page and line numbers. The major goal of qualitative data analysis is to identify in an objective yet rigorous manner any ideas and themes that are predominant and recurring among evaluation participants' comments. While computer word recognition software programs are available that will assist and expedite this content analysis process, the method favoured by the author involves multiple transcript readers (or "raters") and the constant comparative method first developed by Glaser and Strauss

(1967). In this approach, the evaluator recruits individuals external to the volunteer program and organization (yet who are familiar with the topic/focus of the program) to serve as "raters" who carefully read each transcribed interview. The raters individually submit the themes they identify to the evaluator, who reviews them and then collapses the individual themes into overarching themes, which are then resubmitted to the raters. The raters review the researcher's suggested collapsed themes and either: (1) indicate that they agree with them; or (2) suggest revisions to the themes based upon their individual original ideas. The process is repeated as many times as needed in order to reach an agreement level that is established ahead of time by the evaluator.

Safrit, Schmiesing, King, Villard, and Wells (2003) used a qualitative case study methodology and focus groups to collect data in order to evaluate impacts of a teen volunteer program in Ohio upon teen program participants. Resources that were developed by the author for use with that specific evaluation (and which the author has used extensively since) may be found in the Appendices. They include: Appendix A: A Quick Guide for Conducting Effective Interviews and Focus Groups; Appendix B: Analyzing Interview and Focus Group Data; and Appendix C: A Data Anaylsis Worksheet to Identify Recurring Themes from Interview and Focus Group Transcripts.

Quantitative Approaches

Quantitative evaluation designs are overwhelmingly the most prevalent approach to collecting impact evaluation data, and the most common method is survey research involving a questionnaire to collect data. While quantitative designs may seek to accomplish various evaluation goals including establishing causation and correlation between various aspects of a volunteer program (Bamberger, Rugh, & Mabry, 2006), VAs would most often use survey methods to collect data so as to describe impacts of volunteer programs in numeric terms. According to Thomas (2003, p. 42):

> Conducting a survey usually involves specifying the characteristic (target variable) of interest, identifying the collectivity that would display the variable (people, institutions, places, events, and the like), deciding how best to gather information from the collectivity, gathering the information, and summarizing the results in a readily comprehensible form.

Translated into volunteer program terms for our purposes, conducting a survey to evaluate impact involves: identifying the volunteer program of interest; identifying all program clientele who have participated in the program and selecting participants for the evaluation; developing a survey instrument (questionnaire) to collect data; collecting the data; and analyzing the data so as to reach conclusions about program impacts.

Participant Selection

When using a survey design, the VA evaluator must identify the target population of the volunteer program. The resulting list of all program participants is termed a census, since it includes everyone. In deciding from whom to collect data, the VA should most often include everyone in the evaluation study so as to avoid appearances of bias or attempting to "skew" the evaluation findings. Usually, using a census to collect data is most feasible when the number of program participants is manageable (say, 100 or fewer), and the VA knows how to contact all participants. Additionally, by using a census the VA avoids having to use higher level statistical analysis to determine levels of significance for the resulting findings since the statistics reported are all descriptive and there was no chance that the evaluation excluded any specific group either on purpose or by sheer randomness. The resulting evaluation findings may (with an adequate response rate) be applied or inferred to the total population of program participants, including those who did not respond to the survey.

However, when large numbers of program participants are involved, time and financial resources may not provide for the VA gathering information from every member of the census. In such situations, the VA must pull a sample from the total population. A sample is simply that — some smaller part of the larger total population. Most VAs who have had any exposure to statistics immediately assume that a random sample must be used, in which every member of the population had an equal chance of being selected as a member of the sample. Random samples are important in higher level statistical analysis of evaluation data collected for mathematical and statistical purposes beyond the scope of this chapter. However, many times a non-random sample may suffice in which the sample members were so selected on the basis of purpose (*e.g.*, collecting data from program clientele who benefitted from the efforts of volunteers who attended a specific training not required of all volunteers) or convenience (*e.g.*, collecting data from program clientele who happened to attend a specific program session on a convenient date or at a convenient location). The caution with purposeful or convenience samples is that the VA evaluator may only apply the evaluation findings to the participating/responding sample members and not the larger census of program participants. As such, the findings section of the evaluation report (to be discussed later in this chapter) would simply begin with a statement of the evaluation's limitations, such as: "The evaluation used a non-random sample drawn from the larger program population; as such, the reader is cautioned against making any inferences from the following evaluation findings to any group other than the evaluation participants."

The most important aspect of identifying and using either a census or sample in a volunteer program impact evaluation is for the VA evaluator to thoroughly and accurately describe and define whichever is used. This allows the evaluation reader to determine for himself/herself the rigor and validity of the evaluation findings as related to the evaluation's implications and conclusions.

Instrumentation

The research instrument utilized in survey research is called a questionnaire (NOTE: it is common in non-academic circles to call the research instrument itself a "survey" when in the purest definition it is actually a "questionnaire" being used in a "survey design"). Survey questionnaires are developed based upon the key foci of the evaluation, and thus (as discussed in the section on logic models) are usually developed based upon the volunteer program's measurable program objectives and targeted outputs and outcomes. The questionnaire may measure knowledge (*e.g.*, items that ask the respondent to provide an answer by filling in a blank, or to select the most appropriate response from a list of responses by circling a number next to the desired response) and/or attitudes (*e.g.*, items that ask the respondent to provide an answer by circling the number that best represents their response on an ordinal scale of 1 to 10, with end point labels such as "totally disagree" or "not at all" and "totally agree" or "always").

Entire texts are devoted to constructing survey questionnaires (Dillman, Smyth, & Christian, 2008) and that discussion is beyond the space limitations of this chapter. However, two critical aspects of developing any questionnaire involve establishing the questionnaire's validity and reliability. Validity refers to the degree to which a questionnaire actually measures the concepts it is designed to measure; validity may be established by sharing the draft questionnaire with a panel of experts in the subject of the evaluation and asking them whether they believe the questions measure what they are intended to.

Reliability refers to the questionnaire's ability to collect consistent data over time, and may be established through a number of means including test/retest and split-half approaches. Again, the reader is advised to seek out additional resources in establishing the validity and reliability of a new questionnaire to use in survey-based impact evaluations.

Data Collection Methods

Once the survey questionnaire has been developed and validated, and its reliability established, the VA evaluator must decide on exactly how to use the questionnaire to collect data. The earliest form for survey data collection still in use today is the written or mailed survey wherein evaluation participants received a print copy of the questionnaire and complete it either in person with the evaluator present to receive the completed instrument or at their leisure at home or wherever, returning their completed questionnaire to the evaluator by mail. In the later decades of the twentieth century, telephone surveys were popular means of collecting evaluation data; however, by the end of the century, the explosion in prevalence of pagers, answering machines, caller identification (ID), cell phones, *etc.*, resulted in telephone surveys being used less and less. However, the corresponding development and prevalence of the Internet and e-mail offered new avenues for administering surveys, and several "do-it-yourself" programs are now available whereby a VA evaluator may post a questionnaire and collect data all from the web, and at minimal expense. As an example, Safrit, Edwards, and Flood (2003) used a web-based questionnaire to collect evaluation data from teen volunteers in North Carolina.

Data Analysis Methods

Once the quantitative data are collected through the survey, the VA evaluator must analyze the data and calculate appropriate statistics to achieve the evaluation objectives. If the survey method sought to use a census, or a purposeful or convenience sample from the larger population, to describe participants' responses to specific aspects of a volunteer program, basic descriptive statistics will suffice including descriptions of central tendency (*e.g.*, means, modes, medians) along with corresponding measures of variance among responses (*e.g.*, ranges, standard deviations; Bamberger, Rugh, & Mabry, 2006). However, if a random sample was used to describe participants' responses to specific aspects of a volunteer program, then higher level statistics are required to analyze the data accurately (*e.g.*, tests for significance) that vary according to the types of data collected and/or specific analysis sought. In this situation, the VA evaluator is advised to seek out the support of a resident researcher or statistician at an area college or university.

Today, the prevalence of personal computers and data analysis software programs renders data analysis much easier than the days before they existed. Data collected using face-to-face and mailed questionnaires are simply entered into a data analysis program ranging from ubiquitous programs such as Excel® (that allows the VA to calculate basic statistics such as means, standard deviations, medians, *etc.*) to more esoteric yet user-friendly programs such as the Statistical Package for Social Sciences® (SPSS) that provides for higher level data analysis.

In closing, the volunteer resource management literature is filled with excellent examples of survey methods in volunteer programs, and VAs are encouraged to search out, read and copy such examples in their own volunteer programs so as to avoid "reinventing the wheel." Stein used a survey methodology and questionnaire instrument to evaluate a volunteer program as early as 1967. In 1978, Woog described a scale he developed to measure attitudes toward volunteers. Singletary, Smith, and Hill (2003) used a quantitative survey methodology to assess impacts on volunteers who participated in a collaborative program to manage water disputes.

Mixed Methods Approaches

Many times, neither qualitative nor quantitative methods alone are adequate to conduct an in-depth, holistic impact evaluation of a volunteer program. Thus, evaluators often develop a mixed methods approach that involves some aspects of both qualitative and quantitative methods (Creswell, 1994). The most common type of mixed methods approach to impact evaluations of volunteer programs involves a "two-phase design" in which the evaluator first uses qualitative methods in a first phase to identify and describe key themes describing a volunteer program's impacts upon clientele, and subsequently quantitative methods to be able to quantify and compare the intensity and pervasiveness of the impacts among the clientele.

The use of mixed methods in volunteer program impact evaluations has two major strengths. First, and most obvious, it provides two parallel and complimentary types of evaluation data for subsequent use in reports: qualitative data attesting to the importance and influences of the volunteer program upon the target clientele, and quantitative data describing the intensity and pervasiveness of specific changes and effects the volunteer program has brought about among clientele. Second, remember that the data collection instruments most commonly used in both qualitative methods (the interview schedule) and quantitative methods (the questionnaire) are each developed based upon the volunteer program's measurable program objectives. Often, volunteer program impacts upon clientele may manifest themselves that were never considered when the program was developed. By using mixed methods, and qualitative methods in the first phase, an unintended yet beneficial volunteer program impact may be identified that can be subsequently studied in greater depth during the second quantitative phase. If the evaluator had only used one or the other method, he/she would either have (1) never been made aware of this unintended impact (by using a quantitative methodology based upon the original program objectives only), or (2) been unable to describe the unintended impact in greater depth or to a larger extent (since it had simply been identified qualitatively).

QUESTION 3: WHO WANTS (OR NEEDS) TO KNOW THE IMPACT EVALUATION FINDINGS?

VAs invest enormous energies and passions into the programs we implement through the use of volunteers, and become the *de facto* experts on the entire program from conceptualization, to development and implementation, through impact evaluation. Probably one of the most difficult realizations a VA faces is that unlike himself/herself, not everyone associated with the volunteer program wants to know everything about it. This reality has been discussed earlier in this chapter. This phenomenon also has important implications for the fourth and final question to be discussed shortly: how to communicate the evaluation findings to specific stakeholders and stakeholder groups.

Consequently, the third question that a VA acting as a volunteer program evaluator must address is who exactly wants to know specifically what about the volunteer program in question. Considering the enormous biases that any VA would naturally have toward a volunteer program with which they are associated, the question is not as easy to answer as one would initially expect.

The Volunteer Program Accountability Matrix

To assist in the development of an objective and rational response to Question 3, the author developed and used for many years a Volunteer Program Accountability Matrix (Figure 3). Basically, the Matrix is a rubric in which specific types of volunteer program evaluation information (that parallel a logic model) are connected to specific types of internal and external volunteer program stakeholders. To use the Matrix, the VA simply answers the following question for each type of evaluation information, for each type of stakeholder: "If time and resources are limited, does this stakeholder really want to know this type of evaluation information?" If the answer is "yes," then the VA simply places a mark [X] in the cell where the specific stakeholder and evaluation information intercept; if the answer is "no," then the cell is left empty. The caveat for developing an effective Accountability Matrix is that the VA *must be brutally honest and frank in responding to the question for each stakeholder group and each type of evaluation informa*tion; he/she must recognize and manage the previously described bias that everyone wants to know everything about a specific volunteer program.

Figure 3: The Volunteer Program Accountability Matrix

Type of Volunteer Program Stakeholder	If time and resources are limited, does this stakeholder really want to know specifics about the volunteer program's . . .			
	Inputs	Activities	Outputs	Outcomes
Internal Stakeholders				
Volunteer Resource Manager				
Program Director				
Organization's Executive Director				
Organization's Board of Directors				
Program Volunteers				
Other Stakeholder? (identify)				
Other Stakeholder? (identify)				

External Stakeholders				
Program Clientele				
Program Funders				
Program Collaborators				
Community Leaders				
Government Leaders				
Other Stakeholder? (identify)				
Other Stakeholder? (identify)				
TOTALS				

The resulting completed Accountability Matrix can be of enormous value to the VA. By summing each particular column (*i.e.*, type of evaluation information), the VA may objectively ascertain where he/she would be wisest to invest time and energies into collecting evaluation data. By analyzing each separate row of the Matrix (*i.e.*, type of program stakeholder), the VA may easily identify what type and how much evaluation data and findings should be communicated to the specific type of volunteer program stakeholder. (The row analyses will also assist in answering Question 4 momentarily.) By reflecting upon the Matrix as a whole, the VA can compare and contrast what types of evaluation information are more targeted to internal stakeholders (*i.e.*, organizational peers) and which are more targeted toward external stakeholders.

As an example, Figure 4 illustrates a completed Accountability Matrix for a volunteer program focused upon decreasing teen obesity. Based upon the completed Matrix, the VA would be wise to spend most of his/her time collecting evaluation data focused in the two categories of outputs and outcomes. Furthermore, it appears that internal stakeholders would be much more receptive to holistic, all-encompassing information about the teen obesity program (spanning the gamut from program inputs to outcomes), while external program stakeholders appear to want more focused (and less encompassing) evaluation data and findings regarding program outputs and outcomes.

Figure 4: A Sample Completed Accountability Matrix for a Volunteer Program Focused upon Decreasing Teen Obesity

Type of Volunteer Program Stakeholder	If time and resources are limited, does this stakeholder really want to know specifics about the volunteer program's . . .			
	Inputs	Activities	Outputs	Outcomes
Internal Stakeholders				
Volunteer Resource Manager	X	X	X	X
Program Director	X	X	X	X
Organization's Executive Director	X			X
Organization's Board of Directors				X
Program Volunteers		X	X	
Other Stakeholder? (Advisory Committee Members)	X			X
External Stakeholders				
Program Clientele			X	X
Program Funders			X	X
Program Collaborators				X
Community Leaders				X
Government Leaders (County Commissioners)			X	X
Other Stakeholder? (County Health Department)			X	X
TOTALS	4	3	7	11

© 2009 R. Dale Safrit, All Rights Reserved.

Monetizing Impacts

In response to increasing demands for accountability, and myriad public/governmental budgeting and fiscal reporting systems, nonprofit managers and administrators have been challenged during the past decade to translate seemingly intangible program outputs and outcomes into financial terms. This "monetizing" of volunteer program impacts has at times been characterized as being cold, cruel, ineffective, and unreliable, yet it continues and expands as a fiscal reality of today's economic realities. Furthermore, it is closely correlated with the response to Question 3; very often, the "who" that wants to know "what" about the volunteer program evaluation includes program funders and decision-makers who more and more often elect to translate all program inputs, activities, outputs, and outcomes into the least common denominator of dollars.

The initial step in monetizing volunteer program impacts is, of course, to identify them. If a VA has developed a logic model for the program being evaluated, then program impacts and benefits are immediately identified in the Outputs and Outcomes sections of the model. However, according to Key (1994, p. 470):

> There are numerous potential sources of data for analysis of program benefits: 1. Existing records and statistics kept by the agency, legislative committees, or agency watchdogs ...; 2. Feedback from the program's clients ... obtained through a questionnaire or focus group; 3. Ratings by trained observers; 4. Experience of other governments or private or non-profit organizations; and 5. Special data gathering.

However, the idea of converting volunteer efforts into financial figures is not new to volunteer organizations. As early as 1982, Karn (1982) proposed a system to convert volunteer time into monetary value. More recently, Anderson and Zimmerman (2003) describe five methods to estimate the dollar value of volunteers' time:

1.   average wage (*i.e.*, the average wage of all wage earners in an identified profession, municipality, or geographic region, usually as gleaned from census data);

2.   comparable worth (*i.e.*, the hourly wage that a paid professional would earn doing the same type of work as a volunteer performing a specific task or job);

3.   independent sector figure (*i.e.*, the average dollar value of an hour of a volunteer's time that is calculated and published annually by The Independent Sector based upon United States Bureau of Labor statistics);

4.   living wage (*i.e.*, the United States federal government's estimated hourly wage required for an individual to maintain a standard of living above the current poverty level); and

5.   minimum wage (*i.e.*, the minimal hourly wage that any employer must pay any employee as established by a state government or the federal government).

Any student in a public administration course taught at the university level has been exposed to standard processes and parameters through which potential intangible outcomes from the expenditures of public dollars are translated into monetary amounts, thus allowing a public administrator to ascertain whether the potential benefits and outcomes justify the proposed outlay of public dollars.

As a result, the process of converting volunteer program metrics (*i.e.*, anything that is measured, or evaluated, as part of the volunteer program) begins with assigning a valid and defendable dollar amount to each and every aspect of the volunteer program being evaluated. However, this is easier said than done, especially for nonprofit programs.

Pulling from Anderson and Zimmerman (2003), the author most often uses the approaches of comparable worth and minimum wage. This position is supported by Key (1994), who stated: "Most economists argue that despite their imperfections, market prices are the best valuation of a benefit. Therefore, the evaluator should always use a market value when one is available" (p. 470). Current minimum wage is such a market value. Both the average wage and living wage are often difficult to document based upon public records, not reflective of specific geographic regions, and almost impossible for a VA to calculate independently. While most VAs in the United States are familiar with The Independent Sector's (<www.independentsector.org>) annual estimate of the value of a volunteer's time, the figure represents a national average that is not reflective of specific geographic regions or the level of complexity and specialization of particular volunteer tasks. Similar estimates and procedures for calculating the value of a volunteer's time in Canada are available from Imagine Canada's website: <www.imaginecanada.ca>.

Returning to our example of the volunteer-based teen obesity program, Figure 5 demonstrates how the VA could convert each specific aspect of the program's inputs, activities, outputs, and outcomes into dollar amounts. Note that the VA used actual receipts and financial records to monetize total Input costs. For Activities and Outputs, the VA used his/her actual salary to estimate the costs of his/her time devoted to the volunteer program (including benefits at a rate of 23 per cent of total salary), and the minimum wage of $6.50 per hour (that was accurate at the time of the original calulations) to calculate the costs of time contributed by the program's volunteers and Program Advisory Committee members, as well as the time required of participants' parents to get their children to the program. In reality, the VA could have requested actual salary amounts from his/her professional peers serving as Advisory Committee members and calculated the value of their time using actual wages; the total figure would most likely have been greater.

The most challenging aspect of any volunteer program to monetize is always Outcomes (or impacts). Three immediate realities contribute to this challenge. First, VAs seldom come into direct contact with the actual clientele of a volunteer program for which they recruit and supervise volunteers; thus, they may not have automatic access to statistics regarding the clientele, nor an opportunity to collect data directly from the clientele. They instead may have to work with the overall program director or organization's executive director to identify and proactively plan for such data collection. Second, even when such data are collected, VAs often do not have a readily available conversion figure or statistic to use in converting the data collected into monetary amounts; thus, the VA must often look to some external entity (*e.g.*, a professional association, government entity, private industry, *etc.*) in order to secure a valid and reliable conversion factor. In the example given, the volunteer-delivered day camp's goal was to educate obese teens about proper nutrition and the role of diet and exercise in a healthy lifestyle. The VA researched the issue of diabetes among children, and found the metric of $2.5 million per year as the estimated medical costs to treat a single obese youth, as estimated by the State Department of Health Services. This metric is defendable as both valid and reliable since it originates with a recognized expert regarding the issue of teen obesity, a government entity in this case. And third, even when clientele data and valid/reliable conversion metrics are available, many VAs feel uncomfortable using them to estimate the monetary value of observed and potential volunteer program outcomes and benefits of volunteer programs. Many argue that they cannot "prove" that the volunteer program directly "caused" any actual change in the program's clientele since such changes can only be documented years into the future. The VA in the example given did not attempt to claim causality between the volunteer program and medical costs saved for the specific program participants. Rather, he/she evaluated immediate clientele outcomes of the program (*e.g.*, increased knowledge, demonstrated new skills, and documented aspirations) and used those figures to estimate a minimal long-term clientele impact (in this case, "a mere 10% of participants"). Thus, the VA is not claiming to have dramatically changed the lives of each and every program participant who benefitted from volunteers' contributions, but instead is offering a logical and defendable proposition about what could long-term impacts could result at a minimum as a result of volunteers contributing their time and energies to the day camp program. In doing so, a VA should keep the following two important points in mind: (1) Always have some documented immediate or short-term outcome to use in calculating potential cost savings; one may not simply material-ize such metrics out of thin air. (2) Always research and document a conversion factor used based upon an expert regarding the program or issue being addressed; government agencies and private foundations are excellent sources of such conversion factors.

Figure 5: Examples of Converting Metrics in a Volunteer Program Focused upon Decreasing Teen Obesity into Dollar Amounts

Inputs	Activities	Outputs	Outcomes
$350 (in nutrition curricula purchased) $750 (use of the day camp facility; in-kind) $3,600 (total costs of day camp supplies, meals, snacks, equip-ment, *etc.*)	$1,800 (VA's salary devoted to program; 3 work weeks = 120 hours for planning and implementing the program @ $15.00/hr. salary rate) $414 (VAs work benefits calculated as 23% of salary) $1,170 (Program Advisory Committee members' time; 3, 2-hour meetings conducted for 10 members @ $6.50/hr. minimum wage[*]) $4,095 (cost of volunteers' time for training; 3, 3-hour volunteer training sessions for 21 volunteers @ $6.50/hr. minimum wage[*])	$2,320.50 (21 adult volunteers contributed 357 total hours during the actual day camp @ $6.50/hr. minimum wage[*]) $266.50 (8 Program Advisory Committee members volunteered 41 total hours to teach program topics during the day camp @ $6.50/hr. minimum wage[*])	84% (n = 30) of teen participants increased their knowledge of proper nutrition and/or the importance of exercise along with diet as evaluated using a pre/post-test survey 75% (n = 27) of teen participants demonstrated new skills in preparing healthy snacks and meals as evaluated by direct observation by program volunteers 54% (n = 19) of teen participants aspired to eat more nutritious meals and to exercise daily as indicated by a post-test survey

Inputs	Activities	Outputs	Outcomes
	$1,404 (costs of participating 36 obese teens parents' costs to transport participants to day camp; 2 hrs./day @ 3 days @ 36 parents @ $6.50/hr. minimum wage[*])		
Total Estimated Program Costs		**Total Estimated Program Benefits**	
$4,700	**$8,883**	**$2,587**	**If, as a result of the program, a mere 10% of obese teens who demonstrated new skills in preparing healthy snacks and meals (n = 3) had to make one fewer visit to a doctor each year for the next 5 years, at an average doctors' visit cost of $120, then the program would have saved a minimum of $1,800 in medical costs.**
			If, as a result of the program, a mere 10% of obese teens who aspired to eat more nutritious meals and exercise regularly (n = 2) did not develop Type II diabetes, at a cost to society of $2.5 million as estimated by the State Dept. of Health Services, then the program would have saved a minimum of $5.0 million.

$13,583	$5,002,587
Estimated CSA: $8,602 Estimated BCA: 368:1 Estimated ROI: 3,673%	

* NOTE: this $6.50 figure is used by the author for illustrative purposes only. As of July 24, 2009, the official U.S. federal hourly minimum wage was increased to $7.25.

© R. Dale Safrit, All Rights Reserved.

Once all volunteer program metrics have been converted into dollar amounts, the VA may borrow from the field of applied economics in order to calculate three very powerful statistics that may support (or discount!) the monetary value of the volunteer program being evaluated. The three statistics include cost savings analysis (CSA), benefits cost analysis (BCA), and return on investment (ROI).

Cost Savings Analysis (CSA)

Cost savings analysis is simply the estimated monetary value of any potential program costs that were not required to be expended by program implementers as a direct result of the involvement of volunteers in the specific program. In the example program, the CSA was $8,602 that includes the contributed value of the day camp rental as well as the value of all time required of and contributed by the volunteers involved in the program. The argument here is that the day camp could not have been conducted without the contributed value of the day camp rental, and without volunteer (as opposed to paid) staff working during the three-day program; no funds existed to cover these costs, especially if it had been necessary to have hired camp staff.

Benefit-Costs Analysis (BCA)

As early as 1978, Moore proposed applying benefit-cost analysis to volunteer programs. Basically, benefit-cost analysis (also called cost-benefit analysis and benefit-cost ratio) is the estimated ratio comparing the net benefits of a volunteer program to the total costs of the program (Key, 1994; Royce, Thyer, & Padgett, 2010). A benefit-cost ratio of one means that the program benefits equal the program costs; a benefit-cost ratio of two (written as 2:1) indicates that for each $1.00 spent on the program, $2.00 were returned as benefits. In the example program, the total program benefits are estimated to be

$5,002,587, and total program costs $13,583. Thus, the calculated BCA would be 368:1, or for every $1.00 in program costs, the program generated an estimated $368 in real and potential benefits.

Return on Investment (ROI)

Taking calculations of volunteer program benefits and costs to a third and higher level, the return on investment "is the discount rate that would make the present value of the project equal to zero" (Key, 1994, p. 461). ROI compares the net program benefits and costs; it is the total benefits minus the total costs, divided by the total costs, and multiplied by 100 (Phillips, 2002; Phillips, 2003; Phillips & Phillips, 2005). The resulting ratio is usually expressed as a per cent by multiplying the ratio by 100. Thus in the example given, the ROI would be $4,989,004 (*i.e.*, $5,002,587 minus $13,583) divided by $13,583, multiplied by 100, or 3,673 per cent. Thus, for every $1.00 invested in the volunteer delivered teen obesity program, a net monetary benefit of $3,673 was generated for the larger community; this ROI would equate to a BCA of 368:1.

QUESTION 4: HOW WILL I COMMUNICATE THE IMPACT EVALUATION FINDINGS?

The fourth and final question that should guide a VA in conducting a volunteer program impact evaluation may at first glance seem superfluous; however, even the best planned and conducted volunteer program impact evaluations are virtually worthless if key program stakeholders do not read and benefit from them. As was identified in the discussion of the Volunteer Program Accountability Matrix, not all stakeholders want (or need) to know the same information gathered from a volunteer program impact evaluation. According to Hendricks (1994, p. 549):

> If a tree falls in the forest and no one hears it, does it make a sound? If an evaluation report falls on someone's desk and no one reads it, does it make a splash? None whatsoever, yet we evaluators still rely too often on long tomes filled with jargon to "report" our evaluation results.

In deciding how to communicate the findings of a volunteer program impact evaluation, a VA should consider three important aspects of the accountability function: (1) the communication recipient, (2) the message to be communicated, and (3) the format and medium used to communicate. We have already discussed the first two aspects in the section addressing the Volunteer Program Accountability Matrix. Using the Matrix, the VA would identify major internal and external stakeholders who need to be informed about the volunteer program's impacts, and what specific impacts and outcomes the stakeholders are most interested in.

Report Formats and Approaches

Regarding the third aspect, the format and medium used to communicate the impact evaluation findings, VAs usually fall into the dominant paradigm of developing a holistic and all-encompassing written final report. Based upon the sample Accountability Matrix in Figure 4, such a report may be warranted for specific internal stakeholders such as the organization's executive director, the VA him/herself, and the volunteer program director. Such a final report serves as a detailed and documented record of the total volunteer program, from its inception (and the identified clientele need that the program was designed to address), through its design and implementation (including planning activities and delivery strategies), through its evaluation of impacts achieved. According to Royse, Thyer, and Padgett (2010), such holistic final reports usually include the following sections:

- Executive Summary: A brief description of the program and evaluation findings (an abstract).

- Introduction: A description of the clientele problem/issue the volunteer program sought to address; the program's description and questions about it explored in the impact evaluation; and a brief review of necessary and relevant literature related to the program and its evaluation.

- Methodology: A detailed and complete description of the evaluation design and data collection procedures including (as appropriate) the target population or sample, instruments used to collect data, and procedures used to analyze the data.

- Results (Findings): Factual information resulting from the evaluation including tables and charts/graphics, identifying those findings of statistical, clinical, or practical significance.

- Discussion: An explanation of the findings including applications and implications to the target clientele, the volunteer program, and/or the sponsoring agency/organization, along with a description of any limitations of the evaluation.

However, again referring to Figure 4, few (if any) of the volunteer program's external stakeholders (and even some internal stakeholders) appear to desire or be interested in such a large and holistic final report. For such stakeholders, an executive summary is probably the most feasible and practical (and politically astute!) format for a VA to use in communicating specific and targeted impact evaluation findings. According to Royse, Thyer, and Padgett (2010, pp. 373-74),

> An executive summary is generally short (2-4 pages) ... use the same headings [as in a final report] in writing one. Use language that is not overly complicated. Aim for sentences to be short (under 30 words); most people don't want to take the time to decipher a convoluted report with many complex, compound sentences.

The VA should be certain to highlight in the executive summary any advanced impact evaluation analyses that have been calculated related to the evaluation findings, such as cost savings, benefit-cost analyses, or return on investment analysis. Appendix D illustrates an executive summary from a real-life volunteer-based youth development program in North Carolina.

In summary, in deciding how to communicate the findings of a volunteer program impact evaluation, a VA should keep in mind the following utilization-focused reporting principles suggested by Patton (2008, p. 509):

1. Be intentional about reporting, that is, know the purpose of the report and stay true to that purpose.

2. Stay user-focused: Focus the report on the priorities of primary intended users.

3. Organize and present findings to facilitate understanding and interpretation.

4. Avoid surprising primary stakeholders.

5. Prepare users to engage with and learn from "negative" findings.

6. Distinguish dissemination from use.

THE FUTURE OF IMPACT EVALUATION IN VOLUNTEER RESOURCE MANAGEMENT

Hopefully, the information, ideas, and resources presented in this chapter will empower VAs to be more positive in their attitudes toward impact evaluation in volunteer programs, competent and confident in their knowledge and abilities to evaluate volunteer program impact, and proactive in aspiring to do so. However, while individual VAs' competencies as impact evaluators are fundamental to our profession, the future of impact evaluation in volunteer resource management will depend on our collective capacity as a profession to advocate for such evaluations.

The profession of volunteer administration is in itself as diverse and colourful as the individual professionals who practise it. This is, indeed, one of the strengths of our profession — our respect for individual volunteer programs and resource managers seeking to bring about positive change in the lives of a pluralistic continuum of unique individuals and communities. However, this respect for diversity and pluralism is also one of our greatest challenges in attempting to focus and consolidate the myriad requisite knowledge and skills needed across the continuum into a single set of professional competencies and standards. The professional organization that is the impetus behind this text has worked diligently toward this end, with enormous success.

But while the future of impact assessment in volunteer programs is grounded in the responsibility of each individual VA to accept the personal challenge to become competent in impact evaluation, and marketed in the recognition by our profession of the importance impact evaluation plays in any volunteer program regardless of breadth or scope, it is dependent upon our abilities as individual VAs to educate our organizational peers and administrators regarding the inherent role of impact evaluation in volunteer program development and implementation. According to Hoole and Patterson (2008, p. 95):

> If evaluation is not tied to the organization's mission and does not contribute to the fundamental understanding of the people and issues the organization serves but is instead undertaken from accountability pressures or conflicting stakeholder demands, evaluation fails the social sector.

This author concurs; the future of impact evaluation in volunteer programs lies in our personal abilities as innovators and leaders, and our professional vision as VAs, to once again educate our organizational peers and steward a process of innovation and acceptance. The ultimate impact of our efforts will be a new, sustained volunteer organizational culture wherein volunteer program impact evaluation is seen as integral to continual quality improvement and organizational learning rather than necessary for resource development and funder accountability.

REFERENCES

Anderson, P.A., & Zimmerman, M.E. (2003). Dollar value of volunteer time: A review of five estimation methods. *The Journal of Volunteer Administration, 21*(2), 39-44.

Bamberger, M., Rugh, J., & Mabry, L. (2006). *Real world evaluation: Working under budget, time, data, and political constraints.* Thousand Oaks, CA: SAGE Publications.

Bennett, C., & Rockwell, K. (1994, December). *Targeting outcomes of programs (TOP): An integrated approach to planning and evaluation.* Retrieved June 14, 2009, from http://citnews.unl.edu/TOP/english/.

Boone, E.J. (1985). *Developing programs in adult education.* Englewood Cliffs, NJ: Prentice-Hall, Inc.

Boone, E.J., Safrit, R.D., & Jones, J.M. (2002). *Developing programs in adult education* (2nd ed.). Prospect Heights, IL: Waveland Press.

Brizius, J.A., & Campbell, M.D. (1991). *Getting results: A guide for government accountability.* Washington, DC: Council of Governors Policy Advisors.

Carman, J.G., & Fredericks, K.A. (Eds.). (2008). *Nonprofits and evaluation.* San Francisco: Jossey-Bass.

Combs, W.L., & Falletta, S.V. (2000). *The targeted evaluation process.* Alexandria, VA: American Society for Training & Development.

Council for Certification in Volunteer Administration. (2008). *Body of knowledge in volunteer administration.* Retrieved August 12, 2009, from http://www.cvacert.org/certification.htm.

Creech, R.B. (1968). Let's measure up! A set of criteria for evaluating a volunteer program. *Volunteer Administration, II*(4), 1-18.

Creswell, J.W. (1994). *Research design: Qualitative & quantitative approaches.* Thousand Oaks, CA: SAGE Publications.

Culp, K., & Nolan, M. (2000). Trends impacting volunteer administrators in the next ten years. *The Journal of Volunteer Administration, 19*(1), 10-19.

Daponte, B.O. (2008). *Evaluation essentials: Methods for conducting sound research.* San Francisco: Jossey-Bass, a Wiley Imprint.

Dean, D.L. (1994). How to use focus groups. In J.S. Wholey, H.P. Hatry, & K.E. Newcomer (Eds.), *Handbook of practical program evaluation* (pp. 338-349). San Francisco: Jossey-Bass Publishers.

Dillman, D.A., Smyth, J.D., & Christian, L.M. (2008). *Internet, mail, and mixed-mode surveys: The tailored design method.* Hoboken, NJ: John Wiley & Sons, Inc.

Dunn, C., Feaster, T., Guion, L.A., Jayaratne, J., Safrit, R.D., & Sykes, W. (2006). *North Carolina Cooperative Extension Program Development Institute: Reinforcing the solid foundation of extension programming in North Carolina.* Raleigh: North Carolina Cooperative Extension.

Ellis, S.J. (1996). *From the top down: The executive role in volunteer program success.* Philadelphia: Energize, Inc.

Fetterman, D.M. (1996). Empowerment evaluation. In D.M. Fetterman, S.J. Kaftarian & A. Wandsersman (Eds.), *Empowerment evaluation: Knowledge and tools for self-assessment & accountability* (pp. 3-46). Thousand Oaks, CA: SAGE Publications.

Fisher, J.C., & Cole, K.M. (1993). *Leadership and management of volunteer programs.* San Francisco: Jossey-Bass Publishers.

Frechtling, J.A. (2007). *Logic modeling methods in program evaluation.* San Francisco: John Wiley & Sons, Inc.

Gay, L.R. (1985). *Educational evaluation and measurement: Competencies for analysis and application.* Columbus, OH: Charles E. Merrill Publishing Co.

Glanz, J. (2003). *Action research: An educational leader's guide to school improvement.* Norwood, MA: Christopher-Gordon Publishers, Inc.

Glaser, B.G., & Strauss, A.L. (1967). *The discovery of grounded theory: Strategies for qualitative research.* Chicago: Aldine Publishing Company.

Grinnel, R.M., & Unraau, Y.A. (Eds.). (2008). *Social work research and evaluation* (8th ed.). New York: Oxford University Press.

Guerra-Lopez, I. (2008). *Performance evaluation: Proven approaches for improving program and organizational performance.* San Francisco: Jossey-Bass.

Hendricks, M. (1994). Making a splash: Reporting evaluation results effectively. In J.S. Wholey, H.P. Hatry, & K.E. Newcomer (Eds.), *Handbook of practical program evaluation* (pp. 549-575). San Francisco: Jossey-Bass Publishers.

Holden, D.J., & Zimmerman, M.A. (2009). *A practical guide to program evaluation: Theory and case examples.* Los Angeles: SAGE Publications, Inc.

Honer, A.S. (1982). Manage your measurements, Don't let them manage you! *Volunteer Administration, 14*(4), 25-29.

Hoole, E., & Patterson, T.E. (2008). In J.G. Carman & K.A. Fredericks (Eds.), *Nonprofits and evaluation* (pp. 93-113). Hoboken, NJ: John Wiley & Sons, Inc.

Joint Committee on Standards for Educational Evaluation. (1994). *Standards for evaluations of educational programs, projects, and materials.* New York: McGraw-Hill.

Joint Committee on Standards for Educational Evaluation. (2009). *The program evaluation standards.* Kalamazoo, MI: The Evaluation Center. Retrieved June 14, 2009, from http://www.wmich.edu/evalctr/jc/.

Karn, G.N. (1982). Money talks: A guide to establishing the true dollar value of volunteer time. *The Journal of Volunteer Administration, 1*(2), 1-17.

Kearns, K.P. (1996). *Managing for accountability: Preserving the trust in public and nonprofit organizations.* San Francisco: Jossey-Bass Publishers.

Key, J.E. (1994). Benefit-cost analysis in program evaluation. In J.S. Wholey, H.P. Hatry, & K.E. Newcomer (Eds.), *Handbook of practical program evaluation* (pp. 456-488). San Francisco: Jossey-Bass Publishers.

Kirkpatrick. D.L. (1959). Techniques for evaluating training programs. *Journal of the American Society for Training and Development, 13*(11-12), 23-32.

Krueger, R., & Casey, M.A. (2000). *Focus groups: A practical guide for applied research* (3rd ed.). Thousand Oaks, CA: SAGE Publications.

Medaugh, B. (1999). Volunteer evaluations – From a volunteer's perspective. *The Journal of Volunteer Administration, 17*(2), 6-10.

Merrill, M., & Safrit, R.D. (2000, October). Bridging program development and impact evaluation? *Proceedings of the 2000 International Conference on Volunteer Administration* (p. 63). Phoenix, AZ: Association for Volunteer Administration.

Miles, M.B., & Huberman, A.B. (1994). *Qualitative data analysis: A sourcebook of new methods*. Beverly Hills, CA: Sage Publications.

Moore, N.A. (1978). The application of cost-benefits analysis to volunteer programs. *Volunteer Administration, 11*(1), 13-22.

Morley, E., Vinson, E., & Hatry, H.P. (2001). *Outcome measurement in nonprofit organizations: Current practices and recommendations.* Washington, DC: Independent Sector.

National Human Services Assembly. (2004, October). *From research to action: A unified response to the 2004 Volunteer Management Capacity Study.* Retrieved August 12, 2009, from http://www.nassembly.org.

Naylor, H.H. (1973). *Volunteers today: Finding, training and working with them.* Dryden, NY: Dryden Associates.

Naylor, H.H. (1976). *Leadership for volunteering.* Dryden, NY: Dryden Associates.

O'Connell, B. (1976). *Effective leadership in voluntary organizations.* Chicago: Follett Publishing Company.

Patton, M.Q. (2008). *Utilization-focused evaluation* (4th ed.). Los Angeles: SAGE Publications, Inc.

Phillips, J.J. (2003). *Return on investment in training and performance improvement programs* (2nd ed.). Amsterdam: Butterworth Heinemann.

Phillips, P.P. (2002). *The bottomline on ROI: Basics, benefits, & barriers to measuring training & performance improvement.* Atlanta, GA: CEP Press.

Phillips, P.P., & Phillips, J.J. (2005). *Return on investment: ROI basics.* Alexandria, VA: American Society for Training & Development.

Rossi, P.H., & Freeman, H.E. (1993). *Evaluation: A systematic approach.* Newbury Park, CA: SAGE Publications.

Royse, D., Thyer, B.A., & Padgett. D.K. (2010). *Program evaluation: An introduction* (5th ed.). Belmont, CA: Wadsworth.

Safrit, R.D., Edwards, H.C., & Flood, R.W. (2003, September). An initial assessment of an interactive Web-based Extension curriculum to engage and prepare rural adolescents for active civic involvement: The North Carolina 4-H TRY-IT! project (Teens Reaching Youth through Innovative Teams). In J. Kozari (Ed.), *Proceedings of the 16th European Seminar on Extension Education, ESEE 2003* (pp. 141-146). Eger, Hungary: ESEE.

Safrit, R.D., & Lopez, J. (2001). Exploring Hispanic American involvement in community leadership through volunteerism. *The Journal of Leadership Studies, 7*(4), 3-10.

Safrit, R.D., & Merrill, M. (1998). Assessing the impact of volunteer programs. *The Journal of Volunteer Administration, 16*(4), 5-10.

Safrit, R.D. & Merrill, M. (2001, November). A comparative study of human resource management in the non-profit sector: Two grassroots organizations, two countries, two continents, many insights. In N. MacDuff (Ed.), *Proceedings of the 30th Annual Conference of the Association for Research on Nonprofit Organizations and Voluntary Action (ARNOVA)* (p. 48). Miami, FL: ARNOVA.

Safrit, R.D., & Merrill, M. (2005, November). The seven habits of highly effective managers of volunteers. *Proceedings of the 10th International Association of Volunteer Efforts (IAVE) Asia-Pacific Regional Volunteer Conference* (p. 67). Hong Kong, China: IAVE.

Safrit, R.D., & Schmiesing, R.J. (2002, October). Measuring the impact of a stipended volunteer program: The Ohio 4-H B.R.I.D.G.E.S. experience. *Proceedings of the 2002 International Conference on Volunteer Administration* (p. 16). Denver, CO: Association for Volunteer Administration.

Safrit, R.D., & Schmiesing, R.J. (2004). A suggested model for contemporary volunteer management: Qualitative research bridging the professional literature with best practices. *The Journal of Volunteer Administration, 22*(4), 34-39.

Safrit, R.D., & Schmiesing, R.J. (2005). Volunteer administrators' perceptions of the importance of and their current levels of competence with selected volunteer management competencies. *The Journal of Volunteer Administration, 23*(2), 4-10.

Safrit, R.D., Schmiesing, R.J., Gliem, J.A., & Gliem, R.R. (2005). Core competencies for volunteer administration: An empirical model bridging theory with professional best practice. *The Journal of Volunteer Administration, 23*(3), 5-15.

Safrit, R.D., Schmiesing, R., King, J.E., Villard, J., & Wells, B. (2003). Assessing the impact of the three-year old Ohio Teen B.R.I.D.G.E.S. program. *The Journal of Volunteer Administration, 21*(2), 12-16.

Schmiesing, R., & Safrit, R.D. (2007). 4-H Youth Development professionals' perceptions of the importance of and their current level of competence with selected volunteer management competencies. *The Journal of Extension, 45*(3). Retrieved May 2010 from http://www.joe.org/joe/2007june/rb1.php.

Singletary, L., Smith, M., & Hill, G.C. (2003). Assessing impacts of volunteers who participate in collaborative efforts to manage environmental disputes. *The Journal of Volunteer Administration, 21*(2), 24-32.

Spaulding, D.T. (2008). *Program evaluation in practice: Core concepts and examples for discussion and analysis.* San Francisco: Jossey-Bass, a Wiley Imprint.

Steele, S. (1970). Program evaluation: A broader definition. *The Journal of Extension, 8*(Summer), 5-18. Retrieved June 13, 2009, from http://www.joe.org/joe/1970summer/1970-2-a1.pdf.

Stein, M. (1967). Toward an assessment of the volunteer workers program at Osawatomie (Kansas) State Hospital. *Volunteer Administration, I*(1), 37-52.

Stenzel, A.K., & Feeney, H.M. (1968). *Volunteer training and development: A manual for community groups.* New York: The Seabury Press.

Stufflebeam, D.L. (1987). The CIPP model for program evaluation. In G.F. Madaus, M.S. Scriven, & D.L. Stufflebeam (Eds.), *Evaluation models: Views on educational and human services evaluation* (pp. 117-141). Boston: Kluwer-Nijhoff.

Taylor, M.E., & Sumariwalla, R.D. (1993). Evaluating nonprofit effectiveness: Overcoming the barriers. In D.R. Young, R.M. Hollister, & V.A. Hodgkinson (Eds.), *Governing, leading, and managing nonprofit organizations* (pp. 93-116). San Francisco: Jossey-Bass Publishers.

Thiede, W. (1971). Evaluation and adult education. In G. Jensen (Ed.), *Adult education: Designing an emerging field* (pp. 13-26). Washington, DC: Adult Education Association of the USA.

Thomas, R.M. (2003). *Blending qualitative & quantitative research methods in theses and dissertations.* Thousand Oaks, CA: Corwin Press, Inc.

Tyler, R.W. (1949). *Basic principles of curriculum and instruction.* Chicago: University of Chicago Press.

W.K. Kellogg Foundation. (2000). *Logic model development guide.* Battle Creek, MI: W.K. Kellogg Foundation.

W.K. Kellogg Foundation. (2004). *Using logic models to bring together planning, evaluation, and action: Logic model development guide.* Retrieved May 2010 from http://www.wkkf.org/~/media/475A9C21974D416C90877A268DF38A15.ashx.

Wells, B., Safrit, R.D., Schmiesing, R., & Villard, J. (2000, October). The power is in the people! Effectively using focus groups to document impact of volunteer programs. *Proceedings of the 2000 International Conference on Volunteer Administration* (p. 59). Phoenix, AZ: Association for Volunteer Administration.

Wilson, M. (1979). *The effective management of volunteer programs.* Boulder, CO: Volunteer Management Associates.

Wilson, M. (1981). *Survival skills for managers.* Boulder, CO: Volunteer Management Associates.

Woog, P. (1979). Development of a scale to measure attitudes toward volunteers. *Volunteer Administration, 12*(3), 28-37.

APPENDIX A: A QUICK GUIDE FOR CONDUCTING EFFECTIVE INTERVIEWS AND FOCUS GROUPS[*]

Interviews and focus groups are information (*i.e.*, data) gathering methods that are particularly useful for exploring participants' in-depth concerns, ideas and opinions. Both methods use pre-determined open-ended questions to guide either face-to-face or distance (*e.g.*, telephone) discussions with either a single individual (interview) or small groups of individuals who share specific attributes or characteristics (focus group). The set of predetermined questions is called the Interview Schedule and should be developed ahead of time based upon specific ideas and opinions that the researcher seeks to explore. Normally, interviews should last no longer than 30-45 minutes, and focus groups no longer than 60-90 minutes.

Preparing for Interviews and Focus Groups

1. Call potential participants to invite them to the session.

2. Send participants a written follow-up invitation with a proposed agenda, session time and list of questions the group will discuss. Plan to provide a copy of the report from the session to each member and let him/her know you will do this.

3. About three days before the session, call each participant to remind him/her to attend.

4. Choose a setting with little distraction. Avoid loud lights or noises, ensure the interviewee is comfortable (you might ask them if they are), *etc*. Often, they may feel more comfortable at their own places of work or homes.

5. Assure participants that their responses will be treated confidentially.

6. Explain the format of the interview/focus group to be used. Indicate how long the session is expected to take.

7. Tell them how to get in touch with you later if they want to, and ask them if they have any questions before you both get started with the session.

8. Don't count on your memory to recall comments and answers. Ask for permission to record the interview and/or bring along

---

[*]

someone to take notes. Bring extra batteries for use with the tape recorder.

9. Hold sessions in a conference room, or other setting with adequate air flow and lighting. Configure chairs so that all members can see each other. Provide name tags for members, as well. Provide refreshments, especially box lunches if the session is held over lunch.

Conducting the Actual Session

1. Introduce yourself, and ask participant(s) to introduce himself/ herself.

2. Occasionally verify the tape recorder (if used) is working.

3. Ask one question at a time.

4. Attempt to remain as neutral as possible, and avoid showing strong personal reactions to participants' responses.

5. Encourage responses with occasional nods of the head, "uh huhs", *etc.*

6. Be careful about the appearance when note taking. That is, if you jump to take a note, it may appear as if you're surprised or very pleased about an answer, which may influence answers to future questions.

7. Provide transition between major topics, *e.g.*, "we've been talking about (some topic) and now I'd like to move on to (another topic)."

8. Don't lose control of the session. This can occur when respondents stray to another topic, take so long to answer a question that time begins to run out, or even begin asking questions to the interviewer.

9. It's critical that all members participate as much as possible, yet the session move along while generating useful information. Because the session is often a one-time occurrence, it's useful to have a few, short ground rules that sustain participation, yet do so with focus. Consider the following three ground rules: a) keep focused, b) maintain momentum and c) get closure on questions.

10. After each question is answered, carefully reflect back a summary of what you heard (the note taker may do this).

11. Ensure even participation by all. If one or two people are dominating the meeting, then call on others. Consider using a round-table approach, including going in one direction around the table, giving each person a minute to answer the question. If the domination persists, note it to the group and ask for ideas about how the participation can be increased.

12. In closing the session, thank all participants and indicate that that they will receive a copy of the report generated from their answers, and adjourn the meeting.

Immediately After the Actual Session

1. Make any expanded notes on your written notes, *e.g.*, to clarify any initials notes, ensure pages are numbered, fill out any notes that don't make senses, *etc.*

2. Write down any special or unique observations made during the session (for example, was the respondent particularly nervous at any time? Were there any surprises during the interview?)

3. Have notes and/or recordings transcribed.

APPENDIX B: ANALYZING INTERVIEW AND FOCUS GROUP DATA[*]

Interviews and focus groups result in very meaningful qualitative data that may be analyzed objectively by following the steps below. However, note that this analysis requires time and must be planned for proactively.

1. Record the actual session (especially with focus groups).

2. Take written notes to supplement/back-up session recordings.

3. Following the session, have recordings transcribed. Give each separate transcription a unique identification number. (NOTE: often, the number will be the numeric date on which the session was conducted.)

4. Format transcriptions in double-spaced, number pages documents, with a separate document for each individual interview and focus

---

group. (NOTE: it also helps the reader to number each line on each individual page.)

5. Identify and recruit 3 to 5 individuals who may serve as objective "readers" of the transcriptions. (NOTE: readers should be familiar with the session focus, but not involved/connected directly to the specific topic/session. Thus, VAs from other organizations are excellent potential readers!)

6. Deliver the written transcripts to each reader, along with a copy of the Data Analysis Worksheet. Ask the readers to read each transcription thoroughly at least twice: (1) first for an initial overview, and (2) secondly for more in-depth analysis and theme identification.

7. Allow a minimum of 10 working days for readers to return completed Data Analysis Worksheets.

8. Review carefully each individual Data Analysis Worksheet and identify overall resulting themes.

APPENDIX C: A DATA ANALYSIS WORKSHEET TO IDENTIFY RECURRING THEMES FROM INTERVIEW AND FOCUS GROUP TRANSCRIPTS[*]

Please read, and re-read, carefully the transcribed qualitative data that has been sent to you. Based upon your interpretation of the responses, identify any reoccurring themes that you believe are represented by the data. Please give a 3-6 word title to each theme to identify it and its meaning, and document what specific data in the transcript you are basing your suggested theme on by citing appropriate page and line numbers to reference specific responses supporting your proposed theme. Please record and document your themes as a document using this form. You may duplicate this page as much as required so as to document all reoccurring themes you identify from the transcribed data. Please e-mail your completed worksheet(s) to [evaluator's name here] as a single document that is labeled by your name and date of submission. Thank you!

****

EXAMPLE: Theme title: Colors of the rainbow

Documentation from the data: Page: <u>3</u> Line(s): <u>12-13</u>;
Page: <u>3</u> Line(s): <u>21</u>
Page: <u>4</u> Line(s): <u>1-2</u>
Page: <u>5</u> Line(s): <u>16-9</u>

****

Theme 1:

Documentation from the data: Page: _____ Line(s): ___

Page: _____ Line(s):

Page: _____ Line(s):

Page: _____ Line(s):

Page: _____ Line(s):

Theme 2:

Documentation from the data: Page: _____ Line(s): ___

Page: Line(s):

Page: Line(s):

Page: Line(s):

Page: Line(s):

Theme 3:

Documentation from the data: Page: _____   Line(s): ___

Page: Line(s):

Page: Line(s):

Page: Line(s):

Page: Line(s):

Rater's Name and Date: _____

APPENDIX D: A SAMPLE IMPACT EVALUATION EXECUTIVE SUMMARY FOR A VOLUNTEER PROGRAM[*]

2006 and 2007 Executive Summary
Targeted Impacts of the Bladen County 4-H
"Mission Possible: Get Fit for Life!" Day Camp

The Situation

North Carolina is the 16th in adult obesity and 5th in adolescent obesity. According to a 2008 report from the Trust for America's Health and the Robert Wood Johnson Foundation, the number of overweight and obese children has been steadily increasing over the past 20 years and the Center for Disease Control does not expect this trend to plateau until the year 2040. More than 19% of North Carolina students ages 10-17 are obese, a condition that can eventually lead to chronic health problems such as heart disease and Type 2 diabetes. North Carolina Nutrition and Physical Activity Surveillance System (NCNPASS) 2004 data show that 20% of Bladen County youth ages 12 to 18 and 38.3% of Bladen County youth ages 5 to 8 are overweight. In addition to obesity, poor dietary quality is a concern among

---

[*]   Duplicated with permission, © 2009 Angela Shaver, North Carolina Cooperative Extension – Bladen County Center, All Rights Reserved.

Bladen County's children and youth. Bladen County scores 10% higher than the state rate for childhood obesity. Costs to Bladen County for poor nutrition, overweight, obesity and physical inactivity are over $7 million annually. Given the fact that Bladen County is a Tier 1 poverty county, the growing obesity epidemic and its high costs are a serious threat to the county's economy, as well as its health.

Address the Issue

Mission Possible: Get Fit For Life! day camp is a collaborative strategy to reduce rates of Type 2 diabetes in Bladen County by identifying youth at risk for developing this debilitating chronic disease and providing them with the tools to improve their lifestyle and reduce their individual risk factors. Participants and their families experienced a multi-faceted approach to improving their health. Through participating in educational workshops, behavior challenges, regular health screenings, and a one-week day camp, Mission Possible teaches new knowledge and skills to at-risk youth while giving them realistic opportunities to practice desired behaviors in the long-term. The camp is staffed almost entirely by community and agency volunteers. Commitment to this project requires attendance at the week long day camp by identified at-risk youth participants age 5 to 12, participation in provided health screening opportunities by participants and family, and participation in family follow-up wellness workshops.

Program Goals, Objectives, and Impact Indicators

The primary goal of Mission Possible included assisting youth and families with adopting behaviors that contribute to their total health and well-being, and reducing the rate of Type II Diabetes. Additional program goals consisted of getting youth and families to eat smart and move more.

Program objectives included (all as measured by participant written pre-post tests):

- ✓   At least 50% of participating youth will increase knowledge of the importance of fruit and vegetable consumption;
- ✓   At Least 25% of participating youth will increase knowledge of different ways to be physically active;
- ✓   At least 50% of participating youth will increase skills in preparing and eating healthy meals and snacks;

✓ At least 25% of participating youth will be willing to try new foods;

✓ At least 25% of participating youth will learn to read nutrition food labels; and

✓ At least 10% of participating youth will aspire to eat smart and move more.

Specific measures of progress in the areas of knowledge, attitude, skills and aspirations included:

✓ Number of youth gaining knowledge of the impact of screen time on health and well-being;

✓ Number of youth gaining knowledge of the effect of large portion sizes on healthy eating;

✓ Number of youth increasing knowledge of the importance of fruit and vegetable consumption;

✓ Number of youth with increased knowledge of different ways to be physically active;

✓ Number of youth increasing knowledge of the effect of reducing sugar sweetened beverage consumption on healthy weight;

✓ Number of youth increasing skills in preparing and eating healthy meals and snacks;

✓ Number of youth willing to try new foods;

✓ Number of youth learning to read nutrition food labels; and

✓ Number of youth aspiring to eat smart and move more.

Measurable Outcomes Achieved

2006 program outcomes (as measured by pre-post tests) included:

✓ 22 youth increased knowledge of the importance of fruit and vegetable consumption;

✓ 11 youth increased knowledge of different ways to be physically active;

✓ 41 youth increased skills in preparing and eating healthy meals and snacks;

✓ 32 youth were willing to try new foods;

✓   12 youth learned to read nutrition food labels; and

✓   8 youth aspired to eat smart and move more.

Similarly, 2007 program outcomes included:

✓   21 youth gained knowledge of the impact of screen time on health and well-being;

✓   24 youth gained knowledge of the effect of large portion sizes on healthy eating;

✓   5 youth increased knowledge of the importance of fruit and vegetable consumption;

✓   9 youth increased knowledge of different ways to be physically active;

✓   15 youth increased knowledge of the effect of reducing sugar sweetened beverage consumption on healthy weight;

✓   17 youth increased skills in preparing and eating healthy meals and snacks;

✓   6 youth were willing to try new foods;

✓   17 youth learned to read nutrition food labels; and

✓   14 youth aspired to eat smart and move more.

Cost Savings Analysis

The North Carolina Division of Health Services estimates the additional health care services and medical treatment for every obese youth of at least 10 years of age to be approximately $2.5 million dollars, supposing that that 10 year old will live to an early age of 55 before succumbing to his or her illness. That $2.5 million dollars will cost someone, either the youth's family, the youth themselves (as an adult), insurance companies, or other taxpayers. So if as a long-term impact of the 2006 and 2007 Mission Possible: Get Fit For Life! day camps just 1 of the 76 participating youth (41 in 2006 and 35 in 2007) succeeds in battling his or her obesity and overweight, then the resulting Cost Savings is $2.5 million dollars.

However, based upon the measured facts that 58 total youth increased actual skills in preparing healthy meals during the two years of the program, and 22 total youth aspired to actually change their behaviors by eating and moving more, a more realistic Cost Savings may be calculated. The average of the preceding two metrics is 40.

Assuming a minimal long-term success rate for the Program of 10% (*i.e.*, 10 out of 100 participating youth will avoid Type II Diabetes as a direct result of his/her participation in Mission Possible), a more realistic long-term success number would be 4 youth. Thus, a more realistic Cost Savings is $10 million (*i.e.*, 4 @ 2.5 million).

Cost Benefits Analysis

Based upon auditable data, total program costs for the two years of Mission Possible included:

- Program Development/Implementation $ 17,254.64
- Materials (76 youth × $250/youth   19,000.00
- Equipment/Hardware (included in facility rental)   0.00
- Facility Rental (2 weeks × $2,377/week)   4,754.00
- Travel/Subsistence (76 youth × 2 weeks × $40/youth/week) $ 6,080.00

$$\text{TOTAL COSTS:} \qquad \$ 47,088.64$$

Based upon 76 youth participants in both years, the Mission Possible Program cost $619.59 per participant. With total Program costs of $47,088.64, and estimated Program benefits of $10 million, the Cost Benefit Analysis (CBA) for the program would be:

$$CBA = \frac{\text{Total Program Benefits}}{\text{Total Program Costs}} = \frac{\$10,000,000}{\$47,088.64} = \$212.37$$

Thus, for every $1.00 spent on the Program in 2006 and 2007, Mission Possible returned $212.37 in monetary benefits to Bladen County.

Return On Investment

With total Program costs of $47,088.64, and estimated Program benefits of $10 million, the Return On Investment (OI) for Mission Possible would be:

$$ROI = \frac{\text{Total Benefits} - \text{Total Costs}}{\text{Total Costs}} \times 100 = \frac{\$10,000,000 - \$47,088.64}{\$47,088.64} \times 100 = \$21,136.55$$

Thus, for every $1.00 spent on the Program in 2006 and 2007, Mission Possible returned $21,137 in *net* monetary benefits.

Chapter 12

RISK MANAGEMENT

Melanie Lockwood Herman
Nonprofit Risk Management Center

INTRODUCTION

Every volunteer administrator brings optimism about the contribution of volunteers to his or her job. Volunteers truly make a difference in the institutional lives of nonprofit organizations and in the very real lives of persons served by nonprofits. While no volunteer administrator looks forward to missteps or harm resulting from volunteer service, errors of judgement and accidents sometimes occur. Risk management is a discipline that empowers volunteer administrators to plan for "performance" and plan for "trouble." Spending time on likely risks will increase opportunities for success both by the nonprofit sponsor and participating volunteers.

CONCEPTS AND TYPES

Risk management is a discipline leaders turn to for help predicting the future, managing opportunities and adverse events, and putting in place systems, policies and a culture that creates a solid foundation for success in a volunteer program. Risk management activities occur at all stages in a volunteer program; however, ensuring the integration of sound risk management during the planning stages of a volunteer program is vital.

What Is Risk Management?

The Nonprofit Risk Management Center (<www.nonprofitrisk.org>) has adopted the following definition of risk management: "a discipline for dealing with uncertainty." Lack of understanding about risk management is itself a risk in a sector where "uncertainty" is commonplace. This definition dispenses with an academic approach. Leaders of volunteer programs are grounded in the practical worlds in which they and their organizations exist. To a large extent, we can never be certain about the future. Professional volunteer administrators should take time to reflect on the "what ifs" associated with each bold step the nonprofit organization takes, from expanding the geographic area or population served, to recruiting a celebrity spokesperson, to accepting a gift with entangling "strings" attached.

Often, risk management is viewed through a narrow lens, as a discipline for preventing and addressing accidents. This perspective prevents the appreciation of activities that can allow a volunteer program to focus the bulk of its resources on mission-related programs. Rather than limiting your view to the accidents that could occur or your agency's exposure to liability for negligent conduct, it is better to think broadly about what events, circumstances, or actions stand in the way of achieving the mission of your volunteer program.

Ideally, risk management activities empower a volunteer program by enabling the program to both identify risks and take specific steps to minimize the chance that volunteers, clients and the volunteer program itself will suffer accidental or intentional harm. Failing to take these steps may increase the likelihood of harm and threaten the ability of the organization to raise funds, retain enthusiastic volunteers or even survive. Managing risks help a volunteer program focus on its mission — not the unintended consequences of a loss.

An effective risk management program provides a *framework* for:

* balancing and understanding what risks are inherent within the organization; and

* empowering the board and staff to make good choices in dealing with these risks.

Ideally, risk management creates an environment where a volunteer program can take *more risk*, not less. For example, an organization that has focused on risk management issues may decide to proceed with a community-service project that other area nonprofits view as too risky.

Risk management is an integral part of good management. To be most effective, risk management should become part of the culture of a volunteer program. When risk management is integrated in a volunteer program's philosophy, outreach, recruitment, service delivery and planning activities, it becomes the responsibility of every volunteer.

An effective risk management program is helpful on three levels:

1. it can reduce the likelihood of injuries and mishaps by integrating safety measures into the day-to-day operations of an organization;

2. it can minimize the adverse effects of any losses that do occur; and

3. it can enable an organization to demonstrate that it followed the appropriate steps or procedures in its activities — evidence that could help the volunteer program prevail in a lawsuit.

Variations on Risk Management

Strategic Risk Management

Various off-shoots of the general discipline of risk management have emerged in the past decade. One example is *strategic risk management*. The Nonprofit Risk Management Center defines this term as: "Using an organization's resources and activities to counter potential losses and seize potential gains" (Head & Herman, *Enlightened Risk Taking: A Guide to Strategic Risk Management*, 2002, p. 8). Strategic risk management differs from traditional risk management in that it invites leaders to look at the upside dimension of risk — as well as the downside. In a traditional risk management program it is customary to ask: "What could go wrong?" In a strategic risk management program it would be important to also ask: "What could go right?" Leaders committed to taking a strategic approach to risk management should explore steps that could increase the chances of success, such as risk-taking to improve the results of a fundraising campaign or achieve better than average attendance at a special event.

Enterprise Risk Management

Another example of a variant on traditional risk management is the discipline of *Enterprise Risk Management*. Enterprise Risk Management or ERM has been embraced widely by organizations throughout the world, including some nonprofit organizations. The essence of ERM is to systematize risk awareness, identification, and strategy across all areas of an organization.

Enterprise Risk Management is:

> ... a process, affected by an entity's board of directors, management and other personnel, applied in strategy setting and across the enterprise, designed to identify potential events that may affect the entity, and manage risk to be within the risk appetite, to provide reasonable assurance regarding the achievement of entity objectives.

(Committee of Sponsoring Organizations of the Treadway Commission, online: <www.coso.org>.)

Crisis Management

The topics of crisis management, business continuity planning, and disaster preparedness often arise during a discussion of risk management in the nonprofit sector. Sometimes the terms are used interchangeably, but they refer to different issues and processes.

The discipline of *crisis management* refers to the steps and strategies an organization might employ to avoid a crisis and manage an ongoing crisis. A crisis may be caused by human action or inaction, by a natural disaster or by the loss of critical funding. One way to distinguish risk management from crisis management is by thinking of risk management as being principally concerned with *preventing harm* and crisis management with a focus on *extreme circumstances when preventive efforts have failed*. The distinction is not necessarily helpful. For example, a solid risk management program should encompass what a volunteer program is doing to cope with the uncertainty facing your organization as well as how a volunteer administrator will cope if the risk materializes (the worst case scenario).

A solid crisis management program should address both what is being done to address the most likely causes of a crisis before they strike as well as what the response will be should the crisis occur. Both disciplines look at strategies before and during a crisis, or potential crisis. Perhaps the distinction is subtler — with risk management tending to focus on strategies for mundane as well as truly urgent matters, and crisis management emphasizing the most dramatic events and circumstances that could disrupt an organization's operations.

Whatever the volunteer program's mission, crisis management planning should help the volunteer administrator deal with the unthinkable in the present and so that the organization and its activities can be sustained into the future. One thing that is true for both risk management and crisis management: it is difficult, if not impossible, to approximate a value for the disruption and disasters that were averted through awareness and planning. That is one of the reasons why it is very hard for any volunteer program to set aside precious time for crisis management planning and activities.

Some general rules for crisis management include:

1. *Before the Crisis*

    •   Do what you can, when you can — Do not establish an unrealistic plan to avert or manage the crises facing your nonprofit. Use available resources and be practical.

    •   Be flexible — Crises rarely emerge in the way that you will have envisioned. This means that leaders must be nimble and flexible and prepared to deal with a crisis at hand, rather than the "scenario" that has been rehearsed beforehand.

    •   Involve a diverse group of people — Tapping the perspectives of a diverse group of people is beneficial in brainstorming the types of crises most likely to occur and the most effective strategies for averting or managing a crisis.

    •   Focus on the most probable crises first — When a planning group discusses possible crisis exposures it is likely to consider some crisis exposures that are extremely remote. If time is limited, focus on those crisis risks that are, in the group's opinion, the "most probable."

- Revise and revisit — Exposure to crisis situations varies over time as a nonprofit expands programs, serves new constituencies, works with new partners and more. The list of crisis risks should be revisited and updated annually.

2. *During the Crisis*

- Remember that compassion is your business.

- Do what you can.

- Act with unity.

- Call on others for help.

- Be flexible.

- Document everything.

Business Continuity Planning

The discipline of *business continuity planning* concerns the need to prevent the interruption of mission critical services, or if that is not possible, ensure the restoration of mission-critical services in a timely manner.

Disaster Preparedness

Disaster preparedness refers to the preparation that an organization may take to "weather" a disaster. A "disaster" may be an event caused by nature or by human conduct (*e.g.*, terrorism).

Process, Strategies, and Tools

There are various ways to describe the risk management process. The framework developed by the Nonprofit Risk Management Center is presented here as one option for thinking about the steps in an ongoing process that can be replicated or applied in any volunteer program. This framework contains five key steps:

Figure 1: The Risk Management Process

Risk Management Process

establish
the context

follow up
and adjust

appraise
risks

act on your
decision

decide
what to do and
communicate

Reprinted with permission from the Nonprofit Risk Management Center, 2009.

Establish the Context

The risk management process begins with a focus on things other than risk. "Establish the context" refers to the culture, history, resources, services and nature of the organization — factors that influence the volunteer program's capacity for risk-taking, it's tendency to be risk averse, its ability to successfully implement sound risk management, and overall receptivity to policy and programmatic changes that will protect the mission and assets of the organization while positioning to pursue its mission. For example, leaders of a nonprofit with a long history of workplace accidents, volunteer complaints and growing insurance costs may be open to steps to move the organization down a new path. The leaders of a nonprofit that has never experienced the sudden departure of a valuable staff member or volunteer or tragedy involving a client is likely to place less value on contingency planning and a focus on planning for the possibility of negative publicity. Organizational history and experience with loss are powerful motivators for risk management and the absence of such a history may cause some leaders to believe that reflecting on risk and drafting responses are a waste of time.

Another consideration in the first step of this framework is how important the practice of risk management is to the organization and the level of resources the organization is willing and able to commit to the process. Ideally, the board and staff should support and encourage the use of effective risk management techniques. Many experts in the field note that sound risk management starts with the "tone at the top" while recognizing that organizations that are best prepared to deflect or cope with life's "what ifs" are those where addressing hazards is a shared responsibility.

Establishing the context for risk management within an organization also includes considering the relationships between the organization and its environment (for example, the relationship the nonprofit enjoys with key stakeholders). Every nonprofit relies on stakeholders — those persons and institutions that hold a "stake" in the nonprofit's activities, services, mission and outcomes. A nonprofit that is widely respected and held in high regard by donors, clients, sister agencies and regulators alike may focus on reputation preservation as a key aspect of the risk management program, in contrast with a nonprofit that is working to rebuild its reputation after a loss in stakeholder confidence.

Some of the questions leaders should ask in identifying the context for risk management in a nonprofit include:

- What is the organization's view of risk — something to be avoided or a natural part of the organization's operations and mission?

- What barriers or potential barriers exist to the development of a risk management program? What issues will make it particularly challenging for this organization to establish a risk management program?

- Are there any signs or motivating factors that will increase the organization's receptivity to risk management activities?

- Which internal stakeholders should be involved in the development of a risk management program?

- Which external stakeholders should be involved in the creation of a risk management program?

- What resources are available to support our risk management efforts?

- How supportive is the board of directors and staff to developing a risk management program? Will they have to be "sold" on the idea?

- What similar organizations can we consult with about establishing a risk management program?

- What organizational strengths will support a risk management program?

- What organizational weaknesses may impair our ability to establish a risk management program?

Identify Risk

Risk identification is essentially the process of determining what can happen, why, and how. In many small to mid-sized nonprofits this process begins with the creation of a Risk Management Committee whose role includes risk identification. It is important to first lay the groundwork for this step by considering or establishing the context for risk management. Most groups tasked with risk identification grapple with the challenge of making certain that all of the major exposures facing the organization are included, and nothing is left out. There are several ways of making certain you address a breadth of areas where risks exist (*e.g.*, programs, buildings, equipment) and the types of risk (*e.g.*, risk to people, property, reputation) when undertaking the process of identifying risk in an organization. Three approaches are discussed below.

The first approach is to first identify the functional areas in the organization, such as governance, fundraising, community service initiatives, special events, administrative operations, *etc.* Use these functional categories as headings for the risks identified in the brain-storming process. The second approach is to first identify major asset categories, such as people, property, income and goodwill. Then identify and group risks by these major categories of assets. A third approach is to simply ask: "What uncertainties threaten our mission?" After a long list of risks has been identified, the team working on the project can assign appropriate headings. There is no right or wrong way to go about the process. The goal of risk identification is to consider and articulate the risks facing the organization, without neglecting any potentially serious risks. For example, a closer examination of a campus-based social services group might reveal a host of risks, such as:

- the risk of a student volunteer causing injury to an elderly client while participating in a service project;

- the risk of serious injury occurring during an event organized by the nonprofit;

- the risk of fatality occurring during a sponsored "road trip"; and/or

- the risk of a student volunteer contracting a serious or fatal disease while participating in an alternative spring break to a third world country.

Evaluate and Prioritize Risk

So how do we make sense of risk? How do we set priorities? Even if leaders could identify every single risk facing their nonprofits (an impossible task), it would remain impossible to address — through management controls, policy changes or other methods — every identified risk. There would be no time remaining for the core mission of the nonprofit and the need for a risk management program would dissipate. Given that reality, how do leaders and volunteer administrators in particular make appropriate decisions about where to invest the nonprofit organization's financial and other resources? Do some risks rise to the top as priorities because of their emotional content (*e.g.*, the risk of client injury or death)? Are management's perceptions of what is risky reasonable or based on a purely emotional response? Not every risk facing a nonprofit is likely to materialize. Other risks may be likely but their consequences not especially severe. The third step in the risk management process is to evaluate the likelihood of a risk materializing and its potential severity.

The fundamental goal of risk prioritization is to create a workable, practical list on which to focus risk management efforts. Many newcomers to risk management feel overwhelmed after completing a risk identification exercise. No wonder! A group of four or five creative individuals can easily compile a list containing several dozen risks. If a group spends hours at this exercise the list can easily cover several pages. At first glance, all of the items on the list may appear to be high priority risks requiring the organization's immediate attention. It is essential to take a closer look and begin to prioritize identified risks. Here is a suggested approach.

- Review each identified risk to determine how often it might occur (frequency). Ask the following question:

How often or likely is this risk to materialize? Think in terms of the risk actually happening, not the fact that it exists. For example, if the risk is theft of petty cash by a staff member, is this likely to occur twice a year or once a decade?

- Assign a frequency grade based on your answer to the above question.

  Consider using 1 to 10 as your grading scale. You could also use HIGH – MEDIUM – LOW. For example, if you decide that the theft of monies in petty cash is likely to occur less than once a year, you might assign a LOW frequency grade, or a "2" using the 1 to 10 scale.

- Review each risk and ask how much it might cost both in monetary and non-financial terms (severity). Ask the following question:

  How significant would it be if it did happen? Think again in terms of the actual risk happening. For example, if the maximum amount kept in petty cash is $25, then theft occurring twice a year would mean a maximum loss of $50 (the loss could be less).

- Assign a severity grade based on your answer to the above question.

  Consider using 1 to 10 as your grading scale where 1 represents a low risk. You could also use High – Medium – Low. For example, if the maximum financial loss to the organization would be $25 or $50, then a grade of Low or "1" would probably be appropriate.

- Add the frequency and severity scores for each identified risk to determine a total score. Re-rank the list of identified risks based on the total score (frequency + severity). Consider addressing the risks with the highest combined scores first.

Decide How to Control Your Risks and Implement the Risk Management Program Using Available Tools

This is the most active phase of the process whereby the leaders of an organization develop strategies to minimize the likelihood of a risk materializing and responses that will be activated should an incident occur. These strategies are then tested by the organization. Risk retention — deciding not to take action — is selected for low-priority risks.

Some managers in organizations wrongly believe that implementing risk management strategies is beyond their budgets and staffing resources. The opposite is often true. Some of the most effective risk management strategies require little or no financial investment and minimal staff or volunteer time. Examples of inexpensive risk management strategies that are common in nonprofit organizations include:

- Adopting a *code of conduct* to clarify prohibited conduct and warn employees/volunteers/participants/clients about the nonprofit's expectations and the consequences of violating these expectations or standards. Keep in mind that it's always best to involve people "on the ground" in identifying risks as well as strategies.

- Developing *position descriptions* for the board, staff and volunteers in order to provide guidance about the expectations of persons serving in these positions and increase each individual's likelihood of succeeding in their role.

- *Responding with compassion* to an individual who has suffered an injury while participating in the nonprofit's programs or serving on the nonprofit's behalf.

- *Equipping private vehicles* driven on the nonprofit's business (behalf) *with disposable cameras*, an easy to use accident reporting form, and a pencil.

- *Including reference checks* as part of the nonprofit's screening process for paid and volunteer positions.

- *Ensuring that the terms of partnerships with other nonprofits are memorialized in a written contract or "memorandum of understanding."*

- *Designating a Media Spokesperson* and making certain that key personnel in the nonprofit know the nonprofit's policy for handling media inquiries.

Key considerations in designing and selecting risk management strategies include:

- Does the strategy, policy change or approach suit the culture of the nonprofit?

- Can the strategy be implemented consistently?

- Does the nonprofit have the resources required to implement the strategy?

- What barriers to implementation exist and how will the organization overcome those barriers (*e.g.*, the barrier of training hundreds of volunteers in remote locations may be addressed by offering an online training system with 24/7 access)?

Monitor and Update the Risk Management Program as Needed

Risk management is a circular process (see Figure 1). Each of the five steps of the risk management process is connected to the steps that precede and follow it. The team assigned to risk management in a nonprofit organization should review the techniques it has implemented on an annual basis to make any revisions that may be needed. Each year the risk management committee can also select a new set of risks on which to focus their attention. One of the most important steps in embracing risk management is to commit to learning from past experience. This is especially important when an organization has faced the consequences of an accident. It is essential to take time to examine what happened in order to determine whether any changes are required in policy, procedure or common practice in order to prevent a similar incident in the future.

RISK MANAGEMENT RESOURCES

The Nonprofit Risk Management Center is a nonprofit organization that is dedicated to helping other nonprofits cope with uncertainty. The Center provides free technical assistance (available by telephone or e-mail) as well as publications, software, training opportunities and consulting help. For more information, visit <www.nonprofitrisk.org>.

- *No Surprises: Harmonizing Risk and Reward in Volunteer Management* is the Center's most popular risk management text. The fifth edition of this easy-to-read and easier-to-use guide was published in September 2009. For more information, see online: <http://nonprofitrisk.org/store/no-surprises.shtml>.

- *Hallmarks of a Risk-Aware Nonprofit* is a free online tool developed by the Nonprofit Risk Management Center with generous funding from the Travelers Foundation. The tool offers easy-to-understand targets and goals for nonprofit leaders aspiring to improve their risk management efforts. Practical suggestions, templates and "tools" are featured throughout. To access the tool, see online: <http://nonprofitrisk.org/tools/hallmarks/intro.shtml>.

- *My Risk Management Plan* is an affordable online tool that walks nonprofit leaders through the process of creating a customized risk management plan. To learn more, see online: <http://nonprofitrisk.org/tools/rm-plan/rm-plan.shtml>.

- *Workplace Safety Is No Accident* is a free, online toolkit on the topic of workplace safety. The toolkit contains hundreds of samples, checklists and narratives on various aspects of workplace safety. Nonprofit and public sector editions are available online: <http://nonprofitrisk.org/tools/workplace-safety/workplace-safety.shtml>.

- *Business Continuity Planning Tutorial* — The Nonprofit Risk Management Center has developed a free business continuity planning tutorial that walks nonprofit leaders through the process of creating a business continuity plan for their organization. To access the tutorial, see online: <http://nonprofitrisk.org/tools/business-continuity/business-continuity.shtml>.

REFERENCES

American Association for Retired People. (2003). *Experience at work: Volunteering and giving among Americans 50 and over.* Washington, DC: Independent Sector and AARP.

Graff, Linda L. (2005). *Best of all: The quick reference guide to effective volunteer involvement.* Dundas, ON: Linda Graff & Associates Inc.

FEMA. (2009). *Citizen Corps volunteer liability guide.* Retrieved from http://www.citizencorps.gov/downloads/pdf/Citizen_Corps_Volunteer_Liability_Guide.pdf.

Head, George L., & Herman, Melanie L. (2002). *Enlightened risk taking: A guide to strategic risk management.* Washington, DC: Nonprofit Risk Management Center.

Independent Sector. (2002). *Engaging youth in lifelong service.* Washington, DC: Independent Sector and the Youth Service Alliance. Available at http://www.independentsector.org.

Nonprofit Risk Management Center. (2009). *State liability laws for charitable organizations and volunteers, State-by-state summary of liability protection laws and analysis of the Volunteer Protection Act.* Leesburg, VA: Nonprofit Risk Management Center. Retrieved April 2010 from http://www.nonprofitrisk.org/library/state-liability.shtml.

Chapter 13

QUALITY IMPROVEMENT

Salvatore P. Alaimo, Ph.D., CVA
Grand Valley State University

INTRODUCTION

Economic, social and technological forces have put quality improvement (QI) front and centre as a priority for government, business and the nonprofit sector. Over the past several decades we have seen methods for QI permeate the business world with such managerial processes as Total Quality Management (TQM) and Continuous Quality Improvement (CQI). Performance measurement and performance management have taken on a more prominent role in government operations (Poister, 2003; Starling, 2008). The increasing call for accountability combined with increasing competition for resources has resulted in program evaluation, performance measurement and overall QI becoming a major focus in the nonprofit sector (Brody 2002; Reamer, 1998; Salamon, 2002). The quality movement that has taken place during this time has been based on approaches that are fact-based, data-driven and focused largely on the quality of service to consumers and consumer satisfaction (Poister, 2003). This chapter will draw on some of these concepts, trends and ideas to discuss improving the quality ("degree of excellence") of volunteer administration.

The core of the definition of quality that is most applicable for this chapter is "the degree of excellence of a thing" (*Webster's New World Dictionary and Thesaurus*, 1996, p. 502).

Why We Should Be Concerned with Improving Quality?

Volunteer administrators, no matter whether they work for formal nonprofit organizations, businesses, government or smaller community groups all have a responsibility to ensure the volunteers they are responsible for and work with are providing the best possible service to the consumers their organizations serve. This responsibility holds true regardless of the situation and who the volunteers are directly or indirectly serving. We can think of many scenarios where people depend on volunteers to perform specific functions or tasks such as homeless shelter residents depending on volunteers for meals; a high school student depending on a volunteer for math tutoring; hospital visitors needing help with directions; a theater company relying on volunteers to be ushers and ticket-takers; senior citizens requiring transportation to their doctor's appointments; or an environmental organization utilizing volunteers to collect petition signatures and engage in advocacy. In all these cases, the quality of the volunteer's work performance directly impacts those who are served and who rely on such efforts. It also is part of the organization's work toward its mission which can be viewed as a promise or covenant with the consumers it serves.

In addition to the consumers served by the volunteer administrator's organization, volunteer administrators should also be concerned with improving the quality of volunteer performance for their volunteers. Volunteers may be motivated by different reasons on an individual basis such as a need for affiliation, social reasons, cause-related reasons, power, or others. Regardless of motivation, volunteers are quite often interested in the quality of their performance or service. They want to know if they have done a good job by meeting the expectations conveyed to them and are fulfilling their responsibilities. Volunteer administrators that incorporate a process to improve quality that is a part of their supervision of their volunteers will be able to regularly communicate with their volunteers, offering positive feedback

and/or suggestions to improve performance. Some volunteer administrators informally and periodically monitor their volunteers' performance, while others conduct regular appraisals using a more formal tool
to evaluate performance, and still others may combine informal and
formal approaches as part of their QI process. Providing feedback to
volunteers on their performance by conveying the importance of their
work and appreciating their efforts can be the most powerful form of
recognition. It also can be an effective motivator when incorporating
goals and objectives for the volunteer's work and performance level.

IMPROVING PERFORMANCE — RECRUITMENT AND RETENTION

Improving the quality of the volunteer administrator's work in
managing volunteers is paramount to the quality of their overall
performance, their efforts to efficiently and effectively utilize resources, and their ability to recruit and retain volunteers. Some have
observed that the majority of the focus driven by traditional models of
volunteer management, discussed by government officials, referenced
in research studies and found on the Internet has been around volunteer
recruitment to the point of neglecting or not emphasizing the importance of volunteer retention (Brudney & Meijs, 2009). Volunteer
administrators should desire to improve the quality of both recruitment
and retention of volunteers because they impact each other. The more
effective volunteer administrators are in recruiting volunteers the more
likely they will positively impact the retention of those volunteers.
Confronting issues such as volunteer motivations; expectations from
both the volunteer and the organization; ensuring the volunteer
engages in what he or she feels is meaningful work; and matching the
volunteer's skills, experience and desires for work with the organization's wants and needs will likely contribute to that volunteer staying
longer in their assignments. Conversely, if a volunteer administrator is
effective in providing ongoing support for volunteers, they will
positively contribute to retaining those volunteers. Such an effort can
contribute to an image or reputation for how the organization manages
volunteers which likely can lead to increased recruitment, especially if
existing, satisfied volunteers are spokespersons for the organization in
efforts to recruit new volunteers. There is not likely a more powerful
recruitment effort than a satisfied, existing volunteer reaching out and
speaking to prospective new volunteers about their experiences.

The concern Brudney and Meijs express for the overemphasis on
recruitment at the expense of retention speaks directly to a volunteer

administrator's ability to efficiently and effectively manage, and be good stewards of, resources. When we think of volunteer recruitment and retention, we can invoke the cliché 80/20 rule. Volunteer administrators must ask themselves if they prefer to spend 80 per cent of their time recruiting new volunteers and 20 per cent of their time contributing to the retention of their volunteers, or vice versa. Brudney and Meijs implicitly suggest our choice would be the latter because they view volunteer energy as a natural, renewable resource that is impacted by human intervention in a way that should sustain and grow that resource (2009). Their regenerative approach to volunteer management sets the context for QI because of its emphasis on a more long-term, sustainable relationship between the volunteer and the organization they're volunteering for. We can add to their recommendations the fact that the effort to recruit new volunteers typically requires more resources and time from the volunteer administrator and the organization they represent than the ongoing support for retention.

The quality of volunteer performance is a reflection of the image and reputation of the organization that the volunteer administrator represents. The types of organizations volunteer administrators may represent can vary greatly from more formal incorporated, nonprofit organizations to more informal, unincorporated community-based organizations. They may also represent small businesses or large corporations who have organized employee volunteer programs or government agencies that address a variety of issues including health education initiatives, disaster preparedness, or local sports and recreation. For any organization utilizing volunteers, the quality of how volunteers are managed contributes to the overall quality of organizational performance and how that organization's constituency and the general public perceive it. Volunteers are in essence acting as agents or representatives of the organization. They often take on high-profile roles where there efforts are open and viewable for all to see such as in direct service, special events and fundraisers, advocacy and others. Quite often this representation is seamless, as consumers and other stakeholders may not know the difference between who is a volunteer and who is a paid employee of that organization. More specifically, this perception is linked to how the organization manages and supports its volunteers and ultimately how well it works towards satisfying its mission.

Performance and the Volunteer Administrator Role

Volunteer administrators also stand to benefit from QI. They typically are at the low end of the compensation chain within organizations and they often have very limited portions of those organizations' budgets. By improving the quality of their work, volunteer administrators can achieve several objectives that will likely enhance their work experience and give new meaning and value to their work. First, a demonstration of improving quality conveys that you are concerned with the organization's mission, service to its consumers, reputation and image, volunteers, the proper use of resources and specifically your work. This raises the value of your work and you as an individual employee in that organization. Second, QI simply can make your job more efficient and effective with regard to how you communicate, allocate and devote your time, and report the results of your work. Third, you can create a work environment where you are an integral part of the organization's culture and effort to learn. This can help you grow as a professional employee and as a person as you try new ideas, engage in professional development and reflect on your work.

Volunteer administration is a profession that is also seeking to enhance its reputation and overall value in society. Improving the quality of volunteer administration on an individual level contributes to the overall quality and reputation of the profession. The UPS Foundation's research conducted in 1998 found that "the primary reason people stop volunteering is because of poor management" (2002, p. 3). The foundation concluded that building capacity and a stronger infrastructure to sustain the efficient and effective volunteers was a critical need, and one that justifies the importance of the volunteer administration profession. The now defunct Association for Volunteer Administration (AVA) surveyed its members and established some key messages to help position the profession of volunteer administration. Some of them include:

> Capable volunteer administrators make the critical difference in focusing volunteer resources to impact on mission, services and safety.
>
> Strong volunteer administrators bring many skills to the whole organization.
>
> The increasing complexity of the work requires a greater investment in the volunteer management process.
>
> Philanthropic institutions are stewards of the public trust, including community resources such as volunteers.

> People working together through voluntary participation is essential for building a civil society.

(AVA, 1999, pp. 9-12.)

Improving the quality of volunteer administration is important for upholding these statements and the Council for Certification in Volunteer Administration's (CCVA) core ethical values. CCVA states that volunteer administrators should do the following:

- Have a philosophical perspective on volunteerism that reflects sound practice, history, diversity, and human needs.

- Be knowledgeable of and familiar with all local, state/provincial, and federal legislation regarding personnel practices, human rights codes and cultural diversity.

- Include volunteers in the development of organizational and departmental goals and objectives.

- Strive to assure that all volunteer recruitment and placements are respectful of each individual's skills and readiness for his/her volunteer role in order to maintain the highest level of integrity and show concern for staff and volunteers.

- Involve paid staff and volunteers in gathering information pertinent to the issues at hand.

- Clearly differentiate between your own personal opinion/philosophy and established organizational policies and procedures guidelines. (CCVA, 2005)

All of these prescriptions for upholding the core ethical values for the profession have clear links to and implications for QI.

Lastly, the community stands to benefit when QI is employed in all facets of volunteer administration. Volunteer engagement is an important contributor to building community and developing social capital. The efforts of volunteers directly and indirectly help address societal needs not adequately dealt with by business and government. In fact, it is volunteers that determine societal needs are inadequately met and take on the role of entrepreneurs to develop initiatives, projects or organizations to address these needs. Volunteers are usually on the front lines helping nonprofit organizations, businesses, and government determine community needs. Improving the quality of volunteer administration directly impacts how efficiently and effectively volunteers work towards serving those in need and address their community's problems.

Building a Culture of Continuous Improvement and Learning

The successful engagement in quality management requires developing and maintaining a culture dedicated to continuous improvement. The culture of an institution and its environment are important factors that drive individual and organizational behaviour. Culture is described as "including ideas and beliefs, the affective/expressive dimension, and an evaluative element consisting of value-orientations" (Parsons in DiMaggio & Powell, 1991). Organizational culture, often referred to as corporate culture especially when referencing businesses, has been characterized as comprising shared values, ideas, beliefs, assumptions, norms, artifacts, and/or patterns of behaviour (Bjerke, 1999; Ivancevich, Szilagyi, Jr. & Wallace, Jr., 1977; Ott, 1989; Schein, 1992). Organizational culture has been more specifically defined as "... the importance for people of symbolism — rituals, myths, stories, and legends — and about the interpretation of events, ideas, and experiences that are influenced and shaped by the groups within which they live" (Frost, Moore, Louis, Lundberg & Martin, 1985, p. 17), and "[a] pattern of shared basic assumptions that the group has learned as it solved problems of external adaptation and internal integration, that has worked well enough to be considered valid and, therefore to be taught to new members as the correct way to perceive, think and feel in relation to these problems" (Schein, 1992, p. 12).

The organizational culture perspective challenges the traditional structural perspective for analyzing organizations in that (1) organizations are more than structures developed to achieve rational ends, and (2) members' behaviour is driven by these factors rather than simply rules or authority and this behaviour drives the social life of the organization (Bjerke, 1999; Ott, 1989). Organizational culture is a social construction that is both a product and a process. It is a product because it is constructed by humans in the form of accumulated wisdom; it is shared with others who learn it, more noticeably regarding new members of the organization; and it is a process because it gets renewed and recreated (Bjerke, 1999; Bolman & Deal, 2003).

Culture has its strength when it is internalized within the personality of the organization, and this overrides attempts to use it strategically for desired ends. This point is relevant and critical concerning "the culture for evaluation" within an organization where the leadership breeds and infuses a culture of being self-critical individually and organizationally. Schein's point about basic assumptions, the things that are engrained in and are a natural part of the organization, is important to understanding how QI may require a supportive organizational culture to be successful to where it becomes embedded in that culture as a continuous, ongoing process. The common phrase "It's just a part of what we do" is a good example of how an organization's stakeholders describe a basic assumption. Bjerke describes this concept as *hidden assumptions* which he defines as "... the fundamental beliefs behind all decisions and actions — that might be nonconscious cornerstones of culture" (Bjerke, p. 34).

In the context of volunteer administration where volunteers are contributing their time, skills, and expertise we can expect the incorporation of values, focus on a mission, and a commitment to address a particular social problem or human need as likely basic or hidden assumptions. We can also expect volunteer administration to be an operational basic assumption. This raises the questions for (1) how quality improvement can be an integral part of an organization's values, norms and work towards its mission; and (2) how it can subsequently become an operational basic assumption that permeates all areas of the organization that in some way impact volunteer administration. We can look to the top-down support of leadership as an important driving factor behind developing and nurturing an organizational culture committed to QI.

Quality Improvement and Leadership

Leadership has been defined in many ways throughout the vast literature on the subject. For the purpose of this chapter Northouse's definition of leadership will be used, "Leadership is a process whereby an individual influences a group of individuals to achieve a common goal" (2004, p. 3). This definition provides us direction in that the common goal here for volunteer administration is QI. The culture of an organization is demonstrated in many ways, but one of the more prominent is the management style of the organization. An organization's ability to successfully attain its goals and objectives while working toward satisfying its mission largely relies on the leadership's ability to effectively work with key stakeholders such as the board, staff and operational volunteers. This involves creating purpose and commitment for these stakeholders which is arguably the leader's most influential impact on organizational culture (Bjerke, 1999). The organization's mission serves as the leader's driver and rallying cry for such purpose and commitment; the guide for strategy, performance and organizational change; and the representation of the social goods the organization provides for society.

The literature tells us how important it is to have the support of the organization's leadership for successful volunteer administration (Bradner, 1999; Brudney, 1995; Brudney, 2005; Ellis, 1996; Fisher & Cole, 1993). The same holds true for successful QI. The leader of an organization can have profound influence on their organization's culture in many ways. The culture of a nonprofit organization is largely built upon the leader's values, activities and tasks which are inculcated to staff and other stakeholders (Hay, 1990). The leader's use of language is a key driver of the acculturation process. The way values and rules of behaviour are communicated, including non-verbal communication, shapes the values and norms of the organization's culture (Bjerke, 1999). A leader can have formal influence based on their position and authority (Ivancevich, Szilagyi, Jr. & Wallace, Jr., 1977) and set the priorities for the organization.

The issue of accountability has garnered much attention recently in the nonprofit sector. While it typically is linked to more top-down approaches to management and leadership within the context of meeting goals or objectives, it also influences the culture of an organization. If a leader communicates the rules of behaviour and the priorities for an organization, this communication has no meaning for the organization's members if there is no accountability for following those rules or satisfying those priorities. Without the proper accountability framework, a leader's voice to the organization becomes rhetoric without any foundation for meaningful action. The leader must provide the organization's members with the level of support and working environment that enables them to deliver on their area of accountability. This involves leveraging the creative capabilities of the organization's members, engaging members through the psychological contract of their expectations combined with those of the organization, aligning members' thoughts decisions and actions with their goals and the roles involved in achieving them, and developing members to help them realize their potential through mentoring and coaching (Kraines, 2001). This conveys that QI is more likely to be successful if it is a part of the organization's accountability framework.

Leaders in and of themselves are symbols, and their patterns of behaviour and leadership can be an artifact for the organization that communicate information about the organization's values, guiding beliefs and ways of doing things (Davis, 1984; Ott, 1989). Congruence must exist between the cultural values and operating norms for an organization to be successful (Anthes, 1987). Impacting an organization's culture will likely influence the organization's strategic direction, and the ability to achieve its goals and objectives (Davis, 1984;

Hay, 1990). Effective leadership and a supportive culture are typical characteristics of high-performing organizations and specific leader practices include: permeating a strong customer (consumer) orientation throughout the organization; demonstrating a strong commitment to quality; involving and empowering staff by ensuring they participate in decisions and that their feedback is used; and ensuring employees have the proper training to perform their jobs well (Wiley & Brooks, 2000).

ORGANIZATIONAL LEARNING

The development of the organizational culture conducive for QI to be continuous and ongoing involves developing organizational learning, as it goes hand-in-glove with QI. Organizational learning involves learning from successes and failures, and changing behaviour due to encountering situations, usually emanating from its environment. It involves individuals learning new ways to achieve their goals and sometimes involves individuals learning to change the goals (Denhardt, Denhardt & Aristigueta, 2002). Organizational learning occurs when "... individuals within an organization experience a problematic situation and inquire into it on the organization's behalf" (Argyris & Schon, 1996, p. 16). Learning resulting from this inquiry must become embedded in the organization's member perceptions, methods for acquiring new knowledge and part of the organization's history for learning (Argyris & Schon, 1996). While organizations are collectives of individuals, we cannot assume that individual learning permeates and takes hold at the organizational level. Individual learning does not guarantee organizational learning, but it is a prerequisite for it (Senge, 1990). Organizations need to be environments for storing knowledge that goes beyond the individual level in files, within policies, regulations, strategic plans, documented decisions, *etc.* (Argyris & Schon, 1996). Argyris and Schon also recommend that organizations "directly represent knowledge in the sense that they embody strategies for performing complex tasks that have been performed in other ways" (1996, p. 13). In a highly competitive and rapidly changing environment organizational learning must occur quickly and be sufficient enough to match or be greater than the change outside the organization (Schwandt & Marquardt, 2000) and in a way that they can sustain their mission and purpose (Dym & Hutson, 2005).

Leaders are challenged with ensuring that individual members learn, grow and adapt in an environment that encourages and rewards them (Ott, 1989). They should also ensure that they have access to information, a feedback loop exists and that the learning process contributes to improved performance (Mesch & McClelland, 2006). Information must flow in both hierarchical directions for a nonprofit to be a learning organization (Drucker, 1990). Organizational learning is a socialization process driven by the structures, systems and culture. Without encouraging, fostering, nurturing, and rewarding an organizational culture for learning that allows for failure and taking risks, an executive director cannot successfully lead a learning organization even with the proper structures and systems in place. Executive directors who wish to lead a learning organization should focus on building an infrastructure for learning that includes recording the organization's history, reflecting on successes, failures and innovation, and incorporating learning into the organization's planning process (Senge, 1996). A culture for organizational learning also involves internal and external collaborative efforts with other stakeholders and organizations, and receptiveness to taking calculated risks (Block, 2004), all arguably staples of volunteer administration and overall nonprofit management.

One particular aspect of organizational learning, "inference of causal connections between actions and outcomes and their implications for future action" (Argyris & Schon, 1996, p. 17) helps describe the process of determining actions for QI. It appears that QI and organizational learning are inextricably linked. QI is an example of a process that can help develop and foster organizational learning, while a culture within an organization that is driven by organizational learning is one that is conducive for QI. The responsibility for becoming a learning organization resides primarily with the organization's internal stakeholders, as in the case of a nonprofit organization the executive director, board of directors, staff and volunteers. Volunteer administrators can play an important part in facilitating organizational learning by taking a learning approach to their work and participating in decision-making, interpreting results and determining next steps. This learning approach involves focusing on important issues and concerns; dialog and reflection about improvement; being able to cope with difficult circumstances for the program and potential "negative" information about the program's effectiveness; and insightful assessments and discussions about the past, present and future (Torres & Preskill, 2001).

QUALITY MANAGEMENT

Volunteer administrators engaging in QI participate in quality management. Quality management is defined as "systematically and continuously improving quality of products, service, and life using all available human and capital resources" (Brocka & Brocka, 1992, p. 4). There are several aspects of any quality management process that are highly recommended for success. First, there must be *commitment from leadership* because the leadership typically drives the organizational culture and ensures quality management is employed at every level of the organization (Berg, 1997; Boyer, 2008; Brocka & Brocka, 1992). Volunteer administrators should not attempt to improve quality by themselves because they will likely not receive the resources and support to implement such an effort and not likely be successful in shaping the organization's culture alone. The leadership controls the organization's resources and is responsible for that organization's systems and processes while embedding its priorities into the culture of the organization.

Second, *employee participation* in managerial decisions is important for the QI to be continuous (Berg, 1997; Boyer, 2008; Stashevsky & Elizur, 1999). This makes sense within the context of volunteer administration given the fact that volunteer administrators, whether their volunteer program is centralized or decentralized, typically rely on other employees and stakeholders in the organization. This reliance may take the form of transferring resources or information or simply other employees working directly with volunteers. QI inevitably involves organizational change, and such change is not likely to happen without broad support and participation from the employees in the organization or other key stakeholders, such as volunteers. Employee or stakeholder participation likely will take various forms including direct participation involving individuals developing the strategy; consultative participation where individuals have a voice in the process but are represented by others such as QI work teams; or delegative participation where employees are empowered to take the necessary actions to improve quality (Berg, 1997). Employees and other stakeholders may participate in a mix of these approaches depending on their time constraints, position within the hierarchy and overall interest in QI.

Third, employees and stakeholders must operate in an environment of *empowerment* (Berg, 1997; Boyer, 2008). They must be able to exploit their past experiences in work processes and situations and convey their ideas for QI. Berg states (1997, p. 41) that:

> Management must still actively supervise the change process, but it also must delegate authority alongside the delegation of responsibility. Mobilizing employees to take responsibility must be met with the possibility of executing it.

The selection of an approach for QI largely is dependent on the organizational quality context which takes into account past quality performance, external demands for quality, the competitive forces that influence quality and the available resources to improve quality (Benson, Saraph & Schroeder, 1991). Adam and Foster identified additional contextual variables including leadership, the role of a quality department, employee relations, training, data reporting and a few others (2000). Let's translate each of these contextual factors for the specific purposes of QI in volunteer administration. Table 1 below provides some examples for each of these factors and considerations for effectively managing them:

Table 1: Contextual Factors for Quality Improvement in Volunteer Administration

CONTEXTUAL FACTORS	VOLUNTEER ADMINISTRATION EXAMPLES	CONSIDERATIONS
Past quality performance	• Marketing of volunteer opportunities • Meeting recruitment goals • Ongoing support for volunteers • Retention rates • Volunteer satisfaction • Volunteer performance • Volunteer administrator performance	• Past quality performance measures must be established to provide a baseline for quality improvement specific to each area of volunteer administration
External demands for quality	• Expectations for quality established by collaborative partners, contracts, accreditation or grants	• External demands represent legal and ethical obligations, and standards and expectations established mutually or solely by the external entity

CONTEXTUAL FACTORS	VOLUNTEER ADMINISTRATION EXAMPLES	CONSIDERATIONS
Competitive forces	• Volunteers have many choices • Competition for volunteers and their time	• How can your volunteer program stand out from others by factoring in quality?
Available resources for QI	• Personnel • Time • Money	• QI incurs direct costs and an opportunity costs
Leadership	• Leadership drives the culture and controls the resources for QI	• Does the leadership personally support and allocate resources for QI? • Does the leadership make an effort to embed QI into the culture of the organization?
Role of quality department	• Can be an *ad hoc* work group, team or committee	• Does the quality team comprise a diverse mix of stakeholders with various perspectives?
Employee relations	• Relations between volunteer administrator and leadership, staff and volunteers • Relations between staff and volunteers	• How can relations between employees be improved to ensure inclusiveness and participation? • How can staff-volunteer relationships be improved?

CONTEXTUAL FACTORS	VOLUNTEER ADMINISTRATION EXAMPLES	CONSIDERATIONS
Training	• The necessary training in the QI process • Training and professional development to improve the quality of individual stakeholder performance	• What type of training is required to cover the QI process for participants? • What training and professional development will directly impact QI for volunteer administration?
Data reporting	• Resource and supply needs — computers, software, printers, *etc.* • Format for reporting • Content for reporting	• Do we have the necessary tools to properly engage in the QI process? • What format should we use for reporting our data depending on our audience? • What is the critical information necessary to report for our QI process?

THE QUALITY IMPROVEMENT PROCESS

Once the contextual factors for quality improvement have been analyzed reviewed, and the implications for each have been documented, the QI process can now be developed. The first step is *forming a quality improvement team* (Bennet and Baker, 1990, Iowa State University, 2009) made up of important stakeholders who are knowledgeable about the volunteer program, have at least a basic, working knowledge of volunteer administration and understand the needs of those being served such as consumers, volunteers, staff, partnering organizations and the larger community. It is advisable to have the volunteer administrator lead the team that should include a mix of staff, direct service and/or administrative volunteers, one or two board members, and a quality improvement expert from the community who may come from government, business, health or academia. The team then *establishes the QI plan* which should contain the next steps from this point forward. It is important for the team to document in the plan as it moves forward with the QI process the types and sources of support that will be needed, required resources, assigned tasks for team members and corresponding deadlines which will ensure the plan is carried out and the QI process is successful (Bennet and Baker, 1990).

Any new QI process needs to *establish quality measures in the current state* to serve as the basis for improvement. This provides a baseline for current quality in the designated areas to be improved. Some areas in volunteer administration that can serve as areas for measured quality improvement include:

- marketing and communications for volunteer opportunities;
- recruitment efficiency and effectiveness;
- effort to provide ongoing support for volunteers;
- retention rates;
- volunteer satisfaction;
- staff satisfaction;
- consumer satisfaction;
- consumer outcomes;
- volunteer administrator performance;
- volunteer performance;
- meeting of goals and objectives for volunteer-driven activities, projects and events;
- how volunteers are recognized;
- evaluation tools, methods and systems;
- data collection and reporting;
- volunteer orientations;
- volunteer training;
- development and revision of policies and procedures;
- use of resources/adherence to the budget; and
- diversity and inclusiveness of volunteer pool.

It is important for the team to discuss and document the benefits of improving quality in each area because it is important for the stakeholders to (1) understand why they are driving organizational change, (2) understanding how the QI for each specific area fits into the overall QI for volunteer administration, and (3) be able to articulate the benefits, particularly financial and mission-based, to the important stakeholders who are in a position to provide support, resources and enable improvement strategies to be implemented.

Once the team has established the measures for the designated areas of improvement, they should *analyze the systems, processes and communication* currently taking place in each area. This information will provide the basis for the specific strategies for improvement in each area by establishing the strengths, weaknesses and obstacles for improving quality and the detailed sub-areas requiring attention. At this point the team can begin *brainstorming and establishing change strategies for producing improvement* (Iowa State University, 2009). The establishment of these strategies should involve checking each for their feasibility and overall what it takes to implement them. Keep in mind that not every strategy may be feasible and not every one may be enacted during the first attempt at QI.

The next step involves *implementing the strategies by collecting and using data for decision-making.* This information should include the carrying out of the strategies for QI, documenting what worked well and not so well in the process. Such documentation helps ensure that the QI process is continuous and that it contributes to organizational learning. Some examples of the specific dimensions for QI in volunteer administration with some possible, corresponding action steps are shown below in Table 2.

**Table 2: Sample Action Steps for Specific Intended Areas
for QI in Volunteer Administration**

DIMENSION FOR QI	ACTION STEPS
Improving the effort to provide ongoing support for volunteers	• Conduct detailed volunteer position needs assessments to ensure the proper work environment, tools and resources are provided for the volunteer to successfully carry out their assignment and accomplish their goals • Revising position descriptions and volunteer assignment descriptions accordingly

DIMENSION FOR QI	ACTION STEPS
	• Periodically checking in with volunteers to make sure they have everything they need
Improving staff satisfaction for the results of volunteer efforts	• Have one-on-one discussions with staff about how volunteers specifically impact their work • Conduct needs (wants) assessments with staff and make sure they are part of the process of developing position descriptions and assignment descriptions • Periodically conduct a staff satisfaction survey to determine how to improve staff's satisfaction with the work of volunteers
Improving the effectiveness of volunteer training	• Incorporate the adult learning model for training volunteers • Link the outcomes for volunteer performance and the meeting of assignment goals and objectives back to training content • Acquire ongoing volunteer feedback on their work experience and how well training prepared them for it • Revise and update training based on staff and volunteer feedback, updated policies and procedures, risk management issues, new programs, *etc.*

The next step of *reporting the results of those changes* can be easily misconstrued as the last step in the QI process. First, Figure 1 reminds us that QI is a continuous, circular or as some call it, serial process.

Figure 1: Continuous Quality Improvement (CQI) Process

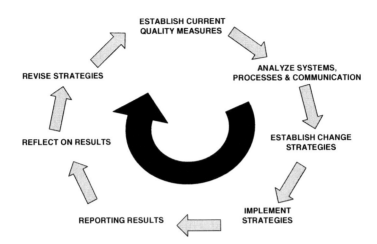

We can see that *reflection on the results of the changes*, which hope-fully do in fact result in QI, is a critical step for *revising the strategies and possibly the quality measures* for the next round of QI in each specific area of volunteer administration. The philosophy behind CQI "contends that most things can be improved" and that it is a "serial experimentation (the scientific method) applied to everyday work to meet the needs of those we serve and improve the services we offer" (Iowa State University, 2009).

Recommended Practices for QI in Volunteer Administration

The following recommended practices for QI in volunteer ad-ministration draw from the QI concepts and apply them directly to the specific aspects of practice and

1. *Enlist the support from the organization's leadership* — The support from the organization's leadership as we have discussed is critical to the success of any QI process. Seek this support before venturing down the path of QI to ensure you will have the right organizational culture and resources to engage in the QI process.

2. *Incorporate feedback loops* — Ongoing feedback from volunteers, staff and consumers is necessary for the QI process, so make sure feedback loops exist for each stakeholder group. These are systems and processes in place by which each individual stakeholder can communicate feedback on how things are going. You want to

make sure that the methods of communication are conducive for each stakeholder group, that feedback is communicated regularly and that you close the loop by getting back to the stakeholders and communicating what has been done with their feedback.

3. *Be aware of the psychological contract for volunteering* — The psychological contract for any new volunteer comprises the expectations you and your organization have for the volunteer's efforts and performance, and the volunteer's expectations for their experience with you and your organization. The volunteer's part of the psychological contract is unique and personal to each volunteer because it is a social construction based on a number of factors. For example, the volunteer may have expectations based on the organization's reputation in the community, a referral from a neighbour, a billboard he or she read while driving into town, your organization's website, cause-related reasons, or a combination of these factors. Your expectations for the volunteer's efforts are most likely based on organizational needs assessments, corresponding position and assignment descriptions and policies and procedures. It is critical to flesh out the psychological contract from the beginning (possibly at the interviewing or screening stage), so that there is a mutual understanding and match of expectations. Beyond this initial conversation, it is important to also provide ongoing support for the volunteer to satisfy their expectations for satisfying their work requirements. Research on the psychological contract for volunteering revealed that when volunteer expectations were not satisfied, it contributed to volunteer withdrawal. When ongoing support was not provided it was even a more significant contributor to withdrawal (Farmer & Fedor, 1999). Understanding and properly managing the psychological contract for volunteering can be a critical component of overall QI in volunteer administration because it impacts multiple areas of your volunteer program.

4. *Proactively seek projects for QI* — This keeps in the theme of QI being continuous because you will not be waiting until a crisis in quality occurs in a specific area to take corrective action. By being proactive, especially in the beginning of your QI journey, you can select the most important areas that need to be improved and possibly the areas most feasible for that point in time.

5. *Select the proper assessment tools and incorporate a mix of quantitative and qualitative data* — When you assess for quality measures, the tools and methods you use may vary depending

upon the timing, location, feasibility and audience you are collecting data from. In some situations one-on-one interviews will be most effective while in others, a written or online survey is most appropriate. Remember that numbers quite often prompt more questions than provide answers as what is behind those numbers is usually a very important determining factor for QI. Observations, quotes and stories from stakeholders and other more qualitative information are important especially when used to complement the quantitative data you have collected. Providing a mix not only enhances the rigor and quality of your assessments but also tells a more well-rounded story of what you're assessing.

6. *Remain grounded in understanding means and ends* — The great Greek philosopher Aristotle stated that the ends will always be superior to the means by their very nature but he also observed that human beings tend to focus, sometimes to obsession, on the means. QI involves determining what means (supplies, personnel, processes, systems, resources, actions, *etc.*) will result in improving quality. The reason for improving quality in a specific area represents our desired ends. Both means and ends will change over time in a continuous process; however remember to stay focused on why we want to improve quality and the ultimate or long-term outcomes we seek.

7. *Be patient* — Organizational change and QI typically does not happen overnight and sometimes does not improve to your desired quality measures. There are multiple factors that determine QI, as we discussed, and some are complex in nature, all impacting the QI process while the environment in which you operate is constantly changing. It is likely at the beginning of your QI process you will have to take small steps to get the process going and come up with some strategies and results to build upon.

8. *Embrace the paradigm for the culture of continuous improvement* — Remember that there is no such thing as negative information, only learning opportunities. This paradigm is not easy to swallow at first especially with the hierarchical, political, and accountability pressures of the workplace. However, once this paradigm is embraced and carried out on an organizational level, it can be extremely empowering and uplifting by allowing safe space to experiment and attempt to improve quality with the understanding that not everything will work right. The paradigm also creates a culture of inquiry where stakeholders inherently and naturally seek

knowledge of what is working well and not so well for the purpose of learning how to improve quality.

9. *Model behaviour* — The most effective way to build support, buy-in and participation in your QI process is for you to model QI as an individual in your organization. Think about how you can improve the quality of your work and increase the value of your position in the organization. It may require changing your ways of work, contributing to the culture of change and learning, participating in professional development or advanced education, or improving relations with your co-workers. Remember that Mahatma Gandhi told us we must be the change we seek in the world.

CONCLUSIONS

The profession of volunteer administration has become more prominent and important to our society as the number of nonprofit organizations and volunteer activity has grown. More organizations now compete for a limited amount of overall resources which has increased competition and elevated the importance of quality improvement as a management mechanism to better serve consumers and prove worthiness for those resources. Volunteer administrators must develop a culture for continuous improvement within their work environments in order to ensure they are serving their volunteers as best they can while meeting internal and external stakeholder expectations for performance. This in turn helps ensure the organizations they represent are serving their consumers in alignment with what is promised in their missions. When volunteer administrators engage in QI they enhance the reputation of the profession while upholding its recommended practices and ethical standards. Ultimately, QI in volunteer administration contributes to increasing the value of volunteer administrators' work to their organizations and their communities, and their organization's contributions to society.

REFERENCES

Adam, E.E., & Foster, S.T. (2000). Quality improvement approach and performance: Multisite analysis within a firm. *Journal of Quality Management*, 5(1), 143-158.

Anthes, E.W. (1987). *Personnel matters in the nonprofit organization.* Hampton, AR: Independent Community Consultants, Inc.

Argyris, C., & Schon, D.A. (1996). *Organizational learning II: Theory, method, and practice* (2nd ed.). Reading, MA: Addison-Wesley Publishing Co.

Association for Volunteer Administration (AVA). (1999). *Portrait of a profession: Volunteer administration.* Richmond, VA: Association for Volunteer Administration.

Association for Volunteer Administration (AVA). (1999). *Positioning the profession: Communicating the power of results for volunteer leadership professionals.* Richmond, VA: Association for Volunteer Administration.

Bennett, G., & Baker, O. (1990). Developing an integrated quality improvement program. *American Journal of Infection Control, 18*(2), 118-125.

Benson, G., Saraph, J., & Schroeder, R. (1991). The effects of organizational context on quality management. *Management Science, 37*(9), 1107-1124.

Berg, A.M. (1997). Participatory strategies in quality improvement programs. *Public Productivity & Management Review, 21*(1), 30-43.

Bjerke, B. (1999). *Business leadership and culture.* Northampton, MA: Edward Elgar Publishing, Ltd.

Block, S.R. (2004). *Why nonprofits fail.* San Francisco: Jossey-Bass.

Bolman, L.G., & Deal, T. (2003). *Reframing organizations: Artistry, choice and leadership.* San Francisco: John Wiley & Sons

Boyer, D.K. (2008). Oklahoma's quality assurance experience: Continuous improvement through employee empowerment, teamwork, diversity and best practices. *Corrections Today*, pp. 38-42

Bradner, J.H. (1999). *Leading volunteers for results.* Winnetka, IL: Conversation Press, Inc.

Brocka, B., & Brocka, M.S. (1992). *Quality management: Implementing the best ideas of the masters.* Homewood, IL: Business One Irwin.

Brody, E. (2002). Accountability and public trust. In L. Salamon (Ed.), *The state of nonprofit America* (pp. 471-498). Washington, DC: Brookings Institution Press.

Brudney, J.L. (1995). Preparing the organization for volunteers. In T.D. Connors (Ed.), *The volunteer management handbook* (pp. 36-60). New York: John Wiley & Sons.

Brudney, J.L. (2005). Designing and managing volunteer programs. In R.D. Herman & Associates (Eds.), *The Jossey-Bass handbook of nonprofit leadership and management* (pp. 310-344). San Francisco: John Wiley & Sons.

Brudney, J.L., & Meijs, L.C.P.M. (2009). It ain't natural: Toward a new (natural resource) conceptualization for volunteer management. *Nonprofit and Voluntary Sector Quarterly, 38*(4), 564-581.

Council for Certification in Volunteer Administration. (2005). *Professional ethics in volunteer administration.* Retrieved on October 16, 2009, from http://www.cvacert.org/documents/Professional EthicsinVolunteerAdministration-2006.pdf.

Davis, S. (1984). *Managing corporate culture.* Cambridge, MA: Ballinger Publishing Company.

Denhardt, R.B., Denhardt, V.J., & Aristigueta, M.P. (2002). *Managing human behavior in public & nonprofit organizations.* Thousand Oaks, CA: Sage Publications, Inc.

DiMaggio, P., & Powell, W.W. (1991). Introduction. In W.W. Powell and P.J. DiMaggio (Eds.), *The new institutionalism in organizational analysis* (pp. 1-38). Chicago: University of Chicago Press.

Drucker, P.F. (1990). *Managing the nonprofit organization.* New York: Harper Collins Publishers.

Dym, B., & Hutson, H. (2005). *Leadership in nonprofit organizations.* Thousand Oaks, CA: Sage Publications.

Ellis, S.J. (1996). *From the top down.* Philadelphia: Energize, Inc.

Farmer, S.M., & Fedor, D.B. (1999). Volunteer participation and withdrawal: A psychological contract perspective on the role of expectations and organizational support. *Nonprofit Management and Leadership, 9*(4), 349-367.

Fisher, J.C., & Cole, K.M. (1993). *Leadership and management of volunteer programs.* San Francisco: Jossey-Bass.

Frost, P.J., Moore, L.F., Louis, M.R., Lundberg, C.C., & Martin, J. (1985). An allegorical view of organizational culture. In P.J. Frost, L.F. Moore, M.R. Louis, C.C. Lundberg, & J. Martin (Eds.), *Organizational culture* (pp. 13-25). Beverly Hills, CA: Sage Publications.

Hay, R.D. (1990). *Strategic management in nonprofit organizations.* Westport, CT: Greenwood Press.

Iowa State University – Facilities Planning & Management. (2009). *Continuous Quality Improvement (CQI)*. Retrieved on July 28, 2009 from http://www.fpm.iastate.edu/worldclass/cqi.asp.

Ivancevich, J.M., Szilagyi, Jr., A.D., & Wallace, Jr., M.J. (1977). *Organizational behavior and performance*. Santa Monica, CA: Goodyear Publishing Company, Inc.

Kraines, G. (2001). *Accountability leadership: How to strengthen productivity through sound managerial leadership*. Franklin Lakes, NJ: Career Press.

Mesch, D.J., & McClelland, J. (2006). Managing for performance and integrity. In D.R. Young (Ed.), *Wise decision-making in uncertain times: Using nonprofit resources effectively*. New York: Foundation Center.

Northouse, P. (2004). *Leadership: Theory and practice*. Thousand Oaks, CA: Sage Publications, Inc.

Ott, J.S. (1989). *The Organizational culture perspective*. Chicago: The Dorsey Press.

Poister, T.H. (2003). *Measuring performance in public and nonprofit organizations*. San Francisco: Jossey-Bass.

Reamer, F.G. (1998). *Social work and evaluation skills*. New York: Columbia University Press.

Salamon, L. (2002). The resilient sector. In L. Salamon (Ed.), *The state of nonprofit America* (pp. 3-61). Washington, DC: Brookings Institution Press.

Schein, E. (1992). *Organizational culture and leadership*. San Francisco: Jossey-Bass Publishers.

Schwandt, D.R., & Marquardt, M.J. (2000). *Organizational learning: From world-class theories to global best practices*. New York: St. Lucie Press.

Senge, P.M. (1990). *The fifth discipline*. New York: Currency Doubleday.

Senge, P.M. (1996). Leading learning organizations. In F. Hesselbein, M. Goldsmith, & R. Beckhard (Eds.), *The leader of the future* (pp. 41-57). San Francisco: Jossey-Bass.

Starling, G. (2008). *Managing the public sector* (8th ed). Boston: Thompson Wadsworth.

Stashevsky, S., & Elzur, D. (2000). The effect of quality management and participation in decision-making on individual performance. *Journal of Quality Management, 5*(1), 53-65.

Torres, R.T., & Preskill, H. (2001). Evaluation and organizational learning: Past, present and future. *American Journal of Evaluation, 22*(3), 387-395.

United Parcel Service Foundation (2002). *A guide to investing in volunteer resources management: Improve your philanthropic portfolio.* Atlanta: UPS Foundation.

Wiley, J.W., & Brooks, S.M. (2006). The high-performance organizational climate. *Handbook of organizational culture and climate* (pp.177-191). Thousand Oaks, CA: Sage Publishing.

Chapter 14

LEADERSHIP FOR NONPROFIT ORGANIZATIONS

Paul Varella, Ph.D.
Bissett School of Business – Mount Royal University

As a leader ... I have always endeavored to listen to what each and every person in a discussion had to say before venturing my own opinion. Oftentimes, my own opinion will simply represent a consensus of what I heard in the discussion.

I always remember the axiom: a leader is like a shepherd. He stays behind the flock, letting the most nimble go out ahead, whereupon the others follow, not realizing that all along they are being directed from behind.

...

It is better to lead from behind and to put others in front, especially when you celebrate victory when nice things occur. You take the front line when there is danger. Then people will appreciate your leadership.

Nelson Mandela (1994), *A Long Walk to Freedom*

INTRODUCTION

The quote by President Nelson Mandela illustrates that effective leaders are unique and rare individuals who are exceptional in bringing direction to their ranks and who must also acknowledge that it is the collectivity that accomplishes the goals instilled by the leader, not the leaders themselves. Outstanding leaders are exceptional individuals who fulfill a critical function in the broader society and inside organizations, and that is especially true within the nonprofit sector. President Mandela himself was a leader of a nonprofit organization, known as the African National Congress, which has evolved from a community and volunteer-based organization to become a political power in present South Africa.

Building up on President Mandela's quote, this chapter includes an appreciation of how the prototype of the twenty-first century leader includes an individual who embraces two different and, sometimes, contradictory set of characteristics. On one side, there is the call for an individual who is self-confident, visionary, creative, charismatic, excellent communicator, experienced, and technically prepared. On the other end, there is the desire that such a leader provides individualized attention to members of the organization and eagerly defers credits for organizational accomplishments; that person also needs to be humble, ethical, and self-sacrificial. This is indeed a very tall order, which allows us to understand why good leadership is something rare. Included ahead is a detailed examination of what constitutes a good leader and some indications about the benefits that such leaders may bring to nonprofit organizations (NPOs).

THEORETICAL BACKGROUND

The question of what constitutes effective leadership has kept many social scientists busy (Yukl 2006); the body of literature on the subject is vast and sometimes contradictory. However, the intention here is not to offer a treatise on leadership; rather, the focus is on a practical framework that could help NPOs and their members develop good leadership practices. Therefore, the next sections revolve around the conceptualization of what constitutes a good and effective leadership process for NPOs.

The perspective here suggests leadership as a powerful mechanism, leading to organizational success. It assumes that there are specific individual behaviours, personalities, and attributes that typify a gifted person to be exceptional in leading an organization. Such leaders develop a relationship between the leader and one or more individuals associated with him or her, based on the leader's behaviours that engender motivation, reactions, and inspiration on the part of people. The term *relationship* broadly includes an emotional or cognitive connection that people can feel toward the leader (Waldman and Yammarino, 1999; House, 1971).

The decision of which texts to include in a short chapter like this is a difficult task. In this process, the reader should also expect some biases from the author. Such biases assume that leadership does matter in organization, and that effective leaders are neither social constructions nor a collective sense-making exercise of the members of high-performing organizations, as some authors believe (for more on this approach see, *e.g.*, Agle *et al.*, 2006; Meindl, Ehrlich, and Dukerich, 1985; Pfeffer, 1977, 1981).

This chapter is supported by a broad theoretical and empirical body of academic work, which is purposefully *harvested* with two goals in mind. The first objective is to offer the necessary academic justification for the ideas in this chapter. The second goal is to suggest a list of texts which may satisfy the curious mind that does not get all the wanted answers from this chapter.

It is important to specify the labels that will be used here when referring to the people under the influence of a leader, since such definitions have caused some misunderstandings in leadership studies. Throughout this chapter, the term *subject* is the name of the individuals who are exposed to leadership effects and may respond differently, depending on their leader's behaviours and actions. Subjects are individuals who are related to an organization, as leaders may influence the behaviours of its constituents (employees, volunteers, board of trustees, and so on), or the external stakeholders of the organization as well. The term *subordinate* represents individuals occupying a specific hierarchical position in an organization who may or may not be under the influence of a leader, as it is clarified ahead. Finally, the term *follower* signifies an individual who displays full acceptance of the leadership influence.

Finally, much of the included ideas come from organizational studies, regardless if the studies included a for-profit or a nonprofit entity. There are not many seminal leadership studies focusing exclusively on the nonprofit sector, since the organizational leadership literature has evolved mostly within the for-profit sector (House and Aditya, 1997). Yet, leadership is a social-psychological process involving leaders and subjects; there may be differences between for-profit organizations and NPOs, but the study of people responding to leadership inside organizations should share more commonalities than differences across both sectors. Having highlighted that, there will be specific mentions to the nonprofit context whenever possible and necessary.

Defining Leadership

The idea of leadership seems to be an elusive concept to define. It is usually confounded with power, management, hierarchical stature, social positioning, or personality. As the intention is to explore organizational leadership specifically, the definition that will best serve such purpose is the one offered by House *et al.* (1999, p. 184):

> [Organizational leadership] *is the ability of an individual to influence, motivate, and enable others to contribute toward the effectiveness and success of the organizations of which they are members.*

Note that this definition is of *organizational leadership* and it does not necessarily intend to explain the leadership processes in the political or broader social contexts. Hence, it assumes that the leadership phenomena inside organizations will evolve through means that differ from general leadership models.

Leaders vs. Managers

In the organizational context, the difference between leaders and managers is a contentious topic, as the field seeks to establish a definition of what organizational leadership is. It is intuitively unmistakable that both leaders and managers are interchangeable yet different concepts; hence, the overlap across them is a tenuous topic. For instance, finding when one stops being a manager and becomes a leader, or vice versa, represents a major debate in the field (Yukl, 2006). Leadership and management are complementary but are two different processes (Bennis and Nanus, 1985). Leadership is associated more closely with its method of inspiring or influencing subjects in order to gain commitment. On the other hand, management is a process associated with hierarchical power in obtaining subjects' compliance. Such a comparison is not necessarily all encompassing; yet, finding a solution for such a problem may be undesirable. Albeit intuitively different, managerial and leadership functions share a large overlap, so by that degree separating the two processes may not help the full appreciation of the issues that are pertinent to organizational leadership. It may serve us better to appreciate the singularities and overlaps of each function.

Not all managers are leaders, but more commonly than not, organizational leaders function as managers. Appreciating the leadership characteristics of a managerial leader is common practice in studying organizational leadership; this chapter follows the same logic in explaining leadership within a NPO.

The two central dimensions that help us understand the varying nature of organizational leadership and managerial processes are:

1. the focus of their actions being alternatively on task accomplishment or subjects' motivation and well-being; and

2. the different sources of power that leaders and managers can draw from.

In order to understand these perspectives we start by appreciating the nature of the work of a manager. The first systemic view of the managerial work was introduced by the seminal work of Drucker (1954, 1967), who originally studied the function of a manager in an organization, proposing that the ability of coordinating tasks and people would be central to the functions of an executive. Building on the original work of the founders of the field, Mintzberg (1973) offered additional insights about the different domains of the managerial work. He suggested that managers' first area of action is the information-processing role, as they have to monitor the internal and external environments as well as fulfilling the role as the spokesperson for their unit then disseminate the information back to it.

Secondly, the decision-making responsibilities are part of the managerial role. In this role, it is up to a manager to allocate resources according to the goals of the organization, manage internal conflict, and negotiate with all constituents. In addition, organizations look for their managers to be creative, entrepreneurial and to offer a sense of direction. The third and final function of a manager is the interpersonal role; it is up to managers to be sure not only that the tasks are not simply completed, but that the stakeholders in an organization are moving forward with their individual objectives as well. In that role, managers work as liaison between their department and the other areas of the organization and external stakeholders. They also function as motivators, figureheads and the public figure of the organization or the division of which they are in charge.

Probably, the most interesting way of separating the work of a manager from the work of a leader is to articulate that management function is about task-oriented activities, as opposed to the leaders who focus on people-oriented activities. In other words, a manager's critical role lies in getting things done; they have to be sure that the different areas of an organization work in sync, the necessary resources are available in a timely manner, and the decisions are coordinated and done in ways to help the organization attain its goals. Leaders, on the other hand, are more people-oriented, since it is through their interpersonal abilities that leaders will influence individuals to be highly motivated and strongly committed to the goals of the organization; as such, leadership processes include people-focused rather than task-focused roles.

Drucker (1990), known as the founding father of the management school, also ventured in examining the specificities of the work of a manager in a NPO. He noted that converting good intentions into results in NPOs follows a rather specific process. The ability of reaching different stakeholders through a clear and inspirational sense of direction is much more critical for a NPO, when compared to a for-profit one. For him the effectiveness of the NPO stems from how able its leaders are in reaching and engaging the organization's stakeholders, from its volunteers and audience to the broad of trustees. He pointedly defended that NPOs are particularly dependent on righteous leaders, given the usual delivery of public goods that is associated with their social mandate. He also acknowledged the challenges to define organizational performance, given the difficulties of assessing organizational efficiency that are inherent in NPOs' usual outcomes, which cannot be measured in bottom-line terms.

From the work of Drucker (1990) with nonprofit managers, it seems clear that the leadership role is going to be even more critical in a NPO when compared to the for-profit enterprises. Task-oriented behaviours — typical of a manager — may be enough influence for those who are pursuing the financial benefit of well-paid jobs. However, such an approach will not be the most effective way in managing the distinctive work force in a NPO, the volunteer workers. This is not to say that NPOs should not strive for efficiency and effectiveness, like its for-profit counterpart; yet, the inherent necessity of being a people motivator is much larger in a NPO. The reasons for that lay in the sources of power at the disposal of the manager of a NPO, as this article will elaborate ahead.

Power in Organizations

Usually the conceptualization of leadership describes a process that entails an agent (the leader) affecting others (the subjects) in ways that those subjects will respond in favourable ways and engage in beneficial actions which they would not probably do on their own in the absence of the leader. As such, leadership is a form of social power over its subjects. It is necessary, therefore, to understand how power evolves inside organizational hierarchies. Power is the capacity (real or potential) that one agent may have to influence another party whose actions and attitudes are affected by the agent's power. Power derives from the authority of the agent and it falls into two broad categories: positional and personal power (Raven and French, 1959).

Positional power derives from the hierarchical position of an individual inside an organization; it tends to be associated with a title or professional designation, rather than resulting from the individual characteristics of the person who holds the position. A chief executive officer (CEO) of a NPO has positional power for being the topmost executive of the organization. CEOs have positional power due to the fact that they hold the highest position in an organization but that power would accumulate to anyone occupying the position (Yukl, 2006), regardless of who is in that post. The sources of positional power result from a few foundations:

1. Legitimate power — which is associated with a specific profession, function, or hierarchical position in an organization, which is the result of institutional agreements in our society that grant decision-making discretion to individuals who fulfill specific functions — e.g., managers have the right of defining the schedule of the people working for them.

2. Reward power — the ability that an agent has to define salaries, promotions, and recognition to others in an organization.

3. Coercive power — the possibility of a manager to fire or penalize others in the organization.

4. Information power — linked to the possibility of using, releasing or controlling the diffusion of information inside an organization.

Personal power, on the other hand, is associated with the characteristics of individuals rather than the characteristics of the position that they occupy. Thus, there are personal qualities associated with some agents that will exert influences over the actions of the members of an organization regardless of the hierarchical posts of such agents.

For instance, Eleanor Roosevelt was a beacon for social causes in the United States, even beyond the presidency of her husband Franklin D. Roosevelt, after he died in office in 1945. Her lifetime achievements and ability to sway the American society and the people who worked with her were impressive. Mrs. Roosevelt was an activist fighting for the rights of African Americans even before the civil rights movement; she was also heavily engaged in the creation of the declaration of human rights at the United Nations, amongst many other initiatives. She was a very likeable person; her demeanour and solid values-based decisions, associated with the credibility and dedication to her causes, allowed her to influence people's actions even though she had no formal positional power. Her ability to influence people was due to who she was and not to her position; that ability results from two different sources of personal power:

1. Expert power — relates to the perception of how knowledgeable an agent is in specific matters. People will mold their own actions by their observation of leaders and how they perceive such leaders to be informed and well prepared in the corresponding matter.

2. Referent power — the power derived from the subjects' desire to be associated with people with whom they developed affective feelings or admiration.

Such a typology suggests six different sources of power that are not mutually exclusive; actually, it is rather common that powerful individuals benefit from several sources. For instance, top executives of organizations (position power) will commonly benefit from higher levels of charisma, since leaders can use the personal power that derives from charisma to influence their way to the top of the organization (Waldman, Javidan, and Varella, 2004). Any one source of power can easily translate into another inside organizations. Another facet from this typology is that it is possible to identify some differences between managers and leaders. It seems clear that *managers* predominantly employ positional power. On the other hand, *leaders* have at their disposal the ability to stress personal power over positional power inside organizations.

An important stipulation of the consequences for power within organizations is that positional and personal power lead to consequences on subjects through different mechanisms (Galinsky, Gruenfeld, and Magee, 2003). Positional power causes subjects' change of behaviour due to *compliance*; they are not necessarily engaged or convinced about the underlying reasons for their actions, but they would still show obedience toward the demands that are put on them. On the other hand, personal power engenders commitment, as subjects will share an identity with the person exerting pressures on them. Subjects will believe the ideas of their leader and will be motivated in accomplishing their tasks as they more fully understand, believe, and share the vision about the future of the organization.

There is the need to look into more details of the consequences inherent in such typology of organizational power as we venture into the NPO context. The motivations of the constituents of a for-profit organization, its employees, are much more open to the influence resulting from positional power, when we compare them to the volunteer workforce of NPOs. Employees have financial dependencies and continuing concerns with their employers, whereas volunteers have reduced continuing concerns on their associations with a NPO and irrelevant, if any, financial incentive. Consequently, much of the reward and coercive sources of power are diminished, if not void altogether. Volunteers need to develop an emotional connection with the NPOs where they work (Drucker, 1990; Simms and Luke, 2009). For managers of NPOs, this offers a major demand on their ability in developing the abilities associated with the personal sources of power, referent and expert. We see then, in the NPO environment, it is very much critical that a manager embrace strong leadership abilities.

Leaders vs. Leadership

The final theoretical component of the phenomena of leadership is to understand the differences between leaders and leadership. Organizational leaders are individuals who are in the position of using the sources of power that are available to them, to sway members within an organization into behaving in ways that help the collective entity in accomplishing its goals. A two-way influencing process however is the true essence of leadership. Hence, leadership is conceptualized as a *dyadic process* (Rousseau and House, 1994); as such, leadership lays neither within the person of the leader nor with the followers; leadership is the relationship between a leader and the respective followers. Such a process considers that leadership happens in the interconnection between a leader and a subject, and it will only progress if there are at least two parties involved. On the one side is an agent with the ability of influencing another party's behaviour. Adding to that, the subjects will, openly or tacitly, accept and agree with such an influence. In that fashion, the leader, the subject (in this case a follower) and the exchange between both parties are all part of the leadership process (Yukl, 2006).

The discussion up to this point in this chapter about the nature of leadership sets the stage for the understanding of the processes that represent effective leadership. After much effort in the field trying to understand *who* would make effective organizational leaders, the end result was that there was actually very little to report. The past effort in linking personal traits and demographic determinants of leaders did not produce much value (House and Aditya, 1997). It was the focus on leaders' behaviours and the subjects' responses, attributions, and reactions to such behaviours that have led to much more interesting findings. In summary, the interesting question here is not *who* are the good organizational leaders; rather, the question should be *what* behaviours represent a superior form of leadership. This is the direction of the remainder of this chapter.

THEORIES OF EFFECTIVE LEADERSHIP

It is necessary to understand that the context in which the dyadic relationship between a leader and subjects evolve is a defining factor. This is a perspective of leadership which articulates that the effects of leaders' behaviours on their subjects are contingent on a situation; this is the foundation of the *contingency theories of effective leadership*. The suggestion is that in trying to find which leader behaviours would lead to the desirable consequent responses from their subjects, the specificities of the subjects and the organizational environment will equally affect that dyadic relationship. There are situational factors that may heighten or void the effects of leaders; for instance, the perception of a crisis or some environmental uncertainty will stress the subjects' perception of how charismatic their leader may be and, consequently, will affect the dyadic effects of the leader over the subject (Waldman and Yammarino, 1999). An interesting illustration of such effect was the boost on the assessments of the leadership perceptions of former New York City's mayor, Rudolph Giuliani, after the tragedy of the World Trade Center in 2001. The sense of an important crisis made subjects much more attentive to some direction from the city's office. Mayor Giuliani was visible and helped create a sense of direction and vision of how New York was going to cope with the crisis, resulting from the terrorist attacks on the World Trade Center. The perception of environmental uncertainty by followers heightened the charismatic leadership process between subjects and the leader.

Subjects' characteristics also affect leadership development; for instance, immature professionals or new organizational members will react differently to a leader's behaviours when compared to seasoned professionals who have been in the organization for some time. For instance, the perception of the charismatic attributes of a leader by the subjects is higher during the initial tenure of the leader in an organization, whereas the length of the tenure of the leader with the organization diminishes these very perceptions (Beyer and Browninga, 1999). Next, the path-goal theory of leadership is introduced as a blue print to help the understanding of the contingency factors of leadership.

Path-Goal Contingency Theory of Leadership

One of the most influential contingency theory formulations is the path-goal theory of leadership (Evans, 1970, 1996; House, 1971, 1996), which builds on the understandings of the expectancy theory of motivation inside organizations (Vroom, 1964). Expectancy theory proposes that individual motivation at the workplace evolves through a two-step process. First, individuals should expect that their effort would lead to the desired level of performance. Second, the reached performance should lead to the intended reward. In other words, organizational members should be under the impression that they have the individual capabilities and the necessary resources to put into their efforts in reaching the necessary level of performance. Next, they would also expect that the attained performance will lead to the desired benefits according to their own perceptions. When such linkages are clear and positive, the subject is more likely to be motivated and to engage in constructive organizational actions. For instance, volunteers would only become engaged in working with a NPO if they perceive that they have the abilities and the means to accomplish the tasks under their responsibilities; if they believe that they cannot perform their duties for whatever reason, their level of commitment and motivation is reduced. Furthermore, if they believe that they can fulfill their duties, the level of commitment and motivation is even stronger when they see how their actions help in attaining the organizational and personal goals linked to the societal mandate of the NPO.

The path-goal theory of leadership clarifies that an effective leader assists subjects through the expectancy motivational path, which will ultimately lead the organization and individual to valued outcomes. The leader has to reinforce the perception of the two-step motivational process, initially, by fostering the subject self-efficacy and by providing the resources that allow subjects to attain the requested level of performance. Next, the leader also needs to clarify the linkages between the performance of the subjects to the individual and organizational rewards that result from the collective outcomes. It focuses on the relationships between a superior and a subordinate in their daily responsibilities, by explaining how formally appointed superiors may affect individually the motivation and satisfaction of subordinates.

The proponents of the path-goal theory suggest that effective leadership should help subjects make the connection between their individual efforts and the expected level of performance; subsequently, it should develop a clear vision of the rewards in attaining the expected level of performance. The rewards should be communicated in such ways that subjects clearly see how their individual contributions would help create a better future for the organization. Moreover, subjects should also be able to see unequivocally how they personally benefit when that better future is reached. Besides making these connections clear, the path-goal process is affected by the characteristics of the environment, especially the conditions of the workplace and the individual characteristics of the subjects (House and Mitchell, 1974). Hence, the leader's behaviours and actions will have to be adjusted to make sure that the motivational path evolves completely, depending on context. Figure 1 illustrates such connections.

Figure 1: Path-Goal Leadership Theory

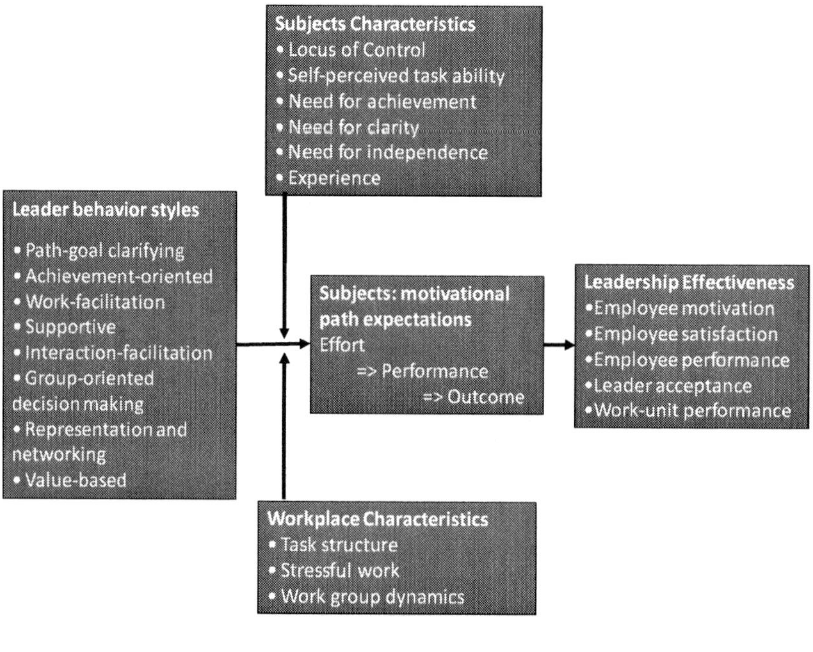

The theory proposes some approaches to effective leadership. A couple of the more elaborated propositions from the theory are related to task characteristics and followers' experience. Specifically the theory proposes that when the work is too repetitive, and workers are inexperienced and lack self-confidence, a supportive form of leadership increases the intrinsic valence of the function; this should also lead subjects to a higher appreciation of their organizational function. Leaders should pay attention to the needs of the subordinates and create a friendly and supportive work environment. However, if working with more experienced workers, achievement-oriented leadership may be more effective, as leaders set equally high standards and challenging but attainable goals.

In a different task environment where it is found that the workers are far too inexperienced for more complex and unstructured tasks, there is the need of directive leadership, where leaders give specific guidelines for the work ahead. However, if the subjects are experienced, participative leadership will be more effective as leaders can then listen to the opinion of the subjects about how to tackle the tasks ahead.

The path-goal theory, as originally proposed, has received mixed empirical support, but it has been an influential framework to suggest ways for conceptualizing effective leadership. Probably the biggest impact of this theory has been on how it framed much of the subsequent conceptualizations of the field. In one way or the other, the latter theories have touched on the issues of leaders' behaviours, contextual factors (subject or work conditions) and the assessment of how that would bring effective organizational results. Furthermore, it is a constant approach of the study of organizational leadership to elaborate on the interconnections of these areas, as firstly introduced by House and colleagues. Summarizing, organizational leadership is a process that helps subjects to understand the central goals of the organization, how their individual actions contribute to such objectives, and what would be the collective and individual benefits of reaching those goals. In such a process, the effectiveness of the leadership process depends on leaders adjusting their behaviours to match the profile of the subjects and the characteristics of the tasks at hand (House, 1996; House and Mitchell, 1974).

In conclusion, leaders should adjust their behaviours to help subjects find the path from their actions to performance and finally to rewards. Despite many suggestions of different behaviours that leaders should depict, a constant element linked to leadership effectiveness is the dimension of a charismatic relationship between leaders and their subjects. From the path-goal theory, we can understand how varying subjects' characteristics and work conditions will associate specific leader behaviours to be charismatic. Although the perception of charisma may vary due to contingencies, the development of charismatic leadership is quite robust and tends to lead to similar dyadic effects (House *et al.*, 2004). The charismatic dyadic relationship will display similar characteristics. In sum, attributions of charisma result from leader behaviours, which are context-specific; but the charismatic relationship is similar, forming a dyadic phenomenon between leaders and subjects.

For instance, Candace Lynne "Candy" Lightner, the founding president of Mothers Against Drunk Driving (MADD), started the organization in 1980, four days after her 13-year-old daughter died at the hands of a repeat offender drunk driver. Her unconventional and outspoken ways helped define a strong charismatic leadership for the NPO. The fresh organization and its inexperienced members looked to the founder's actions as being highly charismatic and energetic, which gave a sense of purpose and defined the organization through its formative years. As the NPO matured, a change in the levels of bureaucracy and the added experience of its constituents changed the situational arrangement for Mrs. Lightner's leadership. Now, the same actions by the leader were no longer seen as charismatic anymore, the organization had grown, new bureaucratic processes were in place, and the work force was different (Weed, 1993). The new situation generated an internal conflict and led to the eventual replacement of MADD's first president.

The understanding is that charismatic leadership is a very robust concept, but enacting such a relationship demands an acute perception of the work and subject situation. To study this further, one must discuss the nature of charismatic leadership.

Understanding Charisma

The concept of charisma in the leadership literature is related but not equal to the pop culture idea of charismatic individuals, which has led to many misconceptions. Public figures and celebrities with strong personalities and communication abilities receive the label of charismatic individuals. The general public sees them as charismatic, but they have no leadership abilities under the perspective of an organizational form. From a leadership standpoint, charisma is a much more complex and multifaceted idea that only shares the communication abilities with their pop culture counterparts. The confusion has been so troubling that many in the field have moved away from the label; nonetheless, this is a critical concept for understanding leadership in organizations.

The groundbreaking work of Max Weber (1947) at the end of the nineteenth century was the first instance where charismatic leaders were seen by their capabilities of reshaping the performance of organizations and their typically ingrained bureaucratic practices. From Weber's work, the idea of leader's charisma has evolved to the neo-charismatic approach to understand leadership. Neo-charismatic theory actually represents an overarching school of leadership theories, which has been broadly associated with leader effectiveness at both individual and organizational levels (House and Aditya, 1997; Judge and Piccolo, 2004; Lowe, Kroeck, and Sivasubramaniam, 1996). This body of work is alternatively referred to as charismatic (Conger and Kanungo, 1998; Waldman and Yammarino, 1999), transformational (Bass, 1985; Tichy and Devanna, 1985), visionary (Sashkin and Fulmer, 1988), and inspirational leadership (Nanus, 1992). Despite some differences, the various theories share the view that outstanding leaders go beyond a simple performance versus reward transaction and have a deep impact on subjects and their units. Since the core of these theories is the concept of charisma, several authors have used the general rubric of charismatic leadership for all of them.

Specifically, charismatic leaders engender a dyadic relationship between themselves and their subjects based on leaders' behaviours that engender intense reactions and inspiration on the part of their followers. In short, charismatic leaders are commonly viewed as inspirational in their relationship with subjects, which includes being seen as energetic and optimistic, having a sense of purpose and vision, and having strongly held values (Conger and Kanungo, 1998; Waldman and Yammarino, 1999). The charismatic leader's vision gives meaning to efforts and goals by connecting a vision to the deeply held values with which subjects can identify (Shamir, House, & Arthur, 1993). Charismatic leaders are usually unconventional and display a strong rebuttal of *status quo*, becoming strong change agents. Followers develop a charismatic relationship with such leaders by attributing to them a higher intellect and a more acute sense of purpose, and by seeing them as individuals who show a clear path to the best way of reaching a better future.

One of the schools of leadership that resulted from the discussion of charismatic leadership is the discussion of transformational versus transactional leadership (Bass, 1985; Burns, 1978; Tichy and Devanna, 1985). As conceptualized by Bass (1985), transformational leaders are articulated as individuals who have an idealized influence and display individualized consideration and motivation towards their subjects, as well as instilling intellectual stimulation in them. The conceptualization of transformational leaders draws a strong parallel with the model of charismatic leaders. Such leaders are seen as change agents in organizations, since they have a much higher emotional appeal over the subjects and become forces in making sure the organization members become committed to a new and better future.

When considering the charismatic leadership process, we can easily see that it is directly linked to the personal sources of power, as referent and expert power become the main sources of influence that they embody. As such, a charismatic leader engenders commitment from subjects, as they are attracted to the new vision of a better future, attribute positive personal qualities to the leader, and appreciate being associated with such an individual. The rationalization of why there is such a wide amount of empirical evidence, showing higher effectiveness of charismatic leadership (DeGroot, Kiker, and Cross, 2000), results from the understanding that committed individuals will lead to stronger organizational outcomes.

As a different form of leadership, leaders can manifest the transactional approach, which suggests the idea that leaders also make use of different behaviours as means to influence subjects (Bass, 1985). Transactional leaders tend to engage in social exchanges with their subjects in a tit-for-tat process, where recompense is central to the way that they seek to influence subjects' behaviour. They develop reward structures and manage their subjects by reinforcing the desired behaviours in them. Consequently, such leaders instill compliance in their subjects instead of commitment because subjects will focus on the rewards for their actions, instead of the emotional appeal that comes from the more charismatic relationship with leaders that is typical of the transformational process. In observing organizational leaders' actions, it is notable that leaders include both traits, transactional and transformational (Bass 1985), and that a leader characterization would be a matter of degree of how much of each behaviour is manifested.

Socialized vs. Personalized Leadership

With that said, we should note that charisma has been under scrutiny in the literature, as scholars seek to differentiate between positive versus potentially negative effects of charismatic leaders (Gardner, 2003; Varella, Javidan, and Waldman, 2005; Howell and Avolio, 1992), since it has been noted that there is a potentially more dark or personalized manifestation of charisma (Sankar, 2003). Exploiting the inspirational attribution towards charismatic leaders that their followers may develop, some of these leaders may be or may become self-centred, narcissistic, exploitative, and manipulative in their relationships with others in the pursuit of their own self-centred objectives (Conger and Kanungo, 1998; Kets de Vries, 1993). Personalized charismatic leaders will manipulate the inspirational effects on their subjects to emphasize allegiance to themselves, rather than the organizational interests. Thus, rather than focusing confidence-building in the direction of the group and its members, these leaders focus on confidence-building more in their own direction as the sole individual who can take the organization to a better future.

The more positive, socialized form of charismatic leadership has received increasing attention in the literature (Brown and Trevino, 2006). These types of leaders apply restraint in their use of power, and they use their charismatic influence to achieve goals and objectives for the betterment of the collective entity rather than for personal gain (Howell and Avolio, 1992). Similarly, Avolio *et al.* (2004) suggested that such leaders set a personal example of moral standards and integrity to their subjects.

Thus, socialized charismatic leadership includes two elements. First, they will include all the inspirational effects of charismatic leaders as explained earlier. Second, socialized charismatic leaders will role-model and stress key values pertaining to integrity. Leader integrity includes behaviours such as: keeping one's word and acting truthfully; acting ethically; serving the interests of followers, rather than oneself; and being open and sharing critical information with followers (Waldman *et al.*, 2006; Craig and Gustafson, 1998). Favourable reactions on the part of followers are likely to include perceptions of selflessness, as well as a leadership process that is perceived as being trustworthy (Gottlieb and Sanzgiri, 1996).

Socialized charismatic leaders are an effective and positive manifestation because they promote a strong vision and sense of purpose for the organization. A highly effective leader articulates a vision that is based on strongly held ideological values, and vivid and powerful imagery (Nanus, 1992). Through a socialized vision, leaders stimulate a sense of purpose that fosters innovative solutions to major problems. They also show determination in the pursuit of goals, and motivate others because of their own role-modelling and success. For instance, there is a major leadership effect on environmentalists when they see the images of Greenpeace activists challenging whalers in high seas, pulling their stunts and even putting themselves in harm's way to stop the hunting of whales. For environmentalists, the leaders of Greenpeace are clearly seen as socialized individuals and their actions are characterized as charismatic.

Further, a leader's vision may generate high degrees of subjects' confidence, trust and admiration in the leader, as well as emotional appeal (Shamir, House, and Arthur, 1993). Thus, it can encourage subjects to subsume their self-interests for the greater collective good and show a willingness to collaborate. Through socialized charisma, leaders are able to inspire organizational members with a strong vision in which they can identify and focus their attention and efforts (Shamir, House, and Arthur, 1993). Such leadership process, which is referred to as visioning, engages the whole organization as members participate in creating their future and develop collective ideas on what that future should be.

An example of the visioning processes is the work of the highly charismatic Benaree (Bennie) Wiley. During the early 1990s, Mrs. Wiley was appointed as the CEO of a NPO in Boston known as The Partnership Inc. (Stearns, 2005; Mahoney, 2000). It was a typically small NPO, without any permanent staff besides the CEO; volunteers ran its operation. The mandate of the NPO was to promote the integration of African American professionals in Boston. Its mission was to increase the representation and develop the leadership potential of African Americans within the business community of that city. She took the helm of what was then a financially frail NPO that was uncertain to last; she turned the organization around and made it one of the most successful organizations of its kind (Lewis, 2004).

Nowadays, the NPO counts six full-time personnel and a board of trustees that reads more like a "who-is-who" list in the African American community in Boston; over 2,000 people and 250 leading companies have used its support in developing the inclusion of African Americans in the business community. Many attribute the current strong position of The Partnership to the clear sense of purpose and the strong vision that Mrs. Wiley brought to the organization. In her own words, the former CEO describes the need for a vision about the future: "Clarity is a key prerequisite of leadership. Where do you see yourself in five years? How does what you currently do fit in with where you see yourself in five years?" (Morrell, 2008, p. 4.) The leader, however, does not unilaterally create purpose and vision for the organization; rather, visioning is a collective process that includes leaders and subjects alike. Through the processes of consultation and exchange of ideas, leaders build new visions for the organization; a leader functions as a catalyst process that motivates the subjects and uses positive leadership power and influence to engage as many stakeholders as possible.

Right after taking over office, Mrs. Wiley tackled what seemed to be insurmountable challenges, starting with a process of consultation with a large number of stakeholder groups (Coleman, 1998), sponsoring corporations, civic groups, board members, alumni, and so forth. The consultation focused on the mandate of The Partnership and on how to generate the social change that the organization wanted. That set the foot of the organization in the right direction, which changed The Partnership Inc. As one of the members of the board described it, "We had long wonderful conversations. We became friends and I had enormous admiration for her. ... I trusted Bennie implicitly as did the other members of the board, the City, and eventually the Mayor. Corporations supported her. Bennie had negotiated through it all. Within a few short years, Bennie had become the way in this city to reach middle-class blacks." (Roberts and Winston, 2006, p. 6.) This perspective of socialized leadership includes the perspective of leaders behaving in ethical ways.

Ethical Leadership

The new focus of the field on the ethical component of leadership exists in other fronts, besides the discussion of socialized charismatic leaders. There is a positive and necessary shift to study and suggest theories about leadership, which includes leaders with more integrity and a stronger ethical compass. Strongly associated with the idea of socialized values is the conceptualization of servant leadership (Greenleaf, 1977). Servant leaders are organizational leaders whose main concern is the development of their subjects. This perspective includes justifications that fall along the same rationale about the need for socialized leaders; as such, the key to effective leadership is a focus on subjects and the progress of the organization as a whole. As Helene Gayle, CEO of CARE – USA, describes:

> To me it is about being a servant leader and listening to people, having them feel that everything I do is to enable them to do the things they need to do. I constantly remind myself that even though I'm the leader of the team, the people around me know a lot more about their work than I do.

(Welankiwar, 2009, p. 22.)

Along the same line of servant leadership is the idea of level-five leaders (Collins, 2001), who are characterized as charismatic or transformational leaders who not only bring the subjects at the fore-front of their actions, but also are quick in deferring the success of the organization to the subjects. This work has received some initial empirical evidence, showing that level-five leadership helps create organizations with outstanding performance.

A critical read of such propositions may point to a dilemma: Can we be asking too much of our leaders? How can such altruistic leaders progress with their career if they cannot claim the accomplishments to themselves? Can it be possible that egoistic leaders (the ones that are also ethical in their actions) could be more effective than altruistic ones? The reader may want to examine Avolio and Locke (2002), and Waldman and Siegel (2008), for two intellectually stimulating ex-changes of ideas on the topic. As a discussion that is at the forefront of the leadership discussion, there is still much to be determined in the field. This chapter intends to stimulate such a discussion, as it cannot offer strong conclusions for this ongoing debate.

A final framework of leadership associated with ethical values is the work of Brown, Trevino and colleagues (*e.g.*, Brown and Trevino, 2006; Brown, Trevino, and Harrison, 2005). They offer similar rationales, justifying ethical behaviour in leaders as a defining factor for effective leadership. A more rigorous exploration of their approach, however, generates some intriguing questions. Ethics is a relative concept and one that derives from societal values; ethical leadership, therefore, cannot be evaluated as an omnipresent idea because it is highly dependent on context. This highlights the limitation of how much actionable knowledge the conceptualizations around ethical leadership may actually generate. Based on our globalized, culturally diverse, and varied contemporary realities, it seems burdensome to suggest that leaders may enact values that could be seen as ethical by all subjects within an organization. The ethical question presents some additional difficulty in the NPO environment, since different stake-holders will embrace varying ethical perspectives. For instance, firing a large proportion of the employed workforce to improve the survival of the organization will probably be ethical for the financers of the organization; yet, the groups that benefit from the NPO's services may see that as an unethical decision.

Such discussion leads to the next point of this chapter, the understanding of how leadership evolves across different cultures.

Leadership Across Cultures

The Global Leadership and Organizational Behavior Effectiveness Research Program (GLOBE) is a project that included investigators in many corners of the world, examining the relationships between societal culture and organizational leadership. It was a rigorous research undertaking that included around 170 investigators from 61 cultures (House *et al.*, 2004; House *et al.*, 1999). One of the most interesting outcomes of such a massive effort was the identification of a few leadership characteristics that were actually invariant across cultures (Javidan *et al.*, 2006).

Charisma and its socialized manifestation were universally endorsed by all 61 cultures, attesting to the robustness of such manifestation of leadership. Team-oriented leadership was also universally endorsed. The specific behaviours that the study employed to characterize such leaders were: being trustworthy, just, and honest (integrity); having foresight and planning ahead (charismatic/visionary); being positive, dynamic, encouraging, motivating, and building confidence (charismatic/inspirational); and being communicative, informed, a coordinator, and team integrator (team builder). This leads to a clear view of leaders who are universally seen as effective; leaders should exhibit charismatic and integrity qualities, and build effective teams.

The study also points to some leadership characteristics that were universally viewed as *impediments* to effective leadership; self-protective, malevolent, and autocratic were universally viewed as ineffective. The specific assessed behaviours were: being a loner and asocial (self-protective); being non-cooperative and irritable (malevolent); and being dictatorial (autocratic).

Autonomous, status-conscious, risk-taker, and self-sacrificial received mixed results; they were seen as effective leadership behaviours in a few cultures, but were seen as impediments to effective leadership in other cultures. Again, the specific assessed behaviours were: being individualistic (autonomous); being status-conscious; and being a risk-taker (charismatic III — risk-taker: self-sacrificial).

The conclusion is that leaders who display some dimensions that cut across cultural differences lead to effective leadership. Such information is important for the NPO reality in North America on many different fronts. Initially, the increasingly diversified demographic composition represents a new reality for the leaders of NPOs; the volunteer workers, the intended beneficiaries of the NPO activities, and the varying groups of stakeholders are culturally diverse; they will make different demands on NPOs and their leaders. Finally, the globalization of NPO is a reality; for instance, OXFAM, Doctors Without Borders, Greenpeace, and many philanthropic foundations reach across country borders and will have to be able to operate in this uneven environment. The fact that some leadership attributes are universally accepted offers an initial guideline for the budding leader of our current reality. A cautionary point though is that enacting such leadership dimensions may call for concrete actions that should be specific to each situation, as was explored before in this chapter.

CONCLUSION

The challenges in leading NPOs should not be underestimated; the unique design of such organizations creates some difficulties for someone intending to help foster a relevant, stable, and successful cause. The constraints of workforce management that are inherent in its very foundation represent a particularly sensitive environment for managing people. The absence of the usual hierarchical and positional power structures of other forms of organization — e.g., for-profit, governmental, and alike — creates a context in which strong and well-developed leadership is mandatory. A non-motivated volunteer does not exist. If people are not engaged, attracted, and trusting of the NPO, they will not have any reason to work with it. Leaders of NPOs will become more effective as they understand the motivational foundation of volunteers. Moreover, they must fully appreciate how their own leadership abilities help foster the motivation of volunteers.

In seeking the survival and efficiency of NPOs, the fourth sector has seen a tremendous pressure for becoming smartly managed and better-oiled organizations. The reasons for such pressures are legitimate and will certainly help create an industry that is more resilient and better prepared to face the challenges ahead. In many of the other chapters in this book, the reader will find a series of suggestions and techniques that are aimed at creating that sort of NPO, one that is efficient and well administered. The field needs that.

This chapter, however, intends to bring another call, a call for NPO leaders to embrace their vision and instill them throughout the NPO that they lead and the communities that host and depend on it. The sector is replete with examples of highly motivated individuals who, by holding strong values and a strong sense of purpose, ventured into creating fantastic social change. Yet, if such individuals really want to expand their reach to broader audiences and have a stronger social impact, they have to develop their leadership abilities rather thoroughly. Leaders of NPOs will be very effective if they develop the ability of translating their own vision, internal values, and personal sense of purpose into a collective phenomenon. The objective of this chapter was to demonstrate how the development of socialized charismatic leadership inside NPOs could be a far-reaching mechanism of social change, through the creation of outstanding nonprofit organizations.

REFERENCES

Agle, B. R., Nagarajan, N. J., Sonnenfeld, J. A., & Srinivasan, D. (2006). Does CEO charisma matter? An empirical analysis of the relationships among organizational performance, environmental uncertainty, and top management team perceptions of CEO charisma. *Academy of Management Journal, 49*(1), 161-174.

Avolio, B. J., Gardner, W. L., Walumbwa, F. O., Luthans, F., & May, D. R. (2004). Unlocking the mask: A look at the process by which authentic leaders impact follower attitudes and behavior. *The Leadership Quarterly, 15,* 801-823.

Avolio, B. J., & Locke, E. E. (2002). Contrasting different philosophies of leader motivation: Altruism versus egoism. *The Leadership Quarterly, 13*(2), 169-191.

Bass, B. M. (1985). *Leadership and performance beyond expectations.* New York: Harper.

Bennis, W. G., & Nanus, G. (1985). *Leaders.* New York: Harper and Row.

Beyer, J. M., & Browning, L. D. (1999). Transforming an industry in crisis: Charisma, routinization, and supportive cultural leadership. *The Leadership Quarterly, 10*(3), 483-520.

Brown, M. E., & Trevino, L. K. (2006). Ethical leadership: A review and future directions. *The Leadership Quarterly, 17*(6), 595-616.

Brown, M. E., & Trevino, L. K. (2006). Socialized charismatic leadership, values congruence, and deviance in work groups. *Journal of Applied Psychology*, *91*, 954-962.

Brown, M. E., Trevino, L. K., & Harrison, D. A. (2005). Ethical leadership: A social learning perspective for construct development and testing. *Organizational Behavior and Human Decision Processes*, *97*(2), 117-134.

Burns, J. M. (1978). *Leadership*. New York: Harper & How.

Coleman, S. (1998, March 15). Q. & A. With Benaree P. Wiley, President, CEO of the Partnership. *The Boston Globe*.

Collins, J. (2001). *Good to great: Why some companies make the leap and others don't*. New York: Harper Business.

Conger, J. A., & Kanungo, R. N. (1998). *Charismatic leadership in organizations*. Thousand Oaks, CA: Sage Publications.

Craig, S. B., & Gustafson, S. B. (1998). Perceived leader integrity scale: An instrument for assessing employee perceptions of leader integrity. *The Leadership Quarterly*, *9*, 127-145.

DeGroot, T., Kiker, D. S., & Cross, T. C. (2000). A Meta-analysis to review organizational outcomes related to charismatic leadership. *Revue Canadienne des Sciences de l'Administration*, *17*(4), 356.

Drucker, P. F. (1954). *The practice of management*. New York: Harper.

Drucker, P. F. (1967). *The effective executive*. New York: Harper & Row.

Drucker, P. F. (1990). *Managing the non-profit organization: Practices and principles*. New York, N.Y.: HarperCollins.

Evans, M. G. (1970). The effects of supervisory behavior on the path-goal relationship. *Organizational Behavior and Human Performance*, *5* (May), 277-298.

Evans, M. G. (1996). A path-goal theory of leader effectiveness. *The Leadership Quarterly*, *7*(3), 305-309.

Galinsky, A. D., Gruenfeld, D. H., & Magee, J. C. (2003). From power to action. *Journal of Personality and Social Psychology*, *85*(3), 453-466.

Gardner, W. L. (2003). Perceptions of leader charisma, effectiveness, and integrity. *Management Communication Quarterly*, *16*(4), 502-527.

Gottlieb, J. Z., & Sanzgiri, J. (1996). Towards an ethical dimension of decision making in organizations. *Journal of Business Ethics, 15,* 1275-1285.

Greenleaf, R. K. (1977). *Servant leadership: A journey into the nature of legitimate power and greatness.* New York: Paulist Press.

House, R. J. (1971). A Path-goal theory of leader effectiveness. *Administrative Science Quarterly, 16*(3), 321-339.

House, R. J. (1996). Path-goal theory of leadership: Lessons, legacy, and a reformulated theory. *The Leadership Quarterly, 7*(3), 323-352.

House, R. J., & Aditya, R. N. (1997). The social scientific study of leadership: Quo vadis? *Journal of Management, 23*(3), 409-473.

House, R. J., Hanges, P. J., Javidan, M., Dorfman, P. W, & Gupta, V. (2004). *Culture, leadership, and organizations: The globe study of 62 societies, global leadership and organizational behavior effectiveness research program.* Thousand Oaks, Calif.: Sage Publications.

House, R. J., Hanges, P. J., Ruiz-Quintanilla, S. A., Dorfman, P. W., Javidan, M., Dickson, M., & Gupta, V. (1999). *Cultural influences on leadership and organizations: Project globe. Advances in global leadership.* Greenwich, CT: JAI Press.

House, R. J., & Mitchell, T. R. (1974). Path-goal theory of leadership. *Contemporary Business, 3* (Fall), 81-98.

Howell, J. M., & Avolio, B. J. (1992). The ethics of charismatic leadership: Submission or liberation? *Academy of Management Executive, 6*(2), 43-54.

Javidan, M., Dorfman, P. W., De Luque, M. S., & House, R. J. (2006). In the eye of the beholder: Cross cultural lessons in leadership from project globe. *Academy of Management Perspectives, 20*(1), 67-90.

Judge, T. A., & Piccolo, R. F. (2004). Transformational and transactional leadership: A meta-analytic test of their relative validity. *Journal of Applied Psychology, 89*(5), 755-768.

Kets de Vries, M. F. R. (1993). *Leaders, fools, and imposter: Essays on the psychology of leadership.* San Francisco: Jossey-Bass.

Lewis, D. E. (2004). Chief of Boston Diversity Organization to resign. *Knight Ridder Tribune Business News,* p. 1.

Lowe, K. B., Kroeck, K. G., & Sivasubramaniam, N. (1996). Effectiveness of correlates of transformational and transactional leadership: A meta-analytic review of the MLQ literature. *The Leadership Quarterly, 7*(3), 385-425.

Mahoney, C. (2000). Executive profile: Benaree Wiley. *The Boston Business Journal*, p. 3.

Meindl, J. R., Ehrlich, S. B., & Dukerich, J. M. (1985). The romance of leadership. *Administrative Science Quarterly, 30*(1), 78-102.

Mintzberg, H. (1973). *The nature of managerial work.* New York: Harper & Row.

Morrell, D. (2008, Fall). A champion of change: Benaree Wiley discusses leadership, social diversity. *Lead The Way.*

Nanus, B. (1992). *Visionary leadership.* San Francisco: Jossey-Bass.

Pfeffer, J. (1977). The ambiguity of leadership. *Academy of Management Review, 2*(1), 104-112.

Pfeffer, J. (1981). Management as symbolic action: The creation and maintenance of organizational paradigms. In B. M. Staw & L. L. Cummings (Eds.), *Research in organizational behavior.* Greenwich, CT: JAI Press

Raven, B. H., & French, J. R. P. (1959). The bases of social power. In D. Cartwright (Ed.), *Studies in social power.* Ann Arbor: Research Center for Group Dynamics, Institute for Social Research, University of Michigan.

Roberts, L. M., & Winston, V. W. (2006). Bennie Wiley at the Partnership, Inc. Boston: Harvard Business School Cases.

Rousseau, D. M., & House, R. J. (1994). Meso organizational behavior: Avoiding three fundamental biases. In C. L. Cooper & D. M. Rousseau (Eds.), *Trends in organizational behavior.* Chichester, New York: Wiley.

Sankar, Y. (2003). Character not charisma is the critical measure of leadership excellence. *The Journal of Leadership and Organizational Studies, 9*(4), 45-55.

Sashkin, M. R., & Fulmer, M. (1988). Toward an organizational leadership theory. In G. Hunt, B. R. Baliga, H. P. Dachler, & C. A. Schriesheim (Eds.), *Emerging leadership vistas.* Lexington, MA: Heath.

Shamir, B., House, R. J., & Arthur, M. B. (1993). The motivational effects of charismatic leadership: A self-concept based theory. *Organization Science*, *4*(4), 1-17.

Simms, D., & Luke, W. (2009). Fulfill the dream of leading a nonprofit. *Harvard Business Review*, *87*(1), 26-26.

Stearns, S. (2005). Video oral history interview with Benaree Wiley. *The HistoryMakers®*.

Tichy, N. M., & Devanna, M. A. (1985). *The Transformational Leader*. New York: John Wiley.

Varella, P., Javidan, M., & Waldman, D. A. (2005). The differential effects of socialized and personalized leadership on group social capital. In W. L. Gardner, B. J. Avolio, & F. O. Walumbwa (Eds.), *Authentic leadership theory and practice: Origins, effects and development*. Greenwich, CT: Elsevier/JAI.

Vroom, V. H. (1964). *Work and motivation*. New York: Wiley.

Waldman, D. A., de Luque, M. Sully, Washburn, N., House, R. J., Adetoun, B., Barrasa, A., … Wilderom, C. P. M. (2006). Cultural and leadership predictors of corporate social responsibility values of top management: A globe study of 15 countries. *Journal of International Business Studies*, *37*, 823–837.

Waldman, D. A., Javidan, M., & Varella, P. (2004). Charismatic leadership at the strategic level: A new application of upper echelons theory. *The Leadership Quarterly*, *15*(3), 355.

Waldman, D. A., & Siegel, D. (2008). Defining the socially responsible leader. *The Leadership Quarterly*, *19*(1), 117-131.

Waldman, D. A., & Yammarino, F. J. (1999). CEO charismatic leadership: Levels-of-management and levels-of-analysis effects. *Academy of Management Review*, *14*(2), 266-285.

Weber, M. (1947). *The theory of social and economic organization* (1st American ed.) (A. M. Henderson & T. Parsons, Trans.). New York: Oxford University Press.

Weed, F. J. (1993). The MADD queen: Charisma and the founder of mothers against drunk driving. *The Leadership Quarterly*, *4*(3-4), 329-346.

Welankiwar, R. (2009, April). Care CEO Helene Gayle on shaking up a venerable organization. *Harvard Business Review*: Harvard Business School Publication Corp.

Yukl, G. (2006). *Leadership in organizations* (6th ed.). Upper Saddle River, NJ: Prentice Hall.

Chapter 15

ORGANIZATIONAL INVOLVEMENT

Melissa Eystad
World Spirit Consulting

> Individuals involved in volunteer management and development must use creative strategies to continually improve the involvement of volunteers as volunteers are often a critical asset to the organization. Understanding the core elements of the volunteer program through a review of the organizational standards will help to ensure that volunteers are engaged and involved appropriately in achieving the mission and purpose of the organization.

(*The Canadian Code for Volunteer Involvement*, 2006, p. 38)

INTRODUCTION

Volunteer program managers hold a unique, highly-interconnected role within the organization or group that provides opportunities to lead, provide input and influence. Positionally, many volunteer administrators may not find themselves in the "inner circle" of leadership and management at their organizations when it comes to organization-wide analysis and assessment. However, that should not stop them from creatively raising the profile of volunteers as resources and of highlighting their own skills and motivation in building an excellent volunteer support system. In addition, volunteer administrators' links to the broader community put them in contact with people from diverse backgrounds and attributes, requiring skills in cultural fluency and a solid understanding of the importance and challenges of inclusion.

According to the Council for Certification in Volunteer Administration (CCVA), the Body of Knowledge for a certified professional in Volunteer Administration, *organizational management* is defined as "the ability to design and implement policies, processes and structures to align volunteer involvement with the mission and vision of the organization." While a human resource professional needs to understand the work of the organization in order to find, hire and train staff with the skills required, the volunteer administrator must go even deeper to a micro-level to develop smaller tasks and projects that contribute to a greater degree than the effort it takes to involve volunteers. In other words, the tangible and intangible benefits of involving volunteers must exceed real and/or perceived costs to seem worth the effort.

As the external environment changes, the volunteer administrator needs to be aware of how those changes are or could be affecting the organization, its primary beneficiaries and customers, and revise or update strategies for maintaining a viable and dynamic volunteer resource in light of those changes. Therefore, a good working knowledge of the principles and tools of organizational assessment, ongoing involvement in assessment activities and competence in working with diversity and difference will increase the volunteer administrator's value to the organization. This chapter addresses these two topics and related issues, and focuses on how volunteer administrators can demonstrate their value to the organization through skill in and knowledge of organizational assessment, diversity and inclusion.

ORGANIZATIONAL ASSESSMENT: PRINCIPLES, EFFECTIVE PRACTICES AND TOOLS

Organizational assessment at its best, is a constructive step toward health and improved performance. It allows organizations to step back and take stock of their development, their strengths and challenges, and the choices they face for future success.

(V. Hyman, Fieldstone Alliance, *Nonprofit Tools You Can Use Newsletter*, 2006)

There is much debate about nonprofit effectiveness and how it should or even can be measured. An often-heard criticism of the nonprofit sector is that is not transparent enough about how effectively it meets needs and solves societal problems. Funders are increasingly interested in nonprofit capacity and effectiveness, as are volunteers. Because volunteers could feasibly make critical contributions in every area and service of a voluntary organization, the volunteer administrator must not only be able to envision how volunteer resources might contribute organization-wide, but also be able to assess where, how and if those contributions meet expectations and potential. In "The New Volunteer Workforce," Eisner, Grimm, Maynard and Washburn (2009) assert, "most nonprofits do not view their volunteers as strategic assets and have not developed ways to take full advantage of them. In fact, most nonprofits are losing staggering numbers of volunteers each year."

Often there is confusion between the terms "assessment" and "evaluation." For our purposes, we are defining the two activities as different, but related. Organizational assessment refers to the systematic process of gathering key information and measures from across the organization to create a picture of how the organization is functioning and performing. It can be compared with preparing a legal case — assessment is the gathering of evidence in the case. Evaluation is looking at the evidence — as is done in a courtroom — and then applying values and logic to determine what should happen next. Most nonprofits, education and other public services organizations understand the need to regularly assess their status and progress toward achieving mission. The challenge tends to be in finding the time and discipline for rigorous and thorough assessment activities, and/or having the internal expertise to undertake assessment. By using an organizational development approach, nonprofits will develop the internal capacity to be the best they can be in their mission work and to sustain themselves over the long term.

Principles

The first step toward creating effective organizational assessment practices is to have a clear set of principles that will provide a framework through which effective and manageable assessment can take place. The set of principles and practices for responsible nonprofit administration developed by the Minnesota Council of Nonprofits (2005) includes the key accountabilities that not-for-profit organizations hold as institutions created in the public trust and a short description of each accountability. An effective volunteer administrator understands these ten domains of accountability and works to ensure the volunteer program upholds them as relevant and appropriate:

1. Role in Society — Nonprofit organizations are obligated to understand their role as entities that engage and inspire individuals and communities for public benefit, and to conduct their activities with transparency, integrity and accountability.

2. Governance — A nonprofit's board of directors is responsible for defining the organization's mission and for providing overall leadership and strategic direction to the organization.

3. Planning — Nonprofits have a duty to engage in sound planning, define a clear vision for the future, and specify strategies, goals and objectives for plan implementation.

4. Transparency and Accountability — Nonprofits should regularly and openly convey information to the public about their mission, activities, accomplishments and decision-making processes.

5. Fundraising — Nonprofit fundraising should be conducted according to the highest ethical standards with regard to solicitation, acceptance, recording, reporting and use of funds.

6. Financial Management — Nonprofits have an obligation to act as responsible stewards in managing their financial resources.

7. Human Resources — The ability of an organization to make effective use of the energy, time and talents of its employees and volunteers is essential to accomplish the organization's mission

8. Evaluation — An essential responsibility of every nonprofit organization is to assess the impact of its actions and to act upon this information.

9. Strategic Partnerships — Nonprofits should initiate and promote cooperation and coordination between a variety of entities to avoid unnecessary duplication of services and to maximize the resources available to the communities they serve.

10. Civic Engagement and Public Policy — To the extent possible, nonprofit organizations should engage constituents in public policy and advocacy activities as a means to fulfilling their missions and promoting community interests.

Note that program delivery is not included in this list. The account-abilities address *how* the nonprofit is structured and run to deliver its mission, not the specifics of the approach to the issue or need being addressed. It is making sure the foundation of the building is strong and flexible enough to support what you build on top of it.

"Effective organizations periodically take stock of their strengths and weaknesses and the environment in which they work in order to set clear goals, objectives, strategies and tactics" (Philbin and Mikush, 2000, p. 20).

So what is the best way to "take stock"? There are many ways to undertake organizational assessment, depending on the size of the organization, the resources available (financial and human), and purpose of the assessment. As an example, a small nonprofit may have an opportunity to merge with another organization with a similar mission. The gathering of information about its status, services, budget, volunteers, history, *etc.*, will all be critical in determining the feasibility of the merger. Or a nonprofit may want to demonstrate its effectiveness and stewardship of resources with a report to the community and funders to ensure future support and growth.

Assessments typically use tools such as comprehensive questionnaires, SWOT (Strengths, Weaknesses, Opportunities, and Threats) analyses, balanced scorecards, and other diagnostic models along with comparison of results to various "best practices" or industry standards.

Organizational Assessment — Figuring Out What Is vs. What Can Be

Assessing the performance of your organization and your volunteer program will give a current perspective about how things are going at this point in time, or "what is." It will give you data and qualitative information. It will not tell you if your organization has the right mission or goals, or give you strategic direction. That work — moving from "what is" (assessment) to "what we think about what is" (evaluation) to "what can be" (visioning and strategic planning) moves an organization toward continuous learning and improvement.

There are many nonprofit assessment tools available for use or to adapt to a nonprofit's specific assessment interests, including convenient online surveys or questionnaires. Some have detailed assessment questions related to volunteer involvement, while others only examine the volunteer program from a higher human resources capacity perspective. As an example, in the McKinsey Capacity Assessment Grid below (Venture Philanthropy Partners, 2001, pp. 96-97, 102), broad questions are posed about how well volunteers (including board members) are engaged and their contributions:

Table 1: McKinsey Nonprofit Capacity Assessment Grid — Human Resources

HUMAN RESOURCES	1 Clear need for increased capacity	2 Basic level of capacity in place	3 Moderate level of capacity in place	4 High level of capacity in place
Staffing levels	Many positions within and peripheral to organization (*e.g.*, staff, volunteers, board, senior management) are unfilled, inadequately filled, or experience high turnover and/or poor attendance	Most critical positions within and peripheral to organization (*e.g.* staff, volunteers, board, senior management) are staffed (no vacancies), and/or experience limited turnover or attendance problems	Positions within and peripheral to organization (*e.g.*, staff, volunteers, board, senior management) are almost all staffed (no vacancies); few turnover or attendance problems	Positions within and peripheral to organization (*e.g.*, staff, volunteers, board, senior management) are all fully staffed (no vacancies); no turnover or attendance problems
Board – composition and commitment	Membership with limited diversity of fields of practice and expertise; drawn from a narrow spectrum of constituencies (from among nonprofit, academia, corporate, government, *etc.*); little or no relevant experience; low commit-ment to organization's success, vision and mission; meetings infrequent and/or poor attendance	Some diversity in fields of practice; membership represents a few different constituencies (from among nonprofit, academia, corporate, government, *etc.*); moderate commitment to organization's success, vision and mission; regular, purposeful meetings are well-planned and attendance is good overall	Good diversity in fields of practice and expertise; membership represents most constituencies (nonprofit, academia, corporate, government, *etc.*); good commitment to organization's success, vision and mission, and behavior to suit; regular, purposeful meetings are well-planned and attendance is consistently good, occasional subcommittee meetings	Membership with broad variety of fields of practice and expertise, and drawn from the full spectrum of constituencies (nonprofit, academia, corporate, government, *etc.*); includes functional and program content-related expertise, as well as high-profile names; high willing-ness and proven track record of investing in learning about

HUMAN RESOURCES	1 Clear need for increased capacity	2 Basic level of capacity in place	3 Moderate level of capacity in place	4 High level of capacity in place
Board – composition and commitment (*cont'd*)				the organization and addressing its issues; outstanding commitment to the organization's success, mission and vision; meet in person regularly, good attendance, frequent meetings of focused sub-committees
Board – involvement and support	Provide little direction, support, and accountability to leadership; board not fully informed about "material" and other major organizational matters; largely "feel-good" support	Provide occasional direction, support and accountability to leadership; informed about all "material" matters in a timely manner and re-sponses/decisions actively solicited	Provide direction, support and accountability to program-matic leadership; fully informed of all major matters, input and responses actively sought and valued; full participant in major decisions	Provide strong direction, support, and accountability to program-matic leadership and engaged as a strategic resource; communica-tion between board and leadership reflects mutual respect, appreciation for roles and responsibili-ties, shared commitment and valuing of collective wisdom

HUMAN RESOURCES	1 Clear need for increased capacity	2 Basic level of capacity in place	3 Moderate level of capacity in place	4 High level of capacity in place
Volunteers	Limited abilities; may be unreliable or have low commitment; volunteers are poorly managed	Good abilities; mostly reliable, loyal, and committed to organiza-tion's success; volunteers managed but without standards and little accountability	Very capable set of individuals, bring required skills to organization; reliable, loyal and highly committed to organization's success and to "making things happen"; work easily with most staff, but do not generally play core roles without substantial staff supervision; volunteers are managed and contribute to the overall success of the organization	Extremely capable set of individuals, bring complemen-tary skills to organization; reliable, loyal, highly committed to organization's success and to "making things happen"; often go beyond call of duty; able to work in a way that serves organization well, including ability to work easily with wide range of staff and play core roles without special supervision; volunteers managed very well and significantly-contribute to overall success of organization

The McKinsey Capacity Assessment Grid was created by McKinsey & Company and published in *Effective Capacity Building in Nonprofit Organizations* (2001), produced for Venture Philanthropy Partners (www.vppartners.org). It is reprinted, copied, or distributed with the permission of Venture Philanthropy Partners.

Whether or not the organization has a regular and systematic process of assessing its strengths, weaknesses and capacity, a professional volunteer administrator can and should have a plan to regularly review the health of the volunteer program and how well it is maximizing its capacity to support the mission of the organizations. The former United Way of the Minneapolis Area (now the Greater Twin

Cities United Way) developed this assessment tool for agencies that includes a detailed volunteer resources management rating form. While subjective and qualitative in scope, it would provide a quick and broad look at what is working and what could be improved. An additional column could be added to indicate which areas the volunteer program most excels.

Table 2: Volunteer HR Management Assessment Tool

Rating	Indicator	Met	Needs Work	N/A
E	The organization has a clearly defined purpose of the role that volunteers have within the organization.			
E	Job descriptions exist for all volunteer positions in the organization.			
R	The organization has a well-defined and communicated volunteer management plan that includes a recruitment policy, description of all volunteer jobs, an application and interview process, possible stipend and reimbursement policies, statement of which staff has supervisory responsibilities over what volunteers, and any other volunteer personnel policy information.			
E	The organization follows a recruitment policy that does not discriminate, but respects, encourages and represents the diversity of the community.			
E	The organization provides appropriate training and orientation to the agency to assist the volunteer in the performance of their volunteer activities. Volunteers are offered training with staff in such areas as cultural sensitivity.			
R	The organization is respectful of the volunteer's abilities and time commitment and has various job duties to meet these needs. Jobs should not be given to volunteers simply because the jobs are considered inferior for paid staff.			
R	The organization does volunteer performance appraisals periodically and communicates to the volunteers how well they are doing, or where additional attention is needed. At the same time, volunteers are requested to review and evaluate their involvement in the organization and the people they work with and suggest areas for improvement.			
R	The organization does some type of volunteer recognition or commendation periodically and staff continuously demonstrates their appreciation towards the volunteers and their efforts.			

Rating	Indicator	Met	Needs Work	N/A
A	The organization has a process for reviewing and responding to ideas, suggestions, comments and perceptions from volunteers.			
A	The organization provides opportunities for program participants to volunteer.			
A	The organization maintains contemporaneous records documenting volunteer time in program allocations. Financial records can be maintained for the volunteer time spent on programs and recorded as in-kind contributions.			
Indicators ratings: E=essential; R=recommended; A=additional to strengthen organizational activities				

Checklist of Nonprofit Indicators, United Way of Minneapolis Area, 1998. Used with the permission of Greater Twin Cities United Way.

Organizations must establish their philosophy about and commitment to the engagement of people who work in an unpaid capacity before any meaningful self-assessment about volunteer engagement and involvement effectiveness can take place. Volunteer administrators, as lead advocates for quality volunteer resources, often find themselves having to make the case not only for the benefits to the organization for high-quality and effective volunteer engagement systems and strategies, but for even having the volunteer program considered as a key indicator of health and success in organizational self-assessments. But without assessing how well the nonprofit makes use of existing volunteers and seeks to maximize potential volunteer resources, it will not have the information needed to strengthen its human resource capacity for its mission.

Preparing for an Assessment

How are volunteer administrators typically involved in organizational assessment? That varies a great deal depending on the organization, the level of the lead volunteer administrator and where that position resides in the organization. In an article published for Charity Village on "The Evolving Role of a Volunteer Resources Specialist," *one practitioner* says: "Needs are changing internally and things are changing with the economy externally. Just keeping on top of it and making us proactive instead of reactive is the biggest challenge." At the volunteer program level, volunteer administrators must establish the most important key indicators to monitor, and ensure that the data needed is captured and tracked at whatever intervals are appropriate.

Ideally, as one of the organization's key human resource managers, the volunteer administrator would be part of the high-level assessment team and would provide information on all the components of volunteer involvement, from policy development and current strategy and goals, to management processes, volunteer demographics, retention and volunteer relations.

Resource Availability

There is often a concern about the resources available to assist volunteer administrators in assessing the effective integration of volunteers throughout the organization. In review of the many nonprofit organizational assessment tools available, most appear to segment the volunteer program and/or engagement of volunteers for assessment rather than asking questions about how well the organization engages and retains volunteers in all areas of the organization. Whether you use a paper or online assessment survey, one way to possibly gain a broader view of how well volunteers are being integrated would be to develop key questions for each area of the organization that help to assess how or if volunteers are assisting in meeting the goals and objectives of that area. At minimum, it raises the idea that volunteers should at least be considered as resources in each functional area, and will help the organization and the volunteer administrator understand where there may be gaps in effective utilization of the volunteer resource. Another approach might be to have all assessment respondents for each functional area complete appropriate sections of the volunteer program assessment.

DEFINING DIVERSITY AND INCLUSION

What difference does difference make? Can an organization be effective without diverse perspectives and appropriate representation of the cultures, communities and people being served? Demographic changes are occurring rapidly in many of the populated areas of the globe for many reasons, meaning that people of different races, cultures, traditions, life experience and socio-economic situations are now in closer proximity within communities than ever before. Nonprofit organizations by definition exist to serve the community, so it is imperative that nonprofits understand the dynamics of diversity and difference and create environments that foster acceptance, inclusion and intentional and appropriate diversity to be most effective. For the purposes of this chapter, we'll use the following definitions:

Diversity is "full participation by members of many different groups. These could include individual differences that may arise from age, ethnicity, religion, sexual orientation, socio-economic background, working styles, experience, politics, thinking/learning styles, or the types of responsibilities and roles outside the workplace" (Dorothy A. Johnson Center for Philanthropy at Grand Valley State University, 2009). In addition, most current definitions of diversity assume that it brings an added value to any endeavour.

Inclusion is "engaging the uniqueness of the talents, beliefs, backgrounds, capabilities, and ways of living of individuals and groups when joined in a common endeavor" (see, for example, *www.instituteforinclusion.org*). Inclusion moves organizations beyond "token representation" of diversity to having a widely diverse group of individuals working toward common aims, with respect and acknowledgement of the contributions of every person. You can have diversity but still not be inclusive or inclusion without diversity. The Institute for Inclusion has outlined the Key Elements of Inclusion to include:

- Actively including others in collaboration and co-creation processes to maximize individual and collective contributions.

- Involving the right people (regardless of rank or tenure) in innovation, decision-making, market development and leadership toward the common goals.

- Learning to live and work together.

- Promoting values and practices that demonstrate openness, respect, collaboration and appreciation of the validity of different points of view.

- Recognizing and supporting the intrinsic value of all human beings by creating and sustaining conditions that foster awareness, fairness, empowerment and inclusion competences at the individual, group, organizational and societal levels.

Bringing the concepts of inclusion to the volunteer program level, inclusive volunteering can be defined as "the process of assisting any volunteers in obtaining and maintaining genuine and meaningful volunteering placements through the provision of relevant and appropriate supports," understanding that certain volunteers may need extraordinary support in order to participate and the willingness to develop opportunities in an inclusive manner.

Groups of people who could have much to offer but might be excluded in volunteering without some type of accommodation or adaptation of opportunities include:

- homeless people;

- long-term and recent unemployed people;

- new immigrants, refugees and asylum seekers;

- offenders and ex-offenders;

- older or retired people;

- people recovering from addictions;

- people who are not fluent in the mainstream language;

- people with physical or developmental disabilities;

- people with mental health illness;

- people from the Lesbian Gay Bisexual and Transgender (LGBT) community;

- youth; and

- people who are excluded for any other reason.

In order to build a truly diverse and inclusive volunteer program, the nonprofit organization must first and foremost adopt an organization-wide commitment to it and that commitment should be reflected in the mission and goals of the organization and its programs. The volunteer program offers both rich opportunity and challenge for involving volunteers that represent a broad spectrum of attributes, but involving them successfully will take the engagement and support from throughout the nonprofit. Dealing with difference will test a volunteer administrator's human relations, diplomacy and management skills. It will require openness to looking critically at the organization's culture to see where and how barriers exist to inclusion, acceptance and tolerance of "difference". It is often not neat or efficient as there may need to be flexibility on policies, procedures, or volunteer roles may have to adapt to accommodate the different needs of "non-mainstream" volunteers. The unpaid "employee" model of volunteer engagement may be totally unfamiliar to some cultures.

> Voluntary organizations in the United States and globally are faced with the growth of an increasingly diverse population and service base. Methods and approaches that have worked effectively in more homogenous settings may not be as useful in more diverse environments. We need to

identify new ways to reach client groups in a manner comfortable to their cultural styles.

(S. Rodriguez, 1997, pp. 18-20)

A Volunteer Administrator may want to know: what is the current discussion on diversity and inclusion in the voluntary and public sectors, and how is that playing out in how organizations involve volunteers? Lautenschlager (1992) suggests that there are five philosophical issues on which the use of volunteers with disabilities is based. These philosophical issues can relate to any discussion about diversity and inclusion:

1. The universal right to volunteer assumes that all people are potential volunteers, and that all who have the potential to contribute to society should be given the opportunity to do so.

2. Social equality and equal opportunity, which is the basic view that, as a fundamental part of life, everyone should have access to the benefits of volunteering. Barriers that would prevent this from being accomplished are correspondingly required to be diminished and/or eliminated, including the provision of support for volunteers who require it.

3. Diversity as a positive force assumes that a volunteer base that represents the local population is both a rich resource and enrichment to the organization.

4. The position that volunteering is a benefit to the volunteer means that volunteer work is inherently advantageous to those who perform it (mutual benefit).

5. Sensitivity to individual differences means that to act fairly toward all people is not equal to treating everyone the same.

Frameworks

There are a variety of resources available that can help a volunteer administrator gauge how well the organization is attracting and retaining a diverse pool of productive and effective volunteers. One very useful self-assessment tool, "Diversity Continuum – Indicators of Success," has been developed by Planned Parenthood Federation of America (2003). The sections relating specifically to indicators of success for engaging volunteers are reproduced below.

Table 3: Diversity Continuum: Indicators of Success Assessment Tool (Volunteers)

Date:

WORKPLACE: *Employees and Volunteers*

	Culturally Unaware	Culturally Aware	Culturally Aware & Active	Culturally Competent	Assessment			
	1	2	3	4	1	2	3	4
Volunteers	Volunteer pool lacks dimensions of diversity including economic, racial, gender, sexual orientation, age and abilities.	Minimal representation by chance. Limited representation in governance. Discomfort with change is evident.	Deliberate efforts are made to engage, attract, and retain a diverse group of volunteers in particular those working with clients. Diverse representation in key committees such as the nominating committee is seen as Critical.	Clinic, public affairs, and governance volunteers surpass the diversity of the community.				
Board	The board is not diverse	Board members begin discussions on diversification, but are concerned that increasing diversity will diminish board's ability to raise funds. Fear of change prevents action.	Nominating committees actively recruit diverse candidates for the board. The board begins to address board culture for barriers to retention of diverse members. The board is diverse.	The board's leadership and membership are diverse. Multicultural methods and values have been completely integrated into the normal course of business. Board meetings are held in diverse locations and communities.				

SCORE KEY	1-5	6-10	11-15	16-20				
Current Year:								
Previous Year:								

Date:									
WORKPLACE: *Employees and Volunteers*									
	Culturally Unaware	Culturally Aware	Culturally Aware & Active	Culturally Competent	Assessment				
	1	2	3	4	1	1	2	3	
Communications	All communication occurs in the language of the mainstream culture. Staff who are bilingual are not valued for their language skills and are discouraged from speaking languages other than English on the work site with each other.	Bilingual staff and volunteers are hired to address the needs of clients. Their cultural background and language skills are valued and appreciated.	It is recognized that the organization benefits from the diverse cultures, languages, and communication styles of its employees. Benefit brochures, employee handbooks are available in English and other languages.	Multilingualism and multiculturalism are viewed as absolute assets and flexible communication styles are the norm. Various language classes are available during the workday. The whole person is valued.					
Coalition Building	Staff and volunteer efforts focused solely on the organization itself. Issues have a narrow, exclusive focus. There are no	Recognition that relationships with other organizations are needed. Token gestures made to invite others	Relationships based on mutual respect are sought and established with organizations and groups representing diverse	The value and practice of coalition building is institutionalized. The organization is an integral part of multicultural					

	connections to organizations serving culturally diverse communities.	to participate in "our meetings." One or two people are responsible for community outreach.	communities. Agendas are set together and are collaborative efforts.	networks that promote a partnership model. All members of the organization see the value in coalition building. Coalition building is widespread in the organization.				
SCORE KEY	1-5	6-10	11-15	16-20				

RESULTS	
Current Year:	

Previous Year:	

Date:

WORKPLACE: *Policies and Procedures*

	Culturally Unaware	Culturally Aware	Culturally Aware & Active	Culturally Competent	Assessment			
	1	2	3	4	1	2	3	4
Staff and Volunteer Development	Programs to increase awareness of cultural differences do not exist. Outside diversity training	The organization is reactive to the training needs expressed by employees	Diversity training is embraced and seen as essential. Diversity orientations and programs	Multicultural programs such as diversity training are systemic and ongoing. The organizational				

	opportunities are ignored or unknown or seen as unimportant.	and volunteers of different cultures. Few staff and volunteers attend diversity training.	are attended by staff and volunteers. Diversity skills are shared with coalition partners and the community.	structure and delivery of services are multicultural. Trainings are a source of greater understand-ing and team building.			
SCORE KEY	**1-6**	**7-12**	**13-18**	**19-24**			

RESULTS

Current Year:	

Previous Year:	

Date:

WORKPLACE: *Policies and Procedures*

	Culturally Unaware	Culturally Aware	Culturally Aware & Active	Culturally Competent	Assessment			
	1	2	3	4	1	1	2	3
Representations	Mission statement, bylaws, and other guiding statements do not address diversity.	Bylaws and other documents require a specific number of representa-tives from diverse communi-ties to avoid criticism.	Bylaws and other documents explicitly state that becoming an organization inclusive of all cultural groups is a goal. Board members are expected to address diversity.	Policies and practices are aligned and reflect a high degree of commitment to members of different cultures and different models of governance. All board members are willing to embrace diversity.				

Benefits	Management shows no interest or commitment to diversity.	Management minimizes the validity of criticisms pointing to a lack of diversity. Discussions addressing diversity rare.	Management indicates a desire to learn about diversity and to increase the diversity of staff and volunteers by developing programs and allocating resources for these efforts.	Management is diverse and its commitment to diversity is systemic. Management leads the efforts to promote multicultural methods and values within the organization and in the community at large.			
Board	There are no policies that address the organization's involvement in community issues. The focus is solely internal.	Minor involvement exists with community groups through individuals. The organization remains insular.	Policies are created to guide involvement with diverse organizations and communities. Recognition that the organization has a role to play in issues that affect many communities.	Policies and practices reveal an ongoing commitment to social justice. The organization is routinely involved with issues affecting the communities of clients, staff and volunteers.			
SCORE KEY	1-5	6-10	11-15	16-20			
RESULTS							
Current Year:							
Previous Year:							
TOTAL SCORE	1-19	20-38	39-57	58-76			

Strategies for Inclusion

Organizations of every type — for-profit, public and nonprofit — struggle with issues of fairly and appropriately integrating difference in ways that create welcoming and effective organizations. It is ongoing work that is never completed as individuals come and go from organizations, and community demographics continue to change. Volunteer administrators, to be effective in working with diversity and difference, must be aware of their own filters and attitudes first and foremost as that sets the tone for who "gets in" as a volunteer. The following are some practices that volunteer administrators have used to increase their effectiveness in recruiting and retaining a diverse group of volunteers:

- Review policies, processes and expectations to see if all are geared to a particular culture and norms.

- Understand that even effective volunteer management practices can screen out those who might contribute and diversify your volunteer pool. Consider whether regular practices create unintentional barriers to some potential volunteers. For example, does the volunteer role really require a high school diploma? Newcomers in particular may be unable to meet requirements of strict screening practices such as completing a police check and providing immunization records.

- Consider inviting representatives from groups who are currently not volunteering but would add diverse perspectives to your organization to an informal "listening" gathering.

- Reconsider success metrics (*e.g.*, volunteer retention equals success). For example, in many cultures volunteering is a mutual activity rather than "doing for" others for the intrinsic rewards. Making the opportunity more of a "win-win" will be more attractive to some individuals.

- Recognize there is diversity within diversity — age and race, culture and gender, *etc.*

Volunteer programs and tasks often are not designed with the input of diverse or non-traditional audiences, nor in an inclusive manner. In addition, organizations may not have dedicated budgets or internal plans for how to reach out to diverse and non-traditional volunteers as well as to be inclusive in providing opportunities to new audiences of volunteers. It is important to find out what interests potential volunteers may have and want to contribute, what the needs are from the people we are going to serve, not what we think people need (ask them). Do not make assumptions. Take time to learn about the culture and volunteer motivations of the new group.

SUMMARY

Volunteer managers play an important role in an organization. They often interact with all areas of the programme and recruit volunteers for all its aspects. The volunteer manager serves as liaison between the needs and wants of the organization and paid staff and the volunteers' needs and rights. Volunteer managers are internal consultants, helping paid staff identify opportunities for engaging volunteers in the organization's work, developing volunteer-staff relationships, designing strategies for effective integration of volunteers in the organizational work, assess the impact of volunteer services for the clients and the organization, and serving as advocates for the volunteers' rights and for volunteerism within the organization and the community at large.

(Merrill, 2007)

A successful and conscientious volunteer administrator has a complex role to fulfill — she or he not only has a key role in recruiting, training, supervising and retaining volunteers, but must also ensure that the unpaid human resources of the organization build the capacity to achieve excellence in service and contribute to effectively achieving the mission in an ethical and equitable manner.

REFERENCES

Council for Certification in Volunteer Administration (CCVA). (2008). *Body of knowledge.*

Dorothy A. Johnson Center for Philanthropy. (2009). *Grand Valley State University nonprofit good practice guide.* Retrieved from http://www.npgoodpractice.org/Glossary.

Eisner, David, Grimm, Jr., Robert T., Maynard, Shannon, & Washburn, Susannah. (2009, Winter). *The new volunteer workforce.* SSRI.

Greater Twin Cities United Way. (1998). *Checklist of nonprofit indicators.*

Hyman, Vince. (2006, January). Six keys to organizational effectiveness. *Nonprofit Tools You Can Use Newsletter.* Fieldstone Alliance.

Institute for Inclusion. (2008). *Our definition of inclusion.*

Lautenschlager, J. (1992, September). *Bridges to the future: Supported programs for volunteers with special needs*. Ottawa, ON: Voluntary Action Directorate, Multiculturalism and Citizenship Canada.

Merrill, Mary. (2007, December 14). *How volunteers benefit organizations.* Idealist blog.

Minnesota Council of Nonprofits. (2005). *Principles and practices for nonprofit excellence.*

Noseworthy, Karl. (2009, April 16). The evolving role of a volunteer resources specialist. *Charity Village.* Retrieved on June 3, 2009, from http://www.charityvillage.com/cv/research/rcar28.html.

Philbin, Ann, & Mikush, Sandra. (2001). *A framework for organizational development: The why, what and how of OD work – Perspectives from participants in the Mary Reynolds Babcock Foundation's Organizational Development Program 1995-1999.* Winston-Salem, NC: Mary Reynolds Babcock Foundation.

Planned Parenthood Federation of America. (2003). *Diversity continuum: Indicators of success assessment tool.*

Rodriguez, Santiago. (1997). Diversity and volunteerism: Deriving advantage from difference. Presentation at the 1996 International Conference on Volunteer Administration. *The Journal of Volunteer Administration, XV*(3), 18-20.

Venture Philanthropy Partners. (2001). *Effective capacity building in nonprofit organizations* (pp. 96-97). Prepared by McKinsey & Company.

Volunteer Canada. (2006). *The Canadian code for volunteer involvement: An audit tool.*

Chapter 16

ADVOCACY IN VOLUNTEER ADMINISTRATION

Emilie Bromet-Bauer, CVA
Association of Leaders in Volunteer Engagement (AL!VE)

INTRODUCTION

An essential function of the professional volunteer administrator's role is that of advocate. According to the most recent Council for Certification in Volunteer Administration (CCVA) document, *Body of Knowledge in Volunteer Administration* (CCVA, 2008), a core competency for professional volunteer administrators is leadership and advocacy. This is explained as "the ability to advance individual, organizational and community goals, advocating for effective volunteer involvement inside of the organization and in the broader community it serves, through the investment of personal integrity, skills and attitudes" (CCVA, 2008). This document goes on to delineate four subcompetencies in the area of advocacy that cover the breadth of this function in regards to advocating for volunteers within an organization or institution, for volunteerism, and for the profession of volunteer resource management. The document itself and the process of certification reflect what the field considers to be an effective, professional volunteer administrator. That advocacy is explicitly included as a core competency for a volunteer administrator further legitimizes volunteer resource management as a profession.

This chapter is about advocacy, starting with a discussion about the particular importance of advocacy skills for the volunteer administrator. Advocacy skills will be introduced as well as resources for further exploration and development of these skills. Finally, this chapter will introduce strategies for advocating at the different levels of management and leadership in which volunteer administrators generally function, that of the individual volunteer, the organizational level, and the community or societal level.

DEFINITIONS OF CONCEPTS

There are different definitions of *advocacy*, usually depending on the context of the word's usage. However, there are common descriptors within all of these explanations that define the essence of this concept; and which, as we will see, allow us to identify particular skills that are essential to advocacy. Advocacy is a process that is deliberate and that has as its objective a change of some sort. This process is always about influencing what others think or do. We will call these *others* the *audience*. The process of influencing others is about exerting power and includes such methods as arguing, pleading, persuading, and educating. The change that is the objective often has to do with the transference or sharing of power with those who have less power and on whose behalf the advocacy is done. Advocacy can be done on behalf of a person, a group of people, an idea, or a cause or issue. When the objective is a change in power, we are referring to the power to make decisions that impact people or causes — decisions about resource allocation, about what is or is not important, even about who can make decisions.

Within volunteer management, the different kinds of advocacy include advocating on behalf of others, like the volunteers or an individual volunteer. Volunteer administrators also advocate on behalf of volunteer management, which is to say that the organization's leadership recognizes and integrates the volunteer program's systems — the structures, policies, and procedures — in order to build organizational capacity to serve its clients and simultaneously provide quality experience for the volunteers. Often the volunteer administrator must advocate for themselves and for their role managing the volunteer program. In fact, it is important to realize that there is a difference between advocating for good volunteer management and advocating for the importance of the role of the professional volunteer administrator. All of these kinds of advocacy are practised within the boundaries of a particular organization or institution; and will be referred to later in this chapter as internal advocacy.

The volunteer administrator is also responsible for advocating beyond the confines of the organization, in the community or in state, national, or international government. As a leader of volunteers in an organization, the volunteer administrator acts as a role model and represents the values and mission of the organization to the volunteers, and also within the community. Volunteers often are the front line of public relations and advocacy for an organization's cause and values, especially in areas of advocacy and lobbying that are restricted by government regulation and the legal status of the organization. It is the responsibility of volunteer administrators to advocate for volunteerism as an important part of a healthy society. And, finally, it is essential that the volunteer administrator advocate for the profession, educating the public and the nonprofit, civic, corporate, and governmental sectors about the profession and its increasingly important role in society. These kinds of advocacy will be referred to as external advocacy, meaning advocacy in which the targeted audience is primarily outside of the boundaries of the organization.

Having now made these distinctions between internal and external advocacy, it is necessary to point out that, while differing in target audience, in objectives, and strategies, all advocacy is really interrelated and connected. The volunteer administrator must become proficient in advocating both internally and externally, for themselves, their profession, their organization, their program, their volunteers, and for volunteerism. The core sub-competencies indeed reflect the importance of all of these kinds of advocacy.

ADVOCACY AND THE PROFESSION

While there is no readily available research on the importance of advocacy as a function and skill set for volunteer administrators and leaders, there is a growing body of scholarly and practical research on the relationship of advocacy and professionalism in other, relatively new professions, like counselling, health education, pharmacy, and social work. These professions, like volunteer management, are human services that require the professional to work simultaneously at multiple levels — individual, organizational, and societal — to be effective. What research in these professions has found is that advocacy at all levels is interrelated and interdependent, and that the professional in these fields must be proficient in advocacy at all of these levels to be successful (Myers, Sweeney, & White, 2002). *Advocacy in the Human Services* by Mark Ezell (2001) is an excellent textbook that explains human service professional advocacy at all levels, including strategies, tactics, and skills, and how these are interrelated.

As an example, building the capacity to effectively manage volunteers and the integration of those volunteers within the organization do not happen automatically. The volunteer management program — the structures, systems, policies, and procedures — must be developed, institutionalized, and supported for the long run. This process may have been started by a previous volunteer administrator, a board member, the organization's executive director, or volunteers, but the professional volunteer administrator understands that their role is to continually work to expand the volunteer program's capacity to provide value-added support to the organization and to improve the quality of their volunteers' experience. However, the volunteer administrator realizes that rarely is it enough to just know and implement the best practices of their field. The effective volunteer administrator must also have the power and authority to do their job. For example, to successfully advocate for the volunteers in a program or for the program itself, the volunteer administrator or leader must be taken seriously by those in the organization that have the power to make decisions, allocate, and direct resources. They must be credible; their professional knowledge and skills must be seen as legitimate, real, and unique. Otherwise, why should the volunteer administrator be taken seriously when advocating for their volunteers or their volunteer program?

ADVOCACY SKILLS

Just as there are common concepts in all definitions and kinds of advocacy work, there are also basic skills, strategies, and tactics that apply whether one is advocating for one's own position, the volunteers, a cause, or the profession of volunteer management.

Become Knowledgeable

Advocacy is about influence; influence is about exerting power to bring about change; and, as the saying goes, knowledge is power. Regardless of what kind of advocacy or on whose or what behalf the volunteer administrator is advocating, they must be knowledgeable:

*   Know the goals and the objectives of the advocacy. The volunteer administrator must be clear about what they hope to change and to accomplish.

*   Know the facts and the history. If, for example, the volunteer administrator is advocating for a more integrated volunteer program, they should know what makes an effective volunteer program. What is this organization's past history with a structured volunteer program? How do other similar agencies coordinate their volunteers?

*   Know the big picture, the context, and the options. Whether the volunteer administrator is advocating on behalf of an individual volunteer or the volunteer program or the profession of volunteer management, they must be able to understand the particular issue in the context of the larger picture. In the case of internal advocacy, for example, the volunteer administrator must understand the organizational structure, history, and culture, especially in regards to volunteerism, including the attitude of the organization's board of directors about their role as volunteers.

*   Know the audience. What does the audience know about the issue or the facts? What does the audience assume are facts, but are really opinions or are based on their own experience? What do they not know? What are the audience's goals, objectives, and values; what is important to them? What is their perspective or

opinion about the cause or individual for which you are advocating. Finally, what would this audience need to know in order to dialogue with or learn from you, the advocate?

- Know your values and philosophy. The volunteer administrator who is an effective advocate is knowledgeable and confident about their own values and philosophy regarding volunteerism and volunteer management.

Prepare Through Research

Acquiring this knowledge requires thorough research. This is a function of the role of the volunteer administrator as advocate:

- Research the issues. What primary research is available? There are innumerable resources, including scholarly research, about volunteerism and volunteer management available on the web and through several academic journals and sites. There are several sources that focus entirely on issues related to volunteerism and volunteer management. There are other sources that are broader in scope, but very relevant, such as journals and websites about human resource or nonprofit management. It is important that the volunteer administrator becomes proficient in finding these resources. More important, the professional volunteer administrator stays current in accessing these resources as research and knowledge constantly accumulates and changes.

- Connect with others in the profession. An excellent way to stay current in the field is to stay connected with other professional volunteer administrators. The volunteer administrator can join local or national professional networks, attend workshops and conferences, and stay connected through a growing number of professional, web-based organizations, list serves, and social networking sites. Just as with research sources, it is also important to look beyond the field of volunteer resource management for opportunities to network with professionals in other, but related, fields, such as human resources or fund development.

- Research the issues, the organization, or the community through connecting with colleagues and professionals outside of the field of volunteer management. For example, if the volunteer administrator is doing internal advocacy, an effective way to learn about the organization and how the organization's leadership and other staff think about volunteerism and the volunteer program is to participate in activities and functions not related to volunteers or the volunteer program. This is an excellent way to learn about other fields and issues that may appear on the surface not to be relevant to volunteerism, but may, in fact, be.

- Assess assets and deficits of the larger context, the organization, community or sector. For example, there are various tools available to measure an organization's readiness for a volunteer program. Similarly, there are resources that describe how to assess a community's capacity for involving its residents in volunteer and social action activities. The volunteer administrator should know where and how to access and use these tools.

- Critical thinking is essential to process and integrate these various streams of research and information. It is not enough to accumulate this data; the volunteer administrator must also practise critical thinking to apply the information to the advocacy issue. For the volunteer administrator, critical thinking is the process by which they develop their own, personal philosophy about volunteerism and volunteer management, both of which are essential as a foundation upon which to build all advocacy efforts.

Communication Skills are Integral to Effective Advocacy

Advocacy is about influencing others to change the way they think or act. The process of influencing, of exerting power to make this change, regardless of the actual methods used, relies on excellent communication skills:

- Active listening in a non-judgemental way is key to all good communication. Active listening requires the volunteer administrator not only to listen to, but to hear, the others' words without making prior judgements as to the validity or even advisability of what the other person is saying. It is a practice of lifting one's own filters of personal opinion, values, and even knowledge, so that they can truly hear what the other person is saying. It is in this way that the volunteer administrator can learn what the issues are, the larger context of the situation, and what the audience knows and does not know. Fortunately, for the volunteer administrator, active listening is itself a competency of a professional volunteer administrator and is a good example of how these professional competencies overlap and reinforce each other.

- How one communicates is as important — and often more important — than what is communicated. It is assumed by now that the volunteer administrator advocate is armed with knowledge about the issues and the context, and is familiar with their audience. Influencing another is about communicating in a way that the audience not only listens to but also hears what the advocate has to say; and furthermore that the audience becomes open to critically thinking about and processing what they have heard. This does not just happen. It is up to the volunteer administrator as advocate to be self-confident and assertive in their presentation, but not aggressive. Their speech should be clear, concise, and to the point. If they want to educate their audience they may want to learn and practise adult training skills and methods that, based on adult learning theory, are dialogical and not pedantic.

- A particularly useful means of communication in advocacy is persuasion. A textbook on public relations lists characteristics of persuasion as being: "(1) audience analysis, (2) source credibility, (3) appeal to self-interest, (4) clarity of message, (5) timing and context, (6) audience participation, (7) suggestions for action, (8) content and structure of messages, and (9) persuasive speaking" (Wilcox, p. 216). Some of these characteristics have already been mentioned or will be discussed when we speak about advocacy strategies and tactics. While it is not the purpose of this chapter to explain persuasion as an advocacy communication skill, it is interesting to note that the same text explains that some persuasive speaking techniques are based on a dialogue of sorts with the audience, such as mentioned above (Wilcox, 228).

- The website <www.Idealist.org> is an excellent source of practical information about volunteerism and volunteer management, including some handy tips on how to advocate for the profession of volunteer resource management. One of their tips is to learn the "art of translation," which is the practice of learning and adapting one's language to that of the audience. If the volunteer administrator is doing external advocacy about volunteerism in a community, using the language of civic engagement is appropriate. If the volunteer administrator is talking to executive management about the importance of screening procedures for volunteers, referring to risk management and cost benefits to the organization will be more readily received and understood.

- Being aware, knowledgeable, and, above all, respectful of cultural differences of both your advocacy partners and the audience is very important. Having an awareness of others' values and world views will help in understanding their perception of the issues which will help the volunteer administrator in framing the advocacy strategy, translating the message, and communicating with them.

- Communication in advocacy can also be in writing, video, and other forms of media. The same basic principles about persuasion and other forms of influencing apply to these non-verbal forms of communication. Again, by knowing the audience and practising the art of translation, it is possible to craft the advocacy message in such a way as to have greater impact on the audience. For example, while videos and well-written stories will probably go far to influence the attitudes and understanding of a civic group, a concise and well-documented report would communicate better with a busy board of directors.

EFFECTIVE ADVOCACY DEPENDS ON EFFECTIVE STRATEGIES AND TACTICS

The definition of advocacy introduced earlier notes that the process itself is deliberate, indicating that it requires preparation and planning; a constant implementation of advocacy actions; and continuous evaluation, adjustment, and celebration of successful accomplishments.

Preparation is the first stage of the advocacy process. Many of the components of this stage were discussed earlier, including research, assessment, identifying the issues, philosophy, and goals of the advocacy effort. It is at this initial stage that the advocate also begins to identify the allies and potential partners as well as the target audience. Finally, the advocate "… maps the decision making system …" (Ezell, 2001, p. 148), to understand who makes the decisions and how they are made or, in other words, where the power is held and how is it wielded or shared.

This last step is an important element in the next stage, which is the planning stage. It is here that the advocacy strategies and tactics are selected. Strategies are the general frameworks for how to achieve the advocacy goal. In deciding on a strategy or strategies, the advocate takes into account the objective of the advocacy campaign and the target population.

Also, strategies are developed based on the advocate's way of thinking about power and change. If one believes that power resides with the elite, whether it is the political power of politicians or the decision-making power of organizational executive management, then the volunteer administrator will tend towards advocacy strategies that target these audiences, like lobbying or consulting. On the other hand, a volunteer administrator who thinks that decision-making power shared and distributed among the masses is more effective will consider more democratic strategies, like social action or community building. Other examples of strategies are litigation and client empowerment.

There are some best practices in advocacy strategy development to keep in mind. First, as mentioned earlier, collaborations can be very effective. When collaborating, all aspects of the advocacy process can be shared, including these first two stages of preparation and planning. Moreover, it is possible to leverage each partner's strengths, especially when planning tactics, as we will see. Second, it is important to remember that strategies, tactics, and skills can be planned and implemented simultaneously. It is not necessary to think of a strategic plan as consisting of a strict sequence of tactics and steps. In fact, it is more realistic to think of a strategic plan as having sequential and simultaneous elements and as being flexible and changeable. Third, non-confrontational strategies and tactics are the best; the goal is to influence and persuade the audience to change, not to coerce or force or make the audience take a defensive stance.

Once a strategy is determined, the next step in the planning stage is to determine appropriate tactics. Tactics are the specific actions that will move the advocacy along within the planned strategy to achieve the advocacy goal. Tactics include not only what will be done, but by whom, when, and how. Each strategy has certain tactics that are appropriate to it; although some tactics work in more than one strategy. Tactics include: grassroots organizing, action or community-based research, and social marketing. Another increasingly effective group of tactics are technology-based or technology-dependent.

The third stage in the advocacy process is implementation. In this stage the different partners implement the tactics. It is at this stage of the process that the preparation and planning begin to come to fruition. In implementing tactics the communication skills discussed earlier come into play, as well as coordinating, leadership, administrative, and technical abilities. Two functions are especially important during this stage. Maintaining effective communication among all partners is essential, as are monitoring and recording activities.

The latter function is especially relevant for the next stage of the advocacy process which is monitoring the tactics and evaluating the strategies. This advocacy process is learning-focused (Pathfinder, <www.innonet.org>, 2009). It emphasizes the process as much as the goal and objectives. This framework recognizes that change does not happen all at once. Nor is change incremental, occurring in sequential order that builds on the prior activity towards an ultimate goal. In fact, change is very complex; it is iterative. There are many variables that affect the process; these variables interact in ways and over time that are often not anticipated. So, while the advocacy framework introduced here emphasizes the importance of preparation and planning, the true success of an advocacy campaign depends on the ability of the advocates to constantly monitor and adjust tactics and strategies. The evaluation of the effectiveness of tactics and strategies constantly returns the advocate to the planning and implementation stages. Flexibility and adaptability are key.

It should be clear by now that this advocacy process is not linear. Because of the constant evaluation and adjustment, the process circles back on previous stages as it moves toward the achievement of the advocacy goal. So it is inaccurate to refer to a final stage. Indeed, like monitoring and evaluation, celebration of success should be done all along the way, for small as well as significant achievements. It is also important to remember to include all parties, and to design the celebration for each event and each partner much the same way one translates messages for a particular audience.

TYPES OF ADVOCACY

Earlier we introduced the idea that there are different types of advocacy which we broadly categorized as internal and external. Internal advocacy refers to advocating within the organization or group. External advocacy is when the audience or target of the advocacy is outside of the organization. Within these two broad categories of advocacy, there are different kinds of advocacy that differ based on the goal or purpose of the advocacy, the cause or person(s) on whose behalf the advocacy is done, and the audience.

Internal Advocacy

There are three kinds of internal advocacy that the volunteer administrator practises. One thing that is fundamental to internal advocacy is that to be an effective advocate, the volunteer administrator must first build their own credibility. "Personal credibility starts with YOU. Before others will value you and your services, you must first believe in and value them yourself" (Moore and MacKenzie, p. 13). As discussed earlier, advocacy is about influencing others, persuading or educating your audience to change their ideas, beliefs, and actions. To do that requires that the audience believe in what the advocate is saying. This is possible only if the volunteer administrator believes in who they are, what they do, and what they are saying.

In fact, credibility is better stated as "being credible to others" because what is important is how others perceive you to be. In other words, being credible is having others see you as being believable, trustworthy, capable, knowledgeable, reliable, and having integrity. As Moore and MacKenzie (1990) say credibility is based on one's philosophy and principles, and is built on one's presentation, because that is what people see. Presentation is showing the executive management and one's colleagues your values and beliefs about volunteerism and volunteer management and your commitment to the organization's mission. It is also presenting one's knowledge and skills, especially those that are transferable to other functions of the organization, by getting involved in organizational functions outside of volunteer administration, like using one's organizing skills to help coordinate a fundraising event, or sharing one's knowledge of risk management by working on a human resource task force.

Another important aspect of internal advocacy is identifying who is the primary audience for this type of advocacy. The executive director, executive management, and, often, the board of directors are instrumental in creating an organizational culture that is supportive and appreciative of volunteerism, the volunteer program, and the position of volunteer administrator.

Advocacy for the Individual Volunteer

Volunteer administrators are in the unique position of serving both the organization for which they work and the individual volunteers. In a well-run volunteer program, there is usually synchronicity in this, although in any volunteer program in any organization there inevitably are some situations of conflict. Regardless, volunteer administrators advocate for their individual volunteers. This does not include defending a difficult volunteer or one who has not performed or who breached a policy or procedure. Advocating for an individual volunteer is similar to advocating for a client, and utilizes the skills mentioned earlier as well as supervisory skills and knowledge that are part of any volunteer administrator's repertoire. Advocating for a volunteer is about empowerment.

There are four main areas in which a volunteer administrator advocates on behalf of their volunteers. First is when there is a problem, such as a volunteer not getting along with their supervisory staff or fellow volunteers. If, in the course of investigating such a situation, it is apparent that the issue is a difference in personalities or expectations, advocating on behalf of the volunteer may be appropriate, and this may include such tactics as staff development about volunteer supervision or coaching staff and volunteers. Another area of advocacy is when the volunteer has a grievance against a staff person or the organization.

The other two areas of advocacy are really about empowering volunteers. The third kind is advocating on behalf of a volunteer who deserves recognition; it is about influencing staff to show appreciation for a job well done. This might also be advocating for a volunteer's advancement or getting a volunteer increased responsibilities. Finally, facilitating and supporting volunteer advisory groups empowers volunteers to be advocates, for themselves, their program, and their organization.

Advocacy for the Volunteer Program

The purpose of advocacy on behalf of volunteers is to persuade certain persons of the value of the volunteer to the organization. The cumulative value to the organization of all of its volunteers is what volunteer program advocacy is all about. It is that and it is also about showing how building the volunteer corps through effective volunteer management can leverage the individual and cumulative value of volunteers to build organizational capacity. There are a few essential elements to effective volunteer program advocacy.

To effectively advocate for the volunteer program, the volunteer administrator first needs to define the fundamental concepts of volunteerism and the volunteer. It is important to define these in the broadest terms. The broader the definition, the more individuals are included within the arena of influence and responsibility of the volunteer program, and thus there is more contribution in hours, persons, and service to be leveraged. This would also allow the volunteer administrator to better demonstrate the effectiveness and efficiency of the volunteer program, and the complex value of volunteerism to the organization.

A well-run, effective volunteer program is the foundation on which the volunteer administrator builds their advocacy campaign. The development and growth of the volunteer program, in terms of policies, procedures, infrastructure, and systems, is an on-going process. Documentation of the development of the program in the form of narrative reports, newsletters, correspondence, and regular quantitative reports of volunteer numbers and hours, is an excellent way to show the increasing importance of the volunteer program. Many of the assessment and tracking tools and techniques introduced earlier in the book and referenced at the end of this chapter are good for making the advocacy case for the capacity building potential of the volunteer program. In all of these efforts it is advisable to use both quantitative and qualitative approaches, because in internal advocacy the audience will include both those who are more concerned with the financial and administrative costs and benefits of the program and others who are more concerned with programmatic outcomes. For example, an annual volunteer program report that includes the number of volunteers, the total hours, and a dollar sum estimate of their contribution as well as testimonials from satisfied volunteers and stories about successful volunteer effort is best. Another way to demonstrate the effectiveness of the volunteer program is to offer the successful structures, policies and procedures as templates or replicable examples of best practices that can be transferred to other functional areas of the organization.

As discussed earlier, any advocacy effort is more effective if the volunteer administrator prepares and plans the campaign. In advocating for the volunteer program, it is very important that the volunteer administrator identifies and nurtures relationships with potential allies, especially among organizational staff. Seek out and develop relations with staff and management who are known to volunteer outside of their work, who enjoy working with their volunteers, are eager to creatively integrate volunteers into their staffing and truly appreciate the volunteers' contribution. Acknowledging the staff person's strengths in working with volunteers and their special relationship with their volunteers is a good way to do this. If a staff person has strong positive feelings to individual volunteers, they are more likely to support the volunteer program. Advocacy allies among community members, agency volunteers, and board members are also very effective. With all of these, the objective is to share power and responsibilities, both in the development and management of the volunteer program, and, in this case, the advocacy efforts. Staff, board members, and volunteers advocating for the volunteer program is a very powerful advocacy tactic.

The volunteer administrator uses their credibility, especially the transferable knowledge and skills discussed earlier, to actively participate in agency-wide efforts, including task forces and committees. Being involved in strategic planning, fundraising and grant development, and human resource activities gives the volunteer administrator a seat at the table. Once at the table and involved, the volunteer administrator has the opportunity to leverage the capacity building value of volunteers and to advocate for the program.

Advocacy for the Volunteer Administrator Position

Some of the most important advocacy work that the volunteer administrator will do is for the position. As mentioned before, there is a difference between advocating for volunteer management and for advocating for the role of volunteer administrator. Advocating for a volunteer program, including the structures, systems, policies and procedures, does not necessarily imply the need for a professional and knowledgeable volunteer administrator to lead and manage the program. In fact, as government at all levels, funding sources, non-governmental organizations and institutions, the corporate sector, and the general public quickly grow aware of the significant role of volunteerism in a healthy society, there is a slower, but definite, increased acknowledgement of the importance of managing and coordinating these volunteers. However, many of the studies and articles that call for better volunteer management practices do not talk about who would be responsible for developing these structures, policies and procedures much less coordinating the volunteers, implying that this just happens or that anyone in the organization can do this (Eisner, 2009). The reality is that most leaders of public and nonprofit organizations are still unaware that the body of knowledge of best practices of volunteer management and persons knowledgeable and skilled in these practices do exist, or that volunteer administration is a profession.

Advocacy for the role of volunteer administrator, therefore, uses educational tactics to convince executive directors, management, and leadership. This is where the volunteer administrator's personal credibility is so important. The objective is to show the organization's leadership that volunteer resource management is very complex, requiring expertise in a broad range and combination of functional areas that are unique to this profession. Sharing resources about volunteer administration with the executive management, staff development on volunteer management, taking on leadership responsibilities with the board, volunteers, and staff that demonstrate the volunteer administrator's range of expertise are effective tactics.

In many organizations, the value of positions and functions are reflected in job titles, position descriptions, and salaries; and, too often, volunteer administrators, regardless of their title or position in the organization chart, receive a salary that is not comparable with their peers in that organization. In addition to the above actions, the volunteer administrator should consider using local salary survey data as well as the success stories from other organizations that appropriately recognize the role of professional volunteer administrators as tactics within the overall advocacy strategy.

In all of this advocacy work, however, it is important to remember that the volunteer administrator is advocating for the position, not for themselves. The goal is to have a position, including appropriate title, status, compensation, and description, that accurately reflects the requirements and responsibilities necessary to run an effective volunteer program. In other words, advocate for the position such that were the volunteer administrator to leave, the organization would seek to fill it with someone having the same professional background.

External Advocacy

Just as in internal advocacy, the volunteer administrator uses the same knowledge, skills, and advocacy process to advocate for the organization, volunteerism, and the volunteer administration profession outside of the organization. However, in external advocacy, the advocate's leadership is more important than their credibility. Also, there are some advocacy strategies and tactics, like formal collaborations, lobbying, litigation, grassroots organizing, action research, and social activism that are particular to external advocacy. This section will look at the three kinds of external advocacy that are especially relevant to the volunteer administrator. Some resources for information about the different strategies and tactics are listed at the end of this chapter.

Advocacy for the Organization or Cause

The volunteer administrator understands that volunteer recruitment and retention depends in large part or totally on creating and maintaining a meaningful connection between the volunteer and the mission or cause of the organization. In order to develop that strong commitment to the organization, the volunteer administrator must share it as well. It is that commitment combined with the volunteer administrator's leadership skills that come into play when advocating for the organization or its cause within the local community or society. In these situations, the volunteer administrator is often role model, leader, and educator.

Volunteers who are committed to an organization's mission or cause are especially powerful external advocates. Their unique value is they connect the organization to the community. They are from the community and, therefore, external to the organization; however, their volunteer work and their commitment to the organization makes them very much a significant part of the organization. This connection of emotion, dedication, and knowledge about the organization can be leveraged for effective advocacy. The volunteer administrator does this by empowering volunteers to be effective advocates, as individuals and for the organization. The volunteer administrator trains them in advocacy. In the organization's political advocacy campaigns, the volunteer administrator ensures that volunteers are incorporated into the advocacy process, including the preparation and planning stages, and leads them in the organization's advocacy activities, including public relations activities.

Advocacy with External Partners and the Community

A major function of the volunteer administrator is to develop and coordinate partnerships with outside organizations and institutions that not only increase the numbers of volunteers, but expand and enhance the quality of services provided, the effectiveness and efficiency of the volunteer program itself, and, just as important, the transformative experience of the individual volunteers. These partnerships include such programs as intern, service-learning, workfare and vocational programs, and community service. The volunteer administrator in this kind of advocacy not only represents and advocates for their organization, but also for their volunteer program and, in certain cases, for their volunteers. The volunteer administrator's efforts in this kind of advocacy not only reflect on their own work, but also supports the positive reputation of the organization within the community, which, in turn, supports advocacy efforts for the organization and its cause. The actual advocacy activities with partners are discussed in previous chapters.

Advocacy for the Profession of Volunteer Administration

Advocating for the profession of volunteer administration was mentioned several times earlier in this chapter. The importance, however, of advocating for the profession separate from advocating internally for the position of volunteer administrator, cannot be overstated. As was noted earlier, recognition of the unique and essential role of the professional volunteer administrator is the basis of most internal advocacy efforts.

As was mentioned, most leaders in nonprofit organizations do not know or recognize that volunteer resource management is a profession. Other professions tend to see volunteer administration through the filter of a limited education about and experience with working with volunteers. Most people have volunteered a little in their lives and understandably see volunteer coordination through that limited filter. In other words, advocating for the profession is about increasing public awareness and recognition of the profession, its existence and the important role it plays in our society.

Professional development is, of course, basic to advocating for the profession. The volunteer administrator's active involvement in local and national professional associations, certification, continued education and training, attendance at conferences, and subscription to professional journals, are essential to prepare for this kind of advocacy. For one thing, through this kind of involvement, the volunteer administrator can develop those important collaborative partnerships with which to leverage the power of knowledge and numbers.

The purpose of advocating for the profession is, of course, to take the message outside of the realm of the profession itself. Some of the ways this can be done are very individual, including using your professional title. Other tactics include taking on leadership roles within the professional associations and helping organize advocacy activities that target the public and civic, nonprofit, government, and other professions' leaders, such as publicly celebrating International Volunteer Managers Day, making presentations about the profession through local nonprofit training venues and organizations or writing stories for local print and web outlets that emphasize the volunteer administrator rather than the volunteers.

CONCLUSION

This chapter is an introduction to advocacy for the professional volunteer administrator. Any one of the topics discussed could and often have been expanded into full articles, chapters, and books. That there are so many resources about advocacy in general and specifically advocacy relevant to volunteer administrators is a testament to the increasing recognition that advocacy skills, knowledge, and responsibilities are integral functions to any human service profession, including volunteer administration. This is also reflected in the core competencies of the body of knowledge that are fundamental to the certification in volunteer administration, which include: internal advocacy for resources to support individual volunteers and the volunteer program; the integration of volunteerism and volunteer management within the organization; and external advocacy for volunteerism and the profession of volunteer administration. The goal of this chapter is to give the volunteer administrator enough information to inspire and empower them to develop and grow their interest, knowledge, skills, and efforts in advocacy.

ADVOCACY RESOURCES

Online Resources

How to Advocate for the Profession, Idealist.org Volunteer Management Resource Center, online at: <http://www.idealist.org/en/vmrc/howtoadvocate.html>.

Independent Sector, online at: <http://www.independentsector.org/programs/gr/advocacy_lobbying.htm>

Pathfinder, *Advocate Edition: A Practical Guide to Advocacy Evaluation*, Innovation Network, Inc., online at: <http://www.innonet.org/client_docs/File/advocacy/pathfinder_advocate_web.pdf>.

Other Resources

Ellis, Susan J. *From the Top Down: The Executive Role in Volunteer Program Success.* (Energize, Inc., 1996, 2nd edition).

Ezell, Mark. *Advocacy in the Human Services*. (Belmont, California: Wadsworth/Thomson Learning, 2001).

Matusak, Larraine R. *Finding Your Voice: Learning to Lead ... Anywhere You Want to Make a Difference*. (Jossey-Bass, Inc., 1997).

Wilson, Marlene. *Visionary Leadership in Volunteer Programs: Insight and Inspiration from the Speeches of Marlene Wilson*. (Energize Inc., 2008).

REFERENCES

Atlantic Philanthropies. (2009). *Pathfinder advocate edition: A practical guide to advocacy evaluation*. Washington, DC: Innovation Network, Inc. Commissioned by the Atlantic Philanthropies. Retrieved from http://www.innonet.org/client_docs/File/advocacy/pathfinder_advocate_web.pdf.

Boyle, Cynthia J., Beardsley, Robert S., & Hayes, Margaret. (2004). Effective leadership and advocacy: Amplifying professional citizenship. *American Journal of Pharmaceutical Education*, *68*(3).

Bradner, Jeanne H. (1999). *Portrait of a profession: Volunteer administration*. Richmond, VA: Association for Volunteer Administration.

Brudney, Jeffrey L., & Meijs, Lucus C.P.M. (2009). It ain't natural: Toward a new (natural) resource conceptualization for volunteer management. *Nonprofit and Voluntary Sector Quarterly*, *38*(4), 564-581.

Campbell, Katherine H. (2004). *Powerful volunteer connections: A toolkit for maximizing your organization's volunteer resources*. Atlanta: Points of Light Foundation & Volunteer Center National Network.

Carman, Joanne G., & Millesen, Judith L. (2005). Nonprofit program evaluation: organizational challenges and resource needs. *Journal of Volunteer Administration*, *23*(3), 36-43.

Corporation for National and Community Service. (2009, July). *Research brief: Pathways to service: Learning from the potential volunteer's perspective*. Corporation for National and Community Service.

Cowling, Martin. (2005). Sabotage! The five lethal factors volunteer managers employ to harm their programs. *The Electronic Journal of the Volunteerism Community*. Available at http://www.e-volunteerism.com/quarterly/05jan/05jan-cowling.php.

Cowling, Martin J. (2008). Global volunteer management survey 2008: Summary report. *People first – Total solutions*. Retrieved from http://www.pfts.com.au/documents/0805GLOBALVOLUNTEER MANAGEMENTSURVEYDRAFT6-4.pdf.

Cowling, Martin, & Cravens, Jayne. (2007). Sabotage Part Two: How managers of volunteers diminish their role. *The Electronic Journal of the Volunteerism Community*. Available at http://www.e-volunteerism.com/quarterly/07jul/07jul-cowlingcravens.php.

Cowling, Martin, & Fryar, Andy. (2008). Sabotage Part Three: Messing it up: How not-for-profits sabotage their volunteer programs. *The Electronic Journal of the Volunteerism Community*. Available at http://www.e-volunteerism.com/quarterly/08jan/08jan-fryarcowling.php.

Eisner, David, Grimm Jr., Robert T., Maynard, Shannon, & Washburn, Susannah. (2009, Winter). The new volunteer workforce. *Stanford Social Innovation Review*, 32-37.

Ellis, Susan J. (1996). *From the top down: The executive role in volunteer program success*. Philadelphia, PA: Energize Inc.

Ellis, Susan J. (2000, Fall). Should volunteer administration be a "profession"? Yes ... . *The Electronic Journal of the Volunteerism Community*. Available at http://www.e-volunteerism.com/fall2000/profintro.php.

Ellis, Susan J., & McCurley, Steve. (2008). Transferable skills: What makes us invaluable? *The Electronic Journal of the Volunteerism Community*. Available at http://www.e-volunteerism.com/quarterly/08jan/08jan-points.php.

Ezell, Mark. (2001). *Advocacy in the human services*. Belmont, CA: Wadsworth/Thomson Learning.

Fox, Ronald E. (2008). Advocacy: The key to the survival and growth of professional psychology. *Professional Psychology: Research & Practice*, *39*(6), 633-637.

Hick, Steven F., & McNutt, John G. (Eds.). (2002). *Advocacy, activism, and the Internet: Community organizing and social policy*. Chicago: Lyceum Books, Inc.

Idealist. (2009). *Developing your volunteer program.* Idealist.org. Retrieved from http://www.idealist.org/en/vmrc/bestpractices/developingprogram.html.

Idealist. (2009). *How to advocate for the profession.* Idealist.org. Retrieved from http://www.idealist.org/en/vmrc/howtoadvocate.html.

Matusak, Larraine R. (1997). *Finding your voice: Learning to lead … anywhere you want to make a difference.* San Francisco: Jossey-Bass, Inc.

McCurley, Steve, & Ellis, Susan J. (2002). Earning power and respect for volunteer services: A dozen action steps. *The Electronic Journal of the Volunteerism Community.* Available at http://www.e-volunteerism.com/quarterly/02win/pov2b.php.

Moore, Gail, & MacKenzie, Marilyn. (1990). *Building credibility with the powers that be: A practical guide to enhanced personal, program and organizational power.* Toronto: Partners Plus.

Nicholson-Crotty, Jill. (2009). The stages and strategies of advocacy among nonprofit reproductive health providers. *Nonprofit and Voluntary Sector Quarterly, 38*(6), 1044-1053.

Silver, Nora, & Melsh, Margaret. (1999). *Positioning of the profession: Communicating the power of results for volunteer leadership professionals.* Richmond, VA: Association for Volunteer Administration.

Stallings, Betty B. (2001). Building organizational commitment to the volunteer program. *The Electronic Journal of the Volunteerism Community.* Available at http://www.e-volunteerism.com/win2001/orgcommitintro.php.

Stallings, Betty B. (2005). *12 key actions of volunteer program champions: CEOs who lead the way.* Philadelphia, PA: Energize Inc.

Stupak, Ronald J. (2005). The advocacy arena: Who shall lead us? *Journal of Volunteer Administration, 23*(2), 38-41.

Tappe, Marlene K., Galer-Unti, Regina A., & Radius, Susan M. (2009). Incorporating advocacy training in professional preparation programs. *American Journal of Health Studies, 24*(1), 257-265.

United Parcel Service Foundation. (2002). *A guide to investigating in volunteer resources management: improve your philanthropic portfolio.* The UPS Foundation.

Wilson, Marlene. (2008). *Visionary leadership in volunteer programs: Insight and inspiration from the speeches of Marlene Wilson.* Philadelphia, PA: Energize Inc.

Chapter 17

COMMUNITY COLLABORATION AND ALLIANCES

Anita Angelini, MA
Mount Royal University

INTRODUCTION

Consider two comments that emerged from a series of sessions aimed at having rural nonprofit organizations begin to work together to accomplish both their missions and positive outcomes in their community. As a volunteer administrator, you may have heard comments like these:

"I must admit that I don't really know what your organization does in the community."

"When so much time is being spent on figuring out how to save money on our internal processes to stay sustainable for next

year, how am I supposed to be out in the community, spending time looking for new partners?"

Central to effective community collaborations and alliances is a volunteer administrator's ability to: understand and advance individual, organizational, and community goals; advocate for effective volunteer involvement inside the organization and in the broader community it serves; and span the boundaries between organizations in order to engage volunteers towards community ends. While it may be implied, an especially important dimension to any work related to building collaborations, alliances, and partnerships is the fundamental role of relationships, be it between individuals who find that they need to work more closely and cooperatively on an issue of mutual concern or between organizations that find themselves wanting to work together to make the best use of limited human or financial resources.

CULTIVATING AND PROTECTING RELATIONSHIPS

Relationships are powerful tools for any volunteer administrator. One of the first aspects of working with volunteers that a volunteer administrator will recognize is that the volunteers themselves come equipped with a variety of relationships that will influence how the volunteer engages with the organization (Bussell and Forbes, 2006, p. 168). Initial recruitment, retention, and levels and depth of contributions are impacted by the relationships that volunteers hold externally to and in addition to their volunteer role in a particular organization (p. 153). Volunteer administrators will benefit from applying their understanding of the influence that relationships have on volunteers and relate the same kind of thinking to the practice of effective volunteer administration through relationship cultivation and protection.

Relationships take many forms. In this chapter we will discuss collaborations and alliances. This chapter will treat collaborations and alliances as a general concept that is underpinned by relationships regardless of which particular sector the partnering organizations represent. This means the details of who is involved in the collaborations and alliances — for example, between nonprofit organizations, between nonprofit and for-profit organizations, or between nonprofit and government organizations — are not the most salient here. Regardless of the sector being represented, each relationship will produce a particular set of outcomes. The most commonly addressed outcomes in the organizational literature include:

- trust-building (Inkpen and Currall, 2004, p. 588),
- the ability to implement appropriate control mechanisms (p. 588),
- organizational learning (p. 592),
- solidifying of organizational identity (Brickson, 2007, p. 866), and
- broadened capacity for problem-solving (Cross & Sproull, 2004, p. 450).

In terms of trust, the outcomes of relationships can vary from a creation of trust between individuals, individuals and an organization, or between organizations. Williams (2007, p. 595) notes that "the ability of knowledge workers to develop interpersonal trust across organizational boundaries has become an increasingly critical component of trust between knowledge workers who span these boundaries." Reflective learning — learning that is focused on reflecting on the process and content of the collaboration either by a subset of individuals or by a subset of organizations that are part of a collaboration or alliance — may be an intentional or unintentional result of a relationship (Larsson *et al.*, 1998, p. 297). Problem-solving challenges that are introduced to individuals and organizations in a relationship can be approached through multiple perspectives because of the varying experiences and expertise of the people involved (Cross and Sproull, 2004, p. 450). Some relationships will yield problem-solving by referrals to others who have a particular skill set or expertise. Some relationships will yield a new way of viewing the problem, for example, reframing it as an opportunity. The approach is contingent on the strength and type of relationship between the person or organization presenting the challenge and the individuals or organizations reflecting on it. Controls which reinforce authority for decisions and accountability for results, and which bring congruence between individual and organizational objectives (Inkpen and Currall, 2004, p. 588), are also an outcome of a relationship. Clarity about who has the authority for making decisions is important because it is this authority that develops the rules that finally govern the relationship. This is important because the accountability for results and congruence of objectives will form the basis on which you as a volunteer administrator will communicate the results or impact of the relationship to stakeholders. McCurley and Lynch (1996, p. 157) note, "Positive reputations are built from positive achievements, from being 'the one who' made something happen." The reasons for a relationship to exist in the first place and the dynamics shaping the relationship in a continued form will ultimately influence the outcomes of the relationship.

To enter into a collaboration or an alliance means that one will be working with other individuals, and other organizations, in some way that ideally brings about a greater social value to the community and enhances or enriches what your organization can normally achieve on its own (Iyer, 2003, p. 42). One part of the rationale for a relationship is social. It is the idea that the community will be enriched more if organizations worked together than if each organization worked independently. For example, a large urban centre may have several dozen nonprofit organizations providing services for children. Instead of each organization duplicating basic administrative structures (*e.g.*, financial services, human resources, purchasing, leases), efficiencies can be found by sharing a financial expert and financial systems such as payroll across a number of organizations (see Arsenault, 1998).

The other part of the rationale for a relationship is economic and strategic. The idea is that an organization's resources and capacities are limited and if there is another organization that can make the resources and capacities of a partner organization go even further, then the relationship is one worth looking into. There are two unique ways in which inter-organizational relationships produce excellent resource results. The first is the brain trust that can be applied to particular problem-solving or service production that stems from all of the participants in the collaboration or alliance (Barringer & Harrison, 2000, p. 373). For example, Honeywell, an industrial supplies manufac- turer, also has a nonprofit organization through which it runs the Honey- well Retiree Volunteer Program. The website for the Minneapolis chapter of the program, <http://myheart.honeywell.com/eclub/hrvp_story.htm>, makes the call for collaboration in terms of sharing the brain trust explicit: "... what we can do is talk about ourselves ... [a]nd perhaps this will contain an idea or two that you can develop to your own advantage and then show us so we can improve our own operation" (Honeywell, 2009). The second is the advantage that an organization gains when it collaborates or enters into alliance with another organi- zation that carries particularly strong prestige, power, reputation and capacity (Barringer and Harrison, 2000, p. 373).

The way relationships are governed can significantly influence the level of uniquely produced resources gained from engaging in them. When working with others, particularly stakeholders who are external to your organization, the reorganization of how work happens and who is involved is determined somewhat by structural considerations and formal agreements between the individuals and entities involved: "the parties have to agree upon the 'ground rules' on which the relationship is to be organized, continued and possibly dissolved" (Iyer, 2003, p. 42). That being said, "agreements cannot substitute for trust, goodwill, honest intentions and commitment" (Arsenault, 1998, p. 41). An important role that you serve as a volunteer administrator is to actively attend to relationships that already exist. This means three particular activities are required of you as a volunteer administrator:

1. Actively work to ensure that the ground rules or governance of a relationship evolve along the way with the relationship.

2. Attend to the emotional management of others in the relationship so that you mitigate group risk (Williams, 2007, p. 596).

3. Actively scan environmental information that signals to you whether other relationships are strategically beneficial to enter into or to dissolve.

A first consideration in cultivating and protecting relationships are the competencies and resources available to the volunteer administrator to be successful. In particular, what competencies serve you in understanding, initiating, and negotiating your way through collaborations and alliances? "Volunteer Program Managers are in a unique position to argue for, plan for, and train for the alterations in agency operation that will be necessary for receptivity of new audiences, whether they be clients, paid staff, or volunteers" (McCurley & Lynch, 1996, p. 167). To understand one's available competencies and resources will require some reflection on the part of the volunteer administrator. In this chapter there will be many opportunities to reflect on which competencies you may need to spend more time developing. This chapter will also introduce you to new ways of defining what counts as a resource and how resources can contribute to creating and evolving collaborations and alliances.

A second consideration are the goals that your daily work is contributing to. These can be understood to be at three levels:

1. The first is at the individual level to reflect volunteer and staff needs and the needs of other individuals in the community. Volunteer administrators need to ask the question of how collaborations and alliances might bring benefit at the individual level.

2. The second takes into account the organization and its identity in the community. There are certain objectives that the entire

organization operates toward and your job as a volunteer administrator is central to that operation. So, as a volunteer administrator, deciphering what kinds of relationships serve the organizational goals is important.

3. Finally, most nonprofit organizations have goals — and missions — that declare a community outcome. These goals need to also be thought about. Organizations that use volunteers are organizations that tend to exist to bring about some sort of social value. They may span many different sectors, and they all serve to create some sort of broader social benefit and to realize economic rationality through the use of volunteers.

McCurley and Lynch (1996, p. 167) note that volunteer administrators "will make the difference in whether agencies struggle with diminishing resources against overwhelming odds or whether agencies are truly able to involve volunteers effectively enough to mobilize all the resources of the community."

The volunteer administrator is also a champion who needs to communicate successfully. The messaging about the value, importance, and needs of volunteers and volunteer programming are disseminated throughout the organization and the community through the efforts of a volunteer administrator. As a volunteer administrator, you are in the spotlight to communicate what matters most and to explain why. Effective communication is essential to cultivating and evolving collaborations and alliances.

TYPES OF ORGANIZATIONAL RELATIONSHIPS

We frequently hear about partnerships, collaborations, and alliances across various sectors; however, we do not always have a clear idea of what makes each distinct. If we restrict ourselves to the definitions in a narrow sense, we also miss out on some opportunities to create unique opportunities within the collaborations, alliances, and partnerships.

Partnerships

Partnership is a term that can be applied to almost any organizational relationship in which two or more organizations work together. What makes the partnership unique is that it is usually project-based, it exists for a specific and limited period of time, and the organizations working together do not alter their organizational identity or procedures in any way (Shaw, 2003, p. 108). The organizations remain fully independent of each other. This will require some formal arrangements for procedures to follow in the project; however, structurally, culturally, and in terms of governance the organizations will not shift.

Collaborations

Collaborations are a deeper version of partnerships, with two or more participating organizations. Here the organizations jointly create a project or series of projects and jointly apply their own resources to the project. The project is owned by all the participating organizations (Shaw, 2003, p. 108). To collaborate really implies that resources and ownership for results is shared across all collaborating organizations. To make collaborations work, clear controls for accountability and effective communication among the collaborating partners are required.

Alliances

An alliance can be defined as: "the bond or connection between two or more individuals or institutions" (Iyer, 2003, p. 42). Note that the definition is not transactional. It does not require an exchange of resources between the organizations. It does not require that the organizations work on a particular project together. It does not require that the organizations spell out a particular time period for working together either. An alliance can be a type of relationship that is enduring over a long-time scale. An alliance can be a relationship in which questions of ownership for projects are never raised, "… no matter who and how many the partners are, all partners in the alliance realize that their capabilities can be combined to mutual advantage and that the success of the alliance depends on every one of the partners" (Iyer, 2003, p. 43). Notice that tangible resources or assets, like money or equipment, may not be the point of exchange in an alliance. It may be intangible assets, like reputation and organizational branding, that are shared. It may also be intangible capabilities, like "know-how" or networks of relationships, that are used for mutual benefit for the participating organizations.

Regardless of the relationship type the organizational literature is rich with prescriptions for the viability of relationships based on relationship characteristics. Table 1 summarizes the information from organizational literature identifying factors that lead to the building of relationships and identifies suggestions for keeping the relationship successful. Of important note are the similarities between alliances and collaborations. The initiating factors for the relationships and the processes that will keep the relationship going are not all that different. Volunteer administrators will benefit from assessing how they can directly have input into the process either for initiating relationships or for evolving relationships.

Table 1: Launching and Evolving Relationships

Relationship Type	Possible Reasons to Initiate Relationship	What Keeps the Relationship Going
Alliance (Shaw, 2003; Iyer, 2003)	• Seeking cost minimization • Seeking organizational learning • Seeking risk mitigation • Seeking organizational enrichment (for example, image improvement) • Belief that working together can yield greater outcomes than working independently	• Nature of each organization fully understood (size, location, sectoral positioning) • Organizational culture well understood internally and externally • Shared objectives in the alliance • Responsibility of each participating organization to contribute where contributions are complementary or supplemental • Participation which has to do with the type of trust shared between the organizations and the depth of that trust • Communication which has to do with the frequency, formality and level at which communication occurs among the organizations

Relationship Type	Possible Reasons to Initiate Relationship	What Keeps the Relationship Going
Collaboration (Sowa, 2008; Austin, 2009)	• Need to acquire resources that are not available to an organization working independently • Need to find new ideas to apply to organizational services or programs • Need to respond to policy makers and funders exerting pressure to maximize return on investment (dollars vs. services)	• Alignment of strategy, mission, and values between/amongst organizations • Personal connections and relationships strong among the individuals representing the organizations in the alliance • Values driving the generation of a shared vision • Continuous learning of the participating organizations during the relationship-building process • Focused attention of the organization which includes the engagement of senior leaders and high importance of the relationship created and understood internally through each organization in the relationship • Effective communication throughout each organization internally, effective communication amongst the organizations in the collaboration, and effective communication between each organization and external audiences • Strong organizational systems (ground rules and procedures)

Relationship Type	Possible Reasons to Initiate Relationship	What Keeps the Relationship Going
		• Mutual respect and expectations for accountability

KNOWING YOUR DIRECTION AND RESOURCING YOUR WAY THERE

As a volunteer administrator who seeks to enrich and enhance the organizational capacity to support volunteers and volunteerism, you will have to make deliberate choices. That means that you will need to be strategic about the relationships you engage in, why you engage in them, and when. One study (Sowa, 2008) of 20 nonprofit organizations found that there were three primary reasons for organizations to seek-out collaborations. These are:

• to ensure the organization survives through difficult circumstances;

• to gain credibility in the sector or amongst other external stakeholders in the community; and

• to gain more power, a stronger position, an improved reputation, and greater capacity within the sector and community the organization operates (p. 12).

These three reasons are all linked to defining resources and obtaining the most salient resources that are needed at a specific time. So, what counts as a resource? There are several approaches to defining resources. One approach is to look at the form of the resource and the other is to categorize resources according to what the resources enable an organization or individuals to do. Both are worth describing further. Resources come in three forms: tangible assets, intangible assets, and intangible capabilities (Galbreath & Galvin, 2004, p. 2).

Tangible assets include money, and other physical items that carry value like equipment or facilities. Intangible assets include resources that the organization carries with it while it is in operation. This could include intellectual property, reputation, and particular policies or structures used within the organization. Intangible capabilities include those things that managers inside the organization know how to do and the relationships they have built in knowledge-sharing, for example, that differentiate the organization from others. An intangible capability is "… considered a higher-order …" (Galbreath

& Galvin, 2004, p. 3) resource that often lacks internal organizational acknowledgement and the focus of managers when considering what resources need to be supplemented or what resources can be offered in a relationship.

In addition, resources can be defined according to what they assist individuals or organizations to do. This type of definition comes from the fields of sociology and psychology and carries with it an emphasis on the notion of power. This approach to defining resources is also very explicit about the role that relationship cultivation plays in contributing to the asset-richness of an organization. "Resourcing is the creation in practice of assets such as people, time, money, knowledge, or skill; and qualities of relationships such as trust, authority, or complementarity such that they enable actors to enact schemas" (Feldman, 2004, p. 296). Further, "resources are anything that can serve as a source of power in social interactions" (Sewell, 1992, p. 9). Notice that this approach highlights relationships, trust, and social interactions along with the more traditional norms, people, money, and time that volunteer administrators focus on within organizations. Because of ideas like these, the focus of managers seeking to find winning solutions to common organizational challenges has moved to the forefront of management literature. It is because of these changes in the operational and intellectual environment that volunteer administrators are now finding themselves needing to re-conceptualize their work and their roles in their organizations. Indeed, the volunteer administrator will not be able to ignore the transformations that have occurred and that will continue to occur related to fulfilling their responsibilities. "The trick for the future is not just doing things correctly, it also lies in allocating scarce management time towards doing the right things. And that requires being a smart leader, and not just an administrator" (McCurley & Lynch, 1996, p. 165).

Six Relationship Roles

You might be wondering about the ways that a volunteer administrator might begin to acquire or cultivate the tangible and intangible assets described above. Before reading further, take a moment to reflect on the types of relationships that you could see yourself pursuing with an organizational partner — public, private, or nonprofit. Some questions that may help guide this reflection are:

1. What organization can you see yourself partnering with?

2. If you could partner with that organization, what would your organization's role be in the partnership with that organization?

3. How would this role serve the volunteer program and your efforts specifically as a volunteer administrator?

4. What would the partnering organization's role be with your organization?

5. How would this serve the volunteer program and your efforts specifically as a volunteer administrator?

Based on how roles and expected outcomes are set out, there are at least six specific ways that collaborations and alliances may be shaped. These six opportunities may be seen either as specific types of collaborative relationships or as a spectrum of roles that may emerge within alliances. One way of thinking about this set of relationships is in terms of the purpose or the outcomes expected. The six relationship outcomes forming the substance of organizational (or individual) relationships are:

*   advocacy,
*   advisory,
*   contributory,
*   operational,
*   collaborative, and/or
*   catalytic (Lee *et al.*, 2005, p. 56).

If you enter into a relationship with the individual or organizational objective of influencing for social change, whether that influence is directed to government policy makers, business leaders, or other nonprofit organizations, you are taking on an advocacy role. As an adjunct to the advocacy role, you may individually or organizationally begin to advise policy makers, you may begin to have input on the strategic decision-making of other influential organizations, or you may be invited to comment on new program development in other organizations. If so, you are acting in a consultative or advisory role. For some organizations, being invited to the table for input on matters that impact the community is of strategic interest. Operational relationships are in place to enrich the information sharing and capacity of each organization. In the operational role the know-how of one organization is shared, examined, and possibly adapted for implementation in another organization. This type of relationship serves organizations in gaining strength in the functional or process areas of their operations that can stand to be improved. As described earlier, collaborative roles are relationships in which authority for decisions, resources, costs and benefits are shared toward a particular end. In a catalyst role an organization serves other organizations by convening or bringing together groups that would not normally intersect.

Finally, the most common role to be found in relationship development across the nonprofit sector is the contributory role. In this case the partnering organization contributes a tangible asset like money or equipment to support an organization. This is frequently seen in sponsoring and donative programs between businesses and nonprofits. While there is nothing inherently wrong with establishing relationships that are contributory in nature, it does appear that these types of roles are comfortable, frequent, fairly easy to negotiate, and can produce a narrowed vision of the entire resource development playing field available to any one organization. In particular, small nonprofit organizations may become somewhat mission-diminished by agreeing to contributory relationships. "They accept them [the funds for projects and initiatives] because they nominally fall within the organization's broad mission statement, but they are much better aligned with the donor's strategy than with the nonprofit's" (Rangan, 2004, p. 114). In large organizations if capacity is grown over time, funders and supporters of the organization begin to demand even more services and programs to be included under the already existent complement of offerings (Rangan, 2004, p. 114). There is no easy or single way to negotiate the ebb and flow of contributory relationships.

Volunteer administrators may find new opportunities by considering bases for relationships other than contributory (*e.g.*, try thinking of relationships developed around advocacy, advisory, operational, collaborative, or catalytic characteristics). The point of such an activity is to begin to think in an expanded and creative way about a broad spectrum of relationship possibilities.

Organizational Capacity and Sustainability

One of the primary reasons that many relationships are started is to ensure organizational sustainability. The definition of sustainability within many nonprofit organizations has come to be having the resources (human, financial, skills, *etc.*) to function in the immediate future. In some cases this means having the capacity to carry on the work for another few weeks. In others the time-frame may extend out to between three and five years. At the root of this understanding is that the organization is "continuing on" or maintaining what it was doing without change. Volunteer administrators are likely in one of the best positions to see the changes that are needed and that are already taking place in the broader world (*e.g.*, the increasing diversity of communities and of volunteers). It can be a frustration to be in a position to observe change and the opportunities it brings while being in an organization that expects systems and programs to maintain a status quo. By thinking about relationships in a broader way, a volunteer administrator is able to bring an "organizational development" perspective forward.

For the purposes of this chapter, the definition of development includes the ideas of converting the volunteer program and the systems that support it to new purposes so that resources can be used more effectively to produce the outcomes that are desired. Development in this sense is the key to successful volunteer administration. If a volunteer administrator is able to reframe the challenges of their organization, their own skill and knowledge needs, and social objectives, a creative transformation can take place in the nature and quality of the work.

Part of the creative transformation will include relationship cultivation. Through that relationship cultivation the volunteer administrator will likely see an entirely new kind of resource capacity becoming available to the volunteer program and to the organization. By thinking in terms of development you are refocusing your attention on the active creation of resources rather than on relying on resources that are derived elsewhere. It puts the volunteer administrator in a leadership position for the deployment of resources in the most effective ways. Research in the organization literature has demonstrated that a reframing of resources can even lead to internal organizational changes that are beneficial to the organization: "… changes in the internal processes of an organization can take one kind of resource and recreate it as a different resource" (Feldman, 2004, p. 295). The way you seek out resources, define resources, and apply resources to program operations will bring about different outcomes. The volunteer administrator may face the question of how to connect this kind of development work through external relationship cultivation with the internal work of securing organizational support for volunteerism while assisting the organization in meeting its mission and vision. The connection point between the internal and external work can be referred to as organizational and operational strategy.

OPERATIONAL STRATEGY, ORGANIZATIONAL IDENTITY, AND RELATIONSHIPS

As a volunteer administrator you are likely well equipped to recite your organization's mission and values. Some organizations have mission statements and programs but lack the "middle-matter" between the two. The middle-matter is the operational strategy. Operational strategy takes the mission statement and converts it into a unique set of quantitative goals. These goals specify and clarify six aspects to the organization's work. These are:

1. the issue that the organization is addressing through its services and programs;

2. the scope of the activities that the organization will pursue on that issue;

3. the role the organization has in the broader system of organizations also addressing that issue;

4. how the organization is specifically looking to remedy the issue;

5. the impact the organization is looking for on that issue; and

6. an assessment of expected resources and limits for the future (Rangan, 2004, p. 116).

Part of a volunteer administrator's role is to create the middle-matter between the mission and programs. This will involve relationship cultivation internally and externally. It will involve spending time to define resources and ranking and setting priorities to the resources that matter most. It requires that you identify where competency, skill, knowledge, asset, and resource gaps currently exist and where gaps are expected to open up in the future. It also requires that you then select the relationship role or set of roles that are going to be the most effective instruments to helping your organization develop its impact in the community.

The alignment of your activities with the organizational strategy is critical. Organizational strategy determines how an organization will relate to its various stakeholders. Those relationships with stakeholders are based on shared perceptions of the organization and its qualities. The shared perceptions of an organization help create organizational identity, and that identity determines how an organization can act and how other organizations interact with it (Brickson, 2007, p. 866). According to organizational literature, organizational identities come in three orientations: individualistic, relational, and collectivist (Brickson,

2007, p. 868). Individualistic organizational identities are evident when an organization's activities and strategies are directed toward ensuring its own individual success and gaining the most they can from staff efforts. Organizations with this type of identity will be more prone to seek out relationships that are instrumental in achieving the organization's own aims which over time can weaken ties the organization has with others (Brickson, 2007, p. 870). Organizational identities that are relational put emphasis on ensuring the needs of particular internal and external stakeholders are protected and are being met. The focus of these organizations is on preserving and enriching the relationships that hold the most meaning to the organization. For organizations with this type of identity the relationships cultivated are often strong and hold high intrinsic value, regardless of what those relationships help the organization achieve (Brickson, 2007, p. 870). Collectivist organizational identities are membership-based. Organizations with this type of identity have general ties to other stakeholders in the broader community. A collectivist organization views itself as a group member. For organizations with this identity the commonly held agenda or purpose is the main reason that relationships are pursued (Brickson, 2007, p. 871).

These three orientations to identity matter in the discussion of collaborations and alliances because the type of perception the organization has of itself and the type of perception that others hold of it will determine the interactions that are or are not successful. "In deciding whether and how to engage with a certain organization, stakeholders observe how the organization interacts with others" (Brickson, 2007, p. 869). There may be times when major cultural shifts are required in an organization in order to restructure existing relationships or to engage in certain relationship roles with others. This is difficult because identities are inherently resistant to change. To alter the identity, internal and external stakeholder relationships need to go through transformation and renegotiation (Brickson, 2007, p. 869). The identity also defines who matters and who does not in terms of stakeholder significance.

Identifying Stakeholders

Stakeholders are entities that have a direct or indirect interest in the work of a given organization. In the voluntary sector stakeholders are many and may include other sector organizations, for-profit organizations, groups, associations, regulators, funders, policy makers, clients, and individuals. Some stakeholders will have a more direct connection to an organization or more direct role in influencing the organization. These are primary stakeholders. Other stakeholders will have a less direct connection to the organization and fewer opportunities to influence the organization. These are considered secondary stakeholders. For volunteer administrators interested in exploring the cultivation of new relationship roles, it is very important to understand who all the stakeholders are and what their particular relationship with an organization is.

A tool for sorting out who counts as a primary or secondary stakeholder is the Urgency, Legitimacy, and Power (ULP) map represented in Figure 1. This map has been adapted from the work of Mitchell, Agle, and Wood (1997, p. 874) and identifies at least seven stakeholders.

Figure 1: Urgency, Legitimacy, Power Map

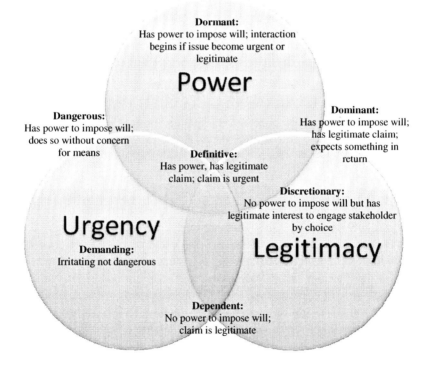

In this map, three stakeholder characteristics mesh in various degrees. To have power a stakeholder has access to money, media, or other forms of direct coercive influence over an organization. Funders, for example, can wield power over an organization and the activities it chooses to pursue. Legitimacy refers to the credibility and appropriateness of a particular stakeholder to raise a concern or make a claim with a particular organization. Clients of a nonprofit organization, for example, have a direct and relevant legitimacy in seeking out services or changes to services offered by an organization. Urgency refers to the extent or degree to which a stakeholder needs to call on an organization to resolve a particular need. Before the green movement experienced across corporate North America, environmental organizations were not viewed as urgent stakeholders. Many for-profit organizations opted to interact with these environmental groups on a discretionary basis. Once the green movement gained momentum, however, for-profit organizations began to view those same organizations with a greater sense of urgency.

The various stakeholders identified in the map should be viewed as fluid rather than static. That is to say that a stakeholder that has been dormant or quiet may suddenly become dependent or may become extremely powerful due to changes in the broader environment. A volunteer administrator, along with senior leaders in the organization, should strive to understand their stakeholder territory — the stakeholders in their map and anticipated changes to the positioning of stakeholders because of environmental changes.

CONCLUSION

This chapter has set out to sketch the foundation and key elements associated with relationships that lead to collaborative activities. The outcomes of relationships that can be important to both the volunteer program and the organization as a whole include trust-building, organizational learning, and improved capacity for problem-solving. Reasons for embarking on a community collaboration or alliance can be diverse. While the majority tend to focus on the acquisition of financial resources, volunteer administrators are in a position to consider potentially more worthwhile reasons for building relationships. For example, expanding advocacy efforts, building advisory capacity, gaining operational advantages, or bringing about broad social change may all be reasons that have high value for the organization, for the volunteer program and for volunteers. Given information on the kinds of possible relationships, potential roles for participants, and a deep knowledge about the mission of their organization, volunteer administrators can make important decisions that can improve communities.

REFERENCES

Arsenault, Jane. (1998). *Forging nonprofit alliances.* San Francisco: Jossey-Bass.

Austin, James E. (2000). Strategic collaboration between nonprofits and business. *Nonprofit and Voluntary Sector Quarterly, 29,* 69-97.

Barringer, Bruce, & Harrison, Jeffrey. (2000). Walking a tightrope: Creating value through interorganizational relationships. *Journal of Management, 26*(3).

Brickson, Shelley L. (2007). Organizational identity orientation: The genesis of the role of the firm and distinct forms of social value. *Academy of Management Review, 32*(3), 864-888.

Bryce, Herrington J. (2007). The public's trust in nonprofit organizations: The role of relationship marketing and management. *California Management Review, 49*(4), 112-131.

Bussell, Helen, & Forbes, Deborah. (2006). Developing relationship marketing in the voluntary sector. *Journal of Nonprofit and Public Sector Marketing, 15*(1), 151-174.

Collis, David, & Montgomery, Cynthia. (2008, July-August). Competing on resources. *Harvard Business Review,* 140-150.

Cross, Rob, & Sproull, Lee. (2004). More than an answer: Information relationships for actionable knowledge. *Organization Science, 15*(4), 446-462.

Feldman, Martha. (2004, May-June). Resources in emerging structures and processes of change. *Organization Science, 15*(3), 295-309.

Galbreath, Jeremy, & Galvin, Peter. (2004). Which resources matter? A fine-grainted test of the resource-based view of the firm. *Academy of Management Best Conference Papers 2004.* Academy of Management.

Inkpen, Andrew C., & Currall, Steven C. (2004). The coevolution of trust, control, and learning in joint ventures. *Organization Science, 15*(5), 586-599.

Iyer, Easwar. (2003). Theory of alliances: Partnership and partner characteristics. *Journal of Nonprofit and Public Sector Marketing, 11*(1), 41-57.

Larsson, Rikard, Bengtsson, Lars, Henriksson, Kristina, & Sparks, Judith. (1998). The interorganizational learning dilemma: Collective knowledge development in strategic alliances. *Organization Science, 9*(3), 285-305.

Lee, Nancy, Aschermann, Kurt, Ehrmann, Rich, & Mintz, Jim. (2005). The challenges and rewards of partnering with the private sector to achieve social marketing objectives. *Social Marketing Quarterly, 11*(3-4), 51-59.

McCurley, Steve, & Lynch, Rick. (1996). *Volunteer management.* Darien, Illinois: Heritage Arts Publishing.

Milward, H. Brinton, & Provan, Keith G. (2003). Managing the hollow state. *Public Management Review, 5*(1), 1-18.

Mitchell, Ronald, Agle, Bradley, & Wood, Donna. (1997). Toward a theory of stakeholder salience and identification: Defining the principle of who and what really counts. *Academy of Management Review, 22*(4), 853-886.

Parker, Barbara, & Selsky, John W. (2004). Interface dynamics in cause-based partnerships: An exploration of emergent culture. *Nonprofit and Voluntary Sector Quarterly, 33*, 458-488.

Rangan, V. Kasturi. (2004, March). Lofty missions, down-to-earth plans. *Harvard Business Review*, ToolKit, 112-119.

Sewell, William H. (1992). A theory of structure: Duality, agency and transformation. *The American Journal of Sociaiology, 98*(1), 1-29.

Shaw, Mary M. (2003). Successful collaboration between the nonprofit and public sectors. *Nonprofit Management and Leadership, 14*(1), 107-120.

Sowa, Jessica. (2008). The collaboration decision in nonprofit organizations. *Nonprofit and Voluntary Sector Quarterly OnlineFirst*, 1-23.

Takahashi, Lois M., & Smutny, Gayla. (2002). Service partnerships-collaborative windows and organizational governance: Exploring the formation and demise of social service partnerships. *Nonprofit and Voluntary Sector Quarterly, 31*, 165-185.

Williams, Michele. (2007). Building genuine trust through interpersonal emotional management: A threat regulation model of trust and collaboration across boundaries. *Academy of Management Review, 32*(2), 595-621.

Chapter 18

A HISTORY OF THE PROFESSION OF VOLUNTEER ADMINISTRATION

Keith Seel, Ph.D., CVA
Mount Royal University

Sarah Jane Rehnborg, Ph.D.
University of Texas

INTRODUCTION

Practitioners in the field of volunteer management today consider what they do to be a professional activity. They have come to hold this belief partly because of communications within the group of practitioners that say that volunteer administration is a profession. Others believe it is a profession because volunteer administration has characteristics associated with a profession such as a peer assessed professional credential, a professional journal, a code of ethics and ongoing professional development training opportunities. For an occupation to be a profession it would have to have characteristics such that others outside the field of practice would also recognize the activity as a profession. It is unclear if this is the case for volunteer administration.

Since the establishment of the earliest professions — law, medicine and clergy — a variety of other practitioner/worker collectives have advanced their particular cause of becoming a profession. Thus, we have more recently established professions related to the disciplines of engineering, teaching, social work, psychology and so forth. One of the challenges in thinking about whether or not volunteer administration is a profession rests on the definition of a "profession." For some a professional is the prima donna of organizational theory (Perrow, 1980); for others a professional is defined by distinctive competences with a network of strategic alliances (Savage, 1994).

This chapter examines the development of volunteer administration over the past six decades. The artifacts of volunteer administration are then compared against different schools of thought regarding the characteristics of a profession. Because volunteer administrators hold that they are a profession and much of the literature produced on their behalf supports that stance, the paper proceeds with the assumption that volunteer administration is a profession. This assumption is tested in the final section of this chapter.

THE DEVELOPMENT OF VOLUNTEER ADMINISTRATION AS A PROFESSION

The Association for Volunteer Administration, which ceased operations in 2006, was the culmination of decades-long sequence of developments aimed at establishing volunteer administration as a profession in the United States and internationally. In one of the Association's core documents, *Portrait of a Profession: Volunteer Administration* (Bradner *et al.*, 1999) traces the history through the following events (pp. 8-13):

Laying the Foundation Post-War to the 1960s

Two early drivers for the profession emerged during this period. First, there was increased publicity around the services available to persons with mental disabilities and mental illnesses in publicly funded organizations. Second, citizens became interested in wanting to assist veterans who returned home with various disabilities.

In 1958, a group of 22 coordinators from 12 states convened prior to the Mental Hospital Institute of the American Psychiatric Association (APA) in Kansas City, Missouri. The purpose of the meeting was to explore interstate exchange of information about volunteer services in mental hospitals. As well, the group expressed a wish to meet periodically under aegis of a national health or welfare organization. In October of that year, this group of coordinators convened at a conference titled "Volunteer Services to Psychiatric Patients," in Chicago. The meeting was co-sponsored by APA, the American Hospital Association, American Red Cross, the National Association for Mental Health and the Veterans Association. As a result of the meeting an early guide for the profession, *The Volunteer and the Psychiatric Patient*, was published in 1959. Also in October of 1958, representatives from other disciplines linked to the treatment of psychiatric patients attended a second pre-Mental Hospital Institute meeting of coordinators in Buffalo, New York.

In February 1960, the National Institute for Mental Health (NIMH), in cooperation with the Menninger Foundation and the Topeka (Kansas) State Hospital, organized the first training institute for coordinators of volunteer services. Grants to support the institute came from the NIMH and the Nathan Hofheimer Foundation. Representatives from 36 states, the District of Columbia and two Canadian provinces attended. While a strong expression of interest in forming an association of people with responsibilities to coordinate volunteers emerged at the meeting, no specific action was taken. "*Volunteer Services in Mental Hospitals*, which became the standard reference on volunteer services program management in psychiatric settings, summarized the institute's presentations."

In October, representatives met in Salt Lake City, Utah and made the decision to form an association for people responsible for what would be known as volunteer management. Officers were elected who in turn created a constitution and by-laws. Committees were formed and representatives identified throughout the United States.

The constitution and by-laws were adopted by 99 "charter members" who met in Omaha, Nebraska in 1961. Thus, the American Association of Volunteer Services Coordinators (AAVSC) became an official organization. "Annual meetings were held prior to the Mental Hospital Institute meeting, and secretarial services were established with the headquarters of the American Psychiatric Association.

AAVSC initiated research to ascertain how volunteer service coordinators functioned, what tasks they completed and how they allocated time. In August, 1963, AAVSC held a planning conference at the APA headquarters in Washington, D.C. to set goals on the standards to be achieved by the organization. '*The Development of Standards and Training Curriculum for Volunteer Services Coordinators*', was published in Psychiatric Studies and Projects, February, 1964."

AAVSC developed the first certification plan for professional personnel in the field of volunteer services in 1967. "The purpose was to certify those individuals who met the prescribed standards and qualifications" (p. 9), including number of years of formal education and experience as well as relevant workshop and seminar participation.

Graduate-level education became possible in 1969 when a master's level degree in Volunteer Services Program Administration was offered at Southern Illinois University at Carbondale. This was the result of extensive planning between AAVSC and the Rehabilitation Institute. Recognition of the value of volunteer services at the political level also occurred in 1969 when the governor of the state of Washington instituted a cabinet-level position for a "Coordinator of Volunteer Services." This move brought increased attention to volunteer engagement and their ability to improve the delivery of human services in that state.

Establishing the Profession — the 1970s

In 1970, the National Institute for Mental Health funded a proposal for a three-year certification training initiative submitted the previous year by AAVSC and Northeastern University in Boston, Massachusetts. The first certification training course ran between February and May 1971. After significant revisions the certification training course ran in 1972 and 1973. Membership rose from 400 in 1970 to more than 600 in 1973 after AAVSC opened its membership to "salaried administrators in all program settings within the human services field" (p. 10).

The year 1973 was a particularly significant year as AAVSC undertook activities to raise political status of the emerging profession and to consolidate the understanding of the training needs of practitioners. First, the membership of AAVSC elected to send a resolution "to the National Governor's Conference requesting the establishment of a cabinet-level coordinator of volunteer services in all states" (p. 10). Second, a national survey of the training needs for the profession as identified by practitioners was undertaken. Also in 1973, "AAVSC notified the APA Institute of Hospital and Community Psychiatry of its decision to become independent" (p. 10). Three publications resulted from the cooperative efforts of AAVSC in the same year: Green Sheets and Portfolios, published with the National Centre for Voluntary Action; a 12-pamphlet volume, *Volunteers in Rehabilitation*, published by Goodwill Industries; and the monograph *The Impact of Volunteerism on the Aging*, published by the NIMH.

In 1975, AAVSC with support from the Lilly Endowment, Inc., elected to create the Alliance for Volunteerism with AAVSC as a founding member. AAVSC had responsibilities for the Alliance Education Task Force which developed a proposal for "professional schools and associations to prepare their students and members to work with volunteers" (p. 11). AAVSC also simplified its name to Association for Administration of Volunteer Services (AAVS). The requirement that members hold a salaried position was dropped as a requirement for membership. The by-laws of the Association were changed to expand the membership to include educators, researchers, and "those actively involved in the field of volunteer administration" (p. 11).

In 1976, an Executive Secretary was hired and the AAVS office moved to Boulder, Colorado. AAVS members now received subscriptions to two profession-specific publications, *Volunteer Administration* and *Voluntary Action Leadership*. Also that year, AAVA, the Association of Volunteer Bureaus and the Association of Voluntary Action Scholars held a first collaborative conference. A pilot study was undertaken by AAVS and the California Council of Directors of Volunteers in Agencies (DOVIAs) to examine how a national organization and local groups of professionals could work together for mutual gain. Results suggesting an affiliate level of membership of DOVIAs in AAVS were presented to the membership at the 1977 conference.

In the last year of this dynamic decade, the Board authorized the hiring of a management consultant to "establish a solid financial base for AAVS, to research grants and write proposals, prepare the AAVA for marketing the Certification Plan and research marketing specialists" (p. 11). Concurrent with these activities the Association embarked upon a process to revise the organization's existing certification system. The revised Certification Plan introduced the concept of performance-based competency system based on an analysis of over 400 surveys completed by volunteer managers. These surveys captured the skills required to effectively engage volunteers in institutional settings (Rehnborg, Cheren, 1979). The revised Certification Plan required that members create written documentation demonstrating their mastery of a majority of the competencies outlined in the plan. The new system was adopted by the membership concurrent with the organization's adoption of a revised set of by-laws. "At the annual meeting, the membership adopted a revised set of bylaws incorporating new board and regional structures. AAVA became the Association for Volunteer Administration (AVA)" (p. 11). Special interest groups within the broad Association membership were recognized and provided scheduled meetings at the annual conference.

Consolidation — the 1980s

Support from the C.S. Mott Foundation allowed AVA to "develop a marketing campaign, increase membership and establish affiliate memberships" (p. 12) in 1980. As a result, four groups became the Association's first affiliate members. In 1981, Adelphi University worked with AVA to field test the performance-based Certification Program and *The Regional Conference Planning Guide* was developed. During the same year, the board realignment and regional structure approved in 1979 became effective. The Board size was reduced to 14 from 28 and four committees formed to reflect the priorities of AVA. A formal awards program was established. Standardized procedures for endorsing educational programs throughout the United States were established. In 1982, AVA became responsible for a peer reviewed journal pertaining to the profession: *The Journal of Volunteer Administration*.

Between 1983 and 1985 the certification program was field tested and the first Certified Volunteer Administrator (CVA) was granted. Other consolidation work included: a survey of post-secondary education institutions offering course work related to volunteer administration (1987); five-year goals for AVA were developed (1988); and the mission statement was revised to read, "The mission of the Association for Volunteer Administration (AVA) is to promote professionalism and strengthen leadership in volunteerism" (p. 12) (1988); piloting course curriculum based on professional competencies outlined in the certification plan (1989); and a second post-secondary survey (1989).

Further Refinements — the 1990s

The 1990s were a period of comparatively little growth and development of the profession. The annual "International Conference on

Volunteer Administration" (ICVA) was a focus for the profession and for AVA. A further survey of the educational needs of volunteer administrators was conducted in 1990 in cooperation with the University of Georgia. AVA awarded "mini-grants for innovative training models" (p. 13) in the following year. Financial pressures were one impetus for an organizational redesign of AVA that saw the focus shift from geographic regions to individual professional members.

The shift to the individual professional set the stage for the revision of the Association's 1970s ethics document. The new consolidated "Statement of Professional Ethics in Volunteer Administration" included a guide for using the ethics statement (Seel, 1995). As well, in 1999, an updated profile of the professional volunteer administrator was produced under the title "Portrait of a Profession: Volunteer Administration" (Bradner, *et al.*, 1999). Outreach and advocacy efforts on behalf of the profession were expanded in 1998 through grants from the St. Paul Foundation, the Leighty Foundation and the Kellogg Foundation.

A pluralism committee of the board crafted a pluralism strategy in 1998 that committed AVA to among other things:

- "… promote professionalism and strengthen leadership in volunteerism and provide opportunities for all segments of our profession to work together to identify the needs of the profession" (p. 14).

- Acknowledge its responsibility "to educate and to learn from the international community about issues/problems that affect the profession as well as to seek their participation in finding solutions" (p. 14).

These two commitments were to energize the AVA's move into the new millennium — and as it turned out, also appear to have created a tragic weakness that was to lead to the dissolution of the Association.

Disintegration and the Promise of Rebirth — 2000 to 2007

The new millennium started off with AVA focused on a bright future centred around a competency-based certification process, a concise ethics statement, and a view to be the global hub for professional development. From 2000 to 2006, large investments were made in strengthening the professional credential and the credentialling process. Competency tests were developed by a test committee; a test bank was developed along with the identification of a requisite body of knowledge. An examination combined with management case studies and the requirement that applicants for the credential have at least three years of experience in the field constituted the credential process in its final form.

In 2005 the final ICVA was held in Jacksonville, Florida. Financial irregularities resulted in the board dismissing the executive director and concluding operations by resolution on June 7, 2006. Prior to dissolution, the professional journal — JOVA — was transferred to the Department of 4-H Youth Development and Family & Consumer Sciences at North Carolina State University in Raleigh, North Carolina, where Dr. Dale Safrit became the Editor-in-Chief.

Also prior to its dissolution, AVA's board transferred ownership of the ethics statement "Professional Ethics in Volunteer Administration, 4th Edition" (AVA, 1999) and the Certified in Volunteer Administration Credential program to the newly formed Council for Certification in Volunteer Administration (CCVA). CCVA "serves as a catalyst to advance the capacity of communities to effectively engage volunteers by promoting and certifying excellence in the professional practice of volunteer administration" (CCVA, 2007).

CCVA's website related the following picture:

> This is the beginning of an exciting new chapter in the history of the CVA credential. Its new home has been created out of the conviction that a collaborative approach will sustain current momentum, preserve high standards of excellence and professionalism, and yield the greatest degree of long-term value and credibility.
>
> It is important to note that, during this period of chaos and transition, the program continued to operate without interruption. Over 120 candidates registered for the 2006 cycle, the exam was conducted on schedule, portfolios were reviewed and all materials were updated. This signaled a high level of commitment to the program and reinforced its perceived value by practitioners in the field.

The long process of development from the 1940s to the present day has a few main highlights:

1.   development of the body of unique knowledge and some theory associated with the profession;

2.   publication of a professional journal to disseminate new information and encourage research supporting professional practice;

3.   development of training and testing procedures to ensure professional standards were met; and

4.   establishment of a competency-based professional credential to recognize an individual's attainment of professional standards.

While there are uncertainties about the direction future developments may take, there can be little debate that these four elements are present. The question remains, however, do the current attainments mean that volunteer administration would be widely recognized as a profession?

EXAMINING CREDENTIALLING AND THE BODY OF KNOWLEDGE

The credentialling process and the body of knowledge of a profession are important defining points for the domain of professional activity and important factors in determining whether or if an activity is professional or not. Therefore, a deeper examination of the credentialling process and the body of knowledge associated with the profession of volunteer administration is important for the discussion that will follow.

Between 1979 and 2006 when AVA ceased operations, a body of knowledge was developed to substantiate both the credentialling process and the claim being made by AVA that volunteer administration was a profession. It is important to note that the first major revision of the Association's certification system which was approved by the membership in the fall of 1979 moved the process to a competency-based format. The competency identification process involved more than 400 surveys of volunteer managers and an analysis of the work performed by those administrators. Table 1 captures the functional areas of work performed by volunteer managers and the competencies that undergird the work. Although the first revision was conceptually sound, the extensive writing expectations associated with performance demonstration, coupled with the absence of adequate centralized oversight and administration greatly diminished participation in the system. Nonetheless, the credential process did serve to outline a body of knowledge necessary for effective administration and spurred Fisher and Cole to develop a text on the subject crediting the competency work of AVA (Rehnborg, 1979).

**Table 1: Original Competency Statements for
the Performance-Based Assessment Program for
Certification of Volunteer Administrators**

Functional Areas	Competencies
I. Program Planning and Organization This is the most basic task in volunteer administration. It involves the development of program goals consistent with the aims of the organization, the selection of objectives and alternative methods to reach those objectives. Effective planning and organization establishes the "map" that allows for the continuous operation of the program.	Program Planning and Organization requires that the volunteer administrator CAN: I.A. Demonstrate knowledge of the agency/organization including its mission/purpose, its structure and the policies or regulations that effect its operation. I.B. Demonstrate the capability to engage in planning activities, armed with adequate information about the community and the agency/organization, to set the course of action for the volunteer program through goals, objectives and action plans. I.C. Make decisions. I.D. Establish structures and procedures to enable the smooth operation of the program. I.E. Assign the activities necessary to accomplish the goals and objectives of the program through effective delegation and coordination.

Functional Areas	Competencies
II. Staffing and Directing Selecting persons to do the jobs that need to be done *and* enabling their performance are staffing and directing responsibilities. This requires the design of job positions, the selection of personnel (both paid and volunteer), developing persons to do the jobs, guiding their performance and recognition for the services performed. Planning and organization is the preparation of the program to meet its goals. Staffing and directing is the actual implementation of the goals.	The Staffing and Directing function requires that the volunteer and administrator CAN: II.A. Demonstrate knowledge and expertise in planning and conducting successful volunteer recruitment. II.B. Demonstrate knowledge and capability in selecting appropriate persons to fill positions. II.C. Demonstrate knowledge of the development needs of personnel to assume or acquire new positions and assure that these needs are addressed. II.D. Demonstrate the ability to motivate, communicate with and lead volunteers and paid staff. II.E. Recognize the accomplishments of personnel. II.F. Facilitate the transition of volunteers away from the program as needed.
III. Controlling This is the process of monitoring and evaluating the program to determine if events and activities have conformed to plans and produced the desired results. Documenting results and revising plans based on evaluation outcomes is part of the controlling process.	The Controlling function requires that the volunteer administrator CAN: III.A. Demonstrate the ability to evaluate total program results. III.B. Demonstrate the ability to document program results and to apply this information in future planning activities.

Functional Areas	Competencies
IV. Agency, Community and Professional Relations Volunteer programs exist within the larger context of the agency/ organization, the surrounding community and the professional field of volunteer administration. Maintaining working relationship in of these areas is vital for successful program administration and the personal career development of the volunteer administrator.	The Agency, Community and Professional Relations function requires that the volunteer administrator CAN: IV.A. Demonstrate the ability to work effectively with many different "types" of people. IV.B. Demonstrate a knowledge of group process and the ability to work with, and as a member of groups. IV.C. Demonstrate knowledge of social organizations, and dynamics of change. IV.D. Demonstrate knowledge of external regulations affecting volunteerism. IV.E. Demonstrate knowledge of the history and philosophy of voluntary action and trends affecting contemporary volunteerism. IV.F. Demonstrate knowledge of the profession of volunteer administration.

The period between 2000 and 2006 was especially active in renewing the development of formal structures centred on developing a "professional credential." The new notion of a professional credential was aimed at achieving three expectations:

1. that employers would begin to selectively recruit for positions with volunteer management responsibilities based on candidates having the CVA credential;

2. that the quality assurance of the processes around the awarding of the credential were sound and based on American credentialling standards. Processes included, the development of a professional knowledge test and associated peer reviewed test item bank, the consolidation of the primary literature base for the profession and the demonstration of a minimum of three years of related volunteer administration experience;

3. widespread acceptance within the practitioner base of the CVA credential as a requirement for professional practice (AVA Board minutes 2000-2006, Credentialing Committee minutes 2000-2006).

The *CVA Toolkit* was developed by AVA for practitioners to begin the process of certification. It is intended as a guide for the aspiring professional to move from practitioner status, or an occupation, to a professional. An examination of this first version of Toolkit provides some important advancements in the development of the profession. The first thing that a candidate encountered was a letter welcoming them to the credentialling process. The letter comes from two people: the chair of a committee and a staff person holding roles with responsibilities for the awarding and oversight of the CVA credential. The existence of a Credentialling Program Manager, backed by a Credentialling Committee, demonstrated to candidates that a system and processes existed to ensure that certain standards were met before the CVA would be awarded. After the letter, the Toolkit opened with the following statement:

> Certified in Volunteer Administration (CVA) is a professional certification in the field of volunteer resources management. Sponsored by the Association for Volunteer Administration (AVA), the CVA credential reflects mastery of the knowledge required of our practitioners in this field as measured through an examination process and a peer assessment process. AVA has established the ethical standards for volunteer resources management, and views these principles as an essential part of one's competence in the field. As a candidate for the CVA credential, you are required to affirm your intent to uphold these ethical standards.

(AVA, 2005, p. 1)

The candidate was informed that "the performance-based CVA program consists of a two-part measurement format to capture your knowledge and application skills based on practical experience" (p. 1). The first part of the measurement was a multiple choice examination consisting of 80 multiple choice questions which was scored as "pass/fail" (p. 1). The examination was worth 50 per cent of the total score required for the credential. The second part of the measurement is the portfolio which consists of a 500-word philosophy statement and a management narrative. The portfolio was also worth 50 per cent of the total score towards the credential. The candidate was explicitly notified that "[y]ou must pass both the examination and the portfolio assessment to earn the CVA credential" (underlining and enlarged print removed from original, p. 1).

Other signals candidates were given about the profession came from four additional processes outlined in the Toolkit. First, the issue of extensions and refunds was addressed. Second, an appeals process was outlined. Third, a recertification process was set out. Finally, candidates were offered three kinds of support from the professional association through the credentialling process: conference calls, a dedicated list serve, and individual support volunteers who already held the credential. As well, a list of primary resources to be read by the candidate was included and a set of readings provided. The impression being made on the candidate is of a profession with a well-conceived and staffed system for professional credentialling.

The current 2010 version is a further refinement. The Council for Certification in Volunteer Administration runs the certification process from its website: <www.cvacert.org>. The Candidate Handbook is a central feature of the process. After a discussion of the credential, core competencies are discussed:

> *A core competency is defined for the CVA program as the knowledge, skills and abilities (KSAs) required for competent/satisfactory practice in the field of volunteer resource management. The CVA Core Competencies were identified by topic experts in the field and verified periodically through a membership survey.*

(CCVA, 2010, p. 2)

Five core competencies were set out and detail provided. The table below presents the CCVA Body of Knowledge (CCVA, 2010a) which specifies the core competencies and content knowledge expected of the candidate:

**Table 2: 2010 CCVA Content Outline Showing
Core Competencies Areas**

Ethics: The ability to act in accordance with professional principles.

1. Understand and commit to CCVA core values and ethical principles for volunteer administration.

2. Recognize the need to honor professional ethics over personal values in fulfilling the role of Administrator of Volunteers.

3. Apply the principles of professional ethics to all aspects of volunteer management.

4. Practice ethical decision-making when confronted with situations involving clients, customers or service recipients, volunteers, and staff who supervise them.

5. Assist beginning practitioners, staff supervisors or leadership volunteers with resolution of ethical dilemmas involving volunteers.

Organizational Management: The ability to design and implement policies, processes and structures to align volunteer involvement with the mission and vision of the organization.

A. Strategy

1. Apply the concepts of strategic planning as they relate to volunteer involvement.

2. Participate in the development of a vision, mission and goals of the organization.

3. Integrate volunteer activity to achieve organizational vision, mission, goals and priorities.

4. Solve organizational problems by deploying volunteers creatively.

5. Collaborate broadly within the organization on projects of mutual interest, seeking to develop strategic internal relationships.

6. Understand and apply effective change management.

B. Operations

1. Apply the principles of operational planning in the design and delivery of volunteer activities.

2. Recognize the culture and norms of the organization in the design of programs and projects.

3. Develop and revise policies and procedures that reflect best practice in the management of volunteers.

4. Apply the concepts and tools of project management.

Human Resource Management: The ability to successfully engage, train and support volunteers in a systematic and intentional way.

A. Staffing

1. Collaborate with management and program staff to design volunteer positions that are mission driven, satisfy agency needs and appeal to potential volunteers.

2. Market the agency, the needs of the client, and volunteer opportunities to build awareness, both internally and externally.

3. Recruit and engage volunteers for assignments that match their skills, interests, abilities, and time availability.

4. Interview, screen, and assign volunteers within the organization.

5. Design and implement orientation and training to meet the needs of volunteers and staff supervisors.

B. Support

1. Direct and coach the effective supervision of volunteer activity.

2. Apply the principles of problem solving and conflict resolution management.

3. Solicit and manage volunteer input and feedback.

4. Apply discipline and dismissal procedures that are fair and equitable.

5. Apply the concepts of team building and group process.

6. Apply the principles of motivation to acknowledge and reward volunteers and their staff partners

7. Plan and lead effective meetings.

Accountability: The ability to collect relevant data and to engage in meaningful monitoring, evaluation and reporting to stakeholders.

A. Fiscal Management

1. Make fiscally responsible decisions related to budgeting, purchasing and staffing.

2. Comply with sound business practices, organizational policy, and relevant jurisdictional legislation related to fundraising and organizational assets.

3. Apply the principles of effective resource management to maximize efficiencies.

B. Data Management

1. Comply with all relevant employment, safety and human rights legislation when collecting data.

2. Adhere to legal requirements, regulatory requirements and best practices regarding confidentiality and privacy of record keeping, data storage and reporting.

3. Collect, analyze and disseminate information about volunteer activity and program to appropriate stakeholders.

C. Evaluation and Outcome Measurement

1. Develop appropriate tools and processes to measure the impact of volunteer involvement.

2. Design and implement a volunteer performance appraisal process.

3. Develop feedback mechanisms to inform volunteers of the results of their activity.

D. Risk Management

1. Understand general legal concepts and comply with specific laws relevant to volunteers and volunteer-based organizations.

2. Design and implement volunteer risk management policy, procedures and tools consistent with the organization's risk management program.

E. Continuous Improvement

1. Apply the concepts of continuous improvement to maximize the impact of volunteer involvement and ensure a positive experience for volunteers.

2. Align improvement initiatives with those of the organization.

3. Apply the results of evaluation to improve future volunteer activity.

Leadership and Advocacy: The investment of personal integrity, skills and attitudes to advance individual, organizational and community goals advocating for effective volunteer involvement inside of the organization and in the broader community it serves.

A. Organizational and Community Engagement

1. Articulate and sustain a vision for excellence in volunteer involvement.

2. Create a climate of mutual respect and inclusion, recognizing diversity.

3. Engage volunteers in decision making, listening carefully to the opinions and concerns of others.

4. Commit to coaching/mentoring others, acting as a role model of superior performance.

5. Share resources and responsibility for moving projects forward.

6. Implement activities that serve the community beyond the walls of the organization.

7. Develop strategic alliances with other organizations to meet shared community needs.

B. Professional Development

1. Develop and implement a focused self improvement plan with goals, action steps and timelines, based on a self-assessment.

2. Participate in formal and informal learning opportunities, integrating learning for personal mastery and program improvement.

3. Seek professional credentials.

4. Design and deliver professional development for peers and colleagues in volunteer administration.

C. Advocacy

1. Advocate through appropriate channels for adequate resources (human, technical and financial) to support volunteer behavior.

2. Develop and implement appropriate advocacy strategies to influence decisions and actions related to positive and effective volunteer involvement within the organization.

3. Develop and implement appropriate advocacy strategies to positively influence the community's attitudes and behavior related to volunteering.

4. Participate in individual and group activities to advocate for the profession of volunteer administration.

Reprinted with permission, CCVA, 2010.

The Body of Knowledge demonstrates the ongoing development and clarification of the core competencies for the profession. Another development in the most recent version of the process leading to the professional credential is the expansion of the CVA Portfolio. In the past the portfolio consisted of two parts, as already mentioned: a statement of philosophy and a management narrative. Added in 2010 is a short ethics case study where, "CVA candidates demonstrate their ability to identify an ethical dilemma and its implications based on the core values of the profession" (CCVA, 2010a, p. 3).

In summary, the long process focused on creating a profession of volunteer administration has produced a number of significant artifacts useful in deliberating the question of whether or not it is a profession. Despite very recent turmoil, the established structures, including the credentialling process, continue on and show evidence of growing demonstrated by both the development of two practitioner-motivated national initiatives in the United States and a growth in the number of people applying to CCVA to begin the credential process. Determining whether or not volunteer administration is a profession is by large measure guided by what one understands a profession to be. We now turn to an examination of central themes about professions within the literature.

WHAT IS A PROFESSION?

Studies on professions highlight foundational sociological constructs. The interplay between society, history, sociological theory, social categories, research and politics is dynamic within the literature on professions. However, as Brante (1988) notes, the trinity driving the exploration of professions is "theory, 'facts', and politics" (p. 120). Depending on the theory, what is taken to be fact and the dominant politics at play, what counts as a profession varies. That stated, it is Parsons (1964) who within sociological theory is generally seen to be the one who framed and set the tradition of American functionalist research into professions.

Parsons introduced the evolutionistic theory of history suggesting that societies progress along a continuum of simple to complex forms. Integration of a society — those things which keep individual actors together — takes place through generalized values among the members of that society. This line of thinking concludes that in a modern society the basic rational values are universalism, specificity and allocation of resources in line with performance. In this light, Parsons regards professions as the conduits of rational values and new technological knowledge that together moves an economy forward. Professionals, in the Parsonian view, play central roles in the advancement of society. In this regard, Parsons takes a divergent view from his peers, believing that it is a strong professional base that is the most significant feature of a modern society and not capitalism, the free market or a business economy (p. 35).

While Parsons' view of the paradigmatic professional was the scientist, his rationalizations have bearing on any discussion about professions. He stressed for example that the profession must emphasize rationality, have a specificity of function, demonstrate universalistic as opposed to particularistic criteria for judgement (pp. 34-49) and adopt affective neutrality as opposed to affectivity (p. 160). In his comparisons between professionals and other occupations — the business man and the bureaucratic administrator, for example — Parsons argues that they share a common characteristic namely that they each seek the best and most efficient method of carrying out their function, choosing to set aside tradition for progress (Menzes, 1976, pp. 48-49). What differentiates the professional from other occupations is the professional's achieved competence in a specific field in addition to the four characteristics mentioned above.

Before we leave Parsons and consider other perspectives on professions, it is important to step back and acknowledge that for Parsons, the context of society in which professions are situated has four broad functional imperatives:

- *Latent pattern-maintenance and tension-management.* This imperative maintains that in "the overall blueprint of the system through time ... [t]here must be some latent memory of how the system works even when it is not actually working and there must also be provision for the remembered elements to be raised to the level of activity" (Waters, 1998, p. 110).

- *Integration.* The imperative here is to "maintain solidarity between units of a system ..., to make sure that the exchanges between them are smooth and orderly and not obstructive and conflictual" (pp. 110-11).

- *Goal-attainment.* Here the imperative is to establish a goal to "modify the environment or to modify internal arrangements. This imperative also includes a requirement that complex goals must be ordered in a hierarchy of priorities and that resources must be allocated so that goals may be realized" (p. 111).

- *Adaptation.* The imperative here is to have the system ensure "the availability of disposable facilities and resources which are procured from the environment" (p. 111). In the situation where there are multiple goals and a complex system, flexibility within resource acquisition and allocation is necessary to avoid facing restraints on the system.

That professions and professionals would be operating within and across each of these imperatives gives some sense of their breadth of scope within the social system. While not stated explicitly by Parsons, it could be argued that a profession would be a significant actor within and across the four social imperatives.

In 1957, Ernest Greenwood while contemplating what the characteristics of a profession were for the purposes of moving the field of social work to professional status, advanced a precisely articulated normative model of a profession that has been widely adopted. By reviewing sociological theory he proposed a scheme by which professionals could be distinguished from non-professionals. He proposed that a profession has to have:

1.   systematic theory,

2.   authority,

3.   community sanction,

4.   ethical codes, and

5.   a culture (p. 45).

His thoughts on each of these are worth reviewing as we consider whether volunteer administration is a profession. To start with, Greenwood did not see professionals and non-professionals as two disconnected spheres of occupational activity. Rather, he envisioned a continuum where the "true difference between a professional and a nonprofessional occupation is not a qualitative but a quantitative one" (p. 46). He saw on one end of the continuum well-recognized and accepted professions such as physicians and attorneys while at the other end were "least skilled and least attractive occupations" such as "watchman" and "scrubwoman" (p. 46). In thinking about professional attributes, those occupations at the professional end of the continuum would exemplify the attributes to a very high degree. As one moved away from the professional end, the degree to which the attributes would be evident would decrease. This means that in the middle area could exist a number of occupations moving towards professionalization.

For Greenwood, systematic theory made clear that "skills that characterize a profession flow from and are supported by a fund of knowledge that has been organized into an internally consistent system called a *body of theory*" (italics in original, p. 46). Because of the presence of systematic theory, the would-be professional was obliged to spend considerable time engaged in formal educational training in an academic setting. Greenwood generalized that "as an occupation moves toward professional status, apprenticeship training yields to formalized education, because the function of theory as a groundwork for practice acquires increasing importance" (p. 47). Furthermore, the rational orientation of a profession to its body of systemic theory encourages professionals to be "critical, as opposed to reverential" of the theoretical system. In other words, professionals evaluate and update the body of theory supporting their profession.

Professional authority derives from the "layman's comparative ignorance" (p. 47) of the body of theory and associated practice of a profession. Greenwood makes an additional point here that non-professional occupations have "customers" while professionals have "clients." The difference is that customers have the power to shop a market to find the services or products he or she wants and that "he has the capacity to appraise his own needs and to judge the potential of the service or of the commodity to satisfy them" (p. 48). In a relationship with a professional, the client "has no choice but to accede to the professional judgment … because he lacks the requisite theoretical background" (p. 48) to assess needs or make choices. As well, the client is not able to "evaluate the caliber of the professional service he receives" (p. 48). Greenwood makes a strong point that the authority of the professional is not limitless but is "confined to those specific spheres within which the professional has been educated" (p. 48).

The powers and privileges of a profession can only be granted by community sanction either formally or informally. Formal authority is often "reinforced by the community's police power" (p. 48). One of the dominant powers of a profession is its control over its training centres. The control is displayed by the profession either granting or withholding accreditation meaning that "a profession can, ideally, regulate its schools as to their number, location, curriculum content, and caliber of instruction" (p. 49).

Confidentiality is to Greenwood one of the most important privileges of a profession. To facilitate the professional's ability to perform, clients need to divulge information they would not normally reveal. The community sanctions this privileged communication as "shared solely between client and professional, and protects the latter legally from encroachments upon such confidentiality" (p. 49). Together the powers and privileges give a profession a monopoly. Greenwood observes that "when an occupation strives toward professional status, one of its prime objectives is to acquire this monopoly" (p. 49). Monopolies can be abused and so a regulating code of ethics is a necessary component of a profession. While regulating codes may be found in many occupations, for Greenwood, "a professional code is perhaps more explicit, systematic, and binding; it certainly possesses more altruistic overtones and is more public service oriented" (p. 50). Two general concepts within professional ethical codes are universalism and disinterestedness. Universalism means that a professional must demonstrate "emotional neutrality" providing the service to whoever requests it even sacrificing "personal convenience" (p. 50). Disinterestedness in the professional-client relationship means that, "the professional is motivated less by self-interest and more by the impulse to perform maximally" (p. 50).

Finally, a profession has three main contributors to formal and informal groups that together create a professional culture: workplaces where the professional performs his or her services; organizations such as post-secondary institutions that replenish the supply of talent for the profession; and formal groups that emerge from the "consciousness-of-kind" such as professional associations (p. 51). Norms, values and symbols make up the culture of a profession. Norms guide the behaviour of professionals in social situations such as the appropriate ways of acquiring clients. Values are the "basic and fundamental beliefs, the unquestioned premises" upon which the profession is built (p. 52). Symbols are a profession's "meaning-laden items" such as "insignias, emblems, and distinctive dress ... its stereotypes of a professional, client and layman" (p. 52).

A third and final perspective on professions is that which has roots in economics. Here the question has more to do with what and how a profession contributes as an economic agent. While there is no economic theory addressing professions as economic institutions, economists have examined the behaviours of professions such as licensing which restricts labour market involvement of people. Savage (1994) asks: "How can we explain the long history, continued existence, and general acceptance of self-regulating professional associations, whose constraints on professional behavior would be unacceptable to any standard neoclassical firm and which current economic theory can comprehend only as a cartel" (p. 130)? Shaked and Sutton (1981) reduce the question of professions to a problem for policy makers who must decide whether professions should "be allowed to retain their monopolistic powers" (p. 217). Another interesting dimension to an economic understanding of professions is that the typical understanding is of professionals being on the production-side of the economy. However, the question of whether or not production is more or less efficient where licensing is a requirement for consumer access to a service is an analysis of demand-side economics. Looked at as a demand-side question of consumer access to services, professions limit access by restricting the number of professionals able to provide the service in question. As a result, economists may in fact reason that "the existence of professions is *prima facie* evidence of market failure" (italics in original, Savage, 1994, p. 130).

Savage moves to advance a different economic perspective on professions as being a network form of organization rather than a firm or occupation. She proposes the following definition, "A profession is a network of strategic alliances across ownership boundaries among practitioners who share a core competence" (1994, p. 131). Within the definition she notes that the idea of core competence is not sufficient to distinguish a profession from the more typical economic notion of a firm. A core competence is simply an ability necessary for the survival of the firm or the profession — it is something put to use in the production of a good or service. So while competencies play a large role in defining different professions "as knowledge-reliant production organizations, the concept is insufficient to differentiate professions from firms" (1994, p. 133). The notion of a network of strategic alliances does differentiate professions from other forms of production. Networks, in the sense used by Savage, mean "an economic organization that accomplishes the exchange of capital, products, and/or knowledge without explicit equity investment or 'ownership'" (1994, p. 133). Applying the concept to professions then, "a network implies a community of practitioners operating separately for many purposes, but dependent on the network for the maintenance and development of core competences that earn them rents" (p. 133).

Professions become the explicit set of exchange relationships between various actors, each a professional within the profession itself. This description of professions suggests that:

- while each professional behaves as an independent actor, all actors are dependent on the network for the evaluation, redevelopment and maintenance of the set of core competencies inherent in the profession;

- lower transactional costs within the profession incline actors to operate within the professional network rather than go outside to the market;

- distributed ownership of the knowledge base of the profession enables broad-based decision-making leading to "successful outcomes-innovations" (Savage, 1994, p. 134);

- the formation of "routines" within the profession allow for the continuation and growth of a body of knowledge that in the domain of practice is far beyond the capabilities of any single professional (differentiation within the legal profession, for example, demonstrates this notion nicely).

The reputation of a profession is an important economic consideration especially in the marketplace. For professions, the question of reputation comes down to how individual professionals link their own "success" with the performance of their peers. With distributed ownership, autonomy is highly valued in professions, so too is the assurance that one's fellow professionals are performing at least satisfactorily. Each professional has a sensitivity to the very real situation of having their reputation in the hands of another — at least in part. Contracts, hierarchical supervision and similar "enforcement-minded" approaches are "virtually impossible to construct and enforce" (Savage, 1994, p. 137). For the network, peer monitoring is a more effective approach to upholding reputation because, peer monitoring "relies on self-interest rather than the availability of third-party enforcement. Individuals want to maximize the value of their membership in the network in order to gain access to its shareable assets. ... Peers are good monitors not only because of what they know, but because they are the ones to whom good monitoring matters most" (Savage, 1994, pp. 136-37).

Remaining on the theme of considering professions from an economic perspective, a rarely mentioned but highly influential force is changing how we understand "professional" in North America. The North America Free Trade Agreement (NAFTA) sets parameters around a trinational market within which numerous professions conduct business. NAFTA defines professionals as "business persons who plan to carry out professional activities ... for an employer or on contract to an enterprise located in a member country other than one's own" (NAFTA, TN-1). To ensure the flow of professional labour within NAFTA, common criteria are established, such as having the minimum educational requirement for all professions to be a baccalaureate degree. The concern of both Canada and Mexico is the "history and needs of each country's professional practices are no longer the key elements defining the content of the profession; instead, professions are defined by a process of homogenization with the other two countries, and especially with the United States" (Arriage Lemus, 1999, p. 3).

The Canadian Department of Foreign Affairs and International Trade sets out the 63 professions allowed to enter a member country in its Guide for Canadian Business Persons (International Trade Canada, 2004). Of the professions listed, the one which comes closest to including volunteer administrators would be the "management consultant" classification which, provides services designed to improve the managerial, operating and economic performance of public and private entities by analyzing and resolving strategic and operating problems. Consultants may assist and advise in implementing recommendations but do not perform operational work for clients. Typically, a management consultant is an independent contractor or an employee of a consulting firm under contract to a client from a member country. The professional services provided must be temporary, periodical or on a fixed consulting basis rather than as full-time employment (International Trade Canada, 2004).

While most professions require a baccalaureate degree, the qualifications for a management consultant within the NAFTA agreement are: a baccalaureate degree or "five years experience as a management consultant, or five years experience in a field of specialty related to the consulting agreement" (International Trade Canada, 2004).

ALIGNING PERCEPTIONS OF A PROFESSION WITH VOLUNTEER ADMINISTRATION

The various perspectives on professions provided above cover a lot of territory and offer multiple and sometimes conflicting views on what it takes for an occupation to move into the professional domain. Table 3 presents the main thoughts related to a profession and links them with the understood current status of volunteer administration.

Table 3: Linking the Attributes of a Profession with Volunteer Administration

Attribute (citation source)	Evidence of Attribute in Volunteer Administration
Conduit of rational values and new technical knowledge; central role in the advancement of society (Parsons)	• There is a network that conveys new technical knowledge pertaining to volunteer management. • Questionable as to its centrality in advancing society.
Emphasizes rationality (Parsons)	• Content outlines, a body of literature, and other dimensions associated with the professional credential provide evidence of rationality.
Has a specificity of function (Parsons)	• Specificity of function defined in core content documents and *Portrait of a Profession*.
Demonstrates universalistic criteria for judgement (Parsons)	• The *Statement of Professional Ethics in Volunteer Administration* introduces universal values and competencies to be used in decision-making.
Systematic theory; body of theory necessitating protracted education (Greenwood)	• While a body of literature has been compiled for certification, there is only a small body of theoretical literature related to volunteer administration. • There is not sufficient theory to require extensive education.

Authority; people served are clients and accede to professional judgement (Greenwood)	• Uncertain. This authority in this sense is influenced by the organization within which the profession is practised. • Customer satisfaction is a frequent interest of volunteer programs to ensure recruitment and retention of volunteers.
Community sanction; confidentiality is protected and privileged; monopoly (Greenwood)	• No evidence of information given to volunteer administrators being privileged and protected. • No evidence of monopoly.
Ethical codes; explicit, systematic and binding; altruistic and public service-oriented (Greenwood)	• There is a professional ethical code. • The code is altruistic and oriented • towards a public service. • The code is not binding on members.
Culture; norms and values exist which guide behaviour; symbols representing the profession (Greenwood)	• Uncertain. Some norms and values do exist but evidence is lacking that they are significant influencers of behaviour. • The "CVA" (Certified Volunteer Administrator) credential, certificate and pins serve to identify members of the profession. Past symbols included "AVA" and "ICVA" as acronyms.
Restrictions on labour market participation in field of activity (Savage)	• Not evident — anybody can be employed as a "volunteer administrator".
"Network of shared alliances across ownership boundaries among practitioners who share a core competence" (Savage)	• Mixed presence of networks that have changed over time. • There is evidence of a sense of identity within practitioners in the field but low.
Professional members dependent on network for the evaluation, redevelopment and maintenance of core competencies (Savage)	• The certification process started with AVA and continuing with CCVA uses the network to consolidate, evaluate, redevelop and maintain core competencies.
Professional members operate within the network and not in the marketplace (Savage)	• Members do not exclusively operate within the network. Consultants and other practitioners are "free agents" to a variety of

	employers. Some of the lead figures in the profession do not hold the CVA credential.
Distributed ownership of knowledge base (Savage)	• Individual members have ownership of volunteer administration concepts and can practise them autonomously.
Broad decision-making leading to successful outcomes innovations (Savage)	• Mixed evidence. Broad decision-making within the known membership did exist within AVA. • The current situation of CCVA and two national initiatives still has the intention of inclusive decision-making but the "membership" profile may have changed.
Existence of routines (Savage)	• Evidence of generally accepted routines such as recruitment, interviewing, evaluation *etc*.
Peer monitoring in place to protect the reputation of the profession (Savage)	• No evidence.
Baccalaureate-level degree (NAFTA)	• No evidence of a full baccalaureate in volunteer administration though it is a component part of a number of post-secondary programs.
Minimum five years' experience (NAFTA)	• Current CVA requirement is a minimum of three years of experience before being eligible for the credential.

DISCUSSION

As Table 3 demonstrates, volunteer administration has some of the characteristics of a profession but would fall short of long-standing well-recognized professions such as law or medicine. It is also evident that there is more to volunteer administration than a simple occupation requiring little or no education or training. In keeping with Greenwood's (1957) thinking, volunteer administration is somewhere on the continuum between occupations and professions. While this may be reassuring, it is hardly a helpful declaration at the end of this kind of analysis. Using Greenwood's five components of profession, we will focus on developments that could further the profession of volunteer administration.

What for volunteer administration and other human-services professions is known as the body of knowledge is in reality a reduction of what Greenwood intended. In proposing systematic theory as part of a profession he goes beyond the accumulated knowledge and introduces the active generation of theory and theorizing by professionals and academics associated with the domain of professional practice. Theory and theorizing move a profession forward by introducing new knowledge, challenging assumptions, identifying and filling knowledge gaps, introducing new conceptualizations of the activity and so forth. Within the profession of volunteer administration, very little systematic theory exists and very few academics are engaged in theory-building or theory-testing. Influential consultants and practitioners offer instrumental information that appears to have no direct link to theoretical work in volunteer administration or even other related disciplines such as human resources. While such contributions should not be discounted, to be a profession volunteer administration will need to see a growth in its theoretically oriented literature base. Furthermore, that theoretical literature should be picked up by the profession and used to refine and advance professional practice. Such literature should also be viewed critically and challenged over time as the profession grows and develops.

Greenwood's dimension of authority is a challenge for the profession of volunteer administration. Intended in this dimension is the profession's authority to exercise exclusivity around the right to practice as a volunteer administrator. In a highly developed profession, an individual is not able to practise without sanction from the professional body. Projecting its authority through its credential, a profession signals to the world that only those persons with the credential are able to practise as a professional. In the case of volunteer administration there are many more practitioners without the professional credential than those having gone through the effort to become credentialled.* Employers do not appear to distinguish between a credentialled and non-credentialled employee. Therefore, there is a real question about the authority of the profession of volunteer administration especially

---

* As of October 2007, there are just over 750 CVA holders. The number of nonprofit organizations in the United States is just over 1.4 million according to the National Center for Charitable Statistics. There are about 161,000 nonprofits in Canada according to Statistics Canada. If just 10 per cent of these nonprofits had a manager of volunteers, there are potentially 156,000 potential professionals practising in North America.

since there are three organizations which to varying degrees have ability to speak on behalf of the profession — though CCVA certainly has the strongest position because it has ownership of the credentialling process and the code of ethics. Efforts by CCVA in particular to consolidate authority in the minds of practitioners and employers would be an important step in advancing the professional status of volunteer administration.

Community sanction in the sense intended by Greenwood simply does not exist for volunteer administration. While various federal, state and provincial laws outline privacy protections in a general way, professional volunteer administrators are not granted any kind of confidentiality protections akin to lawyers and doctors. As well, there is simply no sense of the profession having a monopoly on the practice of volunteer management. An employer can hire any person into the position and disregarding professional standards carries with it no immediate consequence. This is a dimension that requires some additional debate by professional members and credentialled practitioners in the field of volunteer management. It is unclear if establishing a monopoly of practice is a desirable goal for the profession of volunteer administration. Further discussion may serve to clarify what the profession desires by way of a community sanction and the form that might take.

The ethical code developed by AVA and now the property of CCVA was recognized by the Josephson Institute of Ethics as one of the leading codes of its type when it was first widely distributed. One of its unique features is that it was designed to be less a strict set of prescriptive behavioural rules and more of a tool that professionals would use to develop their ethical decision-making competency. As this is a strength of the profession, the ethical code requires ongoing review by professionals to keep it in line with societal changes and changes in professional practice.

The final domain of culture is one that appears to be vulnerable at the present time. With three organizations filling the void left by AVA, there is a real question regarding what the values and norms of the profession will evolve to be. Options include an intentional separation of the credential from the professional development and professional network needs. This would mirror the current situation with the fundraising profession, the Association of Fundraising Professionals (AFP) where the certification — the Certified Fund Raising Executive (CFRE) — is distinct from AFP where a range of activities addressing professional practice occur. A thoughtful and intentional process to consider the benefits and limitations of such an approach would be beneficial to the profession of volunteer administration whose practitioners need to be clear about the divisions, purpose and expected outcomes of their professional network.

CONCLUSION

Volunteer administration is not a profession in the way that medicine and law are professions. It is however well along the continuum and moving towards the highly professional end of the continuum as proposed by Greenwood (1957). Active engagement of credentialled professionals and non-credentialled practitioners by the three organizations now active in the United States is a necessity for the profession at this point in time. Over 50 years of effort have gone into the development of the profession of volunteer administration and for the evolution to continue the various organizations that have come to fill the vacuum left by the dissolution of AVA need to set different agendas aside and articulate the next form that the profession will take. There is a strong and vibrant network of professionals that need to be convened to expand the existing professional framework and ensure that the important contributions made by volunteer administrators continues to be at a truly professional level.

REFERENCES

Arriaga Lemus, M. (1999). NAFTA and the Trinational Coalition to Defend Public Education. *Social Justice, 26*, 145-155. Retrieved August 2, 2007, from Academic OneFile.

Association for Volunteer Administration. (1999). *Professional ethics in volunteer administration* (4th ed.). Richmond, VA: Association for Volunteer Administration.

Association for Volunteer Administration. (2005). *Certified in Volunteer Administration candidate toolkit 2005*. Richmond, VA: Association for Volunteer Administration.

Bradner, J., Hart, J., Hoodless, E., Meijs, L., & Woods, M. (1999). *Portrait of a profession: Volunteer administration*. Richmond, VA: Association for Volunteer Administration.

Brante, T. (1988). Sociological approaches to the professions. *Acta Sociologica, 31*(2), 119-142.

Congress of Volunteer Administrator Associations (COVAA). (n.d.). What is COVAA? Retrieved September 4, 2007, from http://samaritan.com/covaa/info.htm.

Corry, T.O. (2006). Global civil society and its discontents. *Voluntas*, *17*(4), 303-332.

Council for Certification in Volunteer Administration. (2007). About CCVA. Retrieved August 14, 2007, from http://www.cvacert.org/about.htm.

Council for Certification in Volunteer Administration. (2010). *Certified in Volunteer Administration candidate handbook 2010.* Retrieved January 11, 2010, from http://www.cvacert.org/documents/CVA-CandidateHandbook-2010_006.pdf.

Council for Certification in Volunteer Administration. (2010a). *Body of knowledge in volunteer administration.* Retrieved January 11, 2010, from http://www.cvacert.org/documents/CCVABOK2008-Final_000.pdf.

Greenwood, E. (1957). Attributes of a profession. *Social Work*, *2*(3), 44-55. Retrieved July 27, 2007, from EbscoHost.

International Trade Canada. (2004). *A guide for Canadian business-persons. Temporary entry into the United States and Mexico under the North American Free Trade Agreement.* Ottawa: Foreign Affairs Canada and International Trade Canada. Retrieved May 24, 2010, from http://www.international.gc.ca/trade-agreements-accords-commerciaux/assets/pdfs/NAFTAtemp05-en.pdf.

Menzes, K. (1976). *Talcott Parsons and the social image of man.* London: Routledge & Kegan Paul Ltd.

Parsons, T. (1964). *Essays in sociological theory* (rev. ed.). New York: The Free Press.

Rehnborg, S.J. (1979). Assessing skills as a volunteer administrator: A new approach to certification. *Volunteer Administration*, *12(3)*, 10-17.

Savage, D. (1994). The professions in theory and history: The case for pharmacy. *Business and Economic History*, *23*(2).

Seel, K. (1995). *Statement of professional ethics in volunteer administration.* Boulder, CO: Association for Volunteer Administration.

Shaked, A., & Sutton, J. (1981). The self-regulating profession. *Review of Economic Studies*, *48*(2), 217-234.

Tilly, L.A., Tilly, C., & Social Science History Association. (1981). *Class conflict and collective action.* London: Sage.

Waters, M. (1998, 1994). *Modern sociological theory.* London: Sage.

CONTRIBUTORS

Salvatore Alaimo, Ph.D., CVA is an Assistant Professor in the School of Public, Nonprofit and Health Administration at Grand Valley State University, Grand Rapids, Michigan. He previously worked in volunteer administration for the United Way of Metropolitan Atlanta and the Girl Scout Council of Northwest Georgia, and served as President of the Council of Volunteer Administrators (COVA) for metro Atlanta.

Anita Angelina, M.A. is Associate Professor at Mount Royal University. Anita instructs courses in both nonprofit studies and marketing. Anita is an active board member on nonprofit boards of directors and community volunteer.

Emilie Bromet-Bauer is the Volunteer and Intern Resources Manager for a San Francisco nonprofit public health organization and a director on the board of AL!VE (Association of Leaders in Volunteer Engagement). She earned her Certificate in Volunteer Administration in 2006, and is working towards a graduate degree where her research interests include the role of volunteer resource management in transformative volunteerism. Emilie has developed and facilitated workshops on volunteer management, service-learning, and advocacy for local and national conferences.

Jeffrey L. Brudney, Ph.D. is the Albert A. Levin Chair of Urban Studies and Public Service at Cleveland State University's Maxine Goodman Levin College of Urban Affairs. Dr. Brudney has published widely in the areas of public administration, the nonprofit sector, and volunteerism. He has received several international awards for his research, service, and mentoring activities.

Norman A. Dolch, Ph.D. is a Senior Lecturer in the Educational Consortium for Volunteerism at the University of North Texas. He teaches in the online undergraduate and graduate Certificate Program in Volunteer Management and Community Service. His research includes technology usage in nonprofit organizations serving elderly and disabled persons.

Melissa Eystad is founder of World Spirit Consulting, and focuses on helping organizations in the global voluntary sector develop effective volunteer and other resource development strategies. Previously, she served as Chief of Volunteer Services for the Minnesota Department of Human Services, National Director of Volunteer Development for AFS

Intercultural Programs USA, and, most recently, Vice President of Member Services for the Minnesota Council on Foundations.

Mark A. Hager is Associate Professor of Nonprofit Studies in the School of Community Resources & Development at Arizona State University. His research focuses on the scope, dimensions, administration, and financial operations of and reporting by nonprofit organizations. He frequently writes with Jeffrey Brudney on the topic of volunteer management capacity of nonprofit organizations in the United States.

Melissa A. Heinlein, MA, MS, CAVS is Chief, Voluntary Service at the Philadelphia Veterans Affairs Medical Center. She is an adjunct professor at Chestnut Hill College (Philadelphia, Pennsylvania) and is an active member of the Pennsylvania Society of Directors of Volunteers in Healthcare serving in roles such as past vice-president and chair of the education and compliance committee. Melissa writes monthly for VolunteerToday.com under the federal government section and is a certified administrator of volunteers through the Association for Healthcare Volunteer Resource Professionals.

Marianne Kerr, M.Ed., CVA is an associate professor of Cooperative Extension with the University of Alaska Fairbanks. She has worked with volunteers in a variety of professions for over 35 years and has received national recognition from her peers for leading a team effort on the promotion of volunteerism in Cooperative Extension.

Diana Kyrwood, MA, CVA is the President of the New York Association for Volunteer Adminstration. As An Anthropologist, Diana focuses on programs in human service organizations and specializes in training volunteers in effective cross-cultural communication. She has also managed volunteer efforts for large special events in New York City and serves on the test writing committee for the Council for Certification in Volunteer Administration.

Melanie Lockwood Herman is executive director of the Nonprofit Risk Management Center (www.nonprofitrisk.org), a U.S.-based resource organization that advises nonprofits in the U.S., Canada, and countries throughout the world. Melanie is the author or co-author of more than 15 books on various risk management topics and leads the Center's consulting practice. Melanie earned a B.A. degree at American University and a Juris Doctor at George Mason University.

Kathleen McCleskey is an adjunct faculty member at the University of North Texas, Education Consortium for Volunteerism, where she conducts online classes for graduate and undergraduate students.

Kathleen is President of KM Consulting and Training Connection and has worked with nonprofits and managers of volunteer resources for over 20 years. She has a Masters of Human Relations from the University of Oklahoma.

Milena Meneghetti, CHRP, M.Sc., Registered Provisional Psychologist, M4i Consulting, is in private practice in the Family Psychology Centre in Calgary, Alberta. She has over 20 years' experience in Human Resources working in a variety of mid to large organizations, and is a Certified Human Resources Professional with the Human Resources Institute of Alberta. She is also a member of the International and Calgary Coaching Associations. She is a published author, volunteer, public speaker, therapist, counsellor, and life coach. She has an M.Sc. in Applied Psychology, and is a Registered Provisional Psychologist with the College of Alberta Psychologists.

F. Ellen Netting, Ph.D. is Professor and Samuel S. Wurtzel Endowed Chair in Social Work at Virginia Commonwealth University in Richmond, Virginia. She has written extensively in the areas of nonprofit management and faith-based organizations, and about the use of older volunteers. Her practice experience includes supervising volunteers in an office on aging, directing a Foster Grandparent Program, and recruiting and training volunteers for the Long Term Care Ombudsman Program in Tennessee, Arizona, and Virginia.

Sarah Jane Rehnborg, Ph.D. is a Lecturer at the LBJ School of Public Affairs and the Associate Director of the RGK Center for Philanthropy and Community Service at the University of Texas at Austin. Ms. Rehnborg teaches graduate level course work in volunteer administration, nonprofit governance and related courses. As a researcher, she led a cross-disciplinary university team which developed a valid and reliable tool to assess programs engaging volunteers and national service participants for the Corporation for National and Community Service. In addition, she completed a study on volunteer engagement in state agencies and analyzed Texas data collection practices in the field of volunteerism as well as an analysis of the effects of service-immersion programs on the development of Jewish identity among Jewish young people. She served as President of the Association for Volunteer Administration from 1979 to 1981. Prior to assuming leadership of AVA, she developed AVA's initial Performance-Based Certification Program. She received her undergraduate degree from Denison University and her Masters and Ph.D. from the University of Pittsburgh.

R. Dale Safrit, Ed.D. is a Professor, Director of Graduate Programs, and Extension Specialist for Continuing Professional Education in the Department of 4-H Youth Development and Family & Consumer Sciences at North Carolina State University in Raleigh, North Carolina. Dale has an established international reputation as an applied scholar, visionary leader, and motivational educator in the areas of professional development, community-based leadership, and volunteer resource management. He co-authored the community-based text *Developing Programs in Adult Education: A Conceptual Programming Model* (2002, Waveland Press, Inc.) as well as more than 60 peer-reviewed articles in scholarly and professional journals. Dale is Editor of *The International Journal of Volunteer Administration*, and he has been invited to present sessions in 17 different countries, 43 of the 50 United States, and 5 Canadian provinces.

Allan Serafino was an executive with Scouts Canada for nearly 30 years. He currently teaches nonprofit studies at Mount Royal University in Calgary, Alberta, and consults with nonprofit organizations on organizational learning, program planning, and board governance. He is a Ph.D. candidate at the University of Calgary, where his thesis is "The Meaning of Learning in the Workplace for Nonprofit Leaders." He is also the author of several books of poetry and young adult fiction.

Pamela J. Sybert is the Director of the Educational Consortium for Volunteerism at the University of North Texas. She developed the first online academic certificate in Volunteer and Community Resource Management and teaches volunteer management and fundraising courses.

Paul Varella is Associate Professor of Strategy and Organizational Studies at Mount Royal University. Before coming to the academia, Dr. Varella gained 12 years of experience in different businesses. His research focuses mainly on the social capital of organizations, and on how leadership at the upper echelons generates organization-wide consequences, especially in relationship to organizational social networks.

Cheryle N. Yallen, President of CNY Enterprises, is an international trainer/consultant, bringing over 25 years of social service experience to the consulting field. This experience includes working with nonprofit organizations as a consultant, Executive Director, Board member and volunteer. An active member of the social service community, she currently consults with numerous organizations, in addition to being the Executive Director of a private foundation. As a current practitioner, as well as consultant, she brings up-to-date solutions to today's challenges.

INDEX